Credit to Capital: The Complete 10-in-1 Wealth-Building Series

Master Credit, Eliminate Debt, Build Business Funding, and Create Legacy Wealth — All in One Powerful Bundle

By Joe Correa

CREDIT TO CAPITAL

Published by Live Stronger Faster

This book is for educational and informational purposes only. The author and publisher are not engaged in rendering legal, financial, or other professional advice. Readers should consult a qualified professional before making any financial decisions.

First Edition

TABLE OF CONTENTS

TRANSFORMING YOUR CREDIT TO IGNITE YOUR FINANCIAL LIFE

Welcome to *Credit to Capital*—a guide that's not just about fixing your credit… it's about transforming your future.

My name is Joe Correa, and I wrote this book for families like yours—families who work hard, love harder, and are ready to stop surviving and finally start building.

Let me ask you something:
Have you ever felt like no matter how much you earn, you're always one emergency away from starting over?
Have you ever looked at your kids and thought, *I want to give them more—but I just don't know how?*
Have you been told to fear credit… instead of being taught how to use it to fund your future?

If so, you're in the right place.

This book will flip the script on everything you thought you knew about credit, income, and family wealth.

Here's what you'll learn:

- How to **build or repair your personal credit fast**—even if your score is low or nonexistent

- How to **establish powerful business credit** using only your EIN, so you can access tens of thousands in funding without using your Social Security number

- How to use credit to **start or acquire income-generating assets** like online businesses, real estate, vending routes, or Airbnb properties

- How to **protect your wealth** with LLCs, trusts, and insurance—without needing a legal background

- How to **teach your kids and teens** the credit and money strategies no school is ever going to teach them

- How to **automate and delegate** tasks using smart software and credit-funded systems—so you can get your time back

- And how to **scale** your income without burnout, turning your household into a thriving, mission-driven business

What makes this different?

This isn't theory. It's action.
It's not written for financial experts. It's written for busy families.
It's filled with real-life stories of people who started with almost nothing and now own businesses, rental properties, and financial peace—because they stopped fearing credit and started using it like the wealthy do.

Whether you're a single parent trying to stretch your income, a couple tired of working two jobs, or a teen ready to build credit the right way—this book gives you the **playbook**.

You'll walk away with:

- Real strategies

- Step-by-step actions

- Credit templates
- Wealth habits you can apply immediately
- And a mindset that puts you back in control

Why now?

Because the system isn't going to teach this.
Because inflation is real.
Because your job may not be secure.
Because your kids are watching.
Because your legacy can't wait.

So, if you're ready to stop trading hours for dollars…
If you're ready to use credit to build, not borrow…
If you're ready to create time freedom, income, and legacy—starting with what you already have…

Then press play, take notes, and get ready.

Because *Credit-Funded Wealth for Families* isn't just a book.

It's a blueprint.

Let's build.

Introduction to Volume 1: How to Establish Credit in the U.S.

Welcome to **Volume 1** of the *Credit to Capital* series—your ultimate roadmap to transforming credit into real, long-term wealth.

This first volume is titled **How to Establish Credit in the U.S.**, and it's where everything begins.

Whether you're brand new to credit, recently arrived in the U.S., or simply starting over, this volume will teach you exactly how to build a strong personal credit foundation—step by step.

What You'll Learn in Volume 1:

In this foundational volume, you'll discover:

- What credit really is, how it works in the U.S., and why it matters
- The exact steps to build your first credit profile—from no credit to a high score
- How to open your first secured credit card, credit-builder account, or rental-reporting tradeline
- How to manage credit responsibly from day one and avoid the biggest beginner mistakes
- The difference between FICO and VantageScore—and why lenders care

- How to use credit for opportunity, not obligation
- And how to prepare yourself for everything coming in future volumes: business credit, real estate investing, automation, and wealth scaling

Why This Volume Matters Most:

This is where the chain reaction begins.

Without personal credit, it's nearly impossible to qualify for business funding, buy a home, or access the financial tools that allow you to grow wealth. This volume removes the confusion and gives you a **clear, simple plan** that works even if you've never had a credit score before.

It's not about borrowing—it's about **building**.

So if you're ready to unlock the U.S. financial system,
If you want to qualify for more—without co-signers or sky-high interest,
And if you're ready to turn your credit into capital, freedom, and ownership…

Then let's begin.

This is **Volume 1**: *How to Establish Credit in the U.S.*

Let's build your future—one credit move at a time.

VOLUME 1: HOW TO ESTABLISH CREDIT IN THE U.S.

Chapter 1: Understanding the U.S. Credit System

In this chapter, we'll cover the basics: - What credit really is and why it matters in the U.S. - How credit reports and credit scores work - What the credit bureaus are and how they collect your data - The 5 key components of your credit score - How to check and read your credit report Let's start with the concept of credit. In simple terms, credit is your ability to borrow money and your history of repaying it. In the U.S., lenders rely heavily on your credit history to determine your eligibility for loans, rental agreements, even some jobs. That's why it's not just important—it's essential. Credit reports are detailed records of your borrowing and repayment behavior. These reports are compiled by three major credit bureaus: Experian, Equifax, and TransUnion. Each one collects and maintains your credit data based on your activity with lenders, banks, and other financial institutions. Your credit score is a three-digit number typically ranging from 300 to 850. This number summarizes the data in your credit report and tells lenders how likely you are to repay borrowed money. Higher scores lead to better loan terms, lower interest rates, and easier approvals. Here's how your score is calculated: - 35% Payment History: Do you pay your bills on time? - 30% Credit Utilization: How much of your available credit are you using? - 15% Length of Credit History: How long have you been using credit? - 10% Credit Mix: Do you have a variety of credit types, like credit cards and loans? - 10% New Credit: Have you recently opened new accounts or applied for loans? These five factors work together to create a snapshot of your creditworthiness. Knowing them helps you focus your efforts and build your score more effectively. It's also crucial to review your credit reports regularly. You're entitled to one free report per year from each of the three major bureaus through AnnualCreditReport.com. When reviewing your reports, check for errors like incorrect balances, unfamiliar accounts, or outdated information. Disputing these errors can quickly improve your score. By understanding the U.S. credit system and monitoring your reports, you take control of your financial future.

Ana's First Lesson in American Credit

Ana stepped off the plane at Miami International Airport with two suitcases and a heart full of hope. After 12 years of teaching literature in Bogotá, she had finally made the move to the United States to start a new life near her cousin Camila. Her plan was clear: find a job, rent a small apartment, and slowly rebuild her life in this foreign but promising land.

By the second week, Ana had applied for a modest apartment in Little Havana. The landlord smiled politely as she handed over her paperwork, but an hour later, Ana received a text: "Application denied due to no credit history." She was stunned. She hadn't expected to get everything on the first try, but what did "no credit history" even mean?

The same thing happened when she tried to finance a used car. And again when she attempted to get a phone plan. "You need to build credit," said the sales associate, handing her a brochure she couldn't make sense of.

Ana had been financially responsible her whole adult life. She always paid bills on time, never borrowed more than she could afford, and managed her money carefully. But here, none of that mattered. In the eyes of American banks and businesses, Ana was invisible.

One Sunday, over coffee with her cousin Camila, Ana poured out her frustration. "I feel like I'm starting from zero—worse than zero. Back home, I had a reputation. Here, I can't even rent an apartment."

Camila nodded sympathetically. "That's because, here in the U.S., your financial trust is measured by something called a credit score. It's not about how much money you have, it's about how well you've handled credit in the past."

Ana leaned forward, eager to understand. "But I've never missed a payment in my life!"

"Yes, but they don't know that. You have to show them here," Camila replied. She pulled out her laptop and walked Ana through the basics.

She explained that credit in the U.S. is built through borrowing and repayment activity, which is tracked by three main credit bureaus—Equifax, Experian, and TransUnion. These companies collect data from banks, lenders, and even landlords. That data is used to generate a credit report and score.

Camila showed Ana how her credit score was calculated: 35% payment history, 30% credit utilization, 15% length of credit history, 10% credit mix, and 10% new credit inquiries. "Think of it like your financial GPA," she said.

Ana's head swirled. "So, I have to borrow money just to prove I can be trusted with money?" "Exactly," Camila laughed. "Sounds backwards, but it works. Once you understand it, you can use it to your advantage."

They visited AnnualCreditReport.com, where Camila showed Ana how to pull her first free credit report. As expected, it was blank. No accounts, no history, no score.

But something shifted for Ana. Where there had been frustration and confusion, there was now a spark of determination. "If this is how the system works," she said, "then I'll learn the system."

The next day, Ana went to a local credit union and asked about secured credit cards. With Camila's help, she opened one using a $300 deposit. "Only use it for what you can pay off in full," Camila reminded her. Ana nodded. "Groceries only."

She also began keeping a notebook where she tracked every payment and due date. She wasn't just spending—she was building. She even downloaded a credit tracking app that let her check her score for free each month.

At her new job as a bilingual teaching assistant, Ana struck up a friendship with a fellow immigrant from Venezuela named Lucia. Over lunch one afternoon, Ana shared what she was learning about the credit system. Lucia confessed she had never applied for credit either, fearing rejection. Inspired, she asked Ana to help her get started.

Three months later, Ana saw her first credit score: 687. It wasn't perfect, but it was hers. She had created it. That same week, she was approved for a basic cell phone plan. By month five, she qualified for an apartment rental on her own—no co-signer needed.

Ana didn't stop there. She read articles on credit-building, signed up for a financial literacy workshop, and even joined a Facebook group for immigrants navigating the U.S. financial system. She started mentoring others who were in the same shoes she had worn just months earlier.

What Ana learned most was that credit wasn't just about getting approved—it was about access. Access to choices. Access to fair rates. Access to independence. It wasn't personal—it was math, logic, behavior, and timing.

One day, after helping Lucia pull her first report, Ana looked back at the blank credit report she had seen months ago. "Back then, I felt like I didn't exist here," she said. "But now I know—I just had to speak the financial language."

She smiled as she thought about her old students in Bogotá. If they could see her now, learning a brand new system in a brand new land, they'd be proud. And she was proud of herself. Ana didn't just learn credit—she mastered it. And with every on-time payment, every smart decision, she was writing a new story—one of resilience, empowerment, and hope.

Chapter 2: Building Credit from Scratch

Now that you understand the system, let's talk about how to begin: - Open your first secured credit card - Become an authorized user on a trusted account - Take out a credit-builder loan - Pay bills on time and manage utilization - Track your progress using credit monitoring tools These simple steps will lay the foundation for strong, lasting credit. Let's start with the secured credit card. A secured card is one of the easiest credit products to qualify for. You pay a refundable deposit—typically $200 to $500—and that amount becomes your credit limit. Use the card for small purchases and pay off the balance in full every month. This demonstrates responsibility and helps build a positive credit history. Another great strategy is to become an authorized user on someone else's credit card. If you have a trusted family member or friend with good credit, they can add you to their card as an authorized user. You benefit from their credit history on your credit report, even if you don't use the card yourself. This can be a fast way to establish a positive credit record. A third option is applying for a credit-builder loan. These loans are designed specifically for people who are new to credit. Here's how they work: the loan amount is held in a bank account while you make fixed monthly payments. At the end of the term, you get the money—but more importantly, your on-time payments are reported to the credit bureaus. Regardless of which option you choose, the key is to make every payment on time. Payment history is the biggest factor in your credit score, and even one missed payment can set you back significantly. Also, keep your credit utilization low. This means using less than 30% of your available credit. If you have a secured card with a $300 limit, try not to carry more than a $90 balance. Lower utilization signals to lenders that you are managing credit wisely. Finally, monitor your progress. Use tools like Credit Karma, Experian, or your bank's app to check your score regularly. Watching your progress keeps you motivated and allows you to catch issues early. Building credit from scratch takes a few months of consistency—but it works. Stick with these steps, and you'll be on your way to excellent credit.

Samir's Path from No Score to Strong Score

Samir stepped onto the balcony of his new apartment in Austin, Texas, sipping his morning chai. He had earned his master's degree in computer science just three months earlier and landed a job at a promising tech startup. Everything was falling into place—except for one frustrating reality.

He still didn't have a credit score.

Despite earning a respectable salary and being responsible with money, Samir quickly learned that having no credit was just as limiting as having bad credit. He found out the hard way when he applied to rent a car for a weekend trip to San Antonio. "Sorry," the agent told him. "You need a credit history for that." Even when he tried to sign up for a monthly gym membership, the company ran a credit check. Rejected again.

Samir was stunned. "I have the money," he told his friend Neha over dinner. "I've never been in debt. Isn't that supposed to be a good thing?"

Neha smiled knowingly. "In India, yes. In the U.S., not really. Here, lenders want to see that you've borrowed money and paid it back responsibly. No history means no score—and no trust."

It felt unfair. Samir had grown up with a culture of saving, avoiding debt, and paying in cash. Now, all that financial discipline seemed invisible in his new home.

But Samir wasn't one to give up easily. He took Neha's advice and started researching how to build credit from scratch. He quickly came across the concept of a secured credit card . It sounded strange at first—putting down a cash deposit just to borrow his own money—but he saw the logic. It was a foot in the door.

He applied for a secured card through his local credit union and was approved for a $300 limit. The bank held $300 of his own money as collateral. Samir made a promise to himself: he would use the card only for necessities, pay off the balance in full every month, and never carry debt.

The first thing he charged was a $42 internet bill. Then a tank of gas. He paid it off before the due date and kept going. He didn't touch more than $90 a month—keeping his utilization below 30%—and always paid in full.

Two months later, Samir asked his cousin Rohan, who had been in the U.S. for five years, if he could add him as an authorized user to one of his long-standing credit cards.

"Sure," Rohan said. "I've had this card for six years and always paid it on time." Being added to Rohan's account meant Samir could benefit from the card's history, even though he wouldn't actually use it. It was like inheriting financial credibility.

Samir's next move was opening a credit-builder loan from a local online bank. The loan amount was only $500, but the funds were held in a secured account while Samir made monthly payments of $45. It felt a bit silly at first—paying a loan for money he couldn't access—but he realized it was about building a payment history. Each month, the bank reported his on-time payments to the credit bureaus.

Around the same time, Samir also made a budget. Not just for tracking spending, but to stay disciplined with credit. He created a spreadsheet where he tracked his card balances, due dates, payment confirmations, and current score estimates from apps like Credit Karma.

Three months later, Samir logged into his credit monitoring app and saw a score for the first time: 689.

He nearly dropped his phone. He called Neha right away.

"I have a score!" he said, laughing. "And it's not terrible!"

"You built it, one responsible step at a time," she replied. "Now keep it going."

With his score established, Samir received his first pre-qualified credit card offer in the mail. It wasn't flashy, but it had no annual fee and a $1,000 credit limit. He applied and was approved. This gave him more available credit, which helped lower his utilization rate even further.

He used the new card to pay for recurring expenses like Netflix, Spotify, and a few grocery runs, making sure everything was paid in full each month. His spreadsheet remained updated. If his balance ever climbed above $100, he paid it early—even before the statement closed.

Six months later, Samir had a credit score of 734. His financial behavior hadn't changed much—he still lived simply, saved diligently, and avoided unnecessary purchases—but now the system recognized his efforts.

That fall, Samir decided to lease a car. The dealership finance officer reviewed his credit profile and nodded in approval.

"You're in the 700s," she said. "You'll get a great rate."

For Samir, it was a turning point. He was no longer invisible in the system. He had built credibility the American way—not by chance, but by strategy.

And he wasn't done yet. He subscribed to a credit tracking service and began setting new goals. First, he would get his score above 760. Then, he'd start building business credit for a side project he was planning. Eventually, he wanted to buy a condo—and now, he was on track.

But Samir wasn't just building credit for himself. He became the go-to person in his immigrant community for credit questions. He gave workshops at the local community center, wrote blog posts in Hindi and English, and even helped his older brother open a secured card when he moved to the U.S. six months later.

"Your score isn't about showing off," he often said. "It's about access—to homes, jobs, even opportunities you haven't thought of yet. Build it wisely, and it'll serve you for life."

Samir's journey from no score to strong score didn't happen overnight. But with patience, planning, and purpose, he turned a system that once shut him out into a tool that opened doors.

Chapter 3: Improving Your Credit Score

If you've already started building credit or need to repair it, this chapter is for you. We'll discuss: - How to spot and dispute credit report errors - How to lower your credit utilization - The importance of payment history - Avoiding unnecessary credit inquiries - And building consistent habits that raise your score over time Let's start with credit report errors. Mistakes can happen, and when they do, they can seriously impact your credit score. Common errors include accounts that don't belong to you, incorrect balances, or payment statuses that are wrongly reported. Reviewing your credit report regularly can help you catch these issues early. If you find an error, you can dispute it online directly with the credit bureau—Experian, Equifax, or TransUnion—and they are required by law to investigate and respond within 30 days. Next, focus on lowering your credit utilization ratio. As we discussed earlier, utilization accounts for 30% of your score. If you're using a high percentage of your credit limit, lenders may see you as a higher risk. Try to pay down balances and avoid maxing out your cards. You can also request a credit limit increase—but only do this if you're confident you won't increase your spending. Third, make on-time payments a top priority. Set up auto-pay or calendar reminders to ensure every bill gets paid by the due date. Even one late payment can stay on your report for up to seven years. Consistently paying your bills on time is the single most effective way to improve your credit score. Avoid applying for too much new credit in a short period. Each application results in a hard inquiry, which can temporarily reduce your score. Multiple inquiries can signal to lenders that you're desperate for credit, which may hurt your approval chances. Lastly, build positive credit habits. Keep old accounts open to maintain a longer credit history. Diversify your credit mix by responsibly using both revolving credit (like credit cards) and installment credit (like auto loans or credit-builder loans). Monitor your credit regularly to stay informed. Improving your credit score doesn't happen overnight. But with consistency, discipline, and the right strategies, you'll start to see results—and with a stronger score, more financial opportunities will open up.

Maya's Road to Recovery

CREDIT TO CAPITAL

Maya stood in line at the grocery store, holding a half-full basket and hoping her debit card wouldn't get declined again. At 29, she had a good job, a car, and a modest apartment in Queens, New York. But behind the scenes, her financial life was crumbling.

She wasn't new to credit. In fact, that was part of the problem.

At 21, Maya got her first credit card on her college campus. "Build your credit today!" the representative promised, handing her a free t-shirt and a folder. Maya didn't know much about interest rates or utilization, but she figured if she made the minimum payment, everything would be fine.

By the time she was 25, Maya had five credit cards. She never missed a payment—at first. But when her mom got sick back in El Salvador and Maya had to cover medical bills and travel expenses, the debt piled up fast. She maxed out two of her cards, fell behind on payments, and opened a new store card just to buy groceries.

Eventually, the late fees started to snowball. Calls from collections came daily. Maya felt overwhelmed and ashamed. "I'm not irresponsible," she would tell herself. "I just didn't know better."

By the time she turned 28, her credit score had dropped to 520. She couldn't qualify for an apartment without a co-signer. Her auto loan had a 17% interest rate. Even her employer's finance department questioned her when she applied for a relocation benefit.

Maya knew something had to change. One night, she Googled, "How to fix my credit score." What she found surprised her. There were blogs, YouTube channels, free credit counseling services, even community classes. She signed up for a free credit workshop at a local nonprofit, and that workshop changed everything.

The instructor was a soft-spoken woman named Gloria, a former banker who now volunteered teaching financial literacy. Gloria explained how payment history made up 35% of Maya's credit score, and how utilization, credit age, inquiries, and credit mix filled out the rest.

"But most importantly," she said, "you need to know what's on your credit report. Pull it. Read it. Own it."

Maya left the class with a checklist and determination. That night, she went to AnnualCreditReport.com and requested her reports from all three credit bureaus.

What she found stunned her.

There were three collection accounts she didn't recognize. One was from a medical lab she'd never used. Another was an old phone bill she'd already paid but never disputed. There were also two late payments on a student loan she hadn't realized were reported 60 days late during her forbearance period.

The next day, Maya filed disputes on all three accounts. She uploaded bank statements, payment confirmations, and letters. Thirty days later, two of the items were removed, and her score jumped by 41 points.

Encouraged, Maya kept going. She made a spreadsheet with all her accounts: balances, minimum payments, interest rates, and due dates. She used color coding—green for current, yellow for nearing limit, red for delinquent.

Her first goal: catch up on all late accounts. She picked up extra shifts at work, sold some designer bags online, and used the money to pay off a $450 overdue card that had been collecting interest for months.

Then she focused on credit utilization . She had $3,200 in total available credit and was using more than $2,800—an 88% ratio. Her goal was to bring it down to below 30%, ideally under 10%.

She started by paying off her smallest balance—just $280 on a store card. Then she tackled her highest interest card, a gas card with a 27% APR. Slowly, she watched her balances drop and her score climb. She also set all her cards to automatic minimum payments , so she'd never miss a due date again. On top of that, she added calendar reminders on her phone to make additional payments mid-month to further lower her balances before the statement cut-off.

Maya didn't just work on paying things down. She also started building new, positive habits . She signed up for Experian Boost, which added her phone and utility payments to her credit report. It gave her a quick 18-point bump.

At her bank's suggestion, she asked for a credit limit increase on one of her oldest cards. To her surprise, they approved it, raising her limit from $1,000 to $2,500. That change alone dropped her utilization by 15%.

But Maya wasn't looking for quick fixes—she wanted real change. She began tracking her progress monthly. In a notebook, she wrote down her score, total debt, and payment dates. She celebrated small wins: when her score hit 600, when her total debt fell below $2,000, when a collection account aged past the statute of limitations.

By the time her 30th birthday arrived, Maya's credit score was 673.

She applied for a new apartment—no co-signer needed. She refinanced her auto loan and cut the interest rate in half. She even got approved for a travel rewards card, which she used only for groceries and gas, paying it off every week.

But perhaps the most meaningful change was emotional.

Maya no longer felt afraid to open mail or answer unknown calls. She no longer avoided looking at her bank account. She had gone from feeling ashamed to feeling empowered.

She started mentoring younger colleagues at her job, hosting lunchtime sessions on budgeting and credit. She even helped her cousin dispute an old medical bill that had been dragging down her score.

"Credit isn't about being perfect," Maya told them. "It's about being consistent, being aware, and making the system work for you."

Today, Maya's score hovers near 730. She checks her report every few months, keeps her utilization under 10%, and hasn't missed a payment in over two years.

But more than the number, Maya values the confidence she gained—the peace of mind, the sense of control, and the opportunity to create a future on her own terms.

Chapter 4: Financing Major Purchases

In this chapter, we explore how to responsibly use your credit to finance a car, a home, or even start a business: - How to prepare for and qualify for a car loan - What you need to know before applying for a mortgage - Steps to financing a new or growing business - Understanding loan terms, interest rates, and hidden fees Let's begin with financing a car. A car loan is often one of the first major loans people take out. Before visiting a dealership, check your credit score and shop around for loan pre-approval from banks or credit unions. Pre-approval helps you understand your borrowing power and interest rate options. Make sure to set a realistic budget—not just for the car price but also for insurance, taxes, and ongoing maintenance. When you apply for a loan, lenders will look at your credit score, income, employment status, and debt-to-income ratio. The higher your credit score, the lower your interest rate is likely to be. Consider making a down payment to reduce your loan amount and improve your approval odds. Now, let's talk about financing a home. Buying a house is a significant step and requires careful financial planning. Before applying for a mortgage, check your credit report for errors and work on improving your score if needed. Lenders prefer a credit score of 620 or higher, but better rates are offered at 700 and above. You'll also need to save for a down payment—anywhere from 3% to 20% of the home's price, depending on the loan type. Get familiar with different mortgage options such as conventional loans, FHA loans, VA loans, and USDA loans. Each has different requirements and benefits. Get pre-approved by a lender to show sellers you're serious, and compare offers to find the best interest rate and loan terms. For those starting or expanding a business, credit can also play a critical role. Business loans, lines of credit, or business credit cards can provide the funding needed to grow your operations. Before applying, write a solid business plan, register your business entity, and separate personal and business finances. Building business credit alongside personal credit strengthens your financial standing and opens up more opportunities. Lastly, no matter what you're financing, always understand the loan terms. Review the interest rate, repayment period, monthly payment, and any additional fees. A low monthly payment might seem attractive, but a longer term means more interest paid over time. Read the fine print and ask questions before signing anything. Using credit to finance major purchases can be empowering, but only if done wisely.

David's Dream Car and First Home

David leaned back in the plastic chair at the car dealership in Houston, nervously flipping through a brochure for a 2020 Honda Civic. The salesman, all bright smiles and optimism, had just stepped away to "run the numbers." It was David's first time financing a vehicle, and while he felt proud, he also wasn't entirely sure what to expect.

Just two years earlier, David had paid cash for everything. Growing up in Lagos, Nigeria, his parents taught him that debt was dangerous and credit cards were a trap. "If you can't afford it in cash, don't buy it," his father used to say.

But that belief didn't translate well when David moved to the United States at 26 to work as a civil engineer. Here, building credit wasn't optional—it was essential. It started when he tried to lease an apartment downtown. Despite having $10,000 in savings and a steady paycheck, the landlord declined his application. "No credit history," they said.

That moment changed everything.

David began learning about the U.S. credit system. He opened a secured credit card with a $500 deposit and used it carefully, never spending more than $100 per month and always paying it in full. He became an authorized user on his cousin's long-standing card and later took out a small credit-builder loan from his local bank. Within six months, he had a score of 702.

Now, two years later, he was ready for his first major purchase: a car.

The salesman returned, waving a printout.

"Good news! With your credit score at 748 and stable income, we can offer 3.4% APR on a 60-month term. And no co-signer needed."

David exhaled. Relief and pride mixed in his chest. "Let's do it," he said.

The dealership processed the paperwork, and by that evening, David was behind the wheel of his first financed car. The monthly payment fit within his budget, and he even opted for additional gap coverage just to be safe.

But David didn't stop there. With the car successfully financed and his credit profile growing stronger, his sights shifted to an even bigger dream: homeownership.

He'd been renting a one-bedroom apartment near his office and paying $1,400 per month. It wasn't terrible, but he wanted stability. He wanted to invest in something permanent.

The first step was research. David dove into online articles, YouTube videos, and even visited local first-time homebuyer workshops. That's where he first learned about FHA loans—government-backed mortgages that allowed lower credit scores and down payments as low as 3.5%.

At the workshop, he met a mortgage broker named Sheila who offered to run some preliminary numbers for him.

"With your current credit score and employment history, you're a strong FHA candidate," she said. "But you'll need to show two years of consistent work and save for the down payment and closing costs."

David went home and mapped out a savings strategy. He cut unnecessary expenses—eating out, streaming services, and weekly game purchases. He opened a high-yield savings account and labeled it "House Fund." Every paycheck, he deposited $400 without fail.

Within nine months, he had saved $12,000—enough for a down payment, moving costs, and a cushion for emergencies.

The next step was getting pre-approved for a mortgage. David gathered his tax returns, W-2s, bank statements, pay stubs, and identification. Sheila submitted the application to several lenders and got him pre-approved for $270,000 with a 4.1% interest rate.

Pre-approval in hand, David started house hunting.

It was more emotional than he expected. The first house he saw smelled like mildew. The second was too far from work. The third had neighbors who blasted music all day. But the fourth—an older brick home with a renovated kitchen and fenced yard—felt right.

He made an offer below asking, and after a short negotiation, the seller agreed. The home inspection showed only minor issues. The appraisal came back clean.

Then came the final hurdle: closing.

David was bombarded with documents: loan disclosures, settlement statements, title insurance agreements. But he was ready. He had done his homework. He understood the mortgage terms: 30-year fixed, 4.1% APR, $1,335 monthly payment including taxes and insurance.

On closing day, David signed 42 pages and handed over a cashier's check for the down payment.

As the agent handed him the keys, David stood still for a moment.

He'd done it. He had used credit—wisely, patiently, strategically—to finance a car and a home. He had turned numbers and paperwork into real, tangible assets. The first night in his new home, he walked from room to room, still in disbelief. He cooked dinner in his own kitchen and ate at a folding table in the living room, surrounded by boxes. It was quiet. It was his.

Over the next few months, David automated his mortgage payments and set up alerts for due dates. He checked his credit report quarterly and kept his utilization low. His credit score continued to climb, reaching 765 by the end of the year.

He also started mentoring younger colleagues at his firm who were new to the U.S. "Start early," he'd tell them. "Don't wait until you need credit to begin building it."

He shared his story—how he had gone from no credit to owning a car and a home within three years. He explained how credit wasn't about debt—it was about leverage, responsibility, and long-term thinking.

David didn't stop there. He began reading about real estate investing. He took a weekend course on rental properties and even attended open houses for duplexes. His dream now included owning rental units—passive income that could support him in retirement.

But for now, he was content. He had achieved two milestones that once felt impossible.

And he did it not by chasing shortcuts or gaming the system, but by learning, planning, and applying what he'd learned one decision at a time.

David's story wasn't just about buying a car or a house.

It was about building a foundation.

And now that he had it, there was no limit to what he could build next.

Chapter 5: Avoiding Common Credit Pitfalls

Many people unknowingly damage their credit. Let's talk about how to avoid the most common mistakes: - Missing payments and how to set up payment reminders - Carrying high balances and the impact on utilization - Applying for too much credit in a short time - Closing old accounts and how it affects your score - Ignoring your credit report and missing errors Missing payments is one of the most damaging credit mistakes. Even one late payment can drop your score significantly and stay on your report for years. Use reminders, calendar alerts, or automatic payments to ensure every bill is paid on time. Carrying high balances also harms your score. Try to keep your credit utilization below 30%, and if possible, below 10% for optimal results. Paying off high-interest cards first can help reduce debt faster and save money. Be cautious about applying for multiple credit cards or loans in a short period. Each application creates a hard inquiry, which can lower your score temporarily. Multiple inquiries may raise red flags with lenders. Closing old accounts may seem like a good way to simplify your finances, but it can actually shorten your credit history and increase your utilization. Unless a card has high fees or you're at risk of overspending, consider keeping old accounts open. Lastly, don't ignore your credit report. Review it regularly for errors or signs of fraud. Disputing inaccuracies quickly can prevent long-term damage. By avoiding these common mistakes, you can protect the credit foundation you've worked hard to build.

Lina's Lessons from Mistakes

Lina closed her salon early that Friday evening, flipping the "Open" sign to "Closed" and drawing down the security gate with a long sigh. The shop had been unusually quiet all week. Fewer clients meant fewer tips, and fewer tips meant trouble.

She walked to her car, a compact SUV with three missed payments, and sat in the driver's seat a few moments before turning the key. The dashboard lit up with a check engine light—again.

Lina was exhausted—not just from working on her feet all day, but from the stress that had crept into every part of her life. And at the center of it all was one thing: her credit.

She wasn't new to credit. In fact, she had built good credit when she first moved to New Jersey from the Dominican Republic. When she opened her salon six years ago, she had a credit score in the high 700s. She was approved for three business credit cards, financed salon equipment, and even helped her younger sister get her first auto loan.

But then came 2020.

The pandemic hit small businesses like a tsunami. Her salon, once buzzing with customers and chatter, was empty for months. She tried to pivot—offering at-home kits, Zoom consultations, even TikTok tutorials—but the income dried up. Rent was still due. Utilities piled up. Credit card bills went unpaid. "I'll catch up next month," she told herself. But next month turned into the next quarter, and before she knew it, her credit score dropped from 783 to 586.

She maxed out two of her cards and missed five payments. One account was sent to collections. Her salon lease renewal was denied due to her business credit, and she had to move locations—losing a chunk of loyal customers in the process.

By the time things began reopening, Lina was buried in debt, and her phone buzzed daily with creditor calls.

The worst part wasn't the debt—it was the shame.

She stopped answering unknown numbers. She ignored mail. She even turned down a date because she didn't want to explain why her credit card was declined.

One afternoon, while waiting at the DMV to renew her license, she overheard a woman talking about a free credit counseling workshop at the community center.

Lina jotted down the details and attended the following week.

The workshop was small—just eight people and a speaker named Rafael, a former loan officer turned educator. He spoke in both English and Spanish, making everyone feel comfortable.

He started with a simple truth: "Credit isn't about being perfect. It's about recovery."

Lina felt seen.

Rafael explained the five components of a credit score : payment history (35%), utilization (30%), credit history length (15%), new credit (10%), and credit mix (10%). He emphasized that late payments were the most damaging—but also, the most fixable.

That night, Lina went home, opened her laptop, and pulled all three of her credit reports for free. The numbers were worse than she expected—late payments, a collection account, and high balances on all cards. But for the first time in a while, she felt ready to face it.

She made a list:

1. Pay off the smallest balance first – $312 on a store card.

2. Call all creditors to negotiate – especially the one in collections.

3. Set up automatic minimum payments – to avoid missing any more.

4. Create a budget – and stick to it, no matter how tight. She used her next weekend tips to pay off the store card entirely. Then she called the collection agency.

"I'd like to pay in full," she said. "But only if you'll agree to remove it from my credit report after payment."

To her surprise, they agreed. Two months later, the account disappeared from her report.

Her confidence grew.

She created an Excel tracker with due dates, balances, and interest rates. She highlighted every payment made and watched her progress over time.

One of the biggest lessons came from credit utilization . She had three cards, all over 85% usage. Rafael had said to aim for under 30%, and ideally under 10%. Lina called her longest-standing credit card company and requested a credit limit increase. She was approved—from $1,000 to $3,000—which instantly lowered her utilization percentage.

Then she set calendar reminders three days before each due date. No more late payments.

Six months into her recovery plan, her score climbed from 586 to 645.

It wasn't perfect, but it was progress.

She qualified for a lower-interest consolidation loan and used it to pay off two high-interest cards. Her monthly payments dropped by nearly $150, giving her breathing room in her budget.

That Christmas, she gifted herself peace of mind: no collection calls, no new missed payments, and—for the first time in two years—hope.

But Lina didn't stop with her own recovery.

She began sharing her story with other women in her community—stylists, nail techs, makeup artists—many of whom had also been hit hard by the pandemic. She held a "Credit & Coffee" meetup at her salon once a month, where they reviewed reports, disputed errors, and encouraged each other.

One stylist, Jessica, discovered a fraudulent account on her report. Lina helped her write the dispute letter. Another woman had a 580 score and didn't know she could rebuild it. Lina showed her how to get a secured card and use it smartly.

"Your credit doesn't define you," she told them. "But it can empower you."

By the end of the following year, Lina's score reached 703. She applied for a small business credit card again—not out of desperation, but as a tool. She used it for supplies and paid it off monthly, building both personal and business credit together.

She even financed a new salon chair—her first financed purchase in two years—and proudly paid it off early.

Looking back, Lina realized that her biggest mistake wasn't falling into debt.

It was ignoring it.

Once she faced her financial truth, the power came back into her hands. She didn't just rebuild her score—she rebuilt her identity as a confident, informed business owner.

And now, every time she sees a new stylist struggling with bills or avoiding credit entirely, she shares her story.

Because in Lina's eyes, knowledge isn't just power.

It's freedom.

Chapter 6: Long-Term Credit Strategies

Now let's look at how to use your credit for long-term wealth building: - Maintaining healthy credit habits for the long haul - When and how to refinance for better terms - Leveraging credit to build wealth through real estate and business - Building a financial safety net to avoid dependency on credit - Protecting your credit profile from identity theft and fraud Let's start with maintaining good credit habits. Long-term credit success is built on consistency. Always pay your bills on time, keep your credit utilization low, and monitor your credit reports regularly. These habits not only help you maintain a strong score, but also signal to lenders that you're a responsible borrower. Next, consider refinancing opportunities. As your credit improves, you may qualify for lower interest rates on existing debts, like your mortgage, car loan, or student loans. Refinancing can save you thousands over time, but it's important to compare lenders, calculate total interest savings, and watch out for fees. Only refinance when the long-term savings outweigh the costs. Credit can also be a tool for wealth building. Once your credit is strong, you can leverage it to purchase appreciating assets, such as investment properties or business expansions. For example, using a mortgage to buy a rental property can generate cash flow and long-term equity. Similarly, using a business loan to grow your operations can increase income and asset value. The key is to borrow strategically and with a clear repayment plan. Another critical part of long-term success is building a financial safety net. This includes creating an emergency fund with at least 3–6 months of living expenses. A safety net helps you avoid going into debt when unexpected expenses arise, like car repairs or medical bills. It also gives you the flexibility to manage credit proactively instead of reactively. Finally, protect your credit profile. Identity theft and fraud can quickly damage years of careful credit building. Freeze your credit when not applying for new accounts, use strong passwords, and enable alerts for any suspicious activity. Check your credit reports regularly for unfamiliar accounts or inquiries, and act quickly if you suspect fraud. Long-term credit success doesn't require perfection—just consistency, awareness, and smart financial planning. Use these strategies not just to maintain your credit, but to turn it into a tool for true financial independence.

Luis Builds a Credit Legacy

CREDIT TO CAPITAL

Luis leaned back on his worn-out couch, watching a YouTube video titled, "How to Build Wealth in America." His 12-year-old son, Mateo, was doing homework at the kitchen table. The video host said something that stuck with Luis:

"Credit is more than a number. It's a tool. If you know how to use it, it can change your family's future."

That sentence echoed in Luis's mind. He hit pause and looked around his small apartment in Kissimmee, Florida. He and his wife, Carla, had immigrated from Honduras eight years earlier. Luis worked construction; Carla cleaned houses. They made just enough to cover bills, send money back home, and keep food on the table.

But Luis had dreams. Big ones.

He wanted to buy a house. Start a business. Build something that would outlast him.

The problem? He didn't know where to start. He had never borrowed money. He paid for everything in cash and had no debt—but also no credit.

One day, while eating lunch on-site, Luis overheard a coworker talking about refinancing his house. "My credit score is up to 785," the guy bragged. Luis felt a pang of envy. That number—whatever it meant—seemed to open doors.

That night, Luis went online and searched, "How to get a credit score with no history." He stumbled across the idea of a secured credit card . He could pay a deposit—say $200—and use it just like a regular card. The bank would report his usage to the credit bureaus, and over time, he'd build a history.

He applied the next day.

Two weeks later, his card arrived. He felt nervous using it, but he committed to buying only gas and paying it off every Friday. "Slow and steady," he told himself.

Six months later, he had his first credit score: 662.

Encouraged, Luis took the next step. He visited a credit union and asked about a credit-builder loan . He didn't need to borrow money, but he understood now that this wasn't about cash—it was about proving consistency.

He took a $1,000 loan held in a savings account and paid $90 a month for 12 months. Each payment got reported to all three credit bureaus. He also became an authorized user on Carla's retail credit card, which had a five-year history.

Luis created a notebook where he wrote down due dates, balances, credit score updates, and even motivational quotes. Every time he paid early, he gave himself a gold star sticker—like a kid in school.

By the end of year one, Luis had a credit score of 710.

He was ready for his first big leap: buying a home.

He spoke to a mortgage broker, who walked him through the process. She recommended an FHA loan , which required a smaller down payment and accepted credit scores as low as 580—but Luis wanted the best rate possible.

He kept saving.

In six more months, he had $12,000—enough for a 3.5% down payment and closing costs. He was approved for a $250,000 FHA mortgage at 4.2%.

He and Carla found a three-bedroom home in a quiet neighborhood near Mateo's school. They were outbid on the first offer, but the second one stuck.

Luis had never signed so many papers in his life. But as the mortgage agent handed him the keys, he felt something deeper than excitement.

He felt power.

Two years after buying their home, Luis refinanced the loan at 3.3% as his credit score climbed to 765. He used the monthly savings to start investing in tools and gear for a side hustle—installing fences and patios on weekends. With consistent income and a strong credit profile, he opened his first business credit card under an LLC. He used it only for business expenses and paid it in full each month. It helped him separate personal and business finances—and slowly build business credit too.

By his fourth year in the U.S. credit system, Luis owned a home, operated a side business, and had three credit cards—all paid in full. His credit report had zero missed payments.

But Luis wasn't finished.

One Saturday, Mateo came into the kitchen holding a college brochure.

"Dad, will my student loans mess up my credit?"

Luis smiled. "Not if you learn now what I had to learn the hard way."

He sat Mateo down and explained what a credit score was, how to check it, and how to start small. They opened a student credit card together, with a $300 limit, and Luis co-signed. He taught Mateo the same golden rules: keep your balance under 10%, pay early, never miss a bill.

Together, they made the first payment.

It was a proud moment—not because of the dollar amount, but because of what it represented.

Legacy.

Luis began volunteering at a local community center teaching "Credit 101" to other immigrants. He shared his journey, his systems, and his mistakes. He told them not to be afraid of credit—just to respect it.

He taught families how to read credit reports, dispute errors, and build a plan. He translated letters into Spanish, called customer service on behalf of nervous parents, and even helped one woman negotiate a collection account down from $1,400 to $580.

"You don't need to be rich to build credit," he told them. "You just need to be consistent."

Luis's story became a beacon for many who thought credit was out of reach. He showed that with patience, knowledge, and community, even someone starting from zero could rise above.

Today, Luis's credit score holds steady above 770. He owns a duplex and is looking for a third rental property. Mateo is in his second year of college and has a score of 712. Carla runs her own cleaning business and just got approved for a $10,000 business line of credit.

The best part? Luis never became a slave to credit.

He used it intentionally, carefully, and with the bigger picture in mind.

He didn't just build a score.

He built a future.

And that future would outlive him.

Chapter 7: Turning Credit Into Capital – The Power of Financial Leverage

Most people think of credit as just a number—a score that gets you a loan, a car, or a credit card. But what if I told you that credit can be much more than that? What if, instead of just borrowing for purchases, you learned how to use credit to create income, wealth, and freedom?

In this final chapter, we'll explore a topic that goes beyond the basics—how to leverage your credit into capital, and turn that capital into long-term opportunity. This is where credit stops being just a tool to buy things and starts becoming a gateway to building wealth, investing in yourself, and funding your dreams.

Let's get creative.

Credit as Leverage – Not Just a Score

Once you've established good credit—meaning a score in the mid-700s or higher, low utilization, and a strong payment history—you have something incredibly valuable: trust in the eyes of lenders.

That trust can be converted into capital—real, usable money in the form of:

• Business credit cards • Personal lines of credit • Installment loans • Home equity loans • 0% APR intro offers • And in some cases, even grants or SBA-backed loans

The power of that capital depends on how you use it. Many people waste their borrowing ability on short-term gratification—TVs, vacations, impulse spending. But the most successful individuals use their credit to create cash-generating opportunities.

Smart Ways to Turn Credit Into Income

Here are a few strategic examples of how people have turned good credit into opportunity:

1. Starting a Small Business

Once you have strong personal credit, you can access 0% APR business credit cards or lines of credit. Many entrepreneurs have launched online stores, tutoring services, or freelance businesses using just a few thousand dollars in startup funds—all funded by their credit.

Example: Angela, a recent immigrant from Brazil, used her 750 credit score to open two business cards with 12 months at 0% interest. She bought inventory, created a Shopify store, and reinvested profits. Within six months, she was making $2,000/month in profit—with no interest paid.

2. Real Estate Investing

With good credit, you can qualify for low-down-payment FHA loans, or even home equity lines of credit (HELOCs) if you already own property. Some investors even use 0% APR cards to fund renovations, flip properties, or furnish rentals.

Example: Jamal used his credit score of 780 to buy a duplex with 3.5% down. He lived in one side and rented out the other. His tenant covered 80% of his mortgage, giving him cash flow and appreciation.

3. Credit Arbitrage

Though risky if misused, credit arbitrage involves borrowing at 0% APR and investing in assets that yield more than the cost of borrowing. Some do this with high-yield savings, inventory for resale, or even purchasing equipment for a side hustle.

Warning: Only attempt this with a solid plan and the ability to pay back before interest kicks in.

Building a Funding Plan Using Your Credit

If you're ready to take your credit beyond consumer spending, here's a step-by-step framework to responsibly leverage it for growth:

Step 1: Know Your Limits

Request credit limit increases on your existing accounts (without hard pulls where possible). This increases your available credit, reduces utilization, and gives you more flexibility.

Step 2: Create a Business Idea or Investment Goal

What would you do if you had access to $5,000 tomorrow? Fund a course and start freelancing? Build a digital product? Buy equipment for your cleaning business? Clarity is power.

Step 3: Apply for Strategic Credit

Research business credit cards with long 0% APR offers, or apply for a personal line of credit with your bank. Don't use this credit for consumption—only creation.

Step 4: Use Capital for Asset-Building

Spend only on things that can return income: marketing, inventory, equipment, training, or systems. Avoid depreciating items or personal luxuries.

Step 5: Track ROI and Set Payback Timelines

Always set a deadline to repay the borrowed capital—even before the 0% interest period ends. If your project fails to create income, stop spending and pay off what you owe.

The Credit-Opportunity Flywheel

As you start to successfully use credit to fund profitable projects, something powerful happens: your credit improves further, your income grows, and you gain access to even more capital. This creates what we call a credit-opportunity flywheel:

You build credit.

You use it to create something valuable.

You repay on time and profit from your project.

Your credit improves again.

Lenders offer even better terms.

You scale your opportunities.

It's a cycle that can take someone from $0 to a thriving business, portfolio, or even early retirement.

And it starts with responsible credit habits.

A Legacy Mindset

Luis, from Chapter 6, didn't just use credit to buy a house. He used it to start a family business, mentor his son, and teach his community. That's credit with purpose.

You can do the same.

Start thinking beyond survival and toward legacy. What can you build today with your current credit profile? How can your story inspire someone else?

Ask yourself:

• Can I launch a service business? • Can I publish a book or course? • Can I rent a property and build equity? • Can I invest in education that pays off?

If the answer is yes, you have everything you need.

Final Thoughts

Credit is not just a score. It's not just a loan. It's not just a card.

Credit is permission to create.

You've learned how to establish credit, improve it, and now—how to turn it into something greater. This is your invitation to think big, act smart, and use your credit to not just finance things… but to finance a life of possibility.

The world doesn't just need consumers. It needs creators. Builders. Leaders.

Your credit can help you become one.

So go out there. Dream boldly. Plan wisely. And remember: you're not just building credit—you're building a life that lasts.

Elena's Leap from Credit Score to Capital

Elena sat at the edge of her bed, staring at the balance in her bank account: $672.14. She had enough to cover groceries, her phone bill, and maybe gas for the week—but there was nothing left for dreams. She sighed and refreshed the screen again, as if willing the number to rise.

It wasn't that Elena was careless with money. Quite the opposite. Since moving from Guatemala to Phoenix five years earlier, she had lived frugally, worked full-time as a medical assistant, and slowly built a life she could call her own. But despite her efforts, she felt stuck—renting a small apartment, working extra shifts, and wondering if she'd ever be able to afford anything bigger.

Then one night, while scrolling TikTok, she came across a video that changed her trajectory.

The creator said, "If you have a good credit score, you're sitting on opportunity. Not debt. Not limits. Leverage."

That word hit Elena like lightning: leverage.

She clicked the profile, then the link to a free credit-building workshop. It was the first time she'd heard someone explain that credit wasn't just for buying—it could be used to build. Build businesses. Build assets. Build income.

Elena had spent the last three years improving her credit. She had started with a secured credit card, paid every bill on time, kept her balances low, and now had a FICO score of 741. But she hadn't done anything with it—she was afraid of going backward.

The workshop host said something she couldn't forget: "If your credit is strong and your mindset is smart, you're in a better position than most. The next step is to turn that score into capital—and that capital into something valuable."

Elena stayed up all night researching business ideas. She had always loved baking and decorating cakes. She even had a side hustle selling tres leches and cupcakes to coworkers and friends. Could she turn that into something more?

She wrote a list of everything she'd need:

• A commercial mixer • Packaging supplies • A small website • Licensing and permits • A second refrigerator for ingredients

The total came to just under $3,000.

Elena didn't have that in savings—but her credit offered a path forward.

The next week, she applied for a business credit card with 12 months at 0% APR. She was approved for $4,000. For the first time, credit didn't feel like a trap—it felt like a tool.

Elena used it wisely. She purchased only what she needed to scale. She built a simple website using a free template. She took orders online and arranged weekend pickups from her apartment kitchen.

Within two months, her weekend baking income surpassed her weekday job.

But Elena didn't stop there.

She applied for a business license, joined a local women's entrepreneur group, and took a free class on bookkeeping and taxes. She made a repayment plan and set auto-payments on her credit card to eliminate the debt before interest kicked in.

By month nine, her card was paid off.

Her credit score? Still above 740.

Her new problem? Too many customers.

That fall, she applied for a small business line of credit—$15,000—this time backed by a combination of personal credit and new business revenue. She used it to put a deposit on a shared commercial kitchen space and hired her cousin part-time.

What started with a credit card had turned into a full-fledged baking business.

By year two, Elena was earning $6,500 a month in revenue and had opened a storefront. She named it Cielo Dulce—Sweet Heaven.

But what made Elena the proudest wasn't the money.

It was the freedom.

She was able to reduce her hours at her day job and spend more time with her daughter. She helped her mom get approved for her first credit card. She hosted a workshop at her local library on how to build credit and fund side hustles.

And one Saturday morning, when her daughter asked how she started her bakery, Elena didn't hesitate.

"I started with good credit," she said. "But more importantly, I believed I could use it to build something."

CREDIT TO CAPITAL

Elena's story proves that credit is not the destination—it's the bridge. The question isn't whether you should use credit—but whether you'll use it wisely, with purpose and a plan.

She used hers to build a business. Others use it to invest, to scale, to create.

Because when credit meets clarity and courage?

Anything is possible.

VOLUME 2: PERSONAL CREDIT REPAIR BLUEPRINT

Welcome to *Personal Credit Repair Blueprint*, the second book in the *Credit to Capital* 10-in-1 series.

If you've ever felt embarrassed about your credit score, been denied a loan, or just felt stuck financially, you're in the right place. Whether you're recovering from financial hardship, medical bills, a messy divorce, or just didn't learn about credit early in life—this book is for you.

My name is **Joe Correa**, and I've spent years in the financial world—helping people get mortgages, qualify for funding, and build thriving businesses. But none of that matters if your credit holds you back. Credit is the foundation of your financial life. Without it, everything costs more. With it, you gain access, freedom, and options. It's that simple.

Let me say this clearly: **You do not need to be perfect to have excellent credit.**

You just need a strategy, patience, and a few powerful tools. In this book, I'm giving you everything you need to repair your credit from the inside out—without wasting money on overpriced credit repair companies or shady online promises.

Let's be honest—credit can feel intimidating. The numbers, the letters, the acronyms—FICO, Experian, 609 letters, charge-offs—it can seem overwhelming. But it doesn't have to be. I'm here to simplify it.

Credit repair is not magic. It's a process. A very doable, repeatable process that anyone—yes, even you—can follow and succeed with. And in this book, I'll walk with you step-by-step through it.

Here's what we're going to cover:

- **First**, I'll show you how credit really works behind the scenes. This includes what credit bureaus are legally allowed to report, and what they're not. We'll bust the myths you've been told about "bad credit" and show you how the law actually protects *you*.

- **Second**, you'll learn how to pull your full credit reports—the right way—and analyze them line by line to identify errors, outdated accounts, or even fraudulent activity. This is one of the most empowering things you can do.

- **Third**, I'll guide you through writing dispute letters, understanding what to say—and what NOT to say—and how to escalate when the bureaus don't cooperate.

- **Fourth**, we'll cover how to handle collections, charge-offs, judgments, and debt that's been sold multiple times. You'll understand your rights and how to negotiate, settle, or remove these accounts from your report.

- **Fifth**, while you're repairing, we'll also talk about **rebuilding**. I'll share how to use credit builder accounts, secured cards, rent and utility reporting, and other smart tools to actively grow your score—even while working on the negative items.

- **Sixth**, we'll go over long-term credit habits—so once your score is strong, you never fall back again. I'll show you how to manage your utilization, automate payments, and monitor your score for life.

And finally, I'll give you a **90-day action plan** you can follow starting today. Step-by-step. Week-by-week. Designed to deliver real results—even if you're starting with a low score, collections, or no recent credit activity at all.

Why am I so passionate about this? Because I've seen what happens when people get their credit back. They don't just get approved for a credit card or a car loan—they breathe easier. They walk taller. They go after bigger dreams. They stop settling for scraps and start building wealth.

Credit isn't just about numbers. It's about power. And too many people give that power away because they don't know how the system works. I'm here to help you take that power back.

I've seen clients raise their credit scores by 100 points or more—just by following this blueprint. I've helped people go from being denied everything to owning homes, starting businesses, and getting funding they never thought possible. You can be next.

Now, here's what I ask of you:

- Listen actively. Take notes if you can.
- Don't rush the process. You're not here for a quick fix—you're here for permanent results.
- And most importantly—**don't skip chapters**. Each one builds on the last, and this system only works if you follow it in order.

This is your blueprint. Your roadmap. Your way out of credit problems—and into financial freedom.

So take a deep breath. You're not behind. You're not too late. You're not stuck.

You're starting now. And I'm with you.

Let's begin.

"Maria's Credit Comeback"

Let me tell you a quick story.

A few years ago, I met a woman named Maria. She was a single mother of two, working full-time, barely getting by. She'd gone through a rough divorce, and with it came late payments, maxed-out cards, and two collection accounts she didn't even recognize.

Her credit score? 524.

She came to me after being denied for a car loan—even though she was making decent money. The worst part? She was doing everything right now… but her past kept following her.

She thought her only option was to pay a credit repair company $200 a month… for *who knows how long*. But instead of paying someone to send out generic letters, she decided to learn how to fix it herself.

Together, we pulled her full credit report. We found five inaccurate items—one was a collection that had already been paid but was never removed. Another had the wrong dates. Two of the accounts weren't even hers. And the rest? Legit—but she learned how to negotiate and settle them smartly.

She didn't dispute everything blindly. She followed the law. She learned her rights. She sent real letters. She documented everything. She followed a system.

And in just four months, her score jumped from 524 to 678.

She got approved for a new car, dropped her interest rate from 18% to under 7%, and for the first time in her life, she started saving money.

But even more than that—she *felt* powerful again. She realized credit isn't about how "good" you are—it's about how *smart* and *persistent* you are.

That's what this book is about.

It's for the Marias of the world. It's for people who are doing their best, but don't have the tools. It's for those who are ready to stop feeling judged and start taking control.

If she can do it, so can you.

CHAPTER 1: HOW CREDIT REPAIR REALLY WORKS

Let's start with the truth.

Credit repair isn't a mystery.
It's not magic. It's not a secret.
It's a legal, step-by-step process that anyone can do—yes, even you—once you understand your rights and how the system works.

Before you send a single letter or open another credit app, you need to understand what you're up against—and what's working in your favor.

Let's break it down.

The Credit Reporting System: Who's Really in Charge?

In the United States, there are **three main credit bureaus**: *Equifax, Experian, and TransUnion.*

They are *not* government agencies. They are *private companies* that collect and sell your financial behavior to lenders, insurers, and sometimes even employers. Their business is information—and they profit from it.

But that also means they have a legal responsibility to report **accurate** and **verifiable** information.

Here's where it gets important:

> Under the **Fair Credit Reporting Act** (FCRA), you have the right to:

- **Access your full credit reports for free**
- **Dispute inaccurate, incomplete, or outdated information**
- **Have unverifiable data removed within 30 days**

Most people don't realize this, but **a large percentage of credit reports contain errors**. According to a study by the FTC, **1 in 5 people** had a verified error that negatively affected their score.

That's not just unfair—it's expensive. Errors can cost you thousands in higher interest rates, fees, and denied opportunities.

What Counts as a Disputable Error?

So what *can* you dispute?

Here are some of the most common things that can legally be removed:

- Accounts that don't belong to you
- Duplicate accounts (often reported more than once)
- Incorrect balances or payment statuses
- Late payments you actually made on time

- Old collections that should have aged off
- Outdated personal info (wrong addresses, name spellings, etc.)
- Debts discharged in bankruptcy but still showing as active
- Re-aged accounts (creditors illegally restarting the clock)

You don't need to guess. If something doesn't look right, you can challenge it.

And the best part? The **burden of proof is on them**—not you.

The credit bureaus and creditors must **prove** that what they're reporting is accurate and verifiable. If they can't, they're required by law to correct or delete it.

That's the foundation of credit repair.

What Credit Repair Is Not

Let's quickly talk about what credit repair *isn't*—so you don't fall into traps.

- It's **not paying someone $99 a month forever** to "work on" your credit without real results.
- It's **not disputing everything blindly** and hoping things disappear. That can actually hurt you.

- It's **not about hiding from debt collectors** or pretending your credit doesn't matter.

Real credit repair is about **empowering yourself with knowledge**, taking strategic action, and being persistent.

The Shift You Need to Make

If you've had bad credit, you might feel ashamed. Embarrassed. Or like it's just your fault.

Let me stop you right there.

Credit is a system. And it's not designed to educate you.
Most of us weren't taught how credit works in school.
And many of us didn't get the best start financially—especially if you're an immigrant, came from a low-income background, or went through a major life event like divorce, illness, or job loss.

So let's make this shift right now:

> **You're not broken. The system is confusing. And now you're learning how to beat it.**

You have more power than you think—and this chapter is the start of you getting it back.

What's Next

Now that you understand what credit repair is—and isn't—we're going to take the first real step in Chapter 2:

Pulling and reviewing your full credit reports.

That's where the real work begins. You can't fix what you don't see. And I'm going to show you how to pull your reports *correctly*, read them *like a pro*, and start spotting the errors and red flags that are costing you money.

Get ready.
You're about to look at your credit with new eyes—and for the first time, you'll know exactly what to do about it.

The Shift You Really Need to Make

Let's pause here—because before we go deeper into reports and letters and disputes, I need you to make one important mental shift.

This isn't just about fixing your credit. It's about changing how you see yourself.

Because if you're like most people I've worked with, you've probably been carrying some weight with your credit problems. Maybe even some shame. Guilt. Frustration. Embarrassment. You might have told yourself:

"I was unwise with money."
"I ruined everything."
"I'll never be able to buy a house."
"Who's going to trust me with credit again?"
"I'm too far behind to fix this."

Let me stop you right now. **None of that is true.**

Let me say this as clearly as I can:

> **You are not broken. You are not stupid. You are not too far behind.**

You're not alone, either. Millions of smart, hard-working people have bad credit. Why? Because life happens.

People get laid off. They go through divorces. They get sick and medical bills pile up. They co-sign for someone they love and end up paying the price. Or, like so many immigrants and young adults, they simply never got the education to navigate the credit system in the first place.

You're not behind—you were never properly shown how the system works.
That's not your fault. But what happens next? That *is* in your hands now.

This is your moment to stop carrying shame—and start taking power.

Because here's the truth:

Credit doesn't care about your feelings. It cares about your actions.

That means that no matter how bad things might look right now, you can change it. And the system, believe it or not, is actually set up to give you a second chance—*if* you know how to work it.

You don't need perfect credit to be successful. You just need a plan. A system. And someone who's been there and knows the way out.

That's what this book is. Not just a guide—but a roadmap. Not just about fixing your score—but fixing your relationship with money, credit, and your future.

Let this be the shift:

> **"You are not a victim of bad credit. You are now the architect of your comeback."**

That's not a motivational quote. That's a decision. One you're making right now by continuing this book.

You've got this. You've already done the hardest part—starting.

Let's keep going.

David's 180-Degree Turnaround

Let me tell you about **David**.

David was a 38-year-old father of three, working as a skilled tradesman in central Florida. He wasn't lazy. He wasn't reckless with money. But over the years, life had worn him down.

After a back injury, David was out of work for months. Bills piled up, and when the unemployment benefits ran out, he did what many people do—he used credit cards to survive. Groceries. Gas. Even his kids' school supplies went on plastic.

He wasn't splurging. He was surviving.

Then came the missed payments. First one. Then two. Then all of them. His phone was ringing off the hook with collection agencies. His credit score fell into the 500s. And the final straw?

He applied for a small loan to fix his only car—and got denied.

He sat in his driveway that night, head in his hands, wondering, "What now?"

He told me later, **"It wasn't just the car. It was that I couldn't help my family. I felt like a failure."**

But David didn't quit.

He got a second job. And more importantly, he decided to take control of his credit—not by paying a company he couldn't afford, but by *learning* the system himself.

He started with one thing: his credit report.

He pulled all three versions—Equifax, Experian, and TransUnion—and printed them out.

At first, it looked like chaos. Old accounts. Duplicates. A collection that wasn't even his. But slowly, with the help of a basic dispute template and some persistence, David started making progress.

He disputed two items that were inaccurately listed as open when they had already been closed and paid. He wrote to a debt collector and got a settlement in writing—with deletion in exchange. He removed two addresses that didn't belong to him. He tracked every letter and sent copies via certified mail, just like we're going to cover in this book.

And then, something incredible happened.

Within 45 days, two derogatory accounts were removed.
Within 90 days, he was approved for a **secured credit card**.
Within 6 months, his score jumped **from 524 to 663**.

That alone changed everything.

He refinanced his old car loan, saving hundreds in interest.
He got pre-approved for a home loan a year later.
And more importantly—he told me this himself—**"I felt like I could breathe again."**

Now here's the thing:

David didn't do anything you can't do.
He didn't pay a credit repair company.
He didn't need a degree in finance.
He didn't use fancy legal language or threats.

He used the law. He stayed consistent. He educated himself.
He followed a blueprint.

And it worked.

He didn't just repair his credit—he repaired his confidence, his sense of control, and his vision for the future.

That's what I want for you. Not just a higher score. But a new story. So as you go through this book, keep David in mind. When it feels slow, when it feels overwhelming—remember that every small step you take adds up.

The phone calls will stop.
The denials will end.
The confidence will return.

You're not stuck.
You're just one decision away from a completely different financial future.

CHAPTER 2: PULLING AND REVIEWING YOUR FULL CREDIT REPORT

This is where your credit repair journey *truly begins*. Everything until now has been about building the mindset and understanding the system. But now? It's time to take action.

And the first real step is simple but powerful:

Pull and review your full credit report.

You might be surprised how many people try to fix their credit without ever reading their entire report. It's like trying to fix a car without popping the hood.

You cannot fix what you cannot see.

Your credit report is your blueprint. It shows you everything that lenders, banks, landlords, and even employers might see when they evaluate you. That's why this step matters so much.

Where to Get Your Credit Reports for Free

You are legally entitled to a **free credit report from all three major bureaus once a year** through:

AnnualCreditReport.com

This is the only website authorized by federal law to provide free reports from:

- **Equifax**
- **Experian**
- **TransUnion**

Since the COVID-19 pandemic, they've been offering free **weekly** reports, which may still be active depending on when you're listening to this.

Here's how to pull your report:

1. Go to AnnualCreditReport.com.
2. Choose all three reports when prompted.
3. Answer identity verification questions.
4. Download or print each report—don't rely on just viewing them online.

Important tip:
Don't pull only one report. Pull **all three**—because creditors don't always report to every bureau, and errors may appear on one but not the others.

What You're Looking At (Don't Panic!)

When you open your credit reports for the first time, you may feel overwhelmed. That's completely normal.

You'll see multiple sections, including:

- **Personal Information**: Name, aliases, current and past addresses, SSN variations
- **Accounts (Tradelines)**: Credit cards, loans, mortgages, auto loans
- **Collections**: Accounts that went unpaid and were sold or assigned to collectors
- **Inquiries**: Who has pulled your credit and when
- **Public Records**: Bankruptcies, tax liens (these rarely appear anymore)
- **Remarks**: Notes from disputes, fraud alerts, or consumer statements

Take a breath and scan through it slowly. You don't need to understand every code. You're looking for **patterns** and **problems**.

How to Review Your Report (Like a Semi-Pro)

Here's what to look for in each section:

Personal Information

- Are there addresses that don't belong to you?
- Do you see multiple versions of your name?
- Are there unknown phone numbers or employers?

Why this matters: Inaccurate personal data can be linked to false accounts or identity mix-ups. Clean this up first—it lays the groundwork for stronger disputes later.

Accounts Section (Tradelines)

For each account listed, check:

- Is it yours?
- Are the **payment statuses accurate**?
- Are the **open and close dates correct**?
- Are balances and credit limits current?

Highlight any:

- **Late payments you never missed**
- **Accounts showing a balance after being paid**
- **Old negative accounts that should have aged off**

Rule of thumb: Most negative items should fall off your report after **7 years** (except bankruptcy and some judgments).

Collections Section

- Is the debt **legitimate**?
- Has it been **paid but still shows as active**?
- Do you recognize the name of the collector?

Tip: Some collection agencies **re-age** debt illegally to keep it on your report longer. Make sure the **"date of first delinquency"** is correct. This date starts the 7-year countdown.

Inquiries

Soft inquiries don't affect your score. Hard inquiries do.

Look for:

- Inquiries you **don't recognize**

- Multiple inquiries on the same day (could be a car dealership "shopping" your file)

- Inquiries older than 24 months (these should disappear automatically)

Too many hard inquiries in a short time = red flag for lenders.

Create a Credit Repair Tracking Sheet!

Now that you've reviewed your reports, create a **simple spreadsheet or worksheet** to track your findings. You'll use this as your personal "battle plan" moving forward.

Your sheet should have:

- Creditor name

- Account number (last 4 digits only)

- What's wrong (ex: "reported late but paid on time")

- Bureau(s) it appears on

- Date you plan to dispute

- Notes and updates

You'll thank yourself later for staying organized.

Don't Judge—Just Observe

Now, let me tell you something important:

> **"When reviewing your credit report, you may feel frustrated. Angry. Maybe even ashamed." It's ok!**

Please don't let those feelings stop you. You're here now. You're doing the work. You're facing the facts—and most people never get that far.

You are not your credit report.
You are not your old mistakes.
You are not what a three-digit number says about you.

You are someone who is taking control, one line item at a time.

What's Next?

In the next chapter, we'll take the findings from your credit report and start writing **powerful dispute letters** that actually work.

You'll learn:

- How to structure a proper dispute
- What supporting documents to include

- Why wording matters
- And how to avoid common dispute mistakes that delay results

You've now officially crossed the first major milestone.

You've pulled your report.
You've studied the truth.
And now… you're ready to fight for a better financial future.

Let's move forward—together.

"Sofia's Report" – Seeing the Truth for the First Time

Sofia never thought she'd be in this position.

She was 34, smart, driven, the kind of person who always worked hard and made sure her kids had what they needed. She wasn't perfect with money, but she'd never been careless. Life just... hit her hard, and all at once.

It started with her husband's job loss. Then came a series of unexpected car repairs, her daughter's surgery, and a few missed payments that turned into more than a few.

Soon, her phone started ringing constantly. Emails about past-due bills. Letters from collection agencies. She felt overwhelmed, embarrassed, and exhausted. And when she finally tried to refinance her car to lower the payments—they told her "denied due to credit score."

When she logged into Credit Karma, it said her score was 552.

She closed the app and cried.

"I felt powerless," she said later. "Like I'd already failed. Like even if I worked hard, it wouldn't matter."

But then something happened.

One of her close friends sent her a voice note and said, "You don't need to keep suffering. You can fix it. But you need to see the real credit report. Not the app. The real one."

Sofia didn't know what her "real" credit report even was.

So she went to AnnualCreditReport.com, just like you're doing now. It was scary. She worried about what she'd find. But she did it anyway.

She printed all three: Equifax, Experian, and TransUnion.

She sat at her kitchen table with a red pen, a notebook, and a strong cup of coffee.

What she saw surprised her.

There were **14 accounts total**. Some of them were hers. But some… weren't.

There was a **cell phone bill in another city** under her name—but she'd never lived there.

There were **two medical collections**, one of which was already paid but still showing as "open."

There was a **credit card she closed years ago**, but the balance was still listed as active.

There were also **four addresses she never lived at**, and **two employers she never worked for**.

And suddenly, the picture became clear.

> It wasn't that she had "bad credit." It was that her credit report was a mess.
>
> It wasn't just her past—it was a system full of sloppy, outdated, and inaccurate data.

She told me later, "It felt like I was reading a stranger's report, not mine. Like my identity was mixed up with someone else's story."

That night, Sofia started documenting.

She wrote down every account that was wrong or questionable. She marked which ones were on all three reports and which were only on one. She created a simple Excel spreadsheet with colors—red for negative, yellow for questionable, green for accurate.

And for the first time in a long time, **she felt in control**.

Not because her score had changed—it hadn't. Not yet.
But because she had finally taken off the blindfold.
She could see clearly. And now, she could do something about it.

She said, "I didn't cry this time. I felt power coming back. I saw that I wasn't the failure—I was the fixer."

Over the next few weeks, Sofia started writing dispute letters. She contacted a hospital billing department and got one of the collections fully deleted. She submitted identity verification to correct the addresses. She disputed the closed credit card that still showed a balance, and 30 days later, it was updated to $0 and "Paid in Full."

She also took the advice you'll learn in this book—she applied for a secured card and started reporting her rent to the bureaus.

Four months later, her score had risen to **642**.
By month six, she crossed **680**.

But more than that?

- She applied for a new apartment and got accepted with no co-signer.
- She got a low-interest personal loan to consolidate her debts.
- And she started teaching her teenage son about credit—something she was never taught.

That's why this chapter matters so much.

It's not just about the data. It's about **dignity**.

Pulling your credit report doesn't feel powerful at first—but it's one of the most powerful things you'll ever do. Because when you finally see what's working for you and against you, you stop blaming yourself, and start doing something that works.

That's what Sofia learned.
That's what I've seen happen again and again.
And that's what's happening for you—right now.

So take the time.
Print the reports.
Review every line.
Make your list.
And trust this process.

You don't need to have it all figured out today.
You just need to take the next step.

And in the next chapter, I'll show you exactly how to do that—by writing dispute letters that get real results.

Let's move forward.

CHAPTER 3: DISPUTING NEGATIVE ITEMS STEP-BY-STEP

By now, you've pulled your credit reports, reviewed every section, and created your tracking sheet. You've started identifying accounts that don't belong, items that are outdated or incorrect, and you're probably asking yourself:

> "How do I actually fix this?"

This is the chapter where we take action.

This is where the repair begins.

We're going to walk through exactly how to write effective disputes, what to include, what not to do, and how to maximize your chances of success.

The Truth About Credit Disputes

Let's start with a simple truth:
Disputing credit report errors is your legal right!

You don't need a lawyer. You don't need a paid service. You just need the facts and the ability to communicate clearly and assertively.

Under the **Fair Credit Reporting Act (FCRA)**, credit bureaus are required to:

- Investigate disputes within **30 days**
- Verify the accuracy of the information
- Remove or correct unverifiable or inaccurate data

If they can't verify it, they must delete it.

You are not asking for a favor. You are invoking your **federal rights.**

What Can You Honestly Dispute?

You can dispute **any item that is inaccurate, outdated, incomplete, or cannot be verified**. Examples include:

- Late payments that were actually made on time
- Duplicate accounts listed twice
- Accounts that don't belong to you

- Collections already paid
- Incorrect balances or payment statuses
- Outdated accounts (over 7 years old)
- Re-aged accounts (where creditors illegally reset the delinquency date)
- Mixed file errors (someone else's credit data showing under your name)

Don't dispute accounts just to see what disappears. That's called **frivolous disputing**, and it often backfires.
We're doing this the **right way**—with purpose and evidence.

Step 1: Choose Your Method – Online or Mail?

Yes, you *can* dispute online—but I recommend you do it **by mail**, for several important reasons:

Why Mail Is Better:

- You can include **supporting documents** (bank statements, letters, receipts)
- You create a **paper trail**

- You have **proof of delivery**

- You avoid agreeing to certain **terms and conditions** buried in online portals that may limit your legal rights

Send your dispute letters by certified mail with return receipt requested.

That way, you know when they received it, and the 30-day countdown legally begins.

Step 2: Write Your Dispute Letter (The Right Way)

Your dispute letter should be simple, direct, and professional.

Here's a basic structure:

1. **Your Name**

2. **Your Full Address**

3. **Date**

4. **Subject Line**: Dispute of Inaccurate Information on Credit Report

5. **Bureau Name & Address**

6. A short introduction:

"I am writing to dispute the following inaccurate information on my credit report. Please investigate these items and correct or remove them in accordance with the Fair Credit Reporting Act."

7. A clear list of disputed accounts:
    - Creditor Name
    - Account Number (last 4 digits only)
    - Reason for dispute (e.g., "This account is not mine" or "Paid in full but still listed as open")
8. Optional: Attach documentation (cancelled checks, letters, screenshots, etc.)
9. Close with:

   "Please conduct an investigation and send me written confirmation of the results within 30 days, as required by law."

10. Your signature

Keep it short. Keep it clear. **Avoid emotion or accusations.**

Step 3: Include Proof of Identity

Credit bureaus need to verify you're really you. Include the following with your letter:

- A copy of your **driver's license** or government-issued ID
- A copy of a **recent utility bill or bank statement** (to confirm your address)
- A copy of the **credit report page** with the disputed item highlighted

Staple or paperclip these together and include them with your letter.

Step 4: Mail to All Three Bureaus

Each bureau must be contacted **separately**.

Here are the current mailing addresses:

Equifax

P.O. Box 740256
Atlanta, GA 30374

Experian

P.O. Box 4500
Allen, TX 75013

TransUnion

P.O. Box 2000
Chester, PA 19016

Make copies of everything you send. Always send by **certified mail with a return receipt**.

Step 5: Wait… Then Review the Results

Once your dispute is received, the bureau has **30 days to respond**. You'll usually get a letter or email stating whether the item:

- Was **deleted**
- Was **updated**
- Or remains **verified as accurate**

If it's deleted—great!
If it's updated—check that the update is correct.
If it remains—don't give up. You may need to escalate, request more documentation, or dispute directly with the creditor.

***Pro Tip*: Creditors must respond too. If they ignore the bureau's verification request within the 30-day window, the bureau is required to delete the item! (Incredible but true.)**

Common Mistakes Everyone Needs to Avoid

Let's make sure you don't shoot yourself in the foot. Avoid these errors:

- **Disputing everything at once** — Focus on 2–5 items per letter
- **Not keeping records** — Save every letter and response
- **Using "template" dispute letters from the internet** — They look generic and can be flagged
- **Failing to update your address with the bureaus first** — Leads to delays or denials
- **Disputing accurate information** — Don't challenge what you know is correct

Remember, the bureaus have software that looks for patterns. Sloppy disputes get ignored. **Thoughtful ones get results.**

What If They Don't Respond or Fix It?

If you receive no response within 30–45 days, or if the dispute is denied without proper documentation, you can:

1. **Send a follow-up dispute** with stronger wording and more documentation
2. **Dispute directly with the creditor**

3. **File a complaint with the CFPB** (Consumer Financial Protection Bureau) at consumerfinance.gov

The CFPB is your ally. They oversee the credit bureaus and force compliance.

What Success Looks Like

Dispute success can look like:

- A **collection deleted**
- A **late payment updated to on-time**
- A **charged-off account corrected to "paid"**
- A **fraudulent account removed completely**

And over time, these changes lead to **better credit scores, more approvals, lower interest rates, and peace of mind.**

Remember: not every item will be deleted. But every **verified correction** helps. And when combined with rebuilding (covered in the next chapter), your credit score can move dramatically in the right direction.

What to Expect Next

Credit repair is not a one-time event. It's a process.

Start with your **top 3–5 errors**, write clean disputes, and track the results.

Once those are resolved, move to the next batch.

With each step, you build a cleaner credit report—and a stronger financial future.

In the next chapter, we'll go even deeper. You'll learn **how to actively rebuild your credit** while you wait for disputes to process, using proven methods like secured credit cards, rent reporting, and more.

You've done the work. You've written the letters.
Now, let's make that score climb.

"Tyrell's Fight Back" – Winning the Dispute War

When Tyrell first pulled his credit report, he felt like he'd opened a file on someone else's life.

It had been years since he really looked at his credit. In his mind, he knew things weren't perfect. But seeing it in black and white? It felt like a punch in the gut.

He sat in his small apartment in Tampa, eyes scanning line after line—collections, missed payments, charge-offs—and he felt something heavy sink into his chest.

The worst part?

One of the accounts was a **medical bill** from a hospital he'd never been to. Another was a **utility bill** from a place he hadn't lived in over six years. And there was a **credit card in his name**... with an address he'd never heard of.

He called me the next morning. I could hear the frustration in his voice.

> "Joe, I didn't even know half this stuff was on there. How can they just... throw things on your report like that?"

And I told him what I'm telling you now:

> "It happens all the time. But the good news? You don't have to accept it."

That day, Tyrell made a decision: he was going to fight back.

He started with one letter.

He wrote to Equifax to dispute the hospital collection that wasn't his. He attached a copy of his ID, a utility bill to confirm his current address, and circled the item directly on the report.

He followed the format I gave him. Nothing emotional. Just facts.

> "This account is not mine. I have never received care at this facility, nor have I authorized anyone to open this account in my name. Please conduct an investigation and remove this item under the FCRA."

He mailed it certified, with a return receipt requested.

He did the same for TransUnion and Experian.

Then he waited.

At first, it was hard. He kept refreshing his email. He checked the tracking numbers every day like he was waiting on a winning lottery ticket.

And then—day 28—he got a letter back from Equifax.

Deleted.

The hospital bill was gone.

That one win gave him fuel.

He pulled out his tracking sheet and picked the next target: the utility bill from a place he hadn't lived in since his cousin crashed at his old apartment and didn't pay the final balance in his name.

This one felt trickier—because he *had* lived there years ago. But he wasn't the one who racked up the charges after he left.

So he wrote a new letter, this time with more explanation and a copy of the move-out letter he'd saved in an old Gmail folder.

> "The charges on this account occurred after my lease ended and I no longer occupied the unit. I have attached documentation confirming my move-out date. Please correct or remove this account from my report."

He mailed it. Tracked it. Waited.

This time, Experian removed it. TransUnion updated it to $0 and "closed." Equifax kept it—said it was verified.

So he wrote back again.

> "Please provide the method of verification and original billing records."

This time, he escalated.

And 18 days later—Equifax deleted it, too.

Then came the big one: the credit card.

It was in his name, but the address was completely unfamiliar. It had a $2,400 balance. 90-day lates. A charge-off status.

He couldn't believe it.

It felt like fraud—but there was no inquiry on his report. No application trail. No red flags had ever popped up.

Still, he knew it wasn't his.

He called the creditor directly. They said it had been opened six years ago, online, using his name and Social Security number—but a different address and phone number.

That's when it clicked: **identity theft.**

Maybe not the kind you see in movies—but the quiet kind, where someone opens an account, defaults, and disappears.

He filed an **FTC Identity Theft Report**. Then, he sent a copy of it along with a police report, his ID, and a detailed dispute letter to all three bureaus.

This time, he didn't just ask for deletion—he demanded it.

> "This is a fraudulent account. I did not authorize this credit line. Please block and delete this item under FCRA Section 605B and confirm in writing within 30 days."

All three bureaus removed it.

That one deletion? His score jumped **72 points** overnight.

Six months from when he started, Tyrell had:

- Removed 3 major derogatory accounts
- Updated 2 errors
- Added a secured card and reported 6 months of on-time payments
- Jumped his credit score from **534 to 691**

But more than that?

He stopped hiding from his credit.
He started trusting himself again.
He even taught his younger sister how to pull her report—and helped her write her first dispute.

He told me, "I used to think my credit report was a sentence. Like I had to live with it. But now I see it's a story—and I get to rewrite it."

Here's what I want you to take from Tyrell's story:

You don't have to fix it all at once. Don't feel pressured to do it all in one instant!
You don't have to win every dispute immediately.
You just have to **start**, and then keep going.

Disputes are not confrontations—they're corrections. You are not begging. You are exercising your rights. And when you do it the right way—with proof, structure, and persistence—you get results.

So, what's your "Tyrell letter" going to be?

What's the first item you're going to challenge?

You've already done the hardest part—facing your report.
Now it's time to start fixing it.

And I'm right here with you.

Let's move on to Chapter 4—because once you start clearing out errors, the next step is knowing how to handle the **big ones**: collections, charge-offs, and even judgments.

You've got this.

CHAPTER 4: HANDLING COLLECTIONS, CHARGE-OFFS, AND JUDGMENTS

Now that you've pulled your credit report, reviewed every line, and learned how to write effective dispute letters, it's time to talk about the big ones—**collections, charge-offs, and judgments.**

These are the items that often scare people the most. They sound harsh. They look ugly on your report. And they can bring down your score significantly.

But here's the truth most people don't know:

> **You can negotiate with collections. You can challenge charge-offs. And you can even settle or remove some judgments.**

These items are not permanent life sentences.
They are negotiable, fixable, and in some cases—**completely removable**.

This chapter is your roadmap.

Let's Start With Collections

A **collection** happens when a creditor gives up on trying to get you to pay and sells your debt to a collection agency. At that point, the original account is usually closed and a new one appears under the name of the collection company.

So now you've got **two accounts** dragging your score down.

Here's the key question:

> **Do you owe the debt? And can the collector prove it?**

You have the legal right to **request validation** of any debt that's been sent to collections.

Here's how to do it:

1. Write a **Debt Validation Letter** under the **FDCPA (Fair Debt Collection Practices Act)**.
2. Send it within **30 days** of first contact (if possible).
3. Ask the collector to verify:
    - The original creditor
    - The amount owed
    - Proof that they are legally authorized to collect
4. Request that they cease all collection activity until the debt is validated.

If they can't prove it? They must stop reporting it.

If they validate it and it's legitimate, you still have options.

Negotiating With Collections

Once a debt is validated, you can often **negotiate a lower amount** or even a **pay-for-deletion**.

Here's how it works:

> A "**Pay-for-Delete**" agreement means you pay a reduced or full amount **only if they agree in writing to remove the account from your credit report.**

Some collection agencies will do it. Others won't.

Even if they refuse to delete, paying the account will still update the balance to **$0**, which is better than an unpaid collection and may improve your score—especially with newer scoring models like FICO 9 and VantageScore.

When negotiating, keep these tips in mind:

- **Always get agreements in writing before you pay**
- **Never give access to your bank account**—use money orders or one-time payments
- Start low. Many collectors will settle for 30–60% of the amount owed
- Be calm, professional, and persistent

Once paid or deleted, dispute the collection with the bureaus to ensure it updates properly.

Charge-Offs: What They Really Mean

A **charge-off** means the original creditor has written off your debt as a loss—but you may still legally owe it.

This usually happens after 180 days of non-payment.

Here's the mistake people make:

> They think the charge-off means the account is "done." But it still damages your credit—and the balance is often still shown as owed.

You can dispute inaccurate charge-off listings if:

- The **dates** are wrong
- The **balance** is still listed even after a settlement
- The account was **re-aged** to appear newer
- The **status** is incorrect (e.g., marked as "open" when it's closed)

If the account is old, you may want to wait for it to fall off—most charge-offs **age off your report after 7 years** from the original delinquency date.

However, if it's newer and holding your score back, you can:

- **Settle for less and request updated reporting**
- **Dispute outdated or inaccurate information**
- **Request removal after payment if you have leverage (i.e., they want you to pay)**

Pro tip: If you settle a charge-off, try to get the status changed to **"Paid in full"** or **"Settled – Account Closed"** instead of leaving the negative remarks.

Dealing With Judgments and Public Records

Judgments used to appear on credit reports regularly, but thanks to a 2017 change, **most civil judgments and tax liens no longer appear** on consumer credit reports.

That said, if you're still seeing a **judgment** on your report, verify:

- That it is **accurate and belongs to you**
- That it was **entered by a court**
- That the date, amount, and status are all correct

If the judgment is incorrect or expired, dispute it with the bureaus and **attach court records** to prove it.

If it's valid and you can't dispute it, consider:

- **Paying it in full and requesting a satisfaction of judgment**
- **Negotiating a settlement and asking the court to update the record**

- **Working with a legal aid service if you can't afford representation**

Once a judgment is **satisfied**, it holds much less weight—especially if you can get it removed from public records or suppressed in future background checks.

When to Settle and When to Let It Go

This is where strategy matters.

Ask yourself:

- Is the debt **within the statute of limitations**? (Varies by state—typically 3–6 years for most debts)
- Is it **hurting your score right now**?
- Are you planning a major purchase or loan soon?
- Will **paying it restart the clock** and extend its reporting period?

Sometimes, it's smarter to wait out a collection or charge-off that's almost 7 years old.

Other times, settling now makes sense—especially if you're preparing to apply for a mortgage or business funding.

When in doubt, seek help. A qualified credit coach or attorney can review your situation and help you choose the best course of action.

Final Thoughts

Collections, charge-offs, and judgments are scary words—but they are not death sentences.

They are **temporary challenges**. And they are fixable.

Here's what I want you to remember:

> You are not a collection. You are not a charge-off. You are not a judgment.

You are a person taking control of your finances.

You are someone with rights.

You are someone with a plan.

The more you understand how these systems work, the more confident—and free—you'll become.

So take it one item at a time.

Use your credit repair tracker. Stay organized. Follow up.

You'll be amazed how many things that once seemed "permanent" can actually be negotiated, corrected, or deleted entirely.

In the next chapter, we'll take the next step in your rebuild journey—because while you're cleaning up the past, we also want to start building your future.

Let's move forward.

"Jessica vs. the Collection Agencies"

Jessica was a fighter—but even fighters get tired.

She had been through more than most. After putting herself through college while working two jobs, she finally landed a steady position as a licensed massage therapist. She loved helping people. She had built a small but loyal clientele and was doing okay—until COVID hit.

Suddenly, everything shut down.

Her appointments disappeared overnight. She applied for unemployment but waited weeks to receive anything. Bills didn't wait. Neither did the landlord. And when she used her credit cards to pay for food and rent, she thought she was buying time. But in reality, she was falling into a trap.

By the time her industry reopened months later, she was behind on three cards, her car note, and two small medical bills from a trip to the ER with her daughter.

Then came the phone calls.

"Hi Jessica, this is Mike from Midland Credit Management..."

Every day. Every number. Every voice mail with a new name, a new account, a new demand. It was like debt was following her everywhere she went.

She stopped answering the phone. She stopped checking the mail.

And then one day, her bank declined a small loan she applied for to consolidate her bills. That same afternoon, she finally opened a letter she'd been avoiding.

It was a **notice of judgment**.

One of her old credit card companies had sued her and won. She had missed the court date because the notice was sent to an old address. And now, she owed **$2,136 plus interest and legal fees**.

She sat on her couch that night, staring at the letter, holding back tears.

> "I didn't even know I could be sued like that. I felt violated. Exposed. Like they had all the power."

But Jessica wasn't just a fighter—she was also smart.

The next morning, she took a deep breath, pulled out her laptop, and Googled:
"How to remove a judgment from your credit report."

That search led her to learning about credit repair, the FCRA, and eventually—me.

The first thing she did was **pull all three of her credit reports**.

There it was: four collections, two charge-offs, and the judgment.

But what shocked her most?

One of the collection accounts was **already paid**—but still listed as unpaid.

Another was a **utility bill** from an apartment she hadn't lived in for almost six years.
And a third was from a **lab testing company** she didn't even recognize.

She started a notebook. She wrote down the names of the creditors, the amounts, the account numbers, and what looked wrong.

And she got to work.

Her first win came with the paid collection. She called the collection agency, explained the error, and requested they update it to "Paid in Full." They agreed.

But that wasn't enough.

So she mailed a **dispute letter** to all three bureaus with her receipt attached. Thirty-one days later? **Deleted from all three.**

Next, she tackled the lab bill. She wrote a **debt validation letter** and mailed it certified.

Ten days later, the company responded. They couldn't validate the debt. No date of service. No signature. No invoice.

Jessica sent a follow-up to the bureaus. **Deleted.**

Her confidence was building.

Then came the charge-offs.

One was a store credit card with a balance of $1,200. The other was a major card with a $3,600 balance and six missed payments.

She called both creditors, ready to negotiate.

The store card agreed to settle for $450—but they refused to delete it. Still, she got the deal in writing and paid it.

Then she sent a **goodwill letter** asking for deletion due to hardship. They denied it.

But she didn't give up.

Two months later, she sent another letter—this time with a handwritten note about how she used to be a loyal customer, how COVID impacted her, and how she was trying to buy her first home.

That time? They removed it.

Now came the hardest part—the **judgment**.

Jessica was scared. She didn't know how to deal with courts or legal language. But she learned something important:

> If you satisfy a judgment, you can request that the court mark it as "Satisfied" or even "Vacated."

So she called the law firm that won the judgment. She was nervous, but calm.

She said, "I'm ready to settle this judgment. But I want to know what you can do in return."

The attorney offered a payment plan. Jessica negotiated a **one-time payoff for $1,600**, got it in writing, and paid it.

Then, she filed a **Motion to Vacate the Judgment** based on lack of proper service (she never received the initial court notice). She submitted proof of her old and current address, her payment receipt, and a short personal statement.

Thirty days later, the judgment was **vacated**.

Gone.

Eight months after she started, Jessica had:

- Deleted two collections
- Settled two charge-offs
- Vacated a judgment
- Increased her credit score from **518 to 677**

She didn't pay thousands to a credit repair company.
She didn't have perfect knowledge.
She had **determination, documentation, and a plan.**

And today?

She's a homeowner.
She teaches financial literacy workshops for teen moms.
And every year, she reviews her credit report like it's her birthday tradition.

She told me something I'll never forget:

> "I thought collections meant I was irresponsible. I thought the judgment meant I was a failure. But I realized—they were just *temporary problems.* And I didn't need perfect credit. I just needed to believe I had the right to fix it."

You have that same right.

And now, you have the tools.

So take your list. Review your items. One at a time.

You're not just fixing a credit report.
You're fixing your access to freedom. Stability. Options.

Jessica did it. And so will you.

Let's keep going.

CHAPTER 5: REBUILDING CREDIT WHILE REPAIRING

You've made amazing progress so far.

You've pulled your reports.
You've reviewed your history.
You've started challenging false or outdated items.
You've begun settling what's holding you back.

But now it's time for something equally important:

> While you're cleaning up the past... **you need to start building your future.**

This is where credit repair turns into **credit growth**.

In this chapter, I'm going to walk you through how to **build positive credit history**—even if your score is still low, even if you've been denied before, and even if you're working with limited income.

You'll learn:

- What accounts you can open now
- How to build without taking on risky debt
- How to report rent, utilities, and bills that you're already paying
- How to stack small wins that become big gains

Let's start simple.

Step 1: Use a Secured Credit Card

A **secured credit card** is one of the easiest ways to rebuild credit from scratch or after damage.

Here's how it works:

- You make a **cash deposit**, usually $200–$500
- That deposit becomes your credit limit
- You use the card, pay it off each month, and your activity gets reported to the credit bureaus

Think of it as training wheels for your credit.

You're not borrowing the bank's money—they're lending you back your own money to help prove you're responsible.

And guess what?

Most secured cards **graduate to unsecured** cards after 6–12 months of on-time payments.

> Tip: Keep your usage low—ideally under **10–30%** of your limit at all times
> Example: If your limit is $300, never let your balance exceed $90

Even a $300 secured card, paid on time each month and kept under 10% utilization, can **boost your score significantly** in 90–180 days.

Step 2: Report Your Rent and Utility Payments

You're already paying rent, right? And utilities?

But most of that isn't helping your credit score—unless you take a few extra steps.

Here's how to change that:

- Use services like **RentReporters**, **LevelCredit**, or **Experian Boost**

- These tools connect to your rent payments or bank accounts and **report positive payment history** to the credit bureaus

Some of these tools will even **report up to 24 months of past payments**, instantly adding depth to your file.

Think about it—if you've paid your rent every month for two years, that's 24 months of on-time "credit payments" that lenders will now see.

> Bonus: Some services also report utility, streaming services, and phone bills

For $5–$10/month, these tools are a **powerful way to build credit** using the bills you're already paying.

Step 3: Become an Authorized User

This is one of the most **underrated tools** in credit building.

Here's how it works:

- A friend or family member with good credit **adds you to their credit card account**
- You don't need to use the card or even hold it
- The **account's age, limit, and on-time history** can be added to your credit file

It's not a co-signer situation. You're not legally responsible for the debt.

As long as the person trusts you and has:

- A low balance
- A long history (at least 1–2 years)
- No late payments

Then adding you as an authorized user can **increase your score fast**.

> Caution: Only do this with someone who manages credit well. Their bad habits will show up on your file too.

This strategy alone has helped people boost their scores **50–100 points** in 30–60 days.

Step 4: Try a Credit Builder Loan

A **credit builder loan** is designed to help people with poor or no credit **build a payment history**.

Here's how it works:

- You "borrow" a small amount ($300–$1,000)
- But instead of receiving the money, the bank or credit union **holds it in a locked savings account**
- You make monthly payments until it's paid off
- Once you've paid the full amount, they release the money to you

These loans are usually offered by:

- Credit unions
- Community banks
- Fintech companies like Self, SeedFi, or Credit Strong

Bonus: Your monthly payments are reported to all three credit bureaus
That's a **double win**—you save money **and** build credit

If you don't qualify for other credit yet, a builder loan can **kick-start your score** and teach great habits at the same time.

Step 5: Monitor and Adjust

Once you've opened **1–2 new positive accounts**, your job is to:

- Pay every bill on time
- Keep your balances low
- Log in once a week to monitor activity
- Dispute any new errors or unauthorized accounts immediately

Use **free monitoring tools** like:

- Credit Karma (for TransUnion and Equifax)
- CreditWise (from Capital One)
- Experian.com (for full reports and FICO scores)

Think of rebuilding as gardening: You pull the weeds (negative items), but you also **plant seeds** (new, healthy credit accounts).

And if you tend to your garden, your score will grow.

The Power of Positive Data

Here's something the credit bureaus don't always make clear:

> Your score is more influenced by **what you do now** than what happened years ago.

Late payments, collections, and charge-offs hurt. But **they lose power over time.**

New, on-time payments are like fertilizer for your score.

Just **six months** of consistent, on-time payments across a few accounts can move your score **100 points or more**—even if old negatives are still present.

This is how you **outrun your past**.

And as your score grows, more opportunities open:

- Credit card approvals
- Lower interest rates
- Business funding
- Car and home loans

- Peace of mind

You'll stop feeling judged—and start feeling in control.

Final Thought: You're Not Just Repairing, You're Rebuilding

Most people stop credit repair at "deleting bad stuff."
But the real win comes when you also **build good stuff.**

And you're doing that now.

You're using what you've got. You're choosing tools that match your goals. And you're becoming someone lenders **want** to approve—not because you're perfect, but because you're consistent.

> Remember: Credit is less about who you were—and more about who you're becoming.

In the next chapter, I'll show you how to **protect your growing credit** and avoid the most common mistakes that knock people backward.

You've started fresh.
Now let's make sure you don't just fix it—you **keep it strong** for life.

Let's move forward.

"From Broke to 720 – Andre's Second Chance"

Andre wasn't looking to become a credit expert.
He just wanted to stop feeling **embarrassed** every time someone ran his report.

He was 42, worked in HVAC, and had recently gone through a rough patch. After a layoff during the off-season, he'd missed a few payments, defaulted on a small personal loan, and maxed out a couple of credit cards trying to cover his bills.

By the time things settled down, his score had dropped to **524**.

He didn't want to check it. He didn't even want to talk about it.

The real wake-up call came when he applied for a loan to buy a work van—something that would've helped him increase his income. But the dealer ran his credit, looked up at him with that "I'm sorry" expression, and said the words no entrepreneur ever wants to hear:

> "We can't approve this right now."

Andre felt defeated.

Not just because of the loan—but because he knew he was working hard, trying to do things right, but his **past mistakes kept following him**.

He decided he needed to do something—**anything**—to start moving in the right direction.

That night, he pulled his full credit reports, created a spreadsheet, and started listening to every podcast, book, and YouTube video he could find.

He realized something powerful:

> "Even if I can't erase everything from the past, I *can* start building the future."

His First Win: A Secured Card

Andre applied for a secured credit card with a $300 deposit.

He set up auto-pay for $25/month and made sure he never used more than 10% of the limit.

Every month, like clockwork, he paid it down.

Three months in, he saw something he hadn't seen in years:
A green checkmark.
On-time payments.
Utilization below 10%.

It was small—but it was progress.

Turning Bills Into Credit Builders

Next, he signed up for **Experian Boost** to report his utilities and Netflix bill.

He'd been paying those for years—but they never helped him.

Suddenly, three new positive accounts showed up.
His score jumped **23 points in a week**.

He kept going.

He found a program called **RentReporters** and signed up to report his rent payments. He even got 18 months of back payment history included.

His landlord signed the form, and within 30 days, **his rental history appeared on his reports**.

> "I realized I was already doing the hard work—paying on time. I just wasn't getting credit for it."

The Power of an Authorized User

Andre then had a heart-to-heart with his sister.

She had excellent credit, a five-year-old credit card with a $10,000 limit, and never missed a payment. He asked if she'd be willing to add him as an **authorized user**.

She was hesitant at first—but after understanding that he wouldn't even need to use the card, she agreed.

Thirty days later, that account **hit his credit report**.

His score jumped again—this time by **41 points**.

But it wasn't just the number.

It was the feeling.

For the first time in years, Andre felt like **he was winning**.

His Final Move: A Credit Builder Loan

Andre wanted to keep building.

So he signed up for a **Credit Builder Loan** through Self. He committed to $25/month for 12 months. It was a forced savings account—but every payment was reported as an installment loan.

That meant he was now building:

- Revolving credit (secured card)
- Rental history
- Utility history
- Installment credit (loan)
- Authorized user account

He was doing exactly what we've talked about in this chapter—**building while repairing**.

The Results…

After 8 months of rebuilding, Andre's score hit **703**.

A month later, it reached **720**.

He reapplied for the van loan. This time?
Approved. No co-signer.

Decent rate.
He even negotiated the price.

But the biggest win wasn't financial.

It was emotional.

He said to me, "I used to walk into places expecting to be denied. Now, I walk in knowing I'm qualified."

His New Habits

Andre now checks his credit every Sunday.

He keeps all balances under 10%.

He teaches his 18-year-old nephew about credit.
He plans to help him open a secured card as soon as he gets his first job.

Andre didn't have a windfall.
He didn't dispute every negative item.
He just **showed up consistently** and followed a plan.

He told me:

> "I used to think credit was for rich people or people who never messed up. But it's not. Credit is for people who understand the system and respect it."

And now he does.

And now you do, too.

You may not be Andre. You may not have the same setbacks or the same wins. But you *can* follow the same system.

And if you stick with it?

That 500-something score could soon be a memory.

You've already started.
You've already shown up.
Now it's time to keep going.

Let's move on to **Chapter 6**, where I'll show you exactly how to manage your growing credit profile and avoid the pitfalls that send people backwards.

Because rebuilding is great.
But protecting it? That's where the real freedom begins.

CHAPTER 6: MANAGING CREDIT THE RIGHT WAY GOING FORWARD

You've worked hard to clean up the mess.
You've written letters, reviewed reports, opened secured cards, and added positive history.
Now you're finally seeing progress—maybe for the first time in years.

But here's the truth:

> **Rebuilding your credit is only half the battle. The real challenge is keeping it strong.**

This chapter is about **protecting your progress**, managing your credit like a pro, and avoiding the common traps that send people back into the cycle of bad credit.

Because I don't just want you to hit a 700+ score—I want you to **keep it.**

Let's break this down into a system you can stick with for life.

Step 1: Know Your Score—But Don't Obsess

It's important to track your credit—but not to the point where it stresses you out.

You can use:

- **Credit Karma** (for TransUnion and Equifax)

- **CreditWise** from Capital One (for VantageScore insights)
- **Experian** (for FICO scores)

Check it **once a week**—not every day.

Why?

Because credit scores can **fluctuate** a few points here and there. A balance increase or a new inquiry might cause a dip. That's normal.

Focus on **long-term trends**, not daily changes.

And remember:

> FICO is the score most lenders use, but VantageScore gives useful insights too.

Step 2: Automate All Your Minimum Payments

The most important factor in your credit score is **payment history**—it accounts for **35% of your score**.

Just **one missed payment** can drop your score 60–110 points.

Avoid this with one powerful move:

> **Automate your minimum payments** on every card and loan.

Set it and forget it.

Use your bank's bill pay or the lender's autopay feature. Even if you plan to pay more, automation ensures you **never miss a due date**.

And here's a tip:
Set your due dates for the **same day each month** (like the 5th or 15th) to stay organized.

This one step can **save your score**—and your sanity.

Step 3: Keep Your Credit Utilization Low

The second biggest factor in your score is **credit utilization**—how much of your available credit you're using.

Rule of thumb:

- Stay under **30%**, but ideally under **10%**
- If your limit is $1,000, try to stay under $100

High utilization—even if you pay on time—can **drag your score down**.

Here's a pro move:

> Pay down your balance **before the statement closes**, not just before the due date.

This way, the reported balance is low—and your score reflects it.

Also, don't close old cards unless absolutely necessary. The longer your credit history, the better your score.

Step 4: Avoid These 5 Common Mistakes

Many people work hard to rebuild their credit—then lose it all by falling into old habits or making innocent mistakes.

Here are the top traps to avoid:

1. Closing your oldest credit card

You lose history and available credit. Instead, leave it open and use it once every few months for a small purchase.

2. Applying for too much credit at once

Every hard inquiry can lower your score a few points. Too many in a short time looks risky to lenders.

3. Maxing out your cards—even temporarily

Even if you pay it off in full, maxed-out cards hurt your utilization ratio.

4. Co-signing for someone

If they miss a payment, **you're responsible**—and your score suffers.

5. Ignoring your credit reports

Errors happen. Check your reports at least every 3–4 months to spot fraud or inaccuracies.

Step 5: Protect Your Credit Like It's Your Identity

Because it is.

Your credit report affects more than loans. It can affect:

- Job applications
- Apartment approvals
- Insurance rates
- Business opportunities

Protect it by taking the following steps:

- **Freeze your credit** if you're not applying for anything soon
- Use a **credit monitoring service** (some are free with your bank or card)
- Set up **account alerts** for large purchases, logins, or new accounts

- Use **strong passwords and two-factor authentication** on your financial apps

If you ever suspect identity theft:

1. Report it to the **FTC at identitytheft.gov**
2. File a police report
3. Contact all three bureaus
4. Dispute the fraudulent item ASAP

You've worked too hard to let a scammer undo it all.

Step 6: Create Your Personal Credit Calendar

Here's how to make your credit habits sustainable.

Create a monthly or quarterly "credit health check" routine.

Monthly Tasks:

- Pay down all balances
- Check your credit score
- Log new account activity

- Review upcoming due dates

Quarterly Tasks:

- Review your full credit reports
- Dispute any inaccuracies
- Revisit old negative items to see if they've aged off
- Set new financial goals

This makes credit management **part of your routine**, not a crisis management situation.

Set reminders on your phone. Create a spreadsheet. Use your calendar. Whatever works—just make it automatic.

Step 7: Stay Focused on the Long Game

A credit score isn't a destination. It's a tool.

It gives you access to:

- Better rates
- More capital

- Faster approvals
- Greater freedom

But don't chase it for vanity. Chase it for **power**.

And remember:

> A 700+ score with no plan is less valuable than a 680 with direction and discipline.

So now that your credit is healthy—what will you *do* with it?

Buy a home? Launch a business? Refinance bad debt?

Credit is not the goal. It's the **key** to bigger goals.

Final Word: Credit Confidence for Life

Here's the truth:

> The people with the best credit aren't always the smartest.
> They're the most **consistent**.

They show up. They pay on time. They check their reports. They fix what's broken.
And they don't let setbacks define them.

You are now one of those people.

You've done what most people will never do:
You've repaired, rebuilt, and now—you're ready to rise.

In the final chapter, we'll map out a **simple 90-day system** to lock in everything you've learned—and keep your momentum going.

Let's finish strong.

"Maya's Second Scare" – Protecting What She Built

Maya had worked hard to rebuild her credit.

She started at **489**, crushed under the weight of medical debt, a charged-off store card, and a car loan that got repossessed after she lost her job in 2020.

Over the next year, she pulled her reports, cleaned up the errors, disputed accounts that didn't belong to her, and settled a couple of debts that had been haunting her since college.

By the time she was done, her score had climbed to **694**.

She was proud.

She got approved for a new apartment on her own.
She refinanced a used car loan.
She even opened a couple of low-limit credit cards—and promised herself she'd never go back to where she started.

But then… she got comfortable.

It started with a **missed payment**.

Not because she didn't have the money—but because she simply **forgot**.

One of her credit cards had a $500 limit. She used it to buy some holiday gifts, and the balance sat there for two weeks. Then three. Then five.

The due date came and went.

She realized it two days after the grace period.

The late payment? It hit her credit report **within two weeks**.
Her score dropped **46 points**.

That one missed payment undid **months of hard work**.

She told me later, "I felt so stupid. I didn't lose my job. I wasn't broke. I just forgot."

It was a simple mistake—but it came with a heavy price.

That wake-up call pushed Maya to rethink everything.

She went back through all the credit education she'd consumed. She wrote out a system for herself—a "Credit Command Center," she called it.

She started with a **credit calendar**:

- She set all her due dates to the **15th of the month**
- She set **reminders in her phone** for the 13th, 14th, and 15th

- She enabled **autopay** on every card, even if it was just the minimum

Next, she called her credit card companies and asked for her **statement closing dates**—because she wanted to start paying her balances *before* they got reported.

Then, she committed to **never using more than 10%** of any credit limit—even if she could afford more.

> "Credit is like a reputation," she said. "You can build it slowly for years… but one mistake can ruin it."

That wasn't the only scare Maya had.

About three months after that, she got an alert from CreditWise:

> "New inquiry: Capital Bank, Auto Loan Division"

She panicked.

She hadn't applied for anything. She hadn't given anyone permission to check her credit. It wasn't a soft pull—**it was a hard inquiry.**

She froze her credit that night using all three bureaus.

She called Capital Bank the next morning. They said someone had applied using her name and Social Security number from a dealership in South Florida.

But Maya lived in Atlanta.

They flagged it as suspected fraud, canceled the application, and emailed her a fraud packet to complete.

Maya filed an **identity theft report** at IdentityTheft.gov, filed a **police report**, and sent dispute letters to all three bureaus.

She also signed up for **free credit monitoring through Experian** and set up **two-factor authentication** on all her financial accounts.

> "If I hadn't been checking, that inquiry could have turned into a full-blown car loan under my name. And I wouldn't have known until it was too late."

Today, Maya is at **748**.

She's been stable for over a year. She hasn't missed a payment since the holiday mistake. And her credit file is stronger than ever.

Here's what she does every month:

- Logs in to check her balances every Sunday
- Pays her cards **twice a month**—once before the statement closes, and again before the due date
- Prints her **credit report once a quarter** and reviews it line-by-line
- Keeps a "Credit Binder" with every dispute, approval letter, and major financial document

- Uses **calendar reminders** to monitor and update her financial habits

She doesn't obsess. But she stays consistent.

She told me, "I realized that credit isn't just a number. It's a habit. And once you build those habits, you don't go back."

Maya's story is important—not because she's perfect, but because she messed up **and learned from it.**

She didn't panic.
She didn't give up.
She adapted.

And that's what managing your credit the right way is all about.

Credit is not something you check once a year and forget about.
It's something you **actively manage**—just like your health or your relationships.

The goal isn't to be obsessed with your score.
The goal is to build a system that makes it easy to protect your financial future.

Because when you do?

- Credit approvals come faster

- Interest rates drop

- Business doors open
- And you sleep better at night

Maya's second scare could have derailed everything—but instead, it made her stronger.

Let her story be your reminder:

> Don't just rebuild your credit—**respect it.**

And as you move into the final chapter, I'm going to help you create your **90-Day Action Plan**—so everything you've learned turns into real, repeatable momentum.

You've come this far.

Let's finish what you started.

CHAPTER 7: YOUR 90-DAY CREDIT REPAIR ACTION PLAN

You've made it to the final chapter of *Personal Credit Repair Blueprint*—and that means something powerful:

> You didn't just start this journey.
> You stayed with it.
> You showed up.
> You took action.

That alone puts you miles ahead of most people.

But now, it's time to turn all this knowledge into a **simple, clear, step-by-step action plan**—one you can follow over the next 90 days to create real momentum.

This plan is designed for progress, not perfection. Whether you're starting with a 500 score or trying to break into the 700s, this system will give you focus and confidence.

Let's break it down month by month.

Days 1–30: Clean & Confront

This first phase is about **facing your credit** and doing the groundwork.

Your Goals:

- Know exactly what's hurting your score
- Begin cleaning up inaccurate or harmful data

- Set the foundation for rebuilding

Your Action Steps:

1. **Pull All Three Credit Reports**
   - Use AnnualCreditReport.com
   - Download or print all three (Equifax, Experian, TransUnion)
2. **Create Your Credit Tracker**
   - Use a spreadsheet or notebook
   - Track account names, balances, status, issues, and bureaus
3. **Highlight Negative Items**
   - Look for: collections, charge-offs, incorrect late payments, outdated accounts
4. **Dispute Inaccurate Information**
   - Send up to 5 letters to start
   - Mail certified with return receipt

  - Include ID and supporting documentation

5. **Set Up Credit Monitoring**
   - Use tools like Credit Karma, Experian, or CreditWise
6. **Start a Secured Card or Credit Builder Loan**
   - Keep usage under 10%
   - Set up autopay immediately
7. **Use Experian Boost or Rent Reporting**
   - Add positive history from your bills

End-of-Month Goal: Have disputes mailed, 1–2 positive accounts opened, and all payment systems automated.

Days 31–60: Rebuild & Reset

Now that you've started cleaning things up, it's time to **rebuild your credit profile** with consistent, positive behavior.

Your Goals:

- Build new positive payment history

- Set systems that protect your score
- Continue monitoring and disputing

Your Action Steps:

1. **Pay All Bills On Time**
    - Automate minimum payments
    - Set calendar alerts 3–5 days before due dates
2. **Pay Down Balances**
    - Focus on keeping utilization below 10%
    - Pay before the **statement closing date**, not just due date
3. **Become an Authorized User**
    - Ask a trusted friend or family member to add you to their long-standing card
4. **Continue Disputing**
    - Send second round of disputes (if needed)
    - Track responses from the first round

5. **Check for Updates**

    - Log in weekly to review changes to your reports
    - Celebrate small wins like "paid collection" or "item deleted"

6. **Review Judgments or Settlements**

    - If you have court-related debts, begin researching payment or vacating options

End-of-Month Goal: Positive history reported, at least one dispute resolved, utilization improved, and protection measures in place.

Days 61–90: Grow & Guard

You've cleaned. You've built. Now it's time to **grow your credit power**—and put safeguards in place to protect it.

Your Goals:

- Add more positive credit depth
- Secure your identity
- Prepare for future funding or financial milestones

Your Action Steps:

1. **Add a Second Positive Account**
   - Consider a second secured card or credit builder loan
   - Use for small purchases and pay in full
2. **Freeze Your Credit (Optional)**
   - If you're not applying for anything soon, freeze your credit to prevent fraud
3. **Check Aging Accounts**
   - Negative items older than 7 years? Request removal if still showing
   - Paid collections? Ask for deletion confirmation
4. **Create a Credit Maintenance Plan**
   - Credit check every Sunday
   - Payment tracker
   - Quarterly report reviews
5. **Set Financial Goals**

- Buying a home? Applying for funding? Set that target.
- Use your credit power intentionally—not just for vanity.

6. **Avoid New Inquiries**
    - Don't apply for unnecessary credit now
    - Focus on strengthening what you already have

End-of-Month Goal: 3+ positive tradelines, credit protection in place, and credit score steadily rising.

Your Credit Mindset for Life

Here's what I want you to remember—not just for the next 90 days, but forever:

- **Credit doesn't reward perfection. It rewards consistency.**
- Every on-time payment matters more than you think.
- Your past does not define your financial future.
- Credit is not about how much money you make—it's about how well you manage what you have.
- You don't need 800 to win. You need to be responsible, reliable, and aware.

Final Score: You Win by Showing Up

You've made it through seven full chapters.

You now understand:

- How credit works
- How to fix what's broken
- How to build what's missing
- How to protect what you're growing

And now, you have a 90-day plan to make it real.

You don't need luck. You don't need a magic score.
You have something stronger: **knowledge and action**.

You've turned a confusing, intimidating system into something you can navigate. And that makes you powerful.

FINAL WORDS

I want to thank you for trusting me with your time and attention.

As someone who's helped thousands of people through credit repair, mortgage approvals, and business funding—I know what it's like to feel stuck. But I also know what it feels like to come out on the other side.

You're not just fixing your credit.
You're rewriting your financial story.
And you've already started.

Stick with this plan. Share it with someone you care about.
And if you fall off—**get back up.**

You're never too late to fix it.
You're never too far gone to rebuild it.
And you're never alone in this.

I'll see you at the top—because that's exactly where you're headed.

Now, I want to talk about Elena's 90-Day Comeback.

Elena didn't think she had a credit problem—until her dream job slipped through her fingers.

She had applied for a remote sales coordinator role with great pay, full benefits, and the ability to work from home so she could take care of her two young sons. She passed the interviews. Nailed the assessments.

But then she got an email that said:

> "Unfortunately, we are unable to move forward due to information found in your background and credit check."

She didn't know her credit score could affect a job offer.

So she checked it for the first time in years. **546.**

Her stomach dropped. She thought she was doing okay. Her bills were mostly paid. She wasn't being chased by collectors.

But there it was, plain as day:
A paid collection still reporting as open.
A closed utility account she didn't know existed.
Two credit cards she'd maxed out years ago—and forgot about.

> "I felt like my past mistakes had snuck into the present and locked me out of the future."

But she didn't stay stuck.

Elena decided that for the next 90 days, she was going to treat fixing her credit like it was a second job.

Day 1–30: The Clean-Up

She pulled all three of her credit reports, printed them out, and bought a three-ring binder from the dollar store. She called it her "Freedom File."

Each section had tabs: Personal Info, Collections, Cards, Notes, Goals.

She created a spreadsheet with every negative item: who reported it, how much was owed, the status, and the date it first went late.

Then she started writing dispute letters. One to each bureau. For five accounts that looked off.

She took her time. Attached ID. Mailed them certified with return receipts.

At the same time, she opened a **secured credit card** with a $200 deposit. She set it up with autopay. Only used it for gas.

She also signed up for **Experian Boost** and added her phone bill and utilities.

By day 30?

One collection was deleted.
Her phone bill started showing up as an on-time account.
Her credit score jumped to **578**.

Small win—but it felt like a victory.

Day 31–60: The Rebuild

Elena added a **credit builder loan** through Self. $25 a month. She didn't miss a single one.

She also talked to her older brother, who had a great credit card. He agreed to add her as an **authorized user**—just to help her grow her profile.

Within three weeks, that account showed up.

Now her report had:

- A revolving secured card
- A credit builder loan
- Her rent payments
- Her utilities

- A five-year-old credit card from her brother with a perfect payment history

And for the first time in her life, her credit report said something good about her.

She logged in one morning and saw the number: **631**.

> "It didn't seem like a huge number to someone else. But to me, it was freedom."

Day 61–90: The Future

Elena didn't apply for new credit. She didn't rush to spend. She **protected** what she'd built.

She froze her credit to prevent identity theft.
She printed her report and put it in her binder.
She created calendar reminders for every bill, every due date, and every autopay.

She even bought a whiteboard and wrote:

> "On time. Low balance. No excuses."

By day 85, she was ready.

She reapplied to that same company. Updated her resume. Wrote a new cover letter.

Two interviews later, they called her. Offered her the job. Ran her credit again.

This time? **Approved.**

Elena cried.

Not because of the job—though it changed her life.

She cried because she didn't feel broken anymore.

> "It wasn't about the number. It was about feeling in control again."

She stuck to her plan.
She didn't get everything deleted.
She didn't get a perfect score.

But she **won**.

And you can, too.

So if you're listening to this and thinking, *"Can I really do this?"* — let Elena's story answer that.

Yes, you can.

Not in a year.
Not someday.
In 90 days.

One page. One letter. One step at a time.

This is your comeback.

And the only thing between where you are and where you want to be—is action.

You've got the plan.
You've got the tools.
And now… you've got the proof.

Let Elena's story become your story.

Start today.
And I'll see you on the other side of success.

TAKEAWAY

If there's one thing this book teaches, it's this:

> **Credit repair is not just about raising a score—it's about reclaiming your power.**

Whether you're trying to buy a home, start a business, get out of debt, or just breathe easier at night, your credit doesn't have to be a barrier.

You have the tools.
You have the steps.
You have the right to fix what's broken.
And now—you have the blueprint.

You're not just fixing your credit.

You're rebuilding your future.

CONCLUSION: FROM CREDIT CONFUSION TO CONFIDENCE

If you're hearing this now, you've made it all the way through *Personal Credit Repair Blueprint*—and I want to take a moment to recognize what that means.

You didn't just listen to tips.
You didn't just skim ideas.
You committed. You learned.
And most importantly—you showed up for yourself.

That alone makes you different.

Because the truth is, most people don't fix their credit because they **never start**.
They stay stuck in shame, fear, or confusion.
They let their past mistakes define their financial future.
But not you.

You took the time to understand the system.
You took the courage to face your own credit report.
You stopped avoiding—and started taking action.

Let me tell you something from the heart:
That decision will impact not just your credit score, but your **entire life**.

Credit is More Than a Number

We've talked about late payments, utilization, disputes, and secured cards.

But underneath it all, we've been talking about something much bigger:

"Your ability to say yes to yourself."

A strong credit profile opens doors.
It lets you walk into a dealership, a bank, or a landlord's office with confidence.
It means lower interest rates, higher approval odds, and fewer financial headaches.
But more than that? It gives you **freedom**.

Freedom to:

- Start a business
- Rent or buy your dream home
- Rebuild after a divorce or illness
- Move without begging for co-signers
- Stop the cycle of being judged by a number

That's what you've been building here.
That's what this book has helped you unlock.

And even if your score isn't where you want it yet—your mindset has shifted.
You're not guessing anymore.
You have a **blueprint**.

Progress, Not Perfection

Now, here's something you'll need to remember—especially if life throws a few surprises your way again:

Credit is a game of consistency, not perfection.

You're not going to do everything right.
There may be a payment you forget. A dispute that doesn't go your way.
A card that gets declined. A mistake that sets you back 20 points.

That's okay.

This isn't about chasing a perfect 850 score.
It's about building habits that **protect you**, serve you, and support the life you want to live.

The real win is:

- Paying on time
- Staying organized
- Keeping your utilization low
- Fixing problems when they show up
- Never letting shame stop you from moving forward

You've already proven you can do that.

So when a setback comes—and at some point, it might—just go back to the system.

Go back to the binder.
Go back to the 90-day plan.
And keep moving forward.

You Now Have Tools for Life

Let's recap what's now in your hands:

You know how to:

- Pull and read a full credit report
- Dispute inaccuracies using federal law
- Remove collections, fix charge-offs, and deal with judgments
- Rebuild using secured cards, rent reporting, and builder loans
- Set up payment automation and monitoring systems
- Protect your credit with freezes, alerts, and quarterly checkups
- Follow a 90-day roadmap that works—even if you're starting over again

These tools don't just help you fix your current situation.

They prepare you for:

- Buying a home
- Getting business funding
- Teaching your kids about money
- Helping your community
- Avoiding predatory lenders
- Becoming your own financial advocate

This isn't just credit repair.
This is financial empowerment.

You now speak the language.
You now see the game board.
And you're no longer playing defense.
You're on offense.

What's Next for You?

Now that you've repaired and rebuilt your credit, you might be wondering:
"What's next?"

That answer is up to you. But here are some possibilities:

- Want to learn how to **build business credit and access $50K–$250K in funding**?
  Check out my book: *Business Credit Mastery*

- Need help understanding how credit works if you're an immigrant or have no history?
  Listen to: *How to Establish Credit in the U.S.*

- Ready to take your finances to the next level with budgeting, saving, and wealth building?
  Don't miss: *The Personal Finance Playbook for Beginners*

- Curious about how to turn your credit strength into **real estate investment power**?
  Try: *Credit and Loan Strategies for Real Estate Investors*

Each of these titles is designed to take what you've learned and **expand your results** into every area of life—from business to home ownership to long-term wealth.

You're not just building a score.
You're building a strategy.
And I'd love to walk with you on that next step.

If there's one message I hope you take away from this book, it's this:

> **"You are not your credit score.
> But you have the power to change it."**

You can repair.
You can rebuild.
You can rise.

And no matter how bad things may have looked before—you're not stuck.

You've got a system now. You've got support.
And you've got proof that it works.

Thank you for listening to *Personal Credit Repair Blueprint.*
I'm honored to be a part of your journey.

And wherever life takes you next—**take this blueprint with you.**

Because your next big win is just one decision away.

Keep building.
Keep believing.
And I'll see you in the next book.

VOLUME 3: HOW TO BUILD CREDIT FAST WITHOUT DEBT

Let's get one thing straight: you do **not** need debt to build great credit.

That myth has kept millions of people stuck in a cycle of borrowing, paying interest, and hoping their credit score will magically improve over time. It's a broken system that rewards banks, not individuals. And it's time for something better.

That's why I created this book.

Whether you're just starting out with zero credit, trying to recover from past mistakes, or simply looking for a smarter way to boost your score, this guide will show you how to do it **fast**, **safely**, and most importantly—**without going into debt**.

I've worked with thousands of people who believed they had no shot at building credit without loans. But once they followed this system, they watched their scores climb—sometimes by 50, 100, even 150 points in a matter of months. And they did it without borrowing a dollar.

This book is your step-by-step blueprint to do the same.

Who This Is For?

This book is designed for people who want to build or rebuild their credit **without interest, loans, or risk**. It's especially powerful for:

- Young adults with no credit history
- Students who want to build credit before graduation

- Immigrants who are new to the U.S. credit system
- Entrepreneurs preparing for future funding
- Parents and professionals recovering from past financial challenges
- Anyone who wants **control** over their credit without the stress of debt

If you've ever been denied a lease, rejected for a card, or embarrassed by a low score—even when you're financially responsible—this book is for you.

You'll finally understand how the credit system works, what it's really measuring, and how to reverse-engineer a high score using tools you already have access to.

What You'll Learn

In the chapters ahead, you'll learn how to:

- Establish your first credit score with no cosigner
- Add your rent, utilities, and streaming services to your report
- Use secured credit cards and builder accounts *without* paying interest
- Track and grow your score in 30, 60, and 90-day stages
- Avoid costly mistakes that sabotage thousands of people every year
- Leverage other people's credit—safely and ethically
- Maintain a 700+ score without touching a loan

We'll also look at real-life stories from people who went from **invisible** to **credit-approved**, using the same strategies you're about to learn.

This book is full of tools, checklists, and examples you can apply immediately—even if you're starting from zero.

What This Book Is Not

This is not a get-rich-quick scheme.
It's not about hacking the system with shady tricks.
And it's definitely not about borrowing your way to a better score.

This book is about **empowerment**.

It's about learning to play the game of credit the *right* way, so you win long-term—not just for your next apartment or card, but for your future home, business, or investment opportunity.

You don't need to borrow thousands.
You don't need a perfect job.
You don't need to wait years to improve your credit.

You just need a plan. And you're holding it.

Why Credit Without Debt Is the Smart Way Forward

For years, the credit industry pushed the lie that borrowing equals building.

That's not just misleading—it's dangerous.

People get credit cards "just to build credit," then end up carrying balances, missing payments, and watching their scores crash. Others take out small loans they don't need, pay interest for months, and gain just a few points on their report.

That's not smart. That's expensive.

In this book, we flip the model.

You'll learn how to use **what you already pay for**—rent, subscriptions, bills—to build real credit history. You'll learn how to make banks and bureaus **recognize your financial behavior** without putting your money at risk.

And you'll do it in a way that's sustainable, repeatable, and safe.

Let's Build

So, take a breath. You're not behind. You're not disqualified. And you're definitely not the only one who's been confused or frustrated by credit.

By the end of this book, you'll:

- Know exactly what affects your credit score
- Have a simple 3-phase system to follow
- Understand how to grow your score fast without using debt
- And most importantly—feel confident in your financial future

Let's build your credit the right way.

Let's build it **fast**.

Let's build it **without debt**.

Your credit comeback starts now.

CHAPTER 1: THE FAST LANE TO CREDIT GROWTH WITHOUT RISK

Most people believe the only way to build credit is by going into debt.

That was certainly what 27-year-old Andrea believed when she sat across from her bank's credit advisor, nervously clutching a brochure that promised to "improve your credit score fast!" The fine print told a different story—12-month personal loan, 22.5% interest, and a monthly payment she could barely afford on her $38,000 salary as a freelance photographer.

Andrea had always been financially cautious. Raised by immigrant parents who paid cash for everything, she avoided credit cards and took pride in staying debt-free. But when she decided to rent a nicer apartment and her application was denied because of her "thin credit file," her confidence took a hit.

That moment was a wake-up call. She had done everything right—saved money, avoided debt, paid bills on time—but none of it showed up on a credit report. She was invisible to the credit system.

As Andrea scrolled through blogs and videos late into the night, she kept hearing the same advice: get a credit card, take out a loan, finance a purchase. But each suggestion felt like a trap. Was there no way to build credit without taking on risk?

Then she stumbled upon something different—a community forum of people who had built their credit without loans, interest, or debt of any kind. She read story after story of people using tools like rent reporting services, phone bill subscriptions, and secured accounts to grow their scores.

Her curiosity turned to hope.

Andrea started small. She signed up for a rent reporting service that added 18 months of on-time rent payments to her credit report. Next, she linked her

Netflix and phone bills through a free credit reporting tool. She even applied for a credit builder account that held her savings in a locked certificate while reporting payments each month.

In just 90 days, her credit score jumped 70 points.

But what surprised her most wasn't the score boost—it was the sense of control. For the first time, she understood how credit worked. She wasn't relying on debt to prove her worth. She was building a financial identity on her own terms.

Six months later, Andrea applied for a rewards credit card and was approved instantly. She used it for gas and groceries—never carrying a balance—and watched her score continue to rise. When she finally applied again for that apartment, the leasing manager nodded, impressed by her 745 score.

"This is one of the best applications I've seen all month," he said.

Andrea smiled—not because she was proud of the number, but because she earned it without sacrificing her values.

Her story is not an exception.

Every day, thousands of people are rewriting the credit rulebook. They're ditching the myth that you need to go into debt to build credit, and they're doing it faster, safer, and smarter than ever before.

In this book, you're going to learn exactly how.

You'll discover the tools Andrea used—plus a few others you've probably never heard of. You'll learn how to track your progress, avoid common traps, and create a system that works for your lifestyle, your income, and your goals.

Most importantly, you'll learn how to build credit fast… without ever going into debt.

Because in today's world, the best financial power move isn't just having a high credit score—it's knowing you earned it without compromising your future.

Let's get started.

CHAPTER 2: CREDIT MYTHS—WHY YOU DON'T NEED DEBT TO BUILD CREDIT

If you're listening to this book, chances are you've heard at least one of these credit myths—and maybe even believed them. Don't worry. You're not alone. These myths are deeply rooted in our culture and pushed by banks, credit card companies, and even well-meaning friends and family.

But today, we're breaking them down—and more importantly, I'll show you step-by-step how to take smarter actions that actually work.

Myth #1: You Have to Borrow Money to Build Credit

Truth: You need credit activity—not debt.

Most people think borrowing money and carrying a balance is necessary to build credit. That's false.

Step 1: Open an account that reports to the credit bureaus without requiring debt.
Options include:

- Rent reporting services
- Experian Boost (adds utilities and streaming services)
- Credit builder savings accounts (your money is locked and released later)

These accounts report **positive payment history** without requiring you to borrow anything.

Result: You build credit with payments you're already making—zero interest, zero risk.

Myth #2: You Need to Carry a Balance to Boost Your Score

Truth: Carrying a balance can hurt your score and your wallet.

This myth costs Americans billions every year. Credit card companies love it because it means interest charges.

Step 2: Use your card and pay it off in full every month.

- Pay on or before the **statement date**, not just the due date, to lower your utilization ratio.
- Keep usage under **10%** of your credit limit if possible.

Example: If your limit is $500, try not to let your balance exceed $50 when it reports.

Result: You prove you're responsible without paying interest or risking debt.

Myth #3: You Need a Cosigner or a Loan to Start Credit

Truth: You can build independently with the right starter tools.

Step 3: Apply for a secured card or credit-building account with your own money.

- Secured cards are backed by a deposit (usually $200+).
- Some fintech platforms offer "credit lines" against your bank balance or savings.

Bonus Tip: Look for cards that graduate to unsecured after a few months of on-time payments.

Result: You build credit in your name without co-signers or loans.

Myth #4: All Debt Helps Your Score

Truth: Not all debt is treated equally—and some hurts more than it helps.

- Personal loans don't always improve your mix and can increase your debt-to-income ratio.
- High-interest or short-term debt (like payday loans) can tank your score if mismanaged.

Step 4: Avoid unnecessary debt in the name of "building credit."

Focus on the **three credit pillars** instead:

1. On-time payments
2. Low utilization
3. Age of accounts

Result: Your score rises steadily without risking financial setbacks.

Myth #5: You Need a High Income to Have Good Credit

Truth: Credit is about behavior, not income.

People with modest incomes can have excellent credit by simply being consistent.

Step 5: Automate your payments.

- Set up autopay on any reporting accounts.
- Use reminders to check your statement balances and report dates.
- Monitor your credit with free tools like Credit Karma, Experian, or NerdWallet.

Result: You don't have to be rich to build strong credit—you just need a system.

Summary of Steps to Break the Myths and Start Building Without Debt

1. Open reporting accounts that don't require borrowing.
2. Use your card and pay in full—avoid interest traps.
3. Start with a secured card or credit builder tool, not a loan.
4. Skip "fake credit builders" like payday loans or unnecessary loans.
5. Automate your credit behavior and track progress.

By following these steps, you're not just ignoring bad advice—you're building a smarter, stronger foundation for long-term credit success.

Why You Don't Need Debt to Build Credit

When Malik graduated college, he didn't have a job lined up—but he had ambition, a laptop, and a beat-up Honda Civic that could get him to every freelance gig he could find. What he didn't have was credit.

He hadn't taken out student loans, never had a credit card, and his parents always told him debt was dangerous. So when he went to apply for his first apartment, he was stunned to hear his application was denied.

"Sorry," the leasing agent told him. "You don't have any credit history. We need something to show you're responsible with payments."

Confused and embarrassed, Malik walked out of the office and sat in his car. How could he be penalized for *not* owing anyone money?

Later that night, he called his cousin Jasmine, who worked in real estate and finance. "You've got to get some credit activity going," she explained. "Not debt—activity. You need to show the bureaus something."

"But everyone says you have to borrow to build credit," he replied.

"Total myth," she said. "Let me show you how I built mine without a single loan."

Over the next week, Malik followed Jasmine's advice.

First, he signed up for a rent reporting service that let him submit his monthly rent payments from his current sublease. Even though his landlord wasn't part of a big company, the service verified and submitted his on-time payments to the credit bureaus.

Then, he opened a free credit reporting tool that added his phone bill and Spotify account to his credit profile. "You're already paying those," Jasmine said. "Now they'll help your score."

He was skeptical. "That simple?"

"That simple."

Next, Jasmine suggested a secured card. Malik took $200 from his savings and opened one with a company that reported to all three credit bureaus. He set a reminder in his phone: *Use for gas only. Pay off before the statement date.* No balance, no interest, no debt.

He made sure to stay under $20 of use each month—just enough to show activity but low enough to keep his credit utilization below 10%.

At first, Malik didn't think much of it. But three months later, he got an alert: his credit score had gone from 0 to 689.

He stared at the screen in disbelief. "Wait… I didn't borrow anything!"

He logged into the rent portal, the card app, and the reporting tool—and sure enough, everything had been reporting cleanly. On-time payments, low utilization, active accounts. All without a dime of debt.

He called Jasmine that night, nearly shouting. "Why isn't this stuff taught in school?"

"Because schools don't get referral commissions from credit card companies," she laughed. "But now *you* know."

A few months later, Malik went back to that same apartment complex. This time, the leasing agent smiled. "Nice credit score—you're approved."

And when Malik finally had a steady income and started to think about buying a car, he didn't need a cosigner or a high-interest loan. His credit report told a story of responsibility, not risk.

Now, Malik teaches his younger siblings the same truth: You don't need to borrow money to build credit. You just need to understand the game—and play it with strategy.

Because the real myth isn't that you need debt to build credit. The real myth is believing you're powerless without it.

CHAPTER 3: CREDIT BUILDER TOOLS THAT DON'T REQUIRE BORROWING

Diana was a single mom with two kids and a full-time job as a medical assistant. After her divorce, her finances were tight—but she was determined to rebuild her life, including her credit.

There was just one problem: she didn't want to go into debt to do it.

Years ago, she'd made that mistake—maxing out credit cards during hard times, paying the minimums, and watching interest charges grow like weeds. She'd worked hard to pay everything off, and the idea of getting back into that cycle made her stomach turn.

But when her oldest son needed a new laptop for school, she realized she needed access to credit again—just in case. The trouble was, she hadn't used credit in years. Her score was low, her file was thin, and her confidence was shaky.

So, Diana did what she always did when she needed answers: she made a list.

She wrote across the top:
How to Build Credit Without Borrowing Money.

The first item on her list came from a friend who worked in property management:
1. Report Rent Payments to Credit Bureaus.

She had always paid rent on time, but none of it had ever been reported. So she signed up with a rent reporting service. They contacted her landlord, verified her last 24 months of on-time rent, and sent the full history to TransUnion and Equifax. Within weeks, her score went up nearly 40 points.

She was amazed. "I've been paying rent for 10 years," she told her friend. "Why didn't anyone tell me I could get credit for it?"

Next, she checked off item two:

2. Use Your Bills to Boost Credit.

Diana found a free service that linked her bank account and added recurring payments—like her cell phone, water bill, Netflix, and electric bill—to her Experian credit report. These were bills she already paid monthly. Now, they finally counted for something.

Then came number three:

3. Open a Credit Builder Savings Account.

This one felt odd at first. She deposited $25 a month into a locked savings account. She couldn't touch the money until the term ended—but each "payment" was reported as an on-time installment to all three bureaus.

It was a reverse loan—*she* was the lender. But the credit system saw her as someone successfully repaying a loan, and her score ticked upward again.

Number four made her nervous:

4. Use a Secured Credit Card—Cautiously.

Diana used $250 of her tax refund to open a secured card. She promised herself she would use it for one thing only: groceries.

Every month, she used no more than $50 and paid it off before the due date. Her utilization stayed low, and she never paid a cent in interest. Six months later, her card company offered to graduate her to an unsecured card—and refunded her deposit.

Finally, she added one more step to her system:

5. Monitor and Automate Everything.

She downloaded a free app that tracked her credit score, gave her alerts, and reminded her of reporting dates. She set every bill and card on auto-pay and checked in once a week to make sure everything stayed on track.

By the end of the year, Diana's score had climbed 112 points. She had no loans, no balances, and no interest payments—just a clean credit report full of smart activity.

Her friends were stunned when she told them.

"Wait, you didn't borrow anything?" one asked.

"Nope," Diana smiled. "I just figured out how to play the game without losing."

Her journey became the blueprint for her sister, her coworkers, and even her 16-year-old son—who was already asking how he could start early.

These are the same tools available to you right now:

Quick Recap: Tools That Build Credit Without Borrowing

- **Rent reporting services** (like RentTrack or Boom)
- **Utility and subscription reporting tools** (like Experian Boost)
- **Credit builder savings accounts** (like Self or CreditStrong)
- **Secured credit cards with no annual fee**
- **Free credit monitoring tools and automation apps**

You don't need to go into debt to build credit. You need activity, consistency, and tools designed for people who want to grow without risk.

Just like Diana, you can use what you already have—your rent, your bills, your habits—and turn them into credit strength. No loans required.

In the next chapter, we'll take this even further by showing you how to **use rent, subscriptions, and bills in combination** to maximize your credit score gains in just a few months.

You've got the tools. Let's use them with strategy.

CHAPTER 4: USING RENT, SUBSCRIPTIONS, AND BILLS TO BOOST SCORES

Tyrese had been working two jobs—daytime delivery driver and weekend DJ—for nearly five years. He had a good reputation with everyone he worked with. Never late. Always professional. But when he applied for a car loan to replace his aging, 2004 sedan, the bank gave him a short, painful answer:

> "We can't approve this loan because you have an insufficient credit profile."

He stared at the rejection email for a while. "Insufficient?" he muttered. "I pay rent, phone, water, lights… What else do they want?"

That frustration turned into fuel.

Tyrese wasn't going to let an invisible score define his future. He decided to treat his credit like a business. Step one? Research.

He started watching YouTube videos, reading articles, and listening to podcasts. The same tip kept coming up: **You're already making payments that could build your credit—you just need to report them.**

So he grabbed a notebook, drew a line down the middle, and titled one side: **Monthly Bills I Pay.**
On the other side: **Which Ones Can Be Reported?**

Here's what his list looked like:

Left column – Monthly Bills

- Rent: $1,200
- Cell phone: $75

- Internet: $60
- Netflix: $15
- Electricity: $110
- Water: $40
- Car insurance: $135

Right column – Reportable?

- Rent: YES
- Cell phone: YES
- Internet: YES
- Netflix: YES
- Electricity: YES
- Water: YES
- Car insurance: MAYBE (depends on provider)

He realized he was spending nearly $1,600 a month—but none of it was improving his credit score.

The next day, Tyrese signed up with a rent reporting company called **Boom**, which could report both past and future rent payments to the bureaus. They contacted his landlord, verified the lease, and within two weeks, Tyrese had 12 months of on-time rent payments added to his credit report.

He also enrolled in **Experian Boost**, which synced to his checking account and found recurring payments—like Netflix, his phone bill, and even internet—and added them to his credit history. It wasn't magic, but his score jumped 28 points in the first 30 days.

He was hooked.

Now that he had a system, Tyrese wanted to get the most out of every dollar. He called his utility companies and asked, "Do you report to the credit bureaus?" Most didn't, but he learned that services like **LevelCredit** and **Grow Credit** could link some utilities and even streaming services for reporting.

He signed up.

Next, he opened a separate checking account just for bills. That way, he could automate payments, prevent missed due dates, and keep clean records for reporting tools. This not only helped his credit—it helped his sanity.

After three months, Tyrese logged into Credit Karma and couldn't believe his eyes:

Credit score: 714

He took a screenshot and sent it to his mom.

"You did this without a credit card?" she asked.

"Yup," he replied. "Just turned my bills into assets."

His old mindset had been: *Pay bills and forget about it.*

His new mindset: *Every payment is a step toward financial leverage.*

And it was paying off.

Tyrese didn't stop there. He started telling everyone he worked with—especially other gig workers—how to use rent, subscriptions, and bills to build credit.

One of the DJs he trained was only 20 years old, with zero credit. Tyrese helped him set up the same strategy, and within 6 months, that kid was approved for his first apartment—without a cosigner.

Tyrese realized something powerful: credit isn't about borrowing. It's about behavior. And if you pay your bills consistently, you deserve credit for it.

Quick Story Takeaways: How Tyrese Did It

1. **Reported Rent:** Used Boom to report past and future rent.
2. **Used Experian Boost:** Added recurring subscriptions and phone bills.
3. **Used Additional Tools:** LevelCredit and Grow Credit added more utility and service payments.
4. **Opened a Bills Account:** Separated finances for easy tracking and automation.
5. **Watched His Score Climb:** 714 in 90 days—no debt, no loans, no interest.

CHAPTER 5: LEVERAGING AUTHORIZED USER ACCOUNTS SAFELY

Carlos had just turned 21 when he walked into his local credit union to apply for his first credit card. He was working part-time at an auto shop and going to trade school in the evenings. He wasn't looking for anything fancy—just a simple card to help him build his credit.

The bank clerk politely pulled up his file, looked at the screen, and sighed.

> "Carlos, I'm sorry. You have no credit history, so we can't issue a card at this time."

Carlos nodded, disappointed but not surprised. No credit meant no approval—but no approval meant no way to build credit. It felt like a trap.

That night, he talked to his older sister, Natalie, who had a solid financial track record and worked as a nurse. She had a credit score over 800 and used credit cards like a tool—always paying in full, never missing a payment.

Carlos explained what happened.
Natalie paused, then smiled. "You know, I think I can help you out."

She pulled out her wallet and tapped one of her cards.

> "I'll add you as an authorized user."

Carlos blinked. "Wait… I won't have to use it, right?"

"Nope. You don't even need to hold the card. I'll just add your name. My history becomes your history—at least on this account."

Carlos was skeptical. "Is that even allowed?"

Natalie laughed. "It's encouraged. Credit bureaus love seeing positive history—even if it comes from someone else. As long as I keep paying on time, your score goes up. But listen—this only works if we do it smart."

The Rules of the Game

Over the next hour, Natalie explained the rules:

- **Rule 1:** Only use a card with a long, clean history.
  Her card was over 5 years old with a $10,000 limit and 2% utilization.

- **Rule 2:** No missed payments—ever.
  A single late payment would tank *both* their scores.

- **Rule 3:** Carlos wouldn't use the card at all.
  It was purely a tool for reporting history—not for spending.

A few days later, Natalie added Carlos as an authorized user through her card's online portal. It was free. No credit check. No hassle.

Within 30 days, Carlos received an alert:

> "A new account has been added to your credit report."

And just like that, he had a 700+ credit score.

He couldn't believe it. One month ago, he had zero. Now, lenders would see five years of perfect payment history and low usage. All thanks to his sister's responsible habits.

Carlos didn't go on a spending spree. Instead, he followed Natalie's example. He opened a secured card of his own with a $300 deposit and used it only for gas. He paid it off weekly and kept his utilization below 10%.

By the end of the semester, Carlos applied again for a credit card—and was approved instantly, no deposit required.

The Power—and Risk—of Being an Authorized User

This strategy worked wonders for Carlos, but Natalie made sure he understood the risks:

> "If I mess up, your score drops. And if *you* mess up on your own cards later, no authorized user status will save you."

He also learned that not all credit cards report authorized users to all three bureaus. So, before she added him, Natalie confirmed that her card did report to **Equifax**, **TransUnion**, and **Experian**.

Carlos also learned to avoid two big mistakes people make with this strategy:

- **Adding someone you don't fully trust.**
  Natalie knew she could trust Carlos. But too many people add friends or boyfriends who rack up charges and disappear.

- **Being added to a bad account.**
  If someone has late payments, high balances, or a short credit history, being added to their card can actually *lower* your score.

Using This Strategy the Right Way

Carlos shared the idea with a friend at school, David, who wanted to try it too. But David made a mistake—he asked his uncle to add him to a maxed-out store card with three late payments in the past year.

His score dropped 40 points.

Carlos told him what Natalie taught him:

> "It only works if the account is strong. Otherwise, you're better off building credit the slow way than damaging it with the fast way."

Key Takeaways from Carlos' Journey

1. **Choose the Right Person:** Must be financially responsible and have a long, clean history.

2. **Verify Reporting:** Not all credit cards report authorized users to all bureaus. Call and check first.

3. **Keep It Low Risk:** You don't need access to the card—just the history.

4. **Don't Abuse It:** Use the score boost to start your own credit, not to rack up debt.

5. **Be Prepared to Be Removed:** Once your credit is strong enough, ask to be removed to stand on your own.

This strategy isn't about shortcuts—it's about leverage.

Like Carlos, you can use someone else's history as a foundation—but your credit success depends on what you build on top of it.

In the next chapter, we'll explore the **differences between secured cards and alternative credit-building accounts**, so you can choose the best path forward depending on your income, comfort level, and long-term goals.

CHAPTER 6: SECURED CARDS VS. ALTERNATIVE CREDIT BUILDING ACCOUNTS

Emily was proud of how far she had come. Just two years earlier, she was stuck in a job she hated, living paycheck to paycheck with no savings, no credit, and no options.

Now, she had a steady income from her new bookkeeping side hustle, a modest emergency fund, and a clear goal: to buy a reliable car within the next six months—with financing in her name.

But when she checked her credit report, her score was still sitting in the mid-500s. No active accounts. Just a closed utility bill from years ago and a student loan marked as "paid in full." It wasn't bad—it just wasn't enough.

She needed new activity on her credit report.

So she did what most people do: opened a new browser tab and searched,

> "How to build credit fast with low risk."

Almost every article mentioned **secured credit cards**. But a few mentioned **credit builder accounts**, like Self and CreditStrong. Emily was torn. Which one was better? Which one would actually help her reach her goal?

She decided to run her own experiment.

Two Paths, One Goal

Emily took $500 from her savings and split it.

She put $250 into a **secured credit card** through her credit union. It was simple: she deposited the money, got a card with a $250 limit, and promised herself she'd only use it for gas.

Then she signed up for a **credit builder account**. For $25 a month, she'd make "payments" toward a locked savings account, and those payments would be reported as on-time installments to all three bureaus. After 12 months, she'd get her money back—plus interest.

She created two folders in her planner:

1. **Secured Card**
2. **Credit Builder**

Each month, she tracked payments, balances, and changes to her score. She even added alerts on her phone:

- "Pay secured card in full before statement date."
- "Credit builder payment due—auto-pay on."
- "Check credit score update."

She took it seriously. This was her financial comeback story, and she was documenting every step.

Three Months In

By month three, Emily started seeing results.

Her secured card was helping her with **revolving credit**—the type that affects your credit utilization. She always kept her balance below 10%, usually no more than $20 at a time. Her score jumped 34 points in the first 60 days.

Her credit builder account was reporting as an **installment loan**—which helped with her credit mix and payment history. It wasn't as dramatic, but it was steady. Ten more points added to her score by the third month.

She realized both tools were working—but in different ways.

The Difference That Matters

Emily also noticed something important:

- The **secured card** required discipline. If she spent too much or paid late, her score could drop quickly.
- The **credit builder account** was more automated. Payments were fixed, predictable, and reported like clockwork.

Each had its pros and cons.

Secured Card Pros:

- Immediate access to a credit line
- Builds utilization history
- Can eventually graduate to an unsecured card

Cons:

- Requires self-control

- Late payments hurt quickly
- Interest charges if you carry a balance

Credit Builder Account Pros:

- Builds payment history automatically
- Adds installment credit to your profile
- Helps you save money at the same time

Cons:

- No access to funds until end of term
- May take longer to impact score
- Doesn't help with utilization

By month five, Emily's score had risen to **673**—a 68-point improvement from where she started. That was enough to qualify for an auto loan with decent terms.

She walked into the dealership confident, not desperate. And when the finance officer looked at her credit report, he raised his eyebrows.

"You've got a solid credit mix for someone with a short history. Installment and revolving? Nicely done."

Emily smiled. Her experiment had paid off.

Emily's Takeaway: Use Both if You Can

If she had to choose only one, Emily said she'd start with a credit builder account. It was safer and helped her form consistent habits.

But combining both gave her the best results.

Here's What You Can Do Now:

1. **If you have savings to spare,** open a secured card with a low limit.
2. **If you prefer automation and saving,** open a credit builder account.
3. **If possible, do both.** One helps your utilization. The other improves your payment history and mix.
4. **Track everything monthly** and set alerts to avoid missing payments.

Remember: These tools are stepping stones—not lifelong accounts. The goal is to graduate to higher credit and better terms. Once your score improves, you'll qualify for unsecured cards and loans on your terms.

In the next chapter, we'll explore exactly how to **track and optimize your credit growth**, so you know when to take action and when to just stay consistent.

Because building credit without debt is one thing—but building it strategically? That's how you stay in control for life.

CREDIT TO CAPITAL

CHAPTER 7: HOW TO TRACK AND OPTIMIZE YOUR CREDIT GROWTH

If you've made it this far, you've already taken powerful action—activating rent reporting, using subscriptions, opening secured cards or builder accounts. Now it's time to shift from *building* mode to *optimization* mode.

This chapter is all about making sure your credit keeps growing—and doing it efficiently, without guessing.

Step 1: Monitor Your Credit Monthly

To track progress, you need visibility. Fortunately, you don't need to pay for it.

Use these free credit monitoring tools:

- **Credit Karma** (TransUnion & Equifax)
- **Experian.com** (includes free monthly FICO updates)
- **Credit Sesame**
- **NerdWallet**

These platforms allow you to:

- See your score change over time
- Check your credit report for errors
- Monitor utilization and payment history
- Get alerts for new activity or potential fraud

Set a reminder: Check once per month, not every day. Credit changes are slow and steady.

Step 2: Track Key Credit Score Factors

There are five key categories that make up your score. Track and optimize these like a credit professional:

1. **Payment History (35%)**
    - Pay all bills before the due date.
    - Automate payments to avoid human error.
    - Never miss even a $5 payment—it all counts.
2. **Credit Utilization (30%)**
    - Keep your credit card balances below 10% of your total limits.
    - If you can't pay off the full balance early, at least pay it *before the statement closing date*, not just the due date.
3. **Credit Age (15%)**
    - Don't close your oldest accounts unless absolutely necessary.
    - The longer your average age of accounts, the better.
4. **Credit Mix (10%)**

- Include both revolving (credit cards) and installment (credit builder loans or auto loans) accounts.
- You don't need many—just 1–2 of each type is enough.

5. **New Credit Inquiries (10%)**

   - Avoid applying for too many accounts in a short time.
   - Hard inquiries stay on your report for 2 years but only affect your score for about 6–12 months.

Step 3: Use a Credit Tracker or Spreadsheet

Keeping notes will help you stay focused and motivated.

Here's what to include:

Date	Credit Score	Credit Card Limit	Balance	Utilization %	On-Time Payments
Jan 1	580	$300	$20	6%	yes
Feb 1	610	$300	$15	5%	yes
Mar 1	635	$300	$0	0%	yes

You can create this in Excel, Google Sheets, or even a notebook.

Bonus Tip: Some credit apps like Credit Karma or NerdWallet let you track this data visually with graphs.

Step 4: Set Milestone Goals (30-60-90 Days)

Credit growth takes time, but it helps to break it into realistic phases.

30-Day Goal:

- All accounts reporting on time
- Utilization below 10%
- Enrolled in credit monitoring

60-Day Goal:

- Score improves by 20–40 points
- No new hard inquiries
- Automated payments set for all accounts

90-Day Goal:

- Score increases by 50–100 points (if starting from no or low credit)
- Qualify for unsecured credit or better financial products
- Create a plan to graduate or close starter accounts responsibly

Step 5: Avoid These Optimization Mistakes

1. **Paying after the due date but before interest hits**
   - This still risks a late mark. Always pay before the due date.
2. **Maxing out cards and paying off after**
   - Utilization is reported on the *statement date*, not the due date. Keep balances low *before* the statement closes.
3. **Opening too many accounts at once**
   - Every hard inquiry costs you points short-term. Open only what's necessary.
4. **Closing starter accounts too early**

- Keep your first credit accounts open unless there are annual fees or downsides. Age matters.

5. **Ignoring your credit report**

    - Errors happen. Dispute inaccurate info through AnnualCreditReport.com or directly with the bureaus.

Final Thoughts

Building credit is one thing. **Optimizing** it is what gets you to the next level—better rates, better terms, more opportunity.

Consistency is your best friend. Stay automated, stay informed, and celebrate small wins.

In the next chapter, we'll shift focus to something just as important: **How to stay debt-free while your credit continues to grow fast.** Because growth means nothing if it comes with risk—and your financial foundation should always feel stable.

How to Track and Optimize Your Credit Growth

Leah had always been one of those people who avoided credit entirely.

She grew up watching her parents argue about bills—past-due notices taped to the fridge, credit cards with maxed-out balances, and loan officers calling during dinner. So when she moved out on her own at 19, Leah made a vow: no credit, no debt, no drama.

For a while, it worked. She paid for everything in cash, never owed anyone, and didn't even think about her credit score. But then she hit a wall.

At 26, she applied to rent a small house near her new job as a dental assistant. The landlord smiled as she handed over her application—until he ran her credit.

"You don't really… exist," he said gently. "No score. No history. Nothing to evaluate."

Leah was stunned. "But I always pay on time! I don't have debt. Doesn't that mean I'm responsible?"

The landlord shrugged. "It means you're responsible—but it doesn't mean you're creditworthy. At least not in the system's eyes."

That night, Leah sat on her bed, staring at her laptop and wondering how to play this game she never wanted to join.

She didn't want credit for a fancy car or a shopping spree—she just wanted options. A place to live. A way to grow her future without being shut out.

So she made a new vow—not to avoid credit, but to master it on her terms.

The Tracking Begins

Leah opened a free account with Credit Karma and was greeted with the words: "No credit file found." But she also found tools—ones that could help her track every detail going forward.

She ordered her reports from all three bureaus through AnnualCreditReport.com. Blank slates. Not good, not bad—just… empty.

She didn't panic. She created a notebook titled **"Credit Growth Journal"** and wrote on the first page:
Day 1: From Invisible to Unstoppable.

Her first move was to sign up for a secured credit card. She used $300 from her savings and vowed to keep spending under $30 a month. She also activated a rent reporting service that added her monthly rent to her file—and looked into Experian Boost to add her phone and Netflix payments.

Every tool she used, she tracked in her journal:

- Credit Card Balance
- Credit Limit
- Payment Date
- Statement Closing Date
- Rent Reported: Yes
- Utilities Linked: Yes

She even color-coded it like a scrapbook.

Then she set up weekly reminders on her phone:

> "Check credit utilization."
> "Pay off secured card."
> "Log score update."

The First Score

It took about six weeks, but one day, the notification came through.

Your credit score has been updated: 623.

Leah nearly cried. It was a number—just a number—but it meant she existed in the system. Her rent, her bills, her $300 card—they were finally being recognized.

She flipped open her notebook and wrote:
"623. Progress. Proof. Potential."

From that moment on, she became obsessed—not with the score itself, but with understanding *how* it moved.

She noticed that if she paid off her card before the **statement date**, her utilization stayed low and her score climbed faster. When she accidentally let a $120 charge report one month, her score dropped 11 points—even though she paid it off before the due date.

That's when she learned: the **statement date** is more important than the **due date** when it comes to utilization reporting.

She also saw her **credit mix** improve after she opened a credit builder loan—her profile now showed both revolving (credit card) and installment (loan) accounts.

Every time her score moved, she logged the reason why.

From Passive to Proactive

After three months of tracking, Leah had it down to a science:

- She used **less than 10%** of her limit.
- She paid **three days before the statement date**.
- She checked all reports monthly for errors.
- She avoided **hard inquiries** like the plague.
- She didn't open any new accounts unless absolutely necessary.

- She had **auto-pay** set up for every bill.

Her score? **684** and climbing.

Leah knew people with more income and flashier lives who had worse credit than she did. The difference wasn't money—it was strategy.

What started as a panic-driven mission had turned into something empowering.

She was no longer afraid of credit—she respected it. Managed it. Used it.

The Bigger Picture

Leah didn't need a 750 to feel successful. But one day, she got pre-approved for a new apartment—no cosigner, no hassle. She moved into a sunlit studio that overlooked a small park. It wasn't fancy, but it was hers—and she earned it.

She taped a new piece of paper to her fridge:

"684: Built Without Debt. Managed With Discipline."

Then, underneath it, she added a second line:

"Goal: 720 by next summer."

And this time, she knew exactly how to get there.

CHAPTER 8: STAYING DEBT-FREE WHILE SCALING CREDIT FAST

Building credit is important—but staying debt-free while doing it? That's real power.

Too many people fall into the trap of chasing higher scores and better credit cards, only to end up buried in balances, minimum payments, and long-term financial stress. The good news is that you don't need debt to grow your credit—you just need smart strategy and consistent discipline.

This chapter will show you exactly how to scale your credit score fast without falling into the debt trap.

Step 1: Understand the Role of Credit Activity (Not Credit Use)

The credit system rewards **responsible activity**, not borrowing. You don't need to carry a balance or go into debt to grow your score.

Here's what counts:

- On-time payments
- Low credit utilization
- Age of accounts
- Account variety
- Responsible account management

"You don't get bonus points for paying interest."

In fact, carrying a balance hurts your score and your finances. The key is to show you can access credit—but choose not to use much of it.

Step 2: Automate Everything You Can

Automation removes the risk of human error. It's one of the best ways to stay debt-free while building a strong credit file.

Here's how:

- **Autopay the minimum** on every credit card or loan
- Set a **manual reminder** to pay the full balance early (before statement date if possible)
- Automate rent, utilities, and subscription payments from a separate account used only for bills

If your bills are automated, your credit score becomes automatic, too.

Step 3: Use the "1-1-1 Rule" for Smart Credit Card Management

If you want to use a credit card without falling into debt, follow this simple rule:

- Use **1 card** for 1 **type of purchase** (gas, groceries, etc.)
- Use **no more than 10%** of your limit
- Pay it off in full **1 week before the statement closing date**

This ensures:

- Low utilization
- No interest charges
- Positive monthly reporting

Example:
If your card limit is $500, never let your balance go above $50. If your statement closes on the 15th, pay it by the 8th—even if your due date is later.

Step 4: Gradually Increase Available Credit (Without Using It)

Higher limits improve your utilization ratio—but only if you don't increase your spending.

Here's how to raise your limit without increasing risk:

- After 3–6 months of on-time payments, request a credit limit increase
- Use language like "I'm building my credit profile and would like to increase my available credit without impacting my score."
- Don't use the new limit. Keep spending at the same low level.

Tip: Higher credit limits with low balances = better credit scores and stronger lending profiles.

Step 5: Use Credit Builder Tools That Don't Involve Loans

Avoid the temptation to "improve your mix" with unnecessary debt.

Instead, use:

- **Rent reporting services**
- **Experian Boost** (adds utilities and subscriptions)
- **Credit builder savings accounts** (like Self or CreditStrong)
- **Secured cards used for one bill only, paid in full monthly**

These tools build your credit without any risk of revolving debt, compound interest, or impulse purchases.

Step 6: Avoid the "Upgrade Trap"

As your score grows, you'll get offers: unsecured cards, higher limits, even loans or buy-now-pay-later programs. These can be tempting—but dangerous.

Before accepting any upgrade:

- Ask: Will this help my credit profile or tempt me to spend?
- Only accept if it improves your terms (lower APR, no fees) and you can control your usage
- Don't accept cards with rewards that lead to overspending ("Spend $1,000 to earn $50" is a trap)

Smart tip: Keep older, stable accounts open even if you don't use them. They strengthen your average age of credit.

Step 7: Create a "No-Debt Spending Plan"

Credit cards are not emergency funds.

If you're building credit while staying debt-free, you need a cash system that prevents credit reliance.

Create three buckets:

1. **Bills Account** (all automated payments)
2. **Spending Account** (daily expenses)
3. **Emergency Savings** (3–6 months of expenses)

Use your credit card for one fixed item (like your phone bill), and make sure your checking account has the cash to pay it off before it's due.

Step 8: Use Your Score Strategically, Not Emotionally

Your credit score is not a trophy—it's a tool.

Use it to:

- Qualify for apartments or housing with no cosigner
- Refinance high-interest loans if needed
- Open business accounts or utilities without deposits
- Lower your insurance premiums

"Don't use it to justify a lifestyle upgrade or unnecessary spending."

Step 9: Celebrate Milestones—Not Credit Limits

Your score will rise. You'll get offers. But the real win is staying in control.

Celebrate:

- Paying every bill on time for 12 months
- Hitting 700+ without carrying a balance
- Using your credit report to secure better opportunities—not more liabilities

Final Words

Scaling your credit is like building muscle—it happens with consistent, controlled reps. Not with big, risky lifts.

You can build a 750+ credit score without ever carrying a balance, paying a cent of interest, or taking out a loan you don't need. You just need the right plan—and the discipline to follow it.

In the next chapter, we'll look at **the most common mistakes that sabotage credit—and how to avoid them completely.**

Because as your score rises, the risks of missteps grow. But with knowledge and awareness, you can stay one step ahead.

Staying Debt-Free While Scaling Credit Fast

Jonah wasn't new to credit—he was new to using it wisely.

At 24, he'd already made the same mistake millions of people make: thinking a high credit limit meant he could afford more. His first credit card had a $1,000 limit. Within a few weeks, it had a $940 balance.

He promised himself he'd pay it off quickly. Then came an unexpected car repair. Then a missed day of work. Then an interest charge. The snowball started rolling.

Within six months, Jonah had three maxed-out cards and no idea how he'd dig himself out.

By the time he turned 25, he'd paid off most of it through sheer discipline—but his score was wrecked, and his confidence was low. That's when he made a new decision:

> "I'm going to rebuild my credit—but I'm not going back into debt to do it."

He opened a blank journal, titled the first page **"Credit Comeback—No Debt Required,"** and made a promise to himself: *I will grow my credit score without owing a single cent of interest again.*

The Turning Point

Jonah started by canceling all unnecessary subscriptions and building an emergency fund—even if it was just $50 a month. Then, he applied for a secured credit card with a $300 deposit and created a rule:

- Only one charge per month
- Never more than $25
- Pay in full a week before the statement date

He stuck to it like religion.

He called it his "Credit Gym"—small, consistent reps that would make his score stronger without straining his finances.

His friends didn't get it. "Dude, why not just use it for everything and rack up rewards?"

Jonah shook his head. "Because I know how this ends. This card isn't a reward. It's a report card. And I'm not failing again."

The System That Changed Everything

Jonah set up a three-account system:

1. **Bills Account:** Rent, utilities, phone, and the secured card auto-pay came from this.

2. **Spending Account:** Groceries, gas, and day-to-day expenses came from here.

3. **Emergency Savings:** Even if it was small, it was untouchable.

He also set alarms in his phone:

- **Day 7:** Check balance, pay off secured card.

- **Day 10:** Review credit reports.

- **Day 15:** Log credit score.

Each month, he tracked:

- Total credit limit

- Current utilization

- On-time payment streak
- Credit score progress

The funny thing was… the more he tracked, the less he worried. He wasn't guessing anymore. He was managing.

Staying the Course

Jonah's turning point came at the six-month mark. His credit score had climbed from 582 to 702.

He got letters in the mail: pre-approvals, loan offers, cash advance checks.

One night, he got a call from a car dealership.

> "Mr. Diaz, based on your new credit score, we can offer you $20,000 financing—no money down."

He almost said yes. His current car was old, loud, and barely hanging on. The offer was tempting.

But he thought back to that journal entry: *No debt required.*

He thanked them politely and hung up the phone.
Then he made a new journal entry:
"Today I said no to temptation—and yes to my future."

The Real Victory

Jonah didn't buy the car. Instead, he saved $1,000 and bought a reliable used one outright. He kept using his secured card for Spotify and gas. He never carried a balance. Never paid a cent in interest.

By the time he hit his one-year credit comeback anniversary, he was sitting at a 745 credit score.

More importantly, he had peace of mind. No late payments. No minimums. No balance anxiety.

He started coaching his younger brother on how to build credit smart—and became the go-to guy at work for financial advice.

> "You don't need debt to win the credit game," he told people. "You just need discipline, a system, and a reason."

For Jonah, that reason was freedom. Not just from bad credit—but from the stress that came with it.

What Jonah Taught Us

Jonah proved what this chapter is all about:

- You can scale your credit score without debt.
- You don't need to carry balances or open new loans.
- The key is to use credit like a tool, not a temptation.

Because in the end, credit is about *control.* And when you own the system—without letting it own you—that's when you truly win.

CHAPTER 9: COMMON MISTAKES THAT SABOTAGE CREDIT

You've learned how to build credit without borrowing, how to track your progress, and how to stay debt-free. But even the most careful people can stumble into mistakes that undo all their hard work.

In this chapter, we'll cover the most common credit mistakes—what they are, why they happen, and exactly how to avoid them.

Mistake #1: Carrying a Balance Thinking It Helps

The Myth: You need to carry a balance to improve your credit score.
The Truth: Carrying a balance costs you money and lowers your score.

Why it happens: Many people confuse "using credit" with "owing money." But credit bureaus reward *activity*, not *debt.*

How to avoid it:

- Use your card for small purchases.
- Pay the balance in full before the statement closing date.
- Set alerts to pay weekly or biweekly.

Bottom Line: Carrying a balance doesn't help your score—it just earns banks interest.

Mistake #2: Paying Late (Even Once)

The Myth: One late payment isn't a big deal.
The Truth: A single late payment can drop your score by 50–100 points.

Why it happens: People forget due dates, misunderstand statement timing, or wait until the last minute.

How to avoid it:

- Set all bills on autopay for at least the minimum due.
- Use digital reminders to double-check due dates.
- Pay early—especially with credit cards.

Tip: Late payments stay on your credit report for up to 7 years. Protect your payment history at all costs.

Mistake #3: Ignoring Statement Dates vs. Due Dates

The Myth: As long as you pay by the due date, your credit report looks fine.
The Truth: Credit utilization is reported on the **statement closing date**, not the payment due date.

Why it happens: Most people assume payments are only about avoiding fees—not about how your score is calculated.

How to avoid it:

- Find out your card's statement closing date.
- Pay down your balance before this date, not just by the due date.
- Keep your reported balance under 10% of your total limit.

Example: If your limit is $500, keep your balance under $50 *before* the statement closes.

Mistake #4: Closing Old Accounts

The Myth: Closing unused cards is smart because it reduces temptation.
The Truth: Closing accounts can hurt your credit age and increase utilization.

Why it happens: People want to simplify their finances, cut up cards, or avoid fees.

How to avoid it:

- Keep old cards open unless they charge an annual fee.
- Use them for small purchases once every 3–6 months to keep them active.
- If you must close a card, close the *newest* one, not the oldest.

Tip: Your oldest accounts build your "credit age," which impacts up to 15% of your score.

Mistake #5: Applying for Too Many Accounts Too Quickly

The Myth: More cards mean faster credit building.
The Truth: Multiple hard inquiries in a short time signal risk.

Why it happens: People get excited by pre-approval offers or want to jump from 0 to 750 overnight.

How to avoid it:

- Space out applications by 3–6 months.
- Only apply when absolutely necessary.
- Avoid store credit cards that offer "discounts today" in exchange for new inquiries.

Tip: Hard inquiries stay on your report for 2 years but affect your score most in the first 6–12 months.

Mistake #6: Letting Small Bills Go to Collections

The Myth: A $50 bill doesn't matter if you forget it.
The Truth: A $50 collections account can drop your score like a rock.

Why it happens: People overlook old medical bills, parking tickets, or forgotten utilities when moving.

How to avoid it:

- Check your credit report quarterly for unexpected collections.
- Set mail forwarding and close accounts when moving.
- Contact companies before an account goes past due.

Tip: Paid collections may still show on your report, but newer scoring models weigh them less—especially medical debt.

Mistake #7: Misunderstanding Utilization on Multiple Cards

The Myth: As long as your *total* usage is low, you're fine.
The Truth: Each card's utilization is measured *individually* and can affect your score.

Why it happens: People track overall usage but ignore maxed-out individual cards.

How to avoid it:

- Keep each card below 30%, ideally under 10%.
- If one card is maxed, pay it down even if others have zero balances.
- Use balance reminders or apps to monitor usage in real-time.

Mistake #8: Not Reviewing Your Credit Reports Regularly

The Myth: Your credit report is fine if your score looks good.
The Truth: Errors, fraud, or outdated information can hurt your score quietly.

Why it happens: Credit reports are long, complicated, and easy to ignore.

How to avoid it:

- Check your credit report from all 3 bureaus every 3–6 months.
- Use AnnualCreditReport.com for free access.
- Dispute inaccuracies directly with bureaus online.

Look for:

- Incorrect late payments
- Accounts you don't recognize
- Outdated or duplicated information

Mistake #9: Relying Too Much on Credit to Get By

The Myth: Using credit to "float" until payday is harmless.
The Truth: This can lead to a slow debt spiral and missed payments.

Why it happens: Life gets expensive—and credit seems easier than budgeting.

How to avoid it:

- Build a buffer of 1 month's expenses (even if slowly).
- Use your credit card for things you can pay off immediately.
- Treat credit like a tool—not a solution for emergencies.

Final Words

Avoiding these mistakes isn't about being perfect—it's about being **proactive**.

Credit success isn't just built by what you do—it's protected by what you *don't* do. And once you understand these traps, you'll be able to sidestep them for life.

In the next chapter, we'll take everything you've learned and apply it with purpose. You'll learn how to create **30-day, 60-day, and 90-day credit growth plans** to hit your target score—fast, safe, and debt-free.

Common Mistakes That Sabotage Credit

Angela was the first in her family to have "good credit."

After rebuilding her score from the low 500s to a proud 712 over the course of a year, she felt unstoppable. She had a secured card, a credit builder loan, and even a rent reporting service. She followed every tip, paid everything on time, and tracked her progress like a pro.

One Friday afternoon, she sat in her car outside a clothing store, looking at a "You're Pre-Approved!" email on her phone from a retail brand she liked.

"$1,000 credit limit. 20% off your purchase today."

It seemed harmless. She had worked so hard—maybe she deserved to reward herself. Besides, she wouldn't go overboard.

Angela opened the account, got her discount, and bought $250 worth of clothes. She felt a little guilty—but it was still under the limit. What she didn't know was that the card's statement closed five days later—and reported the $250 balance to the credit bureaus.

The Score Drops

The following month, Angela logged into Credit Karma, ready to see another jump.

Instead, her jaw dropped:
Score: 679.

"What?" she gasped. "How did I lose 33 points?"

She scrolled through her report, confused. The payments were still on time. Nothing was in collections. Then she spotted it: the new store card. A $250 balance on a $1,000 limit = 25% utilization. Not terrible—but added to her other small balances, her overall utilization was now above 30%.

It didn't help that her new account also triggered a **hard inquiry**, and her **average age of credit** had dropped from 2 years to 1.5 years.

She was furious—not at the store, but at herself.

"I worked so hard to build this," she muttered. "And I messed it up in a single afternoon."

The Snowball Begins

Angela vowed to fix it quickly. But things got worse before they got better.

The next month, she forgot to pay her secured card *before* the statement closed. It reported a $180 balance on a $300 limit—60% utilization.

Then, she paid her phone bill two days late. Not because she couldn't afford it, but because she thought the autopay was set up—it wasn't.

The result?

Score: 648.

In two months, she lost nearly 65 points.

Angela sat on her couch one night, staring at her planner, tears of frustration forming in her eyes.

> "I didn't max out cards… I didn't miss a loan payment. How did this happen?"

The Turnaround

Determined not to fall back into old habits, Angela decided to start fresh—this time not just building credit, but *protecting* it.

She bought a small whiteboard and wrote in bold letters:
"Credit Safety = Credit Success"

She made a new checklist:

- Don't apply for anything unless it's essential
- Never let a balance exceed 10% of a card limit
- Always check due dates vs. statement dates
- Automate everything—but verify autopay setups
- Pay early—never just on time
- Monitor credit every month—watch for errors, spikes, or new accounts

Angela then called the store card company and paid off the balance. She didn't close the card—she just vowed never to use it again.

Next, she set calendar reminders for every statement closing date. No more late payments. No more balance surprises.

And she gave herself one more rule:
No emotional spending. Credit is for control—not comfort.

The Climb Back Up

Three months later, Angela's score crept back to 692. Not where it was—but getting close.

More importantly, she felt like she had grown. Credit wasn't just numbers on a screen. It was a reflection of habits, awareness, and self-control.

Her cousin asked for help one weekend. "I'm trying to build my score—what should I do?"

Angela smiled.

> "I'll tell you what to do—but I'll also tell you what *not* to do. Because avoiding mistakes is half the battle."

She handed her cousin a notebook and wrote on the first page:
"Don't build a credit score you can't protect."

Angela's Lessons Learned

Angela's story reminds us of what every listener needs to hear:

- A few small mistakes can trigger big score drops.
- Emotional spending or chasing perks can lead to unnecessary inquiries and poor utilization.
- Ignoring statement dates and automation errors can undo months of progress.
- The real power isn't in building a high score—it's in maintaining it through consistency.

Now, she still has great credit. But she's not chasing perfection—she's chasing stability.

And she's helping others do the same.

CREDIT TO CAPITAL

CHAPTER 10: YOUR 30-DAY, 60-DAY, AND 90-DAY CREDIT GROWTH PLANS

If you've followed everything up to this point, you're ready to take powerful, focused action. This chapter is your 3-phase blueprint to build and scale your credit score over the next 90 days—**without borrowing money or going into debt**.

These step-by-step plans will help you:

- Organize your efforts
- Prioritize high-impact actions
- Stay consistent without burnout
- See real, measurable results

Let's break it down by time frame:

Phase 1: The 30-Day Credit Foundation Plan

Goal: Establish a credit footprint and get your first score or a solid point boost.

Week 1: Activate Your Credit Visibility

- **Pull your credit reports** from all 3 bureaus at AnnualCreditReport.com.
- **Sign up for credit monitoring tools** like Credit Karma, Experian, or NerdWallet.

- Note what's on your reports: open accounts, balances, payment history, collections, etc.

Week 2: Add Low-Risk Reporting Accounts

- Sign up for **rent reporting services** (Boom, RentReporters, or LevelCredit).
- Enroll in **Experian Boost** to add phone, utility, and streaming payments.
- Open a **secured credit card** with a deposit of $200–$300, but only use it for one essential bill (like gas or a phone plan).

Week 3: Automate and Optimize

- **Set up autopay** for all bills—credit card, rent, subscriptions, and utilities.
- **Note your credit card's statement closing date** (not just the due date).
- Create a system to pay off your balance 3–5 days *before* the statement closes.

Week 4: Build Your Credit Habits

- Track your credit activity in a spreadsheet or notebook:
    - Utilization %

    - On-time payment status
    - Alerts for due and statement dates

- Avoid applying for any more accounts or loans.

Expected Results:

- Your first score if you had none
- +20 to +40 point boost if you had a thin file
- Clean foundation to build stronger activity in the next 60 days

Phase 2: The 60-Day Credit Acceleration Plan

Goal: Strengthen credit activity, improve utilization, and raise your score more significantly.

Week 5–6: Maintain and Monitor

- Keep secured card spending below **10%** of the credit limit.
- Continue tracking rent and utility payments.
- Log in to your credit monitoring tool weekly to watch for:
    - Score changes
    - Utilization alerts

- Payment history updates

Week 7–8: Strengthen Credit Mix

- If you haven't already, open a **credit builder savings account** (like Self or CreditStrong).
  - These report as installment loans and help diversify your credit profile.
- Make the monthly payment automatic (as little as $25/month).
- Do **not** open any new revolving credit cards unless necessary.

Week 9: Request a Credit Limit Increase

- If your secured card issuer allows it, request a small credit limit increase.
- You can say:

"I'm building my credit history responsibly and would like to increase my available credit to improve my utilization ratio."

- Some issuers will raise your limit without a hard inquiry.

Week 10–12: Clean Up and Consolidate

- Review your credit report for any errors or duplicate accounts.
- Dispute incorrect information directly with the bureaus.
- Check that old collections, if any, are either settled or validated.

Expected Results:

- +40 to +70 point increase, depending on previous activity
- Improved credit mix (installment + revolving)
- More robust credit history with stable reporting

Phase 3: The 90-Day Credit Optimization Plan

Goal: Solidify gains, lower risk indicators, and qualify for better credit products.

Week 13–14: Optimize Utilization Ratios

- If you've received a credit limit increase, **recalculate your new utilization** and keep spending under 10%.
- Pay balances early—not just in full, but before the **statement date**, to keep low balances reported.
- If you have multiple cards, keep each individual card below 10% as well—not just the total.

Week 15: Assess Credit Opportunities (Cautiously)

- Check if you're prequalified (soft pull only) for:
    - An unsecured card with no annual fee
    - A student or beginner rewards card
- If and only if you're above 680, consider upgrading—but avoid store cards or offers that require spending minimums.

Week 16–17: Lock in Positive Behavior

- Maintain 100% on-time payments
- Keep all accounts active with light usage
- Avoid new credit applications

Week 18–19: Plan Your Next Quarter

- Set a new 90-day goal (e.g., hit 720+, refinance auto loan, qualify for a better rental).
- Decide which cards or accounts you'll continue using long-term—and which to keep open just for credit age and utilization.

Expected Results:

- +70 to +120 point total gain (if starting low or thin)
- Pre-approval for credit cards, apartment leases, or low-limit financing

- Sustainable, automated credit system you can use for life

Additional Tips for All 3 Phases

- **Journal Your Progress:** Writing down small wins keeps you motivated.
- **Create a Visual Tracker:** Use a chart or app to monitor score changes, card usage, and milestones.
- **Focus on Behavior, Not Score:** The score will follow if the behavior stays strong.

Your 30-Day, 60-Day, and 90-Day Credit Growth Plans

The day Eric was denied for a used car loan, he felt like someone had punched him in the gut.

He wasn't trying to buy anything fancy—just a reliable car so he could stop taking three buses to work. He had a steady job as a pharmacy tech, a modest income, and a clean history.

But the bank didn't care about that.

> "We can't approve this application. Your credit score is too low, and you don't have enough credit activity."

Eric walked out of that office embarrassed—and angry.

Not because he'd done anything wrong. But because **he hadn't done anything** at all. No missed payments, no debt, no credit cards. Just no *history*.

That's when he made a decision:

"I'm giving myself 90 days to fix this."

Phase One: The 30-Day Foundation

Eric went home that night and started his plan.
He wrote across the top of a blank sheet of paper:
Day 1 – Credit Comeback Plan

He ordered all three credit reports from AnnualCreditReport.com.
What he saw was… basically nothing. Just an old utility account marked paid and a student account that had closed.

He downloaded Credit Karma and Experian, and created a spreadsheet to track:

- Payment history
- Credit usage
- Score updates
- Action items

By Day 3, he had opened a **secured credit card** with a $300 deposit and linked it to just one monthly bill: his cell phone.

Then he found a **rent reporting service**, which allowed him to report 12 months of on-time rent payments. Within two weeks, he was finally on the map.

His score appeared: **612.**
Not amazing—but he existed.

He set calendar reminders for everything:

- Pay off the card on the 10th (before statement date on the 13th)
- Check credit score every 30 days
- Avoid using more than $30 per month on the card

He stuck to it religiously.

Phase Two: The 60-Day Acceleration

By week 5, Eric's score was up to **637**. Small jump—but it was progress.

He didn't apply for anything new. Instead, he added a **credit builder account** through Self. For $25 a month, it would report as an installment loan—helping with his credit mix.

He didn't touch the secured card except for phone bills and gas. Always under $30. Always paid early.

Around week 7, he called his card issuer and politely asked:

> "I've been using my card responsibly. Is it possible to increase my limit?"

They bumped it from $300 to $500 without a hard inquiry.

He didn't spend a penny more—but now his utilization dropped from 10% to 6%.

By week 8, his score hit **668.**

Eric felt like a credit ninja.

Phase Three: The 90-Day Optimization

In month three, Eric went into "maintenance mode."
No new accounts. No overspending. No skipped payments.

He opened a second checking account—just for bills—so there was never a missed payment or overdrawn account. He turned off unnecessary subscriptions and kept his financial life simple.

One day, he got a pre-approval email from a major credit card company.
"$1,500 limit, no annual fee, reward points."

He read the fine print. No hard pull. No gimmicks.

But he passed on it.

"I'm not here to flex—I'm here to fix," he reminded himself.

Instead, he logged his progress and reviewed his goals:

- No debt
- Keep utilization under 10%
- Score over 680 by Day 90

Day 90: The Payoff

On Day 90, Eric opened Credit Karma and stared at the screen.

Score: 691.

He laughed out loud. He'd missed 700 by a sliver—but it didn't matter. He did it. He had built a solid credit score from scratch, with no loans, no late payments, and not a single dollar of interest paid.

More than that—he'd built confidence.

He printed out his plan and put it in a folder labeled: **"Credit Playbook."** Then he wrote another line:
Next goal: 720 by summer.

Eric's Credit Growth Formula

- **Days 1–30:** Add secured card, report rent, automate payments
- **Days 31–60:** Add builder loan, request credit limit increase, keep usage low
- **Days 61–90:** Stop applying, keep accounts active, optimize timing and behavior

Three months ago, Eric was invisible in the credit world.

Now? He was one of the smartest guys in the room—and soon, he'd be one of the most qualified. The next time he walked into a bank, he wouldn't be asking for permission—he'd be showing them a credit report that said *he was ready*.

CHAPTER 11: REAL STORIES OF FAST CREDIT GROWTH WITHOUT LOANS

The path to strong credit doesn't have to run through debt, loans, or high interest rates. These three stories prove that with the right tools and a little commitment, anyone—no matter their age, income, or history—can build a powerful credit profile, completely debt-free.

Let's talk about Naomi for a moment.

Naomi was 32, recently divorced, and starting over in a new city with her two kids. She had always let her ex-husband handle the finances. Now she had to rebuild—on her own terms.

When she tried to lease an apartment in a better school district, the leasing office denied her.

> "Your score is too low, and there's just not enough on your report," the agent said.

Naomi had never missed rent, paid every utility on time, and had a steady job. But none of that mattered because it wasn't *reported.*

Determined not to let her children down, Naomi did her research. Within a week, she signed up for:

- A **rent reporting service** that backdated 24 months of rent payments
- **Experian Boost**, linking her cell phone, electric, and Netflix bills
- A **secured credit card** with a $250 limit that she used only for groceries

She automated every payment, made a spreadsheet to track her progress, and committed to using less than 10% of her available credit. By the end of month one, she had a credit score—**from nothing to 631**.

Three months later, her score was **688**, and the same leasing office that turned her away now approved her with no cosigner.

Naomi didn't borrow a penny. She just leveraged the life she was already living—and made it reportable.

Now, let's talk about Marcus who went from 18 to 710 in 90 days

Marcus was 18 and ready to start his adult life the smart way. His uncle had struggled with bad credit for years, and Marcus was determined to avoid the same trap.

He had a part-time job, a checking account, and a prepaid phone—but no credit history.

Instead of waiting to be denied for his first apartment, Marcus took action early. He followed a strategy he found on a credit-building podcast and set up the following plan:

1. Opened a **Self credit builder account** at $25/month
2. Added his rent and internet through a reporting service
3. Opened a **secured credit card** with a $200 deposit
4. Used it once a week for gas and paid in full before the statement date
5. Tracked his score weekly and never let a single bill go unpaid

By the 30-day mark, he had a score of **645**. By Day 60, it was **682**. And by Day 90, Marcus celebrated his **710 score** with a modest secured credit card upgrade—and a new apartment lease approved on his own.

He had no loans. No debt. No interest payments. Just planning, patience, and discipline.

Let's quickly go over Priya's story now: Fixing What She Didn't Break

Priya was a nurse who had just moved from another country. Although she had years of perfect financial habits back home, her U.S. credit file was empty.

She applied for a credit card. Denied. Applied for a furniture financing offer. Denied again.

> "You have no history here," the rep told her. "You're considered a credit risk."

Priya was stunned. Back home, she had paid every bill early and never carried debt. But in the U.S., she was invisible.

She didn't want to take out a loan. So she found a strategy that worked:

- She signed up with **Nova Credit** to transfer some of her international credit history to Experian
- She added her **U.S. rental payments** and utilities using a rent reporting tool
- She got a **secured credit card** with a $500 deposit and used it to pay her hospital parking fees—just $3/day

She read about credit statement dates and never let a balance report over $40. After 60 days, her score popped up: **652**. Not great—but she existed.

By month three, Priya's score was **705**. She was approved for a better card, and when she applied to finance new appliances for her apartment, she was finally approved—with a smile.

No debt. No games. Just patience and systemization.

What These Stories Have in Common

These three people had different backgrounds and goals—but the same strategy:

- They **started with what they already had** (rent, phone bills, utilities)
- They **used secured cards wisely**
- They **never carried a balance**
- They **tracked their progress**
- They **avoided unnecessary applications**
- And most importantly, they **didn't borrow money to build credit**

Their results?

- Naomi: +100 points and a new apartment
- Marcus: 0 to 710 in 90 days
- Priya: No U.S. credit history to a 705 score in three months

The Big Takeaway

You don't need a bank loan, car loan, or thousands of dollars to build credit fast.

You need a plan.

And these stories prove it works.

In the final chapter, you'll get a powerful summary of everything you've learned—plus your next steps for continuing your credit journey without falling into debt.

CHAPTER 12: FINAL THOUGHTS & SUMMARY

Congratulations. If you've made it this far, you've done more than listen to a credit book—you've taken the first step in transforming your financial future, without falling into the trap of debt.

This final chapter will review the most powerful lessons from this journey, reinforce the habits that protect your score, and show you how to keep building credit safely for the rest of your life.

What You've Learned – The Credit Without Debt Framework

Let's recap the core ideas:

1. You Don't Need Debt to Build Credit

- You need **activity**, not balances.
- Credit scores reward consistency, not interest payments.

2. You Can Use What You Already Pay For

- Rent, subscriptions, and utility bills can be added to your credit profile.
- Services like **Boom**, **Experian Boost**, and **LevelCredit** make this easy.

3. Secured Credit Cards Are Your Friend—If Used Right

- Deposit-based cards offer safe revolving credit.
- Always keep balances below 10% and pay before the statement date.
- These are temporary tools—not permanent necessities.

4. Credit Builder Accounts Add Payment History

- Tools like **Self** and **CreditStrong** report installment loans without actual debt.
- Small monthly payments build your file and help diversify your credit mix.

5. Authorized User Accounts Provide a Head Start

- You can gain credit history from someone else's clean, long-standing card.
- Only use this with people you trust—and who have excellent credit habits.

The 90-Day Plan—Your Roadmap to Results

You also built (or are about to build) your credit using a 3-phase plan:

30 Days – The Foundation

- Open your first reporting accounts (rent, utilities, secured card)
- Start tracking and automating payments

- Create your credit calendar and budget

60 Days – The Acceleration

- Add a credit builder loan to strengthen your mix
- Request a credit limit increase if possible
- Maintain perfect payment history and low utilization

90 Days – The Optimization

- Keep all accounts active
- Avoid new applications unless necessary
- Review and clean up your credit report
- Set new long-term credit goals

Habits That Keep You Safe and Growing

These 10 habits will keep your score rising—and your financial stress low:

1. **Never carry a balance** if you can help it
2. **Pay before the statement date**, not just the due date
3. **Keep credit utilization under 10%**
4. **Review your reports quarterly** for errors
5. **Set all bills on autopay**—then check that they process
6. **Keep your oldest accounts open**, even if unused
7. **Avoid store cards** and rewards traps that encourage spending
8. **Don't apply for too many accounts too fast**
9. **Use credit tracking apps** and review score trends monthly
10. **Celebrate behavior, not the number**—score is a byproduct of discipline

How to Use Your New Credit Power

With a strong credit score, you now have access to:

- **Better housing options** without a cosigner
- **Lower security deposits** on utilities and rentals
- **Approval for credit cards** with rewards or travel points

- **Lower interest rates** if you *do* choose to finance something responsibly
- **Business and investment tools** like business credit cards and funding
- **Emergency peace of mind**—you're no longer financially invisible

Remember: credit isn't about spending—it's about **leverage**. You can now use credit to create more freedom and opportunity, not more stress.

Your Next Steps

Here's what to do after you finish this book:

1. **Review your current credit plan.** Update your goals.
2. **Decide which tools to keep, and which to phase out.**
    - For example: You may want to close a credit builder loan once completed, but keep a long-standing card active.
3. **Set a 6-month and 12-month credit goal.**
    - 6-month: Raise score by 40 points
    - 12-month: Qualify for a rewards card or refinance high-interest debt

4. **Keep tracking. Keep learning.** You've just unlocked a lifelong skillset.

Final Message

You've proven something powerful:
You don't need loans, debt, or a big income to win the credit game.

You just need:

- A strategy
- A system
- And a commitment to financial growth

Whether your goal is to buy a home, launch a business, travel, or simply never stress about money again—strong credit is your foundation. And now you know how to build it without borrowing a dime.

You've got this.
And your future is going to thank you.

EPILOGUE

If you've made it to this point, then you've already achieved what many people still believe is impossible: you've learned how to build real credit, fast, **without taking on debt**.

You didn't fall into the trap of high-interest loans.
You didn't rack up balances in the name of "credit activity."
You didn't rely on someone else to fix your credit for you.
You learned how to do it yourself.

That puts you in the top 10% of people who understand how the credit system really works. And more importantly, you've taken back control.

You're not invisible anymore.

Now, the financial system *knows your name*—and more importantly, it recognizes your behavior.

Maybe you started this audiobook unsure of your score—or unsure if you even had one. Maybe you've been denied in the past, or feared credit because of what it did to someone close to you.

But now you know better.

You've shifted your mindset from fear to strategy. You've turned your rent, your subscriptions, your small purchases, and your habits into credit-building tools. You've learned that credit isn't just for "other people." It's for **you**—and you can manage it on your own terms.

You've gone from wondering if you could qualify… to choosing what you'll qualify *for*.

That shift—from reaction to intention—is one of the most powerful changes you can make in your financial life.

So what now?

Now, you set new goals.

Do you want to:

- Lease a new apartment without a cosigner?

- Get approved for an unsecured credit card with rewards?

- Launch your own business and access capital?

- Buy your first home in a few years?

Whatever your next step is, your credit is ready to support you. All you have to do is continue the same smart habits you built over the last 90 days:

- Automate everything
- Keep utilization under 10%
- Pay before the statement date
- Avoid unnecessary applications
- Track your progress monthly
- Review your reports for errors
- Use credit as a tool—not a temptation

Keep it simple. Keep it steady. And stay in control.

There will be temptations ahead—rewards cards, financing offers, store promotions, and balance transfer games.

You don't need them.

The real power lies in *what you don't owe.* A 720 score that comes with no balances and no interest is worth more than an 800 score with $30,000 in revolving debt.

So guard your credit. Grow it slowly. And use it strategically.

You've proven that you can build credit **without borrowing**. That means you can now qualify for better products **without relying on them**.

You are not dependent. You are empowered.

And you've built a skillset that will last for life.

Most people never learn this.

They continue to believe the lies: that debt is necessary, that balance-carrying is smart, that good credit is only for high earners or people with perfect pasts.

You now know that's false.

So if you know someone struggling with credit, trying to get approved, or living in fear of their score—share this audiobook with them.

Give them the tools. Walk them through the steps. Or simply send them to the next book in the *Credit to Capital* series.

You never know who needs this knowledge. And you never know how much of a difference it can make in someone's life—just like it made in yours.

How to Build Credit Fast Without Debt was just one step in a larger journey.

In the rest of the *Credit to Capital* series, you'll learn how to:

- Repair bad credit and remove inaccuracies

- Build business credit without a personal guarantee
- Start a credit repair business to help others
- Use your credit to fund real estate and business ventures
- Turn personal credit into capital for long-term wealth

Because credit is just the beginning. What you do with it is where the real opportunity lies.

Thank you for trusting me to guide you through this journey. Your credit future is bright, strong, and **debt-free**.

Now go use it wisely.
And I'll see you in the next book.

— Joe Correa

CREDIT-BUILDING CHECKLIST (NO DEBT REQUIRED)

Goal: Build a strong credit score before graduation—without loans or interest.

Step 1: Establish a Credit Profile

☐ Check if you have a credit report at AnnualCreditReport.com
☐ Sign up for free credit monitoring (Credit Karma, Experian, NerdWallet)
☐ If no score appears, don't worry—it's normal at first

Step 2: Open Your First Credit Accounts

☐ Open a **secured credit card** (minimum $200 deposit)
☐ Use it for one fixed expense (e.g. gas, Spotify, groceries)
☐ Apply for a **credit builder loan** (e.g. through Self or CreditStrong)
☐ Enroll in **Experian Boost** to report phone and utility bills
☐ Use a **rent reporting service** if you're renting off-campus or with roommates

Step 3: Set Up Smart Payment Habits

☐ Put all bills on **autopay**
☐ Set reminders to **pay credit card before the statement date** (not just due date)
☐ Keep card usage **under 10% of your limit** (e.g., spend under $20 on a $200 card)

Step 4: Monitor & Track Your Progress

☐ Check your credit score monthly
☐ Track:
- Credit utilization
- On-time payments
- Age of accounts

☐ Keep your oldest account open—even if unused

Step 5: Avoid These Mistakes

☐ Don't apply for store credit cards or multiple accounts at once
☐ Don't close your first card after graduation (it helps your score grow)
☐ Don't carry a balance—**pay in full every month**
☐ Don't co-sign for others unless you're 100% certain of their responsibility

Credit Milestones to Aim For

☐ 1 month: Get your first score (600s+ range is common)
☐ 3 months: Reach 650–680 by using tools and tracking
☐ 6 months: Qualify for better cards or apartment rental approval
☐ 12 months: 700+ credit score with zero debt

VOLUME 4: BUSINESS CREDIT MASTERY

Welcome to Business Credit Mastery: Build Credit Fast & Get Funded. I'm so glad you're here—because this journey could completely transform how you operate, grow, and fund your business.

This book was created for one reason: to give business owners like you the **power to access capital without relying on personal credit**. Whether you're launching a brand-new business or trying to grow an existing one, learning how to build and leverage **business credit** is one of the smartest moves you can make.

Let me start with the truth: most business owners have no idea that business credit even exists. And even fewer understand how to build it. The result? They end up maxing out personal credit cards, taking on high-interest loans, or draining their savings just to keep the business alive.

But that's not your future—because you're about to learn a better way.

In this book, I'll walk you through everything you need to know to start from scratch and build a business credit profile that can qualify you for:

- High-limit credit cards
- Business lines of credit

- Vendor accounts
- And even SBA and bank loans

And here's the best part: many of these options are available **without using your Social Security Number or personal guarantee**. That means you can **protect your personal credit** while unlocking the funding your business needs to thrive.

Throughout this book, you'll learn how to:

- Properly structure your business to meet lender requirements
- Open the right accounts that actually report to business credit bureaus
- Build your credit history even if you're just starting out
- Qualify for business loans and lines of credit
- And most importantly—how to **use business credit to grow, not drown, your business in debt**

Each chapter is designed to give you clear, actionable steps. You'll also hear bonus tips, real-world examples, and strategies that I've personally seen work for small business owners in all industries.

So, whether you're a freelancer, a startup founder, a solopreneur, or running a full team—you're about to gain a competitive edge.

All you need to bring to the table is a willingness to learn and take action.

WHY BUSINESS CREDIT IS SO IMPORTANT TO YOUR SUCCESS

Building business credit isn't just a smart move, it's a game-changing strategy that separates hobbyists from high-level entrepreneurs. Whether you're just starting your business or looking to expand, your ability to access funding without relying on personal credit can transform your financial future. And that's exactly what this book is designed to do for you.

When I started my first business, I had no idea what business credit was. I thought everything had to run through my personal credit cards and personal guarantees. But as I built companies in the mortgage, publishing, and online education space, I discovered the power of leveraging business credit to get vehicles, buy real estate, finance inventory, and even expand operations — all without putting my personal assets on the line. That's the kind of freedom every business owner deserves.

This book is your complete, no-fluff guide to understanding, building, and using business credit the right way. You'll learn everything from setting up your business properly so lenders take you seriously, to getting vendor and net-30 accounts, building strong credit scores with business bureaus, and ultimately qualifying for high-limit credit cards, lines of credit, and even business loans.

We'll also go deep into understanding the key differences between personal and business credit, the specific documentation you need, the credit bureaus that matter, and how to overcome common roadblocks that hold most business owners back. If you've ever been denied credit, overwhelmed by applications, or unsure where to even start, this book will show you a clear, step-by-step path forward.

And don't worry — you don't need to be a financial expert. Everything is explained in simple, easy-to-follow language. You'll be guided through real examples, practical templates, and time-tested strategies used by successful entrepreneurs across different industries.

The truth is, most people don't build business credit because they don't know how. Or worse — they fall for overpriced services and gurus who promise the world and deliver nothing. This book gives you the tools to take control of your business finances without the fluff, scams, or unnecessary confusion.

Inside, you'll also discover:

- The exact steps to separate your personal and business credit
- How to get approved for net 30 and vendor accounts fast
- How to build a Paydex score and DUNS profile that lenders love
- Where to find credit cards and loans designed for your business type
- How to avoid common business credit mistakes that can cost you thousands
- How to qualify for vehicles, equipment, and real estate under your business name

- And how to turn this knowledge into long-term financial leverage

This book was created not just to inform you, but to empower you. Every business owner — from the freelancer to the real estate investor — should understand how to make credit work for them. And with the rise of AI, remote work, and digital entrepreneurship, having access to capital without using your personal credit is no longer a luxury. It's a necessity.

If you're ready to stop relying on personal guarantees, protect your credit score, and build a strong financial foundation for your business, you're in the right place.

Joe's Journey to Business Credit Mastery

I still remember the day I walked into a local bank to ask for a business loan. I had just launched my publishing company, and things were starting to grow. But I needed funds — a few thousand dollars — to produce a new series of books and expand into audiobooks. The banker looked over my application, ran my personal credit, and said the dreaded words: "You don't qualify."

Not because my business wasn't doing well. But because I hadn't established any business credit.

That experience hit hard. But it also lit a fire under me. I went home and started researching everything I could about business credit. What it was. How it worked. Why no one had ever taught me about it before. I found out that I'd been doing everything backward — mixing personal and business accounts, using my own credit cards to cover business expenses, and making decisions that would come back to hurt me.

So I started over.

First, I incorporated my business properly. Then I got an EIN from the IRS, opened a business bank account, and applied for my first vendor account with Uline. I still remember the excitement when it got approved. It wasn't much, but it was a start.

Over the next few months, I followed every step — building trade lines, paying invoices early, monitoring my business credit score, and applying for credit cards in my business name. It wasn't always easy, but with every approval, I grew more confident. And soon, I didn't need to use my personal credit at all.

That same publishing company now funds books, audiobooks, and course creation tools using business lines of credit. I've bought vehicles under the business name. I've even used business credit to invest in real estate, using LLCs that qualified for funding without a personal guarantee.

And I've helped friends, students, and fellow entrepreneurs do the same.

Like my friend Carlos, who used what he learned from me to get $25,000 in business credit within 6 months — even with average personal credit. Or Lisa, a graphic designer who financed her studio equipment entirely through her business and later expanded to two locations.

This book is built on those real-world experiences. It's not theory. It's not fluff. It's what works.

Wherever you are in your journey — whether you're just starting out or looking to scale your empire — business credit can be your silent partner. It works in the background, builds trust with lenders, and gives you leverage when you need it most.

So as you read the rest of this book, remember: if I could do it from a small home office with no financial background and no mentor, you can do it too. And now, you don't have to do it alone.

Let's get to work.

CHAPTER 1: UNDERSTANDING BUSINESS CREDIT

Let's start with a question:
What is business credit—and why does it matter so much?

Business credit is a financial identity for your business. It's separate from your personal credit, and it's built under your business's name and EIN—your Employer Identification Number.

Just like your personal credit shows lenders how you handle money, business credit shows banks, suppliers, vendors, and lenders how your company handles financial responsibility.

And here's the powerful part:
When you build strong business credit, you can access funding, credit lines, and resources **without risking your personal assets or credit score**.

So how is business credit different from personal credit?

Here are a few key differences:

- **Personal credit** is tied to your Social Security Number.
- **Business credit** is tied to your EIN (like a business SSN).
- Personal credit has limits.
- Business credit can offer **much higher limits**, especially as your business grows.

- Personal credit is reported to agencies like Experian, Equifax, and TransUnion.
- Business credit is reported to **Dun & Bradstreet**, **Experian Business**, and **Equifax Business**.
- Personal credit affects your mortgage, car loans, and lifestyle.
- Business credit protects your personal finances and enables **business-only borrowing.**

Here's a quick example:
Let's say you need to buy $5,000 in equipment for your business.
If you use a personal credit card, that debt impacts your personal credit score, increases your utilization ratio, and could even lower your FICO score.

But if you had a business credit card tied to your EIN, that purchase wouldn't touch your personal credit—at all.

Now you're starting to see the power of business credit.

The Benefits of Business Credit

Here are just a few reasons why building business credit should be one of your top priorities:

1. Easier Access to Capital
You can qualify for loans, credit cards, and vendor accounts—even as a startup.

2. Higher Credit Limits
Business credit lines are often 5 to 10 times larger than personal ones.

3. Separation of Finances
Your business debt stays in your business—keeping your personal credit score safe.

4. Better Terms with Vendors
Strong credit can help you negotiate net terms like Net 30 or Net 60.

5. More Credibility
Lenders and partners take your business more seriously when you have a strong credit profile.

Meet the Business Credit Bureaus

There are three major business credit bureaus you need to know:

1. Dun & Bradstreet (D&B)
They manage the **Paydex score**, one of the most widely used business credit scores. The Paydex ranges from 1 to 100. A score of **80 or above** means you pay your bills on time—or early.

2. Experian Business
This bureau assigns an **Intelliscore**, which also ranges from 1 to 100. Lenders want to see a score over **75** to consider you a low-risk borrower.

3. Equifax Business
Equifax gives you multiple scores, including payment index, credit risk, and business failure score.

Understanding how these bureaus track and score your business is key to building a strong profile.

What Is a Trade Line?

A trade line is a record of credit extended to your business. For example:

- If you buy office supplies from Quill on Net 30 terms, that's a trade line.
- If Quill reports that payment to Dun & Bradstreet, it builds your Paydex score.
- Do this with multiple vendors, and you've got a solid credit history.

These vendor accounts are how most businesses start building credit from scratch.

Common Myths About Business Credit

Let's bust a few dangerous myths before we move on:

Myth #1: You need good personal credit to get business credit.
False. Many lenders don't even check your personal credit once your business profile is strong enough.

Myth #2: You need years in business before you can get funding.
Not true. You can start building credit in **your first 30 days** if your business is set up properly.

Myth #3: You can just use your personal credit forever.
Using personal credit for business is risky. If things go south, your personal credit—and financial future—go with it.

Recap

Here's what you've learned so far:

- Business credit is separate from personal credit and tied to your EIN.
- It's tracked by Dun & Bradstreet, Experian Business, and Equifax Business.
- You can build credit through vendor trade lines, business credit cards, and credit lines.
- Strong business credit = funding, growth, and financial safety.

Coming Up Next:

In Chapter 2, we'll set the foundation.

You'll learn how to structure your business to get approved for credit—including which licenses, registrations, and accounts you need to open first.

Let's move forward and **get your business credit-ready** from the ground up.

CHAPTER 2: SETTING UP YOUR BUSINESS FOR CREDIT APPROVAL

Now that you understand what business credit is and why it's so powerful, let's move into the first step of actually building it: **setting up your business the right way.**

Most people skip this part. They go straight to applying for vendor accounts or business loans—and then wonder why they keep getting denied.

But here's the secret:
Lenders and credit bureaus won't even take your business seriously unless you look "fundable" on paper.

In this chapter, I'm going to show you how to structure your business so that credit bureaus can track it, and lenders feel confident approving you.

Step 1: Choose the Right Business Structure

Your business structure is the legal foundation of your company. It impacts everything—from how you're taxed to how lenders view your risk level.

To build business credit, you need to be operating under one of the following structures:

- **LLC (Limited Liability Company)**

- **S Corporation**
- **C Corporation**

While you can technically run as a sole proprietor, it's much harder to separate business and personal credit—and you'll likely need to use your SSN instead of your EIN.

If you haven't formed your LLC or corporation yet, this is your first action step. You can register through your state's Secretary of State website or use a service like LegalZoom, ZenBusiness, or Incfile to do it quickly.

Step 2: Get Your EIN – Employer Identification Number

Once you've registered your business, it's time to get your EIN from the IRS.

Your EIN is like a Social Security Number for your business. You'll use it to:

- Open a business bank account
- Apply for business licenses
- Apply for business credit without using your SSN

Getting your EIN is free and only takes a few minutes. Go to irs.gov and search "Apply for EIN." You'll receive your number immediately upon completion.

Step 3: Open a Business Bank Account

This step is non-negotiable.
You need a business checking account that's tied to your LLC or corporation.

Why? Because lenders will want to see:

- How much money your business earns
- Your average daily and monthly balances
- If you manage your finances responsibly

Plus, many business credit card and loan applications **require** business bank account statements.

Choose a business-friendly bank with low fees. Some great options include Chase Business Checking, Bluevine, Novo, or your local credit union.

Step 4: Get a D-U-N-S Number

Dun & Bradstreet issues something called a **D-U-N-S Number**, which is used to track your business's credit activity.

This number is essential if you want to establish a Paydex Score, which is one of the most widely used business credit scores.

To get your D-U-N-S Number, visit dnb.com. Apply under the "Get a D-U-N-S Number" page. It's free and typically takes 1–2 weeks to process.

Step 5: Set Up a Professional Business Identity

Now, let's make your business look credible. This is what we call **lender-compliant**.

You need the following:

Business Address – Use a commercial office, virtual office, or co-working space (like Regus or Opus). Avoid PO boxes.

Business Phone Number – Get a dedicated business line through services like Grasshopper, RingCentral, or Google Voice.

Professional Email Address – No Gmail or Yahoo accounts. Use something like you@yourbusiness.com.

Business Website – Create a simple website with your domain name. Even a one-page site adds legitimacy.

Matching Business Info Across All Platforms – Your LLC filing, EIN, bank account, D-U-N-S profile, and website should all show the same business name, address, and phone number.

If your business info doesn't match across sources, lenders might reject your applications automatically.

Step 6: Apply for Any Required Licenses or Permits

Depending on your state and industry, your business may need:

- A general business license
- A sales tax permit
- A professional license (for real estate, construction, etc.)

You can usually apply for these through your state or local government's business division. Be sure to check what's required in your area.

Even if a license isn't strictly required, having one can **boost your credibility** with lenders.

Step 7: Set Up Your Business on Google & Business Listings

Lenders often check online listings to verify your business information.

Set up a **Google Business Profile** with your name, address, phone, and website.
List your business on Yelp, Bing, and other online directories.
Make sure your listings match the info you submitted to banks and credit bureaus.

This adds another layer of legitimacy and improves your visibility in search engines.

Step 8: Keep Personal and Business Finances Completely Separate

This is where many business owners go wrong.

You should never use your personal bank account or credit cards for business expenses once your business account is active.

Use your EIN, not your SSN, on credit applications.
Always pay business expenses from your business checking account.
Track your income and expenses using software like QuickBooks, Wave, or Zoho Books.

This separation protects your personal credit and helps lenders trust your business's financial stability.

Recap of Key Setup Steps

Here's a quick checklist of what we covered:

- Form your LLC or Corporation
- Get your EIN from the IRS

- Open a business bank account
- Apply for a D-U-N-S Number
- Create a professional business identity
- Obtain necessary licenses or permits
- List your business online for added credibility
- Separate your personal and business finances completely

Doing this groundwork correctly sets you up for massive success. Without it, you'll struggle to get approved for even basic vendor credit.

What's Next?

Now that your business is fully set up and lender-compliant, you're ready for the **fun part**—actually building credit!

In the next chapter, you'll learn exactly **which vendor accounts to apply for**, how to use them, and how to get your first credit lines reporting to the bureaus.

Remember: This setup process is the foundation. Once it's in place, you'll be amazed how quickly you can begin building and leveraging business credit.

Let's move on to **Chapter 3: Building Business Credit from Scratch.**

CHAPTER 3: BUILDING BUSINESS CREDIT FROM SCRATCH

Now that your business is fully set up and ready for funding, it's time to do what most people never get around to: actually **building business credit**.

Many entrepreneurs think they need to apply for a loan or credit card first—but that's **not the starting point**. The truth is, the fastest and safest way to build business credit is through something called **vendor credit**.

In this chapter, I'll show you step-by-step how to start building credit using **Net 30 vendor accounts**, how to manage them responsibly, and how to track your progress.

Step 1: Start with Net 30 Vendor Accounts

Net 30 accounts are business credit lines offered by suppliers and vendors. The "Net 30" part means you have 30 days to pay your invoice in full.

These accounts are usually easy to qualify for, even if you're a brand-new business. And here's the best part: **many Net 30 vendors report your payment history to business credit bureaus.**

This is how you begin to establish a credit file with Dun & Bradstreet, Experian, and Equifax.

What You Need Before You Apply

Before applying for any Net 30 accounts, make sure the following is in place:

- Your business is legally registered (LLC or Corporation)
- You have an EIN from the IRS
- You have a business checking account
- Your D-U-N-S Number is active
- Your business address, phone, and website are consistent across all documents

If all of these are set up, you're ready to apply.

Step 2: Apply for These Starter Vendors

Here are five popular Net 30 vendors that are known for working with new businesses **and reporting to credit bureaus**:

1. Uline – [uline.com]

Offers shipping, packaging, and office supplies. Easy approval if your business info is complete.

2. Quill – [quill.com]

Office supplies, cleaning products, and more. Often grants Net 30 terms after your first order.

3. Grainger – [grainger.com]

Industrial and commercial products. You'll likely need to call and request Net 30 terms with your EIN.

4. Crown Office Supplies – [crownofficesupplies.com]

Reports to multiple bureaus and has a monthly membership fee for easier approval.

5. NAV Business Boost – [nav.com]

While not a vendor, NAV reports your subscription payments to all three major business bureaus, helping you build credit fast.

How to Use Vendor Accounts

Once approved, make a small purchase—around $50 to $100—and then **pay the invoice early**, not just on time.

Paying early helps you build a **high Paydex score** (80 or higher), which tells lenders your business is low risk.

The key is **repetition and consistency.**
Start with 2 or 3 vendor accounts, pay them on time for at least 60–90 days, and monitor your credit file.

Step 3: Monitor Your Business Credit

It's important to track your credit-building progress.

Use tools like:

- **NAV.com** – Great for monitoring Dun & Bradstreet, Experian, and Equifax scores.
- **Dun & Bradstreet CreditBuilder** – Paid option to add trade lines and monitor your Paydex.
- **Experian Business Credit Report** – Available through their business portal.

You should start seeing trade lines appear within 30–60 days of on-time payments.

Step 4: Expand to More Vendors & Credit Sources

Once your first trade lines are reporting, you can expand to more vendors and move up to **business credit cards** and **store credit**.

Here are a few options to consider:

- **Summa Office Supplies**
- **Strategic Network Solutions**
- **Office Garner**

And for store credit cards:

- **Amazon Business Credit**
- **Home Depot Pro Xtra Card**
- **Staples Business Advantage**

These store cards often require 3–5 trade lines already reporting, so make sure your profile is solid before applying.

Step 5: Move to Revolving Credit

After about 90 days of consistent on-time vendor payments, your business should be ready to move up to **revolving credit**—which means business credit cards.

Some great starter business credit cards include:

Capital One Spark Classic for Business

Low barrier to entry and reports to business credit bureaus.

Divvy Smart Credit Card

No personal guarantee required; ideal for expense management.

Brex Card

No personal credit check, but typically requires $50K+ in your business bank account.

Remember: Use these cards for business purchases only, and keep your utilization **below 30%** to maintain strong scores.

Step 6: Keep Building Trade Lines

Your goal is to build at least:

- **5 trade lines reporting to Dun & Bradstreet**
- **3 to 5 accounts reporting to Experian Business**
- **A Paydex score of 80 or higher**

Once you hit this point, your business becomes much more attractive to traditional lenders.

That's when you can start applying for **lines of credit, term loans, and SBA-backed loans**.

How Long Does It Take?

With consistent effort, you can build a strong business credit profile in **3 to 6 months**.
That's fast compared to building personal credit, which can take years.

Common Mistakes to Avoid

Let's talk about what NOT to do when building business credit:

- **Don't apply for too many accounts at once.** Start with 2 or 3 and work your way up.
- **Don't use personal credit when applying.** Always apply using your EIN, not your SSN.
- **Don't miss payments.** Late payments can tank your score quickly.
- **Don't rely on unverified vendors.** If they don't report to credit bureaus, they don't help your profile.

Recap of Action Steps

Let's summarize everything you've learned:

- Apply for 2–3 Net 30 vendor accounts that report to credit bureaus
- Make small purchases and pay your invoices early
- Monitor your credit reports using NAV or bureau tools
- Add more vendors and expand to business credit cards
- Keep your utilization low and payment history perfect
- Build 5+ trade lines and maintain a Paydex score of 80+

What's Next?

Now that you're building your credit, it's time to unlock **real funding**. In the next chapter, you'll learn how to apply for **business loans and lines of credit**—and how to avoid the common pitfalls that get applications denied.

We'll go over lender requirements, financial documents, and where to get approved even if you're still a young business.

Let's keep building momentum.
Up next: **Chapter 4 – Getting Approved for Business Loans & Credit Lines.**

CHAPTER 4: GETTING APPROVED FOR BUSINESS LOANS & CREDIT LINES

So far, you've learned how to build business credit from scratch—by setting up your business properly and opening trade lines with vendor accounts. Now, it's time for the next level: **getting real funding**.

In this chapter, I'll show you how to qualify for and get approved for **business credit cards, lines of credit, and loans**, even if your business is still new. You'll learn what lenders look for, how to prepare your business profile, and how to avoid the mistakes that lead to denial.

Let's get started.

Why Most Businesses Get Denied

Most small businesses get denied for credit or funding because they apply **too soon**—before they've built a solid business credit foundation.

Others get denied because they:

- Use inconsistent business information
- Apply using their Social Security Number instead of their EIN
- Don't have enough revenue or time in business
- Don't meet the lender's basic requirements

The good news? You can **avoid all of that** with the right preparation.

Types of Business Funding

Let's begin by breaking down the most common types of funding available to small businesses:

Business Credit Cards

These are revolving credit lines with higher limits than personal cards. They help build credit, manage cash flow, and offer rewards or cashback.

Business Lines of Credit

This is flexible funding you can draw from as needed—like a credit card, but with lower interest rates. You only pay interest on what you use.

Business Loans

Lump sum funding repaid over time. These include short-term loans, term loans, equipment loans, and SBA-backed loans.

What Lenders Look For

Different lenders have different requirements, but most look at the same core criteria:

1. Business Credit Score
A Paydex Score of **80+** and an Experian Intelliscore of **75+** show that you're low risk.

2. Time in Business
Some lenders work with startups, but most prefer businesses that are at least **6 to 12 months old**.

3. Business Revenue
Many lenders require a minimum of **$5,000 to $10,000 in monthly revenue**.

4. Bank Account Activity
They'll look at your average balance, number of deposits, and daily cash flow.

5. Financial Documentation
Be prepared to show business tax returns, profit and loss statements, and sometimes personal credit (depending on the lender).

Tiered Funding Strategy

Here's a step-by-step path to move from beginner to advanced funding:

Tier 1: Starter Business Credit Cards

These are great if you've had vendor accounts reporting for 2–3 months and a small revenue stream.

- **Capital One Spark Classic** – Easy approval with modest limits

- **Divvy Smart Credit Card** – No PG and offers spending insights
- **Brex Card** – No personal credit check; best for startups with $50K+ in the bank

Key Tip: Always apply with your **EIN**, not your SSN, when possible.

Tier 2: Business Lines of Credit

Once your business is showing revenue and has 3–6 months of strong banking activity, apply for lines of credit.

Top lenders to consider:

- **BlueVine** – Requires 6+ months in business and $10K/month revenue
- **Fundbox** – Great for newer businesses with less paperwork
- **Kabbage by American Express** – Good for flexible working capital

Lines of credit are useful because they're **revolving**, meaning you can draw what you need and reuse it after repayment.

Tier 3: Business Loans

If you've been in business for over a year and are generating $100,000 or more annually, you may qualify for larger loans.

Options include:

- **OnDeck** – Short-term loans with fast approvals
- **Lendio** – A loan marketplace that matches you with lenders
- **SBA Loans** – Backed by the Small Business Administration, offering low rates and long terms

SBA loans have stricter requirements but offer the best rates if you qualify.

Documents You'll Likely Need

For most funding applications, you'll need the following:

- Business bank statements (last 3–6 months)
- Business tax returns (for loans over $50K)
- Profit & Loss statement or cash flow report
- Business license (if applicable)
- Voided business check

Have these ready before applying to speed up the approval process.

Where to Apply

Here are the best types of lenders depending on your stage:

Startup or New Business:

- Fundbox
- Divvy
- NAV (for monitoring and matches)

Growing Business (6+ months):

- BlueVine
- OnDeck
- Kabbage

Established Business (1–2+ years):

- Lendio
- SBA

- Traditional banks like Chase, Wells Fargo, or Bank of America

Avoid These Funding Mistakes

- **Applying for too much too soon** – Start with small limits and build up.
- **Inconsistent business information** – Ensure all applications match your EIN, business name, and address.
- **Using your SSN when not required** – Always use your EIN to avoid tying funding to your personal credit.
- **Ignoring fine print** – Some lenders charge high fees or use daily payments. Always read the terms.

Tips for Maximizing Approval Odds

✓ Build 5+ trade lines before applying for revolving credit
✓ Keep a consistent business income deposited monthly
✓ Show positive cash flow and avoid negative bank days
✓ Monitor your business credit regularly through NAV
✓ Apply with lenders who report to the business credit bureaus

The more "fundable" your business looks, the more funding you'll qualify for.

Bonus Tip: Use Fintech Lenders

Fintech companies like Divvy, Brex, and BlueVine are startup-friendly and offer fast approvals without the strict requirements of traditional banks.

They're especially useful if your business is newer but you have good cash flow and your credit profile is clean.

Recap of Action Steps

Here's your quick checklist:

✓ Apply for a business credit card using your EIN
✓ Choose a fintech lender for your first line of credit
✓ Prepare your bank statements and documents
✓ Avoid common mistakes like overapplying or using personal credit
✓ Monitor your approvals and build gradually toward larger loans

What's Next?

You've now learned how to **build and access real business funding**—but that's just the beginning.

In the next chapter, we'll focus on **how to use your business credit strategically**. You'll learn how to scale your business, invest wisely, and grow without falling into the debt trap.

Let's move forward to **Chapter 5: Leveraging Business Credit for Growth.**

CREDIT TO CAPITAL

CHAPTER 5: LEVERAGING BUSINESS CREDIT FOR GROWTH

Congratulations! You've built a strong business credit foundation and started accessing funding. But here's where the real opportunity begins—**using that credit to grow your business in a smart, sustainable way.**

In this chapter, I'll show you how to leverage business credit to expand operations, increase profitability, and scale with confidence. We'll also cover how to manage your credit wisely to maintain and grow your approval limits over time.

Because business credit isn't just about getting approved—**it's about what you do with it.**

Why Most Business Owners Misuse Credit

Let's start with a reality check.

Many small business owners finally get access to credit—and then they burn through it. They spend it on untested marketing campaigns, excessive inventory, or non-revenue-generating expenses.

Then they struggle to make payments. They default. Their scores drop. And just like that, the funding dries up.

But that won't be your story—because you're about to learn **how to use credit as a tool, not a trap**.

Smart Ways to Use Business Credit

Here are the most effective ways to use business credit for growth:

1. Invest in Revenue-Generating Activities

Use credit to fund things that bring in more money—like:

- Paid advertising campaigns that have proven ROI
- Building or optimizing a sales funnel
- Hiring freelance help to increase output or productivity
- Ordering inventory for high-demand products

If it brings in more revenue than it costs—it's a smart use of credit.

2. Take Advantage of Vendor Credit Terms

Let's say a vendor gives you Net 30 terms. You get the product today, sell it this week, and pay the vendor 30 days later.

You just scaled your business **without using your own cash**.

This is called **cash flow leverage**—and it's one of the smartest moves you can make using vendor credit.

3. Upgrade Your Tools & Systems

If your business is growing, consider using credit to:

- Upgrade to better software or automation tools
- Improve customer experience
- Streamline processes that save time or reduce mistakes

These investments may not generate direct revenue today—but they **increase efficiency and long-term profit margins**.

4. Expand into New Offerings or Markets

If you've validated your current business model, you can use credit to:

- Launch a new product or service
- Expand into a new city or state
- Build a small team to support fulfillment or customer service

The key is to move **strategically**—not based on emotion or impulse.

What NOT to Do with Business Credit

Now that we've covered the good—let's talk about what to avoid.

☒ Don't use credit for things that won't generate ROI.

Vacations, fancy offices, or the latest tech gadgets don't grow your bottom line.

☒ Don't max out your credit limits.

Try to keep your utilization below **30%**, ideally around **10–20%**.

☒ Don't miss payments or pay late.

Even one missed payment can drop your business credit scores and hurt your future funding chances.

☒ Don't co-mingle personal and business credit.

Keep all business credit activity under your **EIN**, not your SSN.

Managing Business Credit Responsibly

Here's how to maintain your credit profile as your business grows:

☑ Make On-Time or Early Payments
This keeps your Paydex score at 80 or above and builds trust with lenders.

☑ Keep Utilization Low
If you have a $10,000 credit limit, try not to carry more than $2,000–$3,000 at a time.

☑ Request Higher Limits Every 6–12 Months
If you've been making timely payments, call your card issuer and ask for a limit increase.

☑ **Diversify Your Credit Profile**
Use a mix of vendor accounts, business credit cards, and potentially a line of credit or term loan.

☑ **Monitor Your Reports Monthly**
Use NAV.com or go directly to D&B, Experian, and Equifax to keep an eye on your credit health.

Growing Credit Limits Over Time

Your ability to access **larger lines of credit** grows with your:

- Time in business
- Credit history length
- Payment history
- Average account balance
- Monthly revenue and consistency

If you manage credit well, you'll qualify for higher limits—and better terms—without needing a personal guarantee.

Many businesses go from a $1,000 vendor account to a $50,000 credit line in under 12 months with consistent credit-building habits.

Long-Term Credit Strategy

As you continue growing, your credit strategy should evolve.

Here's what to focus on over the next 6–12 months:

➔ Build Relationships with Banks & Lenders

Open a business checking account at a major bank. Apply for a business credit card through them after 3–6 months of activity.

Banks prefer to lend to businesses that already **bank with them**.

➔ Consider SBA Loans for Large Growth Moves

If you plan to buy equipment, expand locations, or need funding over $100K, SBA loans offer:

- Lower interest rates
- Longer repayment terms
- High approval odds if your business profile is strong

Just be ready for paperwork—it's a more detailed process.

➔ Separate Credit Strategies for Each Entity

If you run multiple businesses or LLCs, build credit separately for each EIN.

This allows you to access funding in each business without over-leveraging one.

Leveraging Credit Without Getting Buried

The key to long-term success with business credit is **control**.

Never borrow more than you can reasonably repay—even if you get approved.

Credit should create **financial freedom**, not pressure.

Ask yourself before using credit:
"Will this expense help grow my business or improve profitability?"

If the answer is no—it's better to wait.

Final Thought: Think Like a CEO

As your credit profile grows, think beyond just credit cards and Net 30 accounts. Think like a CEO.

Use credit to fund systems, delegate responsibilities, and build infrastructure.
Use it to unlock opportunities and scale smart.

And always remember—business credit is a tool.
Used wisely, it can fuel your success for years to come.

Recap of Action Steps

Let's summarize this chapter:

- Use business credit for revenue-generating and efficiency-building expenses
- Avoid high utilization and missed payments
- Maintain and monitor your credit profile monthly
- Request credit limit increases every 6–12 months
- Build relationships with banks and apply strategically
- Think long-term and scale with intention

What's Next?

In the final chapter, we'll wrap everything up with your **90-day action plan** and show you how to keep your credit growing long after this book ends.

You've made incredible progress so far—now let's make sure the momentum keeps going.

Let's head into **Chapter 6: Conclusion & Next Steps.**

CHAPTER 6: NEXT STEPS

You've made it to the final chapter of Business Credit Mastery. Congratulations!

By now, you've learned how to **set up your business correctly**, **build your credit profile from scratch**, **get approved for funding**, and **use that credit wisely to grow**.

Now, it's time to pull it all together and create a **clear, actionable plan** so you can move forward with confidence—step by step.

This isn't the end of your journey—it's just the beginning.

Let's walk through your **next 90 days**, give you a recap of everything we've covered, and lay out the strategy to keep building momentum.

The 30 / 60 / 90 Day Action Plan

Let's start with a simple plan you can follow over the next three months.

Days 1–30: Get Your Business Credit-Ready

During your first month, focus on the fundamentals:

- Register your business as an LLC or corporation
- Get your EIN from the IRS

- Open a business bank account
- Apply for your D-U-N-S Number with Dun & Bradstreet
- Set up your business phone number, email, website, and address
- List your business on Google and online directories
- Ensure all information is consistent across registrations

Your goal in this first phase is to **establish your credibility** and make your business "lender-ready."

Days 31–60: Start Building Credit History

Once your structure is in place, it's time to apply for your first vendor accounts:

- Choose 2–3 Net 30 vendors that report to credit bureaus (Uline, Quill, Grainger, etc.)
- Make small purchases—$50 to $100
- Pay invoices early to start building your Paydex score
- Monitor your business credit using NAV or bureau portals

You'll also want to explore **adding a business credit card** such as Divvy, Brex, or Capital One Spark (depending on your eligibility).

By the end of this phase, you'll have **multiple trade lines reporting** to the credit bureaus.

Days 61–90: Apply for Funding & Expand Your Profile

Now that you have credit history, it's time to unlock actual funding:

- Apply for a business credit card with a major bank
- Apply for a business line of credit from BlueVine, Fundbox, or Kabbage
- Keep credit utilization under 30% and continue paying early
- Request credit limit increases if eligible
- Use credit to fund smart, growth-oriented expenses

This is also a great time to **build banking relationships** with lenders you may want to use later for bigger loans or SBA funding.

CHAPTER 7: SCALING WITH MULTIPLE BUSINESS CREDIT PROFILES

In this chapter, we're going beyond the basics. You already know how to build business credit for one company. Now, imagine doing it for **two**, or **three**—and using each profile to access **separate funding**, reduce risk, and scale your financial potential.

That's what Chapter 7 is all about:
Creating and managing multiple business credit profiles—legally, responsibly, and profitably.

Let's get started.

Why Have Multiple Credit Profiles?

Most business owners only build one business credit profile under their primary company. But smart entrepreneurs build **multiple**.

Here's why:

- Each EIN can build its own credit file
- Each profile can apply for its own credit lines and loans
- You can reduce risk by separating ventures
- You can scale funding across different industries

- You can isolate liabilities in one entity without affecting the others

This is a strategy commonly used by real estate investors, agency owners, and entrepreneurs with digital businesses, e-commerce, or franchising models.

How It Works

Each LLC or corporation is treated as a **separate legal entity**. That means:

- It gets its own **EIN from the IRS**
- It builds its own **DUNS number and Paydex score**
- It can open **its own business bank account**
- And it can apply for **vendor accounts, credit cards, and loans**

There is **no legal limit** to how many business credit profiles you can build, as long as each business is legally registered and has a valid purpose.

When Should You Consider Creating Multiple Profiles?

Here are a few signs you might benefit from this strategy:

- You run multiple businesses or brands under one roof
- You want to access more credit without overextending one company
- You're ready to expand but want to protect your existing assets
- You're in a high-risk industry and want to separate liability
- You're investing in real estate or passive income vehicles

Each new profile is a new opportunity to build funding potential.

Step-by-Step: Building a Second Business Credit Profile

Here's how to start your second profile (or third, fourth, and so on):

Step 1: Register a New LLC or Corporation

Start with your Secretary of State. Choose a name, register it, and receive your Articles of Organization or Incorporation.

Step 2: Apply for a New EIN

Visit irs.gov and apply for a new Employer Identification Number. This must be unique to the new business.

Step 3: Set Up a New Business Bank Account

Use your new EIN, business name, and registration documents to open a dedicated business checking account.

Step 4: Apply for a New DUNS Number

Go to dnb.com and apply for a new D-U-N-S number. Remember: one per entity.

Step 5: Create a Professional Presence

Just like your first company, make sure this business has:

- A business phone number
- A professional email
- A website and domain
- A business address or virtual office

Consistency is critical. Make sure all business information matches across documents.

Step 6: Apply for Vendor Accounts

Choose 2–3 vendors that report to business credit bureaus. Start with small purchases and pay early.

Step 7: Build and Monitor

Watch your credit scores grow with each on-time payment. After 60–90 days, you can begin applying for business credit cards and revolving accounts.

Pro Tips for Managing Multiple Entities

Running multiple credit profiles takes organization and discipline. Here's how to stay in control:

✓ **Use a spreadsheet or CRM tool** to track credit accounts, due dates, and limits for each entity
✓ **Use a different bank for each business**, or set up separate online banking portals
✓ **Label all credit cards and accounts clearly** to avoid cross-usage
✓ **Keep detailed bookkeeping records**
✓ **File taxes separately for each entity**, or consult with an accountant for pass-through strategies
✓ **Use a registered agent** if managing multiple states or addresses

What to Avoid

✖ Don't apply for credit with the same email or phone number across all businesses
✖ Don't cross-use credit from one business for another—this could cause reporting or legal issues
✖ Don't mix financial activity; keep each business financially independent

✖ Don't overextend yourself—build one solid profile before starting another

The goal is sustainable growth, not chaos.

Funding Multiplication: How to Stack Credit Across LLCs

Here's an example of how powerful this can be:

Let's say you build business credit for one LLC. After 6 months, you have:

- $15,000 in Net 30 credit
- $25,000 in revolving business credit cards
- $40,000 in available business lines of credit

Now you open a second LLC. You build a similar profile. That's another $80,000 in potential access.

Suddenly, you're managing **$160,000 in business credit access**, across two legally separated, EIN-backed companies.

And remember: this isn't about debt—it's about **leverage and liquidity**.

Use Cases for Multiple Credit Profiles

Here are a few ways people are using multiple credit profiles:

- **E-commerce** – Separate credit for different brands or stores
- **Real estate** – Each property LLC builds its own profile for rehab or rental financing
- **Online education** – Separate funding for content production, marketing, and software
- **Franchising or licensing** – Isolate each unit to reduce liability and maximize funding
- **Agency services** – Use separate LLCs for marketing, consulting, and fulfillment

This is the business version of "not putting all your eggs in one basket."

Is This Legal?

Yes—**absolutely**, as long as each business:

- Has a valid purpose
- Operates independently
- Maintains its own records

- Applies under its own EIN

Thousands of investors, developers, and entrepreneurs use this strategy legally and ethically.

Your Next Steps

Here's how to get started if this chapter resonated with you:

- Write down the new business ideas or brands you could develop
- Register a second LLC and apply for a new EIN
- Follow the same steps you learned in Chapters 2 and 3
- Start with low-risk vendor accounts
- Use the same discipline and timeline—30, 60, 90 days
- Document every account, purchase, and payment for both entities

Final Thoughts

Think of every EIN you create as a key. A key to a new financial profile. A new opportunity. A new funding system.

But just like credit, the power lies in **how you use it**.

You now have a roadmap for multiplying your credit-building success. Whether you stop at one business or expand to many, the principles stay the same:

Build smart. Leverage wisely. Protect your assets. And scale with intention.

CHAPTER 8: PROTECTING AND REBUILDING BUSINESS CREDIT

Even the most well-run businesses hit bumps in the road. Cash flow gets tight. Payments get delayed. Mistakes happen. What matters most is not avoiding every problem—but knowing **how to respond when your business credit takes a hit**.

In this chapter, we'll walk through what to do if your business credit is damaged, how to **rebuild quickly**, and how to protect your profile going forward—so you never lose access to the funding you've worked so hard to build.

Let's begin.

Warning Signs Your Business Credit Is at Risk

Just like with personal credit, there are clear warning signs that your business credit may be slipping:

- You receive fewer credit offers or denials from vendors
- Your Paydex score drops below 80
- You notice new negative items or late payments on your credit reports
- You get calls from collections or past-due notices

- Your lenders reduce your credit limits or raise your rates

If any of these happen, don't panic—**but don't ignore them either.**

Step 1: Check Your Reports Across All Bureaus

Your first step is to pull your business credit reports from:

- **Dun & Bradstreet** (for your Paydex score)
- **Experian Business** (for your Intelliscore)
- **Equifax Business** (for risk scores and trade line data)

Use a tool like **NAV.com** to monitor them in one place.

Check for:

✔ Inaccurate information
✔ Missed or late payments
✔ Accounts in collections
✔ Unreported positive trade lines

Step 2: Dispute Errors or Inaccuracies

Just like personal credit, **business credit reports can contain errors**.

You have the right to dispute those items.

Here's how:

Dun & Bradstreet:

- Log in to your DNB account
- Use the "Update Your Company Information" tool
- Submit corrections with proof (invoices, emails, bank statements)

Experian Business:

- Visit their dispute center at experian.com/business
- Submit written disputes with documentation

Equifax Business:

- Visit their business dispute center online
- Mail or upload dispute forms with supporting details

Errors can take 30–60 days to resolve, so be patient but proactive.

Step 3: Bring Past-Due Accounts Current

If your business has **legitimate late payments**, work quickly to get accounts current:

- Contact vendors directly and request a payment plan
- Ask if they'll **re-age the account** or remove the negative remark after payment
- If an account is in collections, **negotiate a pay-for-delete** arrangement

Tip: Always get payment agreements in writing. Keep all email correspondence.

Step 4: Rebuild Your Trade Lines

If your scores have dropped or your profile looks thin, the best solution is to **start fresh with new vendor accounts**.

Here's how:

- Apply to 2–3 Net 30 vendors that report
- Make small purchases and pay early
- Monitor your score as new trade lines post

Good trade lines can **outweigh old negatives** over time.

Try rebuilding with vendors like:

- **Crown Office Supplies**
- **Summa Office Supplies**
- **NAV Business Boost**
- **Strategic Network Solutions**

Step 5: Add Positive Data (Even Manually)

Some bureaus like Dun & Bradstreet allow you to **manually add trade references**.

This means you can report:

- Office leases
- Utility bills
- Commercial services
- Vendor relationships that don't normally report

If you have a good payment history with these companies, ask them to verify it.
D&B will include them in your Paydex calculations.

Step 6: Ask for Credit Limit Increases

Once your credit is stable again, **ask your active vendors or lenders** to increase your limits.

Why?

Because higher limits reduce your utilization ratio—**one of the biggest factors in your score.**

Even if you don't need more credit right now, higher limits improve your credit profile and buying power.

Step 7: Establish Goodwill With Your Lenders

If you've had a rough month or quarter, be honest—with your lenders, that is.

Reach out. Let them know the situation. Many are willing to:

- Waive late fees
- Offer temporary deferments
- Lower your payments
- Help you avoid credit damage

It's always better to communicate early than to fall behind in silence.

Step 8: Build a Business Emergency Fund

Protect your credit by building a safety net:

- Set aside 1 to 3 months of expenses in a business savings account
- Use credit **only when it makes you money**, not to cover recurring costs
- Diversify your income streams so your cash flow isn't fragile

Credit is a tool, not a crutch. Build financial strength behind it.

Step 9: Separate Risk with Multiple Credit Profiles

As we discussed in the last chapter, having **more than one business entity** can protect you.

If one business runs into credit issues, the other remains untouched—so long as they are legally and financially separate.

This is how entrepreneurs protect themselves without pausing growth.

Step 10: Stay Educated and Engaged

The business credit world changes fast.
Stay up to date by:

- Reading SBA and lender updates
- Monitoring policy changes at NAV, D&B, and major lenders
- Listening to credit or business finance podcasts
- Joining forums or online groups for credit-building entrepreneurs

The more you know, the more you'll catch issues **before** they become problems.

Recap: The Rebuilding & Protection Checklist

Here's what to do if your business credit is damaged—or if you simply want to protect it moving forward:

☑ Pull reports from D&B, Experian, and Equifax
☑ Dispute any errors or outdated info
☑ Pay down or resolve negative accounts
☑ Rebuild trade lines with Net 30 vendors
☑ Add new positive trade references
☑ Ask for higher limits on open credit lines
☑ Communicate with lenders early if problems arise
☑ Build a business emergency fund

☑ Use multiple credit profiles for risk separation
☑ Stay informed and monitor your reports monthly

Final Thought: Credit Is a Long Game

Sometimes, rebuilding takes time. That's okay.

A late payment today **doesn't define you tomorrow**.

Credit is about consistency. Not perfection.

If you keep taking positive steps—every month, every quarter—your scores will climb.
Your credibility will grow.
And the funding you need will become available again.

So stay steady. Stay smart.
You're building more than a score—you're building **a financially resilient business**.

CHAPTER 9: TURNING BUSINESS CREDIT INTO LONG-TERM WEALTH

You've built your business credit. You've used it to access funding, protect your personal finances, and grow your company. But here's the bigger question:

How do you turn business credit into real, lasting wealth?

In this chapter, we'll explore advanced strategies that go beyond credit cards and vendor accounts. You'll learn how to **use business credit to invest, build assets, and create generational wealth**—without ever using your personal credit profile.

Let's move on.

What Is Wealth, Really?

Wealth isn't just about money in your bank account.
It's about **ownership**, **control**, and **cash flow**.

True wealth means:

- You own assets that grow in value
- You control funding and resources
- You have systems that create income without trading time

Business credit is one of the best-kept shortcuts to building that kind of wealth.

Strategy 1: Invest in Cash-Flowing Assets

Once you've built strong credit across one or more businesses, you can use that credit to **buy assets that pay you back monthly**.

Examples include:

- Real estate (rental properties, Airbnb, commercial units)
- Equipment (vending machines, car rentals, business vehicles)
- Content creation (online courses, eBooks, print-on-demand)
- Automated online businesses (e-commerce, affiliate sites)

You don't have to use personal loans or high-interest credit cards.
Use business credit lines, vendor financing, or business installment loans.

- ★ Use business funding to acquire the asset.
- ★ Use the cash flow from the asset to repay the debt.
- ★ Then, reinvest your profits to expand.

Strategy 2: Use Credit to Launch Multiple Income Streams

Your credit profile doesn't just fund one business—it can help you launch **new streams of income**.

You can use business credit to fund:

- ➔ A new coaching or consulting service
- ➔ A digital product (like a course, workbook, or app)
- ➔ A YouTube channel or media brand
- ➔ A mobile business (like a food truck or service van)

If your business credit profile is strong, you can qualify for **$50,000 or more** in funding to test, launch, and grow these ideas—with little or no personal risk.

Strategy 3: Build and Sell Funded Businesses

Want to build wealth fast?

Use business credit to **build companies you can eventually sell**.

Platforms like **Flippa**, **Empire Flippers**, and **Acquire.com** allow you to sell:

- Digital courses
- SaaS tools

- E-commerce stores
- Content websites
- Agency systems

If you use credit to build a business with strong traffic, reviews, or recurring revenue—you can flip it for 3 to 10 times its monthly profit.

That means a side hustle bringing in $5,000/month could sell for $30,000 to $100,000—tax-advantaged, scalable wealth.

Strategy 4: Protect Your Assets with Holding Companies

Once your business or portfolio grows, consider setting up a **parent company or holding company**.

This strategy allows you to:

➔ Build credit in the parent LLC or C-Corp

➔ Lend funds to your other entities

➔ Protect assets under separate legal structures

➔ Centralize profits for reinvestment

- ➔ You can build credit under the holding company as well
- ➔ It can even own equipment, vehicles, or IP
- ➔ It's a smart structure for serious scaling and long-term asset control

Strategy 5: Maximize Rewards & Cash Back

If you've built multiple business credit cards, don't forget about the **free money** they provide.

Examples:

- 2% cash back on advertising, travel, or shipping
- 0% APR intro offers for 12 to 18 months
- Rewards points that convert to free flights or hotel stays
- Exclusive discounts through Visa Business and Mastercard programs

Use these strategically:

✓ Pay off balances monthly
✓ Funnel high-expense categories into the right cards
✓ Reinvest the savings into more asset-building activities

Over time, these benefits add up to **thousands in free cash** each year.

Strategy 6: Use Business Credit to Leverage OPM

One of the best uses of business credit is to access **Other People's Money** (OPM) without traditional investors.

Examples:

- Secure a $50K business line of credit to fund a real estate deal
- Use business credit cards to run ads for a digital product
- Use vendor financing to get products, sell them, then pay later

This is how top entrepreneurs scale without debt stress:
They let the asset pay off the credit—and they keep the profit.

Strategy 7: Rinse and Repeat with New Entities

Now that you've built credit with one business, you can repeat the process:

- Register a second or third LLC
- Build a new credit profile
- Access a second set of funding
- Launch a new brand or income stream

Each EIN is a separate opportunity to access credit, funding, and profit.

Smart entrepreneurs don't rely on one stream—they build a **portfolio of companies**, each with its own credit and income.

Strategy 8: Combine Business Credit with Tax Strategy

Here's where things get exciting.

When used properly, business credit can work **in tandem** with tax strategies to:

- Reduce your taxable income
- Defer taxes on reinvested profits
- Deduct interest, business purchases, and depreciation
- Fund purchases that benefit your business and reduce liability

✓ Work with a business accountant to maximize this.
✓ Use your credit responsibly to fuel legitimate business expenses.

You'll pay less tax, grow faster, and keep more of your profits.

Recap – Business Credit to Build Wealth

Let's summarize the wealth strategies covered in this chapter:

☑ Use business credit to invest in cash-flowing assets
☑ Launch new income streams without personal risk
☑ Build and flip businesses for 3–10X monthly revenue
☑ Set up holding companies for protection and growth
☑ Maximize credit card rewards for free capital
☑ Use OPM strategies to grow without draining savings
☑ Repeat the process under new entities and EINs
☑ Pair credit with smart tax planning for long-term retention

Final Word

Business credit isn't just about funding your company.
It's about **building financial systems** that work for you.

Used correctly, your business credit profile becomes a launchpad—not just for one business, but for a life of leveraged growth, smart investment, and long-term wealth.

You've now completed the blueprint. The next move is yours.

Are you ready to use credit not just to get funded—but to get wealthy?

Let's go.

CHAPTER 10: THE MINDSET OF FINANCIALLY EMPOWERED ENTREPRENEURS

Welcome to the final chapter of Business Credit Mastery—and this one is a little different. We've covered strategy, funding, tools, vendors, and structure. But none of that matters unless you develop the right mindset to **sustain and scale financial success**.

In this chapter, we'll talk about the **mindset shift** that separates those who get stuck in debt from those who build wealth through business credit.

Because the truth is: you can have all the credit in the world, but without the right mindset, you'll never unlock its full potential.

Let's talk about what it means to think, plan, and act like a **financially empowered entrepreneur.**

Wealth Starts in the Mind

Before wealth shows up in your business bank account, it shows up in how you think.

Most people operate from a mindset of:

- Scarcity
- Fear of debt

- Lack of financial education
- Short-term survival over long-term growth

To truly succeed, you must rewire your thinking:

From scarcity → to strategy
From fear → to financial literacy
From reaction → to responsibility
From spending → to investing

Business credit isn't a trap. It's a tool.
Wealthy entrepreneurs use tools. They don't fear them.

Think Like an Investor, Not Just a Business Owner

Business owners think in terms of:

- "What can I afford?"
- "How do I cut costs?"
- "How do I avoid risk?"

Investors think differently:

- "How can I use this money to make more money?"

- "How quickly can I get a return?"
- "What systems can I build to scale this process?"

When you begin using credit to **create cash flow**, **purchase assets**, and **build systems**, you start thinking like a wealthy entrepreneur.

Long-Term vs. Short-Term Thinking

Short-term thinkers use credit to cover gaps.
Long-term thinkers use credit to build bridges.

One uses it to survive.
The other uses it to scale.

Which one are you becoming?

Your goal isn't just to get approved for a credit card or line of credit.
Your goal is to use those tools to build something that outlasts you.

A brand. A portfolio. A company that creates jobs, serves people, and generates wealth—year after year.

Responsibility Before Leverage

Leverage without discipline is dangerous.

Before you go applying for every credit line and maxing out cards, ask yourself:

- Can I track every transaction in real time?
- Do I have a plan for how this credit will grow my business?
- Am I disciplined enough to repay it early and protect my score?
- Do I view credit as power—or as permission to overspend?

Your ability to handle credit responsibly **determines the size of the opportunities that come next**.

Start Small, Grow Smart

You don't need a $100,000 credit line to start.

Start with:

- One Net 30 account
- One revolving business credit card
- One loan you repay early
- One investment that creates recurring revenue

Each small win builds your confidence, your credibility, and your capacity.

Soon, you'll go from testing small purchases to managing **real funding**, deploying it strategically, and stacking profits instead of problems.

Stay Calm in Growth Seasons

As your credit grows, offers will come.

Banks will pre-approve you.
Vendors will offer higher limits.
You'll get more access, more exposure, more risk.

In these moments, stay grounded. Don't rush. Don't overextend.
Ask yourself:

- "Do I need this funding right now?"
- "Will this credit move me forward or just add pressure?"
- "What's the smartest, most profitable use of this capital?"

Calm, focused decisions build long-term wealth.
Emotional, impulsive decisions create setbacks.

Protect What You Build

As you grow, the stakes rise.
So protect what you've built:

✔ Review your credit reports monthly
✔ Keep your utilization low

✔ Never miss a payment—automate everything
✔ Reinvest in your business infrastructure
✔ Use legal protections like LLCs, trusts, and holding companies

Wealth is not just built. It's **protected**—and that takes intention.

Never Stop Learning

Financially empowered entrepreneurs are always:

- Reading
- Listening
- Testing
- Iterating
- Leveling up

Take courses. Read books. Hire coaches. Join communities.

Every level of funding, growth, and opportunity requires a higher level of financial intelligence.
Stay sharp. Stay humble. Stay hungry.

Surround Yourself with Builders

Want to build wealth faster?

Surround yourself with people who:

- Talk about credit, funding, and asset growth
- Think in terms of ROI, automation, and cash flow
- Value financial strategy more than social status
- Push you to build, not spend

Your network shapes your net worth—especially in the business world.

Final Action Plan

Here's your mindset mastery checklist:

✔ Shift from survival to strategy
✔ Use credit only to grow, not to splurge
✔ Treat every dollar like an investment
✔ Track everything—credit, cash flow, ROI
✔ Slow down your decisions but speed up your learning
✔ Celebrate discipline as much as success
✔ Reinvest profits into long-term assets
✔ Stay calm, steady, and consistent

Closing Thought

Business credit is a gateway. A gateway to growth, freedom, wealth, and legacy. But the real key isn't in your EIN. It's in how you **think**.

Think like a builder. Think like a strategist. Think like a CEO who deserves financial independence—and knows how to protect it. If you combine what you've learned with this mindset, there is no limit to what you can fund, build, or scale.

Congratulations.
You've just finished Business Credit Mastery—but more importantly, you've unlocked a **new way of thinking**.

Now go apply it.

EPILOGUE: BUSINESS CREDIT MASTERY: YOUR FINANCIAL LEGACY STARTS NOW

Mastering business credit is not just a financial strategy — it's a shift in identity. You're no longer just a consumer or employee; you are now a strategic operator of a business entity with the power to access funding, protect your personal credit, and scale without limitation. You've walked through the critical steps — from forming your entity and registering for your EIN, to opening Net 30 accounts, applying for business credit cards, and setting up a profile that lenders trust. These are not abstract ideas. They are concrete, actionable steps you can start today.

Many entrepreneurs fail not because their ideas lack merit but because they lack funding. Personal credit often becomes overleveraged and risky. But business credit changes that story. It gives you leverage that doesn't depend on your FICO score, your job history, or even your current income. It gives you control — and control equals confidence. Whether your business is just getting started or has been operating for years, it's never too early or too late to build strong credit under your EIN.

With business credit, you separate risk. You keep your personal finances safe while giving your business the tools it needs to grow. Need to purchase inventory? Book travel for a client event? Pay for a marketing campaign? Secure a short-term line to cover cash flow? Your business credit is your silent partner, allowing you to say yes to more opportunities while keeping personal liabilities at bay.

More importantly, business credit allows you to think bigger. Instead of operating from scarcity — asking, "How much can I afford?" — you begin to operate from abundance: "How can I best deploy capital to multiply returns?" This mindset shift is everything. It's what separates small business owners from scalable entrepreneurs. It's the key that unlocks real wealth. And it all begins with building your first five trade lines and getting them to report to Dun & Bradstreet, Equifax Business, and Experian Business.

Let's be honest — building business credit takes discipline. You must pay on time. You must keep accounts in good standing. You must periodically review your business credit reports, correct any errors, and maintain a low debt-to-income ratio. But once your foundation is built, things begin to snowball. Tier 1 vendors lead to Tier 2 credit cards. Tier 2 leads to revolving lines of credit. Before you know it, you'll have access to $50,000, $100,000, or more — all under your business name.

Many of my clients go on to use their business credit to purchase real estate, invest in digital products, acquire inventory, or even start new businesses. Others use it to bridge cash flow gaps or build financial buffers that reduce stress and increase focus. The uses are endless, but the principle is the same: never again rely on your personal credit for business expenses. That's the past. Business credit is your future.

I've seen entrepreneurs build business credit starting from scratch — no revenue, no team, and no previous business experience. One of my students began with a single Net 30 account and within six months, had four accounts reporting, a business credit card with a $10,000 limit, and a $25,000 business line of credit — all without a personal guarantee. Another used her credit to fund a digital marketing agency that now earns over $300,000 annually.

This is possible because the system works. If you follow the sequence — and avoid skipping steps — your results will be just as powerful. The trick is not to chase funding blindly. Build relationships with banks. Use credit responsibly. Invest in things that grow your income, not just your ego. Business credit can be used to create real leverage — if you use it with wisdom.

After reading this book, you have two options. You can close this chapter and go back to business as usual. Or you can open a new one — the chapter where you become a fundable entrepreneur who no longer relies on personal debt. Start with the basics:

- Check that your business name, address, phone number, and NAICS code are aligned and professional.
- Get listed with Dun & Bradstreet and request your D-U-N-S number.
- Open vendor accounts that report to the bureaus (Uline, Quill, Crown Office Supplies, etc.).
- Use those accounts, pay on time, and track your progress with Nav or CreditSafe.

Once you have 3–5 accounts reporting, move to Tier 2 and Tier 3 options — fleet cards, store cards, and eventually major bank credit cards and lines of credit. Then reinvest what you've learned into your business. This system is repeatable and scalable. One entity. Five accounts. Responsible usage. Strong profile. And repeat.

This isn't just about building a business. It's about building a legacy. A business with strong credit becomes an asset you can sell, scale, or pass down. You can build multiple businesses under your umbrella. You can access funding to launch new ideas, take calculated risks, and protect your personal wealth while building generational abundance.

Let this be the moment you decide to operate differently. Let this be your declaration that you will no longer play small, beg banks for capital, or let a low personal credit score define your business destiny. You have the blueprint. You have the knowledge. And now, you have the responsibility to act.

Thank you for joining me in this journey. I hope this book becomes a reference, a spark, and a turning point in your entrepreneurial journey. If this made a difference for you, I invite you to check out the other books in the Credit to Capital series.

Let's build something unforgettable — together.

THINGS TO REMEMBER

As you come to the end of this book, there are some key principles that you must take with you and revisit often. These are not just helpful reminders — they are the foundational truths that will keep your business financially strong, protected, and positioned for long-term growth.

First, always remember that business credit is not a one-time task. It's a process. You're not just checking boxes — you're building trust with lenders, suppliers, partners, and the business credit bureaus. Every payment you make, every account you open, and every loan you apply for becomes part of your business's financial fingerprint. The more responsible and strategic you are, the more doors will open for you.

Second, consistency is everything. Your business credit file is built over time — not overnight. That means paying invoices early, keeping utilization low on business credit cards, avoiding unnecessary inquiries, and updating your business information regularly across all platforms. Even if you're approved for just one small vendor account, treat it like gold. Use it, pay it off, and repeat. These small steps create momentum that compounds into real credit power.

Next, never mix personal and business finances. This is the number one mistake most entrepreneurs make. It's tempting to use your personal card "just this once," or co-sign for a business loan, but every time you do, you weaken the legal and financial separation between you and your business. If your goal is to truly protect your personal credit and build a business that stands on its own, you must treat your company like a separate entity — with its own accounts, its own EIN, its own credit profile, and its own responsibilities.

Fourth, keep excellent records. Save your approvals, invoices, credit agreements, and proof of payments. Business lenders, underwriters, and even trade suppliers sometimes require proof of account history or business legitimacy — and you want to be ready. It also helps to use accounting software or a simple spreadsheet to track your credit-building progress: when accounts were opened, when payments are due, and how they report to the bureaus. Organized records = faster funding and fewer problems.

Fifth, stay current on your business credit reports. You'll want to regularly monitor your profiles with Dun & Bradstreet, Experian Business, and Equifax Small Business. Look for incorrect data, unreported accounts, or negative marks. Dispute anything inaccurate. Just like personal credit, errors on your business report can hold you back from getting the funding you deserve. And unlike personal credit, not all vendors report automatically — so you may need to call and request that they do.

Another critical reminder: apply for credit strategically. Don't apply for every card, loan, or line you see. Make sure your foundation is strong first — your LLC or corporation is registered, your EIN is active, your business phone and address are set up professionally, and your NAICS code is correct. Then only apply for credit products that align with your stage of growth and industry. Each application creates a record, and too many denials can hurt your business's credibility.

Also, remember to build relationships with banks and lenders — not just chase credit limits. Open a business checking account with a local bank or credit union, maintain a healthy balance, and talk to a small business banker. These relationships can turn into credit lines, business loans, or even funding opportunities you didn't know existed. Relationships matter more than ever in the world of business credit.

One powerful tip most people miss: leverage your business credit before you actually need it. Don't wait until you're desperate for cash to apply. Lenders prefer to extend credit to businesses that appear stable and prepared — not ones that are in a crisis. Build your credit file when things are calm, so you have access to capital when you're ready to grow, invest, or scale.

You should also know that business credit isn't limited to just credit cards or vendor accounts. It includes vehicle financing, equipment leasing, office space, business insurance premiums, and more. Once your credit is solid, you can fund your expansion, invest in assets, or even start new companies — all using the credit history and funding capacity of your original business.

Lastly, never stop learning. Business credit is part of a much larger financial strategy — one that includes tax strategy, investing, debt leverage, and asset protection. The more you learn about these topics, the better prepared you'll be to build real wealth. This book is just the beginning. Make it your mission to become the kind of entrepreneur who doesn't just work for money, but uses credit and systems to multiply it.

You now have the blueprint. You've learned how to structure your business the right way, build strong credit from scratch, get funded without personal guarantees, and unlock a level of freedom most business owners never experience.

But none of that matters if you don't apply it.

So take action. Open your first account. Set up your vendor relationships. Build your DUNS file. Apply for the right credit. Use it responsibly. Repeat the process.

Your future is waiting — and it's funded.

Let's go build it.

VOLUME 5: CREDIT CARD SECRETS FOR BUILDING WEALTH & REWARDS

I never intended to become a credit card expert. In fact, the first time I was offered a credit card in college, I only signed up because they were giving away a free T-shirt. It was red, too big, and had the bank's logo splashed across the front. That shirt cost me almost $3,000 in debt over the next year. That was my introduction to the credit trap—not the wealth-building machine I know today.

Years later, I found myself sitting in the back of a coach flight, knees crushed, dreading the 5-hour trip ahead. Across the aisle sat a man, maybe in his early 40s, sipping champagne in first class. I couldn't help but wonder how some people seem to live in a completely different financial world.

When we landed, I noticed him at the baggage carousel, rolling a sleek carry-on with the American Express Platinum tag hanging from the handle. As we exited, I worked up the courage to say, "Excuse me, can I ask… how do you travel like that?"

He smiled and said something that stuck with me forever:

"It's not money. It's points. I haven't paid for a flight in five years."

That moment triggered an obsession. I dove into everything I could about credit cards, rewards systems, point transfers, 0% APR strategies, and how the wealthy use credit as a *tool*, not a trap. I devoured forums,

YouTube videos, and financial blogs. I tested every strategy. I failed, got rejected, had my credit limit slashed. But slowly, I started winning.

I discovered the real power wasn't just in earning free flights—it was in unlocking capital, funding businesses, stacking credit limits, and converting rewards into cash flow. Most importantly, I learned how to avoid the traps that most people fall into—those hidden fees, interest spikes, and false promises.

One of the biggest shifts happened when I used a 0% interest card to buy inventory for a side business that turned into a six-figure brand. Another time, I earned over $1,200 in sign-up bonuses within a month by timing my applications and expenses just right.

The deeper I went, the clearer it became: Credit cards weren't the enemy. **They were a gateway to financial leverage**, lifestyle upgrades, and even generational wealth—**if** used strategically.

This book isn't just about getting points or avoiding debt. It's about unlocking the systems that banks use to make billions—and flipping them to work for *you*. Whether you want to travel the world for free, launch a business, or just get control over your finances, this book is your starting point.

You're about to learn the secrets the banks *hope* you never discover.

Welcome to *Credit Card Secrets for Building Wealth & Rewards.*
Let's change the way you use credit—forever.

Chapter 1: Understanding the Credit Card System — How Banks Profit and How You Can Flip the Script

"If you don't understand how the system works, you become a victim of it."
— Joe Correa

The True Purpose of a Credit Card

Most people believe credit cards are just a convenience—something to keep in your wallet for emergencies, travel, or impulse purchases. But to banks, credit cards are far more than that. They are **highly profitable financial products** designed to earn money in multiple ways:

- **Interest on carried balances**
- **Annual fees**
- **Late fees and penalties**
- **Interchange fees paid by merchants**
- **Balance transfer fees**
- **Cash advance fees**

Banks are not in the business of giving you credit because they're kind—they do it because **the average American pays hundreds of dollars in interest and fees every year.**

But here's the secret: **You can use the system without falling into the trap.**

The moment you understand the blueprint, you can:

✓ Access capital at 0% interest

✓ Earn thousands in points and cashback

✓ Travel for free

✓ Launch side businesses

✓ Build a 750+ credit score and leverage it for even more wealth

Types of Credit Cards and Their Purposes

There are **five primary types of credit cards** you should be familiar with:

1. **Cashback Cards**

Ideal for everyday spending. Look for:

Flat-rate cashback (e.g., 2% on all purchases)

Rotating categories (e.g., 5% on groceries, gas, etc.)

2. **Travel Rewards Cards**

Best for earning airline miles or hotel points. Key features:

Sign-up bonuses (50,000–100,000 points)

Transfer partners for maximum value

Perks like lounge access and free checked bags

3. **Balance Transfer Cards**

Designed for debt management.

Offer 0% APR for 12–21 months

Ideal for consolidating or eliminating high-interest debt

4. **Business Credit Cards**

Great for side hustles or full businesses.

Higher limits

Track spending by category

Business-specific perks like shipping discounts or office supplies

5. **Credit Building or Secured Cards**
For those with no or poor credit.

Requires a deposit

Reports to all three bureaus

Helps you establish or rebuild your credit profile

Tip: You should never apply randomly. Each card has a purpose, and your selection should match your **financial goals**.

How Credit Card Companies Make Money (and How to Make It Back)

Banks make money in **three main ways**:

1. **Revolving Interest**
The majority of cardholders carry a balance. At an average APR of 20%, the interest compounds fast.
Strategy: Never carry a balance. Pay in full every month.

2. **Merchant Fees**
Every time you swipe, the merchant pays 1.5–3.5% to the card network. That's why cards with rewards are possible.

Strategy: Maximize your return by using the right card for every purchase.

3. **Annual and Penalty Fees**

Annual fees can be worth it—but only if you **use the perks**. Late fees, on the other hand, are to be avoided at all costs.

Strategy: Automate payments and track due dates.

Tools You Need Before Playing the Game

Before you dive in, set up your financial toolset:

1. **Credit Monitoring** – Use platforms like Credit Karma or MyFICO.

2. **Budget Tracker** – Mint, YNAB, or a simple spreadsheet.

3. **Card Benefits Organizer** – Create a table or use an app to track your cards' rewards, due dates, and perks.

4. **Payment Automation** – Always automate at least the minimum payment to avoid late fees.

5. **Spending Goals** – Only use cards for **planned, budgeted expenses**.

Think of your credit card strategy as a business plan. You're not spending emotionally—you're **earning strategically**.

CREDIT TO CAPITAL

Mindset Shift – From Consumer to Wealth Builder

Here's the most important concept of this chapter:

Credit cards are not for spending money you don't have.
They are for **earning rewards on money you're already going to spend.**

This one shift can be life-changing.

For example:

- If you spend $2,000/month on bills, food, gas, and groceries, that's $24,000/year.

- At 2% cashback, that's $480 back in your pocket—without changing your lifestyle.

- With travel cards, it could mean **2–3 roundtrip flights every year.**

- Use multiple cards smartly, and you can earn **over $1,500 in rewards or bonuses** yearly with minimal effort.

And when paired with 0% interest promotions, you can **borrow money for free** and invest it into cash-flowing ventures (covered in later chapters).

ACTION STEPS FOR CHAPTER 1:

1. List your current credit cards and categorize them.

2. Identify which ones have annual fees and which rewards you actually use.

3. Set up auto-pay for all credit card minimums today.

4. Download a credit monitoring tool and track your score.

5. Create a spreadsheet with your card names, due dates, limits, and reward structures.

This is the foundation. In the next chapter, you'll learn **how to apply for new credit cards like a pro**, time your applications, maximize your approval odds, and unlock the **best welcome bonuses** banks offer.

Are you ready to start stacking rewards instead of debt? Let's go.

Marco's story

Marcos always paid with cash. In his mind, credit cards were trouble. He had seen his parents go through it—minimum payments, sleepless nights, collection calls. So when he turned 25 and landed his first steady job in sales, he stuck to the basics: debit card, cash, and a promise to never borrow money.

Every morning, he stopped by his favorite Miami coffee shop before work. The barista, Nikki, would greet him with the same question: "Café con leche, Marcos?" He'd smile, hand over a $5 bill, and head out the door. But one morning, something odd happened. The man in front of him ordered the same drink and scanned a shiny black credit card. The barista handed him a loyalty punch card, and the man nodded, "Put it on the Sapphire. Double points this month."

Marcos tilted his head. Double points?

He watched as the man walked away, sipping his coffee with a confidence that intrigued him. Marcos asked, "What's the deal with that card?"

The barista shrugged. "He's always talking about points. Says he flew to Greece for free last year."

Free? The word echoed in Marcos' head for days.

Later that week, curiosity got the best of him. He went home, opened his laptop, and typed in, "How do credit card points work?" That innocent search led to an all-night rabbit hole—articles, YouTube videos, blog posts. He learned about welcome bonuses, travel hacking, cashback, and 0% APR promotions.

That weekend, he applied for his first real credit card: a no-annual-fee cashback card offering $200 for spending $500 in three months. Simple enough. He figured he could use it for gas and groceries and pay it off immediately.

A month later, he had the $200 bonus in his account and had spent nothing extra to earn it.

That was the beginning.

At work, he started using cards for all reimbursable business travel. He opened a spreadsheet to track due dates, rewards, and limits. Over the next six months, he added a travel card with a 60,000-point bonus and a business card for his side hustle selling custom t-shirts online.

Every purchase became intentional. He stopped seeing credit as temptation and started seeing it as a strategy. His credit score shot from 688 to 742 in less than a year. He used a 0% APR card to buy new printing equipment for his t-shirt business and doubled his sales that quarter.

By year two, Marcos had earned over $3,500 in rewards, taken two trips using points, and never paid a cent in interest.

But the real transformation came one night in December.

His cousin Daniela called him in tears. Her car had broken down, and she didn't have enough for repairs. She had bad credit, no savings, and couldn't get approved for a loan. Without the car, she'd lose her job. Marcos didn't hesitate. He used his 0% card to cover the cost and set up a payment plan with her.

"Why are you helping me like this?" she asked.

"Because I've been learning how to use the system. And now I finally feel like I'm in control."

That Christmas, Marcos flew his parents to New York for the first time in their lives using points. He covered the hotel stay with his card's travel portal and earned another 10,000 points on the spend. His dad, a quiet man with rough hands from years of construction work, leaned over and said, "I never thought this kind of life was possible for us."

"It is," Marcos replied. "If we stop fearing credit—and start using it smart."

The coffee shop where it all started still stood on the corner. But Marcos had changed. Now he ordered his drink with his favorite rewards card, and Nikki would say, "Still stacking points, huh?"

Always, he'd say with a grin.

Because for Marcos, credit wasn't just a tool—it was a second chance, a passport, and a wealth strategy.

And it all started with curiosity and a cup of coffee.

Chapter 2: The Smart Application Strategy – Getting Approved, Maximizing Bonuses, and Timing It Right

"The difference between being denied and being rewarded thousands is all in the timing and the strategy."
— Joe Correa

Why You Shouldn't Apply Randomly

Most people apply for credit cards without a plan. They see a flashy commercial, an influencer post, or a preapproval letter in the mail—and they click apply.

That's a mistake.

Every application results in a hard inquiry on your credit report, which temporarily lowers your credit score by 2 to 5 points. More importantly, too many inquiries in a short period raise red flags to lenders.

But when you apply strategically, you:

✓ Maximize approval odds

✓ Earn the highest welcome bonuses

✓ Increase your total available credit

✓ Build your credit score faster

Timing is everything. And so is knowing which cards to apply for, in what order, and why.

The Approval Formula (Yes, there is a formula!)

To get approved for top-tier credit cards, you need to understand what lenders are looking for. Here are the **five key factors** they analyze:

1. **Credit Score (FICO):**

680+ for mid-tier cards

720+ for premium cards

Scores below 650 will likely require secured or starter cards

2. **Credit History:**

Lenders prefer 2+ years of credit history

No recent delinquencies, collections, or charge-offs

3. **Credit Utilization:**

Keep usage under 30%, ideally under 10%

Example: $1,000 balance on $10,000 limit = 10%

4. **Number of Recent Inquiries:**

0–2 in the past 6 months = strong

4+ = considered risky or "credit hungry"

5. **Total Accounts and Mix:**

A mix of revolving credit (cards) and installment loans (car, mortgage, student loan) helps

Having 3–5 open cards shows experience without being risky

Pro Tip: If your credit isn't quite where it needs to be, focus on increasing your score for 60–90 days before applying. You can do this by lowering utilization, disputing errors, and becoming an authorized user on a high-limit, low-balance card.

The Application Plan — 3 Types of Cards to Target

Before applying, decide what your goal is:

1. **Welcome Bonus Cash or Points**

☑ Ideal for funding a vacation, building emergency funds, or launching a side business

☑ Look for cards offering $200–$750 after spending $500–$4,000 in 3 months

2. **0% APR Offers**

☑ Perfect for big purchases or debt payoff

☑ Many cards offer 0% APR for 12–21 months on purchases or balance transfers

3. **Business Credit Cards**

☑ Higher limits, don't appear on personal report, and offer massive sign-up bonuses

☑ Even side hustles like freelancing or reselling qualify

Rule of Thumb:

- Apply for **personal cards first**, then **business cards**

- Apply for cards from **different banks**, not all from the same issuer

- Space out applications by **at least 90 days**, unless you're executing a stacking strategy (covered in Chapter 6)

Bank Application Rules You Must Know

Each bank has its own internal rules. Violating them often leads to automatic denial, even if you have great credit.

Here are the most important:

Chase 5/24 Rule

- If you've opened **5 or more credit cards** (personal only) in the past 24 months from **any bank**, you will be denied most Chase cards

- Apply for Chase cards **first** in your strategy

Amex "Once Per Lifetime" Rule

- You can only earn the **welcome bonus** for each card **once per lifetime**

- Wait until you can meet the minimum spend before applying

Citi 8/65/95 Rule

- You can only apply for **1 personal Citi card every 8 days** and **2 every 65 days**

Bank of America 2/3/4 Rule

- No more than **2 cards in 2 months**, **3 in 12 months**, and **4 in 24 months**

Knowing these rules helps you avoid denials and wasted hard inquiries.

How to Meet Minimum Spend Without Overspending

Many cards require you to spend $500–$5,000 in 90 days to earn the welcome bonus. But don't panic or overspend—use these strategies:

- **Prepay utilities or insurance** (monthly bills you're paying anyway)

- **Buy gift cards** to places you shop regularly (groceries, gas, Amazon)

- **Pay rent with a service like Plastiq** (with small fees—still worth it for large bonuses)

- **Split large purchases with family/friends and get reimbursed**
- **Use the card for all business or reimbursable work expenses**

Warning: Don't just spend to hit the bonus if you can't pay it off. Remember: the interest is never worth the rewards.

ACTION STEPS FOR CHAPTER 2:

1. **Check your credit report** and score on Credit Karma, Experian, or MyFICO.

2. **Identify your next 1–2 card goals**: cashback, travel, 0% APR, or business.

3. **Choose a card that matches your goal** and current credit profile.

4. **Review the bank's rules** before applying (especially if it's Chase).

5. **Plan how you'll meet the minimum spend** using budgeted, regular expenses.

6. **Apply and track your cards in a spreadsheet** with due dates, bonuses, limits, and category rewards.

Let's talk about Alicia and her journey.

It was a Wednesday evening, and Alicia sat at her tiny kitchen table in a cramped apartment just outside Atlanta, staring at her laptop. On the screen was a Chase Sapphire Preferred card application. Her heart was racing. She'd filled out all the fields, read the bonus offer three times—**60,000 points after spending $4,000 in three months**—but she couldn't bring herself to click "submit."

Her finger hovered over the mouse.

She took a breath and closed the browser.

It wasn't the first time.

Alicia had grown up in a family that feared credit. Her mother called credit cards "debt traps" and warned her never to get one. So for most of her twenties, Alicia operated on cash and a debit card. No credit history, no debt—but also, no opportunities.

Then came the promotion at work. She had just stepped into a marketing manager role and was now traveling for conferences, meeting with vendors, and managing budgets. Her boss used a company credit card. Alicia, however, fronted her travel costs and waited to be reimbursed.

On her first trip to San Diego, she overheard a coworker talking about redeeming points for a five-star hotel stay. Alicia was floored. She had stayed in a basic motel that reeked of mildew just to save money. Her coworker had used points—**earned from spending she already had to do**—and was enjoying oceanfront luxury. That night, Alicia went down the credit rabbit hole.

By the time she was back home, she knew about welcome bonuses, 0% interest periods, and bank approval rules. She signed up for Credit Karma and discovered her score was 712—not bad for someone who'd never had a real credit card.

So why the hesitation?

It was fear. Fear of doing it wrong. Fear of rejection. Fear of debt.

She started small. A week later, she applied for a simple cashback card with a $200 bonus after spending $500. Approved. She used it for groceries, gas, and her Netflix bill. She paid it off every Friday. After three months, her score had jumped to 730. Confidence built.

That's when she pulled the Chase Sapphire back up again. This time, she wasn't nervous. She'd checked her 5/24 status—only one new card in the past 24 months. She'd timed it perfectly. She even wrote out a plan to meet the $4,000 spend: her next flight and hotel, new tires for her car, and helping her sister with a medical bill. All expenses she had already planned—now working toward her goal.

She clicked "Submit."

Approved instantly. $20,000 credit limit.

Her jaw dropped.

That same month, Alicia took another leap—she opened a business credit card under her Etsy side hustle, which she ran on nights and weekends. It sold custom mugs and printables. She'd made only a few hundred dollars a month so far, but now she had a real business checking account and a business credit card. That one came with a $500 bonus after spending $3,000.

Her strategy became airtight:

- Business expenses on the business card
- Personal and travel costs on the Sapphire
- Spreadsheet tracking rewards, due dates, and payment status
- Automation to pay minimums, manual payments every week

In 60 days, she had collected **over $800 in bonuses**, was approved for $35,000 total credit, and still hadn't paid a penny in interest.

Three months later, Alicia stood barefoot on a balcony in Maui, sipping pineapple juice and watching the sunrise. The trip had cost her less than $200 out of pocket. Everything else—flight, hotel, rental car—was covered in points.

She snapped a picture and posted it online. The caption read:
"Debt-free, paid in points, and stress-free. This is how you use credit."

Messages poured in: "How did you do that?" "Teach me!" "What's the trick?"

But there wasn't a trick. It was a strategy. And it had changed everything.

From fear to freedom, Alicia had learned that credit wasn't the enemy.

The enemy was not knowing how to use it.

Chapter 3: Maximizing Credit Card Rewards – Travel, Cashback, and Hidden Perks

"Earning points is just the beginning. The real wealth is in knowing how to use them."
— Unknown

The Three Types of Credit Card Rewards

When used properly, credit cards offer significant rewards that go far beyond cashback. These rewards come in three primary forms:

1. **Cashback**

Flat-rate or tiered percentages back on your purchases

Best for simple, flexible usage

Ideal for people who want real cash without the complexity of points

2. **Points**

Often part of a bank's reward ecosystem (e.g., Chase Ultimate Rewards, Amex Membership Rewards)

Redeemable for travel, gift cards, cash, or transferred to travel partners

Offer the highest potential value when used correctly

3. **Miles**

Airline-specific or flexible miles systems

Great for frequent travelers

Can yield 1.5x to 5x the value of cashback if optimized for premium travel

Quick Comparison:

✓ Cashback = simplicity

✓ Points = flexibility

✓ Miles = maximum travel value

How to Use Points for Free Travel

The average user redeems points for gift cards or statement credits—usually at a value of $0.01 per point. But smart users get **2–5x more** by transferring points to **travel partners**.

Example:

Chase Sapphire Preferred users can transfer points to programs like:

- United Airlines
- Hyatt Hotels
- British Airways
- JetBlue

So instead of redeeming 50,000 points for $500 in gift cards, you might get:

- A roundtrip flight to Europe worth $1,000+
- 3 nights at a luxury Hyatt resort worth $1,500

Redemption Tools:

- **Google Flights**: To find the cash cost of flights
- **AwardHacker.com**: To compare point values across loyalty programs

- **Transfer partners chart** (available from your card issuer's website)

Rule of Thumb: Transfer only when you're ready to book. Once transferred, points can't be reversed.

Cashback Maximization Strategies

Cashback may seem basic, but there are advanced ways to maximize it:

1. **Use Multiple Cards Strategically**

One card for gas, another for groceries, and a third for everything else

Example: Use the **Citi Custom Cash** for 5% back on your top spending category

2. **Stack Rewards with Portals and Apps**

Shop through **Rakuten**, **Honey**, or your card's own portal to earn extra

Some portals offer 10–20% back on specific brands

3. **Redeem for Statement Credits or Bank Deposits**

Avoid redeeming for merchandise or gift cards unless it gives 1:1 value or better

4. **Avoid Annual Fee Cards Unless Perks Exceed Cost**

Do the math: If a $95 card earns you $400/year in cashback, it's worth it. If not, downgrade or switch.

Hidden Perks Most Cardholders Miss

Most people never use the full value of their cards. Here are **high-value benefits** to look out for:

- **Cell Phone Insurance**
 Use a card like Wells Fargo Active Cash to pay your cell bill, and get up to $600 in protection.

- **Extended Warranty & Purchase Protection**
 Many cards extend warranties by an extra year or protect against theft or damage within 90–120 days.

- **Trip Delay & Cancellation Coverage**
 Premium travel cards offer reimbursement if your trip is delayed, cancelled, or interrupted.

- **Lounge Access**

Cards like the Amex Platinum or Capital One Venture X offer access to airport lounges with food, drinks, and Wi-Fi.

- **Global Entry / TSA PreCheck Credits**

Many travel cards reimburse the $85–$100 application fee every 4–5 years.

- **Hotel Status**

Some cards give you instant elite hotel status, which includes free upgrades, breakfast, and late checkout.

Pro Tip: Call your card's benefits line once you're approved and ask for a list of all included perks. They often provide PDFs or online dashboards.

The Rule of ROI — Return on Intent

Before chasing rewards, always ask:

"Am I using this card to earn something on spending I already planned, or am I spending more to chase perks?"

Rewards only work if you:

- Stay within your monthly budget
- Pay the balance in full each month
- Don't fall for marketing that encourages overspending

A $200 cashback reward is not a win if you pay $300 in interest.

The wealth is in the strategy.

ACTION STEPS FOR CHAPTER 3:

1. List all current credit cards and their rewards programs.
2. Organize them into: Cashback, Points, or Miles.
3. Visit your card's reward portal and review transfer partners or cash redemption options.
4. Set a reward goal: Is it travel, cashback savings, or a major purchase?

5. Use a spreadsheet or app (like AwardWallet) to track your rewards and perks.

6. Evaluate each card's annual fee against real benefits used. If the ROI is low, plan to downgrade or switch.

"The Honeymoon That Points Paid For"

Samantha and Jordan had just gotten engaged. She was a school teacher. He was a firefighter. Their dream honeymoon was a two-week trip to Italy—Rome, Florence, and a relaxing finale on the Amalfi Coast. But the price tag was brutal: over $6,500 just for flights and hotels.

"No way we can afford that," Jordan sighed as they scrolled through a travel site at midnight, sitting on their secondhand couch. "We'll just do something local. Maybe a beach weekend."

But Samantha wasn't ready to let go of the dream.

The next morning, while sipping her coffee before work, she remembered something her older sister had mentioned months earlier: "You know, people travel the world for free using credit card points." At the time, it sounded like a scam. But now? It was worth looking into.

She Googled: "How to use credit card points to travel for free."

That search changed everything.

By the time she got home from school, Samantha had a whole notepad filled with terms like "Chase Ultimate Rewards," "airline transfer partners," and "welcome bonuses." She discovered that people were traveling first class for less than what she paid in monthly bills—all because they understood how to **maximize** the credit card game.

That night, she presented her plan to Jordan like a school project.

"Okay, hear me out," she said, flipping open her notepad. "We can get the Chase Sapphire Preferred card. If we each get one, we'll get 120,000 points. That's enough for roundtrip flights to Rome and two nights in a hotel."

Jordan blinked. "Wait. Just for using the card?"

"Well, yes and no. We have to spend $4,000 each in 3 months. But here's how we'll do it: we'll pay all our bills with the card, buy gift cards for groceries and gas, and I already talked to your brother about helping with the down payment for his wedding venue. We put it on the card, he pays us back."

He stared at her. "You're serious about this."

"I'm 100% serious," she said. "We can turn everyday spending into this trip. No debt. No interest. Just strategy."

Three months later, it was working.

Between welcome bonuses, referral points, and cashing in rewards, Samantha had booked two roundtrip flights to Rome for $89 in taxes. She used the Sapphire travel portal to book a boutique hotel in Florence, paying with points. Then, she transferred points to Hyatt for three nights on the Amalfi Coast in a cliffside suite that would've cost over $1,200.

"I feel like a travel hacker," she whispered to herself while confirming the last booking.

They didn't stop there. Samantha signed up for Rakuten and linked it to her card. Every time she shopped for wedding items online, she earned 3%–10% back on top of her card rewards. Jordan used his business credit card for gear and supplies for his woodworking side hustle. More points. More cash back.

By the time the wedding arrived, they had covered:

- All flights with points
- 6 of the 10 hotel nights using transferred miles
- Rental car and excursions with cashback rewards
- Even the luggage, which was bought with a card perk covering 90-day purchase protection

Italy was everything they had dreamed of—and more.

They ate pasta under a canopy of stars in Trastevere, watched the sun set over Ponte Vecchio, and drank espresso on a private balcony facing the Mediterranean. Every moment felt like luxury. And the best part?

They paid **less than $300 total** for the entire trip.

Jordan looked at Samantha while they waited to board their flight home. "You just saved us six grand," he said. "You're like a travel wizard."

She smiled. "Nope. Just someone who read the fine print and followed the rules."

Back home, they didn't stop. They created a spreadsheet, labeled every card they had, tracked benefits, and set reward goals for their next trip—Japan in the spring. Jordan even shared the story with the guys at the fire station, and three of them signed up for cards that week.

Samantha started a little blog on the side: *Travel Like a Teacher.* Within months, she had an audience, affiliate links bringing in passive income, and emails pouring in from people asking, "Can you show me how you did it?"

She always replied the same way:
"Yes. Start by using the money you already spend—and learn the system the banks use to keep us broke."

In less than a year, Samantha and Jordan turned a dream honeymoon into a lifestyle. Not because they made more money—but because they **used their money smarter**.

The rewards were never just about points. They were about freedom, options, and knowing how to make every dollar work harder.

And it all started with a notepad, a cup of coffee, and the courage to click "Apply."

Chapter 4: Building Massive Credit Limits and Leveraging 0% APR for Strategic Growth

"Credit is not just a score. It's a source of capital—and a smart person's bank."
— Joe Correa

Why You Need Higher Credit Limits

The average American has a credit card limit of around $5,000—but people who understand how to build and leverage credit can access **$50,000–$150,000+ in available credit** across personal and business cards.

Here's why higher limits matter:

✓ **Lower utilization = higher credit scores**

✓ **Access to 0% interest capital for large purchases or investments**

✓ **More rewards from higher spending capacity**

✓ **Increased financial flexibility during emergencies**

Think of your credit limit as a **cash reserve** you don't need until you do. The more you have, the less you stress.

How to Increase Your Credit Limits (Without Hurting Your Score)

Here's how to build large credit limits the smart way:

Step 1: Start with your current cards

- Use your card consistently for 3–6 months
- Pay off in full every month (or keep utilization under 10%)
- Request a **credit limit increase online** or call customer service

Pro Tip:
Use phrases like, "I've been using this card for regular expenses and would like a limit increase to support larger purchases and improve my utilization."

Most banks allow **soft pull** requests, meaning no impact to your score.

Step 2: Apply for additional cards strategically

- Space out new applications (every 3–4 months)
- Target banks with generous limits (Amex, Chase, Capital One, Navy Federal Credit Union)
- Consider **business credit cards**, which often offer higher starting limits

Step 3: Combine limits (if allowed)

Some banks, like Chase and Bank of America, allow you to **reallocate credit** between cards. If one card has $10,000 and another has $2,000, you may be able to move $5,000 over—creating higher limits where you need them most.

Step 4: Show income growth

If your income has increased, update it in your credit profile. This often qualifies you for higher limits—even if your score hasn't changed much.

Reminder:
Banks don't verify income unless it's unusually high or you're applying for large loans. Be honest, but know that **your reported income influences your credit limits.**

Using 0% APR Offers Like a Financial Tool

One of the **most powerful advantages** of credit cards is **0% interest introductory periods**, usually lasting **12 to 21 months**. That's up to **1.5 years of free capital**—if you know how to use it.

What You Can Use 0% APR For:

☑ Launching a side hustle or small business

☑ Paying off high-interest debt (via balance transfer)

☑ Buying inventory or equipment to generate income

☑ Covering short-term emergencies without interest penalties

☑ Pre-paying large expenses like insurance, tuition, or property taxes

Caution:
Only use 0% APR offers for **planned, profitable, or essential purposes**. Not for lifestyle upgrades or emotional purchases.

How to Use 0% APR Effectively:

1. **Create a plan** for how the funds will be used and repaid

2. **Set a monthly repayment goal** (e.g., divide total borrowed by number of 0% months)

3. **Avoid adding new charges** to the same card—some issuers apply payments to older balances first

4. **Track the expiration date** of the promotional period to avoid high-interest surprises

Example:
You open a card with a 15-month 0% APR on purchases. You use $4,500 to launch an online course business. You plan to pay $300/month for 15 months. If the business earns $1,000/month, you've used bank money to create leverage—with no interest paid.

Managing Large Limits Without Debt Risk

Getting access to $100,000 in available credit doesn't mean you should use all of it. The **golden rule** of responsible credit use remains:

Only spend what you can pay off—ideally within 30 days.

To stay in control:

- Set up **weekly balance alerts** on each card

- Use **autopay** to avoid missed payments
- Review statements monthly to catch errors or overspending
- Use cards for **planned expenses** only, not lifestyle inflation

Remember: Credit is leverage. Not income.

Tracking and Managing It All

As your credit access grows, you need systems to stay organized:

Use tools like:

✔ **Credit Karma or MyFICO** to monitor score changes

✔ **Spreadsheets** to track card names, limits, due dates, APR periods, rewards

✔ **Personal finance apps** like Mint or Monarch Money to manage spending and payments

✔ **AwardWallet or Travel Freely** to track card perks, travel credits, and expiration dates

ACTION STEPS FOR CHAPTER 4:

1. List all current cards and their credit limits.

2. Request a credit limit increase on 1–2 cards this week.

3. Identify a 0% APR offer you could use for a profitable or essential purchase.

4. Create a payoff plan to use that credit **strategically**, not emotionally.

5. Set up a spreadsheet or app to track your total available credit, usage, and limits.

6. Begin preparing for your next card application by cleaning up your credit report and ensuring your income data is accurate.

"From Broke to Builder: How Malik Used Credit to Launch His Dream"

Malik was tired of watching others win while he barely kept up.

He had a good job—IT support for a hospital network—but it was just that… good. It paid the bills, left little to save, and no room to take risks. And Malik was ready to build *something.* Something of his own.

He'd always dreamed of launching an online tech coaching service—helping everyday people fix computers, set up smart homes, or recover lost files. He already helped neighbors and family members on weekends, for free or fifty bucks here and there.

But to launch it online, he needed equipment—new lighting, a backdrop, a better mic, screen-capture software, a website. Total cost? About $3,200. Malik had $380 in his savings account.

Then, one night while watching YouTube, he stumbled across a video titled:
"How I Used 0% APR Credit Cards to Build My Business."
He clicked.

That video opened a door.

He learned about **introductory 0% APR offers**—credit cards that let you borrow money for 12 to 21 months interest-free. He learned that if he had good credit, he could get approved for $5,000, maybe even $10,000. And if he used that money wisely, he could build something before the promo ended—and never pay a penny in interest.

It didn't feel like debt. It felt like a bridge.

Malik checked his credit score: 738. Solid.

The next day, he applied for the **Chase Freedom Unlimited** card. He was approved instantly—**$10,000 limit and 0% APR for 15 months.** His heart raced. It felt like someone had just handed him a chance he never had before.

Within a week, he ordered everything on his list. He used $2,800 of the available credit and spent every evening building out his coaching website. On weekends, he recorded his first screen-share tutorials: "How to Speed Up a Slow Computer," "Best Free Antivirus Tools," "How to Backup Your Photos to the Cloud."

He wasn't spending recklessly. Every purchase had a purpose. Every dollar borrowed had a job.

He also made a plan: $300 per month, automatically transferred to the card, starting that month. Fifteen months to pay it off completely, interest-free.

By month four, his YouTube channel had 600 subscribers. A local real estate agent hired him to install smart home systems in three rental properties. He made $1,100 in a single weekend.

And the card? He had already paid down $1,200 of the balance—**with business income.**

One day, while logging into his credit dashboard, Malik noticed something new. An offer from American Express: a **business card with a $250 bonus, 0% APR, and no personal credit impact** if pre-qualified.

He applied. Approved again—this time for $15,000.

That's when it hit him.
He now had access to over $25,000 in credit, all because he used it the right way.
No overspending. No interest. Just leverage.

Malik was no longer just an employee. He was a business owner. A content creator. A tech coach.

And it all started with the courage to trust himself—and a card with 0% interest.

But the turning point came the following spring.

His friend Jamal, who owned a local clothing brand, asked how he had funded all this. "Man, I thought you had a big savings stash or something."

"Nope," Malik said, pulling out his phone. "It started right here. 0% APR. I had a plan. I tracked every dollar. I built what I needed without waiting ten years to save up."

Jamal stared at him. "You didn't go into debt?"

"No," Malik replied. "I went into **discipline.** I used the system without letting it use me."

Today, Malik runs a profitable online business. He has five cards—all paid in full—and over $60,000 in total credit access. He teaches others how to launch tech side hustles and helps his community stay away from predatory loans and high-interest traps.

Because he knows what they don't tell you in school:

Credit isn't just about scores or debt—it's **a launchpad**.
If you use it right, it becomes the tool that funds your dreams.

And it all started with one yes.

Chapter 5: Using Credit Cards to Fund Profitable Side Hustles and Income Streams

"Smart credit use isn't about spending—it's about investing."
— Unknown

Credit as Capital, Not Consumption

Most people use credit cards for **spending**—vacations, restaurants, shopping. Wealth builders use credit cards for **funding**—starting a business, building assets, or creating passive income.

What if your next credit card wasn't for buying things you want—but for building the life you want?

Here's the mindset shift:

Don't use credit cards to buy liabilities.
Use them to build **income-producing assets**.

If you're approved for a $5,000–$20,000 credit limit with 0% APR for 12–18 months, you've just been handed **interest-free capital**. That's more powerful than most small business loans—and it's easier and faster to get.

The Best Low-Cost, High-ROI Side Hustles to Launch with Credit

You don't need tens of thousands of dollars to start a business. Here are some of the best ways to turn credit into profit with **low upfront costs** and high scalability:

1. Print-on-Demand E-Commerce (e.g., T-shirts, mugs, journals)

✓ Start-up cost: $300–$1,000

✓ Use credit for: Shopify subscription, design tools, samples, ad budget

✓ ROI: Easily 4x–10x per sale after platform and ad costs

2. Digital Courses or Coaching

✓ Start-up cost: $500–$1,500

✓ Use credit for: Camera, mic, online platform fees, software, ads

✓ ROI: Passive income potential, no inventory required

3. Service-Based Freelancing

✓ Start-up cost: $100–$1,000

✓ Use credit for: Website, branding, scheduling tools, LinkedIn Ads

✓ ROI: High income potential—especially for tech, writing, marketing, or tutoring

4. Short-Term Rentals or Airbnb Co-Hosting

✓ Start-up cost: $1,000–$3,000

✓ Use credit for: Furnishings, cleaning supplies, listing setup

✓ ROI: Monthly recurring revenue after a few bookings

5. Content Creation or YouTube Channel

✓ Start-up cost: $300–$1,500

✓ Use credit for: Camera gear, editing software, thumbnails, promotion

✓ ROI: Long-term growth via monetization, affiliate links, sponsorships

All of these can be funded with a **credit card limit of $1,000–$5,000**, especially if you plan strategically and spend only on essentials.

How to Turn Credit into Cash Flow

Here's how to use a credit card as an **income generation engine** instead of a debt trap:

Step 1: Choose the Right Card

- 0% APR on purchases for at least 12 months
- No annual fee if possible
- Offers a sign-up bonus you can meet with business expenses

Step 2: Create a Budgeted Launch Plan

- Use the card only for launch-related costs
- Avoid subscriptions or recurring expenses unless essential
- Track every dollar and assign it to a specific business purpose

Step 3: Launch and Monetize Fast

- Your goal: earn income **before** the 0% APR window ends
- Start small: One product, one service, one offer
- Reinvest profits back into growth while paying down the card monthly

Step 4: Pay it Back with Profits

- Divide your total spend by the number of 0% months

- Stick to a strict repayment schedule—even if it means delaying personal spending

Example:
If you use $3,600 at 0% interest for 12 months, commit to repaying $300/month.
If your business earns $500/month, you're growing and repaying at the same time.

Red Flags and Risk Prevention

While this is a powerful strategy, here's what to **avoid**:

Using credit with no plan or business model
Don't borrow if you don't know how you'll earn it back.

Overestimating your income potential
Start lean. Test your idea before investing more.

Missing minimum payments
Set auto-pay for at least the minimum payment. One late payment can void your 0% offer.

Mixing personal and business expenses
Open a separate business checking account and keep records.

Letting lifestyle creep in
This credit is for *growth*, not personal upgrades.

When used right, **credit = control**. Used carelessly, **credit = chaos**.

Action Plan to Fund Your Side Hustle With Credit

Here's a 7-step action plan to execute this chapter's strategy:

1. **Choose your hustle:** Pick one income stream from the list above that fits your skillset.

2. **Map out expenses:** Identify startup costs and what you'll spend using the credit card.

3. **Find your 0% APR card:** Apply only after reviewing credit score, income, and current inquiries.

4. **Create a repayment plan:** Divide your spend by the number of months and commit.

5. **Launch fast and lean:** Use only what you need, focus on speed and simplicity.

6. **Track income and ROI:** Use a spreadsheet to monitor card balance, earnings, and breakeven point.

7. **Celebrate and repeat:** Once repaid, you'll have experience and proof—now scale it.

Final Thought:

"You're already spending money. What if that same money built a business instead?"

Credit isn't evil. It's neutral. It becomes **dangerous or powerful based on how you use it**.

And when used for income—not consumption—it becomes the **fuel for your financial independence**.

"The Etsy Empire That Started with a Credit Card"

Nina never saw herself as an entrepreneur. She was a preschool teacher in Denver—organized, soft-spoken, and endlessly patient. But after long days wrangling toddlers, she found peace in something unexpected: designing handmade planners and printable checklists.

Her creations—bright, floral, and neatly structured—weren't just cute. They helped her stay sane. Each time she posted her designs on Pinterest, a few followers would message her: "Where can I buy this?" She'd smile and reply, "It's just something I made for myself."

But one winter afternoon, while sipping peppermint tea and scrolling through TikTok, she stumbled across a video titled:
"I Made $7,000 Selling Printables on Etsy. Here's How I Started With $300."

She watched it twice.
Then a third time.

The woman in the video didn't have a fancy studio or professional design training. Just a Canva subscription, a laptop, and an Etsy account.

"I can do that," Nina whispered.

That night, she dug into research. She found that printables—planners, budget sheets, wall art, goal trackers—were booming. Etsy sellers were making hundreds, even thousands a month. And with digital products, there was no inventory, no shipping—just passive income.

But to start her shop, Nina would need a few things:

✓ A Canva Pro subscription

✓ Listing photos and mockups

✓ A domain name

✓ Etsy seller fees

✓ A marketing budget for Pinterest and Instagram ads

Total startup cost? Around $750.

She had maybe $150 left after rent and groceries. Her savings account was bleak.

That's when she remembered the **Chase Freedom Flex** card she'd been approved for three months earlier. It was mostly untouched, with a $6,000 limit and 0% APR for 15 months.

She'd been afraid to use it.

Now, she saw it differently—not as a trap, but as **fuel**.

The next morning, she made a promise:
"I'm going to build something that earns while I sleep."

She used $497 of her card limit to pay for everything she needed:

- A year of Canva Pro
- A mini photo shoot with her friend's DSLR camera
- An Etsy Plus subscription
- Tailwind for scheduling Pinterest posts
- A domain name and basic website

Every dollar was tracked in a spreadsheet labeled "Project Nina."

She created her first product—a "30-Day Reset Planner" for overwhelmed moms—and uploaded it to Etsy. Her goal was modest: make $200 in 30 days.

Her first sale came on day six. Then another. Then a $40 bundle order.

By the end of the first month, she had $312 in her PayPal account.

It wasn't just the money. It was the **validation**.

As months passed, Nina released more digital products:

- A homeschool planner for parents
- A wedding checklist printable
- A gratitude journal for teens
- Customizable daily routines

Each new listing cost little but expanded her store. She reinvested a small amount of her income into Pinterest and Instagram ads—and used her card's cashback feature to pay for ad boosts. She was careful never to exceed her budget and made weekly payments toward the balance.

By month five, her Etsy income hit $1,200.
Her card balance? Paid down in full.

That's when she realized:
"I used a credit card to build a business, not debt."

At a family dinner, her cousin asked how she suddenly had time off and a new MacBook.

Nina laughed and said, "You know that card the bank gave me last year? The one I was scared to use? It funded my Etsy shop. I paid it back with profits from printable planners."

Her uncle, a small business owner, leaned forward. "Wait—so you started a whole business with a credit card and didn't pay interest?"

"Exactly," she nodded. "I treated it like an investment, not a shopping spree."

Today, Nina's Etsy store brings in over $2,000/month. She spends two hours a week on updates, and most of her income is passive. She's saving for her first home and teaching other teachers how to monetize their creativity.

She still uses her card—but now, only for things that bring returns.

Because she's not just a teacher.
She's a **business owner with a blueprint**—one that started with a decision, a dream, and a little bit of credit.

Chapter 6: Credit Stacking: Unlock $50,000–$100,000 in Interest-Free Capital Without Breaking Your Credit

"Credit stacking is how modern entrepreneurs build fast, grow smart, and fund ideas without asking permission."
— Unknown

What Is Credit Stacking?

Credit stacking is a strategic process of applying for **multiple high-limit credit cards**—both personal and business—in a compressed timeframe to unlock **large amounts of interest-free capital**.

Instead of waiting months or years to build up funding, credit stacking allows you to secure **$50,000 to $100,000 or more** in **under 90 days**.

Why does this work?

Because credit inquiries typically don't show up across all bureaus in real-time, there's a short window—often 24 to 72 hours—where multiple applications can be submitted without the earlier ones negatively impacting the later ones.

Stacking works best when:

- You have good to excellent personal credit (680+)
- You prepare and plan your stack in advance

- You stick to using credit **as a tool**, not a trap

Think of credit stacking as **seeding your business** with zero-interest investment capital. If you treat it seriously, it can change your financial life.

Preparing for the Stack — Clean, Optimize, Strategize

Before stacking, you must prepare your credit profile. Here's how to make sure you're approved for the highest limits possible.

Credit Optimization Checklist:

✓ **Credit Score:** Minimum 700; ideally 720+

✓ **Utilization:** Under 10% across all cards

✓ **Inquiries:** Less than 3 in the last 6 months

✓ **On-Time Payments:** 100% in the past 12 months

✓ **Age of Credit:** At least 1–2 years of credit history

✓ **Credit Mix:** At least 2–3 open accounts (installment + revolving)

Also update your income with current issuers. Your reported income affects limit approvals—even if it's not verified.

Bonus Tip: Remove any outdated or negative accounts from your credit report using tools like Credit Karma or by disputing directly with bureaus.

The 3-Tier Bank Strategy (Apply in This Order)

Different banks have different approval rules. Applying in the right order is **critical** to avoid automatic denials.

Tier 1 – Apply First: Strict Approval Banks

Chase: Follows the 5/24 rule (denied if you've opened 5+ personal cards in 24 months)

US Bank: Conservative approval policy, prefers minimal recent inquiries

Tier 2 – Apply Second: High-Limit Approvers

American Express: Known for generous business lines; won't report business cards to personal credit

Citi: Allows multiple cards if spaced out (8/65/95 rule)

Tier 3 – Apply Last: Easy Approvals or Soft Pull Offers

Capital One: Reports business cards to personal credit—apply last

Navy Federal: Great for high limits if you qualify

Store/Fintech Cards: Apple Card, Petal, or Upgrade—apply only if they're part of your long-term plan

Apply for **3–5 cards in one session**, in the exact order above. Limit yourself to 2–3 personal cards, then move on to 1–3 business cards.

Executing the Stack — Build It, Don't Break It

Once approved, your job isn't done. You need to manage your stack wisely. Log this data as soon as you receive your cards. Set calendar reminders for each due date and promotion expiration.

Use Your Credit for High-Return Investments:

- Launching or scaling a business
- Inventory or equipment for income-generating assets
- Real estate down payments
- Digital ads or brand building
- Coaching, training, or certifications

The rule: **If it doesn't produce income, don't use your stack.**

Avoid These Common Stacking Mistakes

Credit stacking is powerful—but dangerous if used carelessly.

Mistakes to Avoid:

1. **Applying for cards randomly** without planning or bank rules in mind.

2. **Missing payment deadlines**, which can kill 0% APR offers instantly.

3. **Mixing business and personal spending** on the same card.

4. **Carrying balances past the promotional period**—leading to high interest.

5. **Failing to track cards and losing sight of limits, perks, or due dates.**

Remember: You're not using these cards to spend—you're using them to build. Treat every dollar like a seed that must grow.

CREDIT STACKING SUCCESS PLAN (STEP-BY-STEP)

1. **Check your credit** on all three bureaus
2. **Pay down balances** to keep utilization low
3. **Dispute or correct errors** on your report
4. **Plan your stack**: 2–3 personal cards, 2–3 business cards
5. **Apply in one session** following the 3-tier bank strategy
6. **Track every detail** in a spreadsheet
7. **Use cards only for profitable investments**
8. **Set automatic payments** and monitor balances weekly
9. **Pay off or recycle limits** before the 0% period ends
10. **Repeat the stack** in 6–12 months if needed

This is how entrepreneurs use bank capital to build six- and seven-figure businesses—without traditional loans, personal guarantees, or interest.

Real-World Impact:

With smart stacking, you can:

- Fund a business without investors
- Access up to $100K in less than 90 days
- Maintain or even improve your credit score
- Create long-term leverage with short-term action

"Stacking Credit, Stacking Success: How Anthony Unlocked $93,000 in 48 Hours"

Anthony Martinez wasn't broke—he just felt **stuck**.

At 34, he ran a small mobile detailing service in Tampa, Florida. He was good at it. Great, actually. Loyal clients, five-star reviews, a team of two part-time helpers. But every time he tried to expand—buy a van, invest in marketing, upgrade his booking system—he hit the same wall: **no capital**.

Banks weren't lending without a bigger balance sheet. Personal loans came with high interest. His business credit was nonexistent. And the few credit cards he had were small-limit retail cards from his early twenties.

Then, during a late-night YouTube scroll, Anthony heard a word that grabbed his attention:

"Credit stacking."

The video claimed it was possible to get **$50,000 to $100,000 in interest-free capital** without a loan and without hurting your credit—by applying for the right cards, at the right time, in the right order.

Anthony paused the video. Then replayed it. Then took notes.

The next day, he dove headfirst into research. He found blogs, podcasts, even a Reddit group dedicated to credit stacking. He learned that if he optimized his personal credit, applied strategically, and used a mix of personal and **business** credit cards, he could unlock massive funding—without a single loan officer ever saying yes or no.

He spent the next two weeks preparing.

Here's what he did:

- Pulled his credit reports: Experian score was 727
- Paid down two credit cards to drop his utilization below 10%
- Updated his income on existing accounts to reflect recent business growth
- Removed a $45 old phone bill he'd forgotten about

He made a spreadsheet labeled "STACK PLAN" and listed six cards he'd apply for: three personal, three business.

On a Tuesday morning, with a double espresso and nerves kicking in, Anthony launched his plan.

Card 1: *Chase Ink Business Unlimited* – Approved, $20,000
Card 2: *American Express Blue Business Plus* – Approved, $25,000

Card 3: *Citi Custom Cash* – Approved, $12,000
Card 4: *Chase Freedom Unlimited* – Approved, $10,000
Card 5: *Capital One Spark Cash* – Approved, $16,000
Card 6: *Bank of America Cash Rewards* – Approved, $10,000

Total credit approved in less than 48 hours: **$93,000**
All with **0% APR** between 12 to 18 months.

Anthony sat back, stunned.

"I just became my own bank," he whispered.

He didn't go on a shopping spree. He had a blueprint.

He used $6,800 from his new Amex to buy a used commercial van.
$1,200 on branding—logos, business cards, magnetic decals.
$2,300 for a CRM and booking software system.
$4,500 on local Facebook and Google ads.
And $3,000 to hire a virtual assistant for customer service.

He didn't touch the rest.

He created a repayment plan: $800/month toward the balances, starting immediately.

In the next 90 days, his business **doubled**.
He went from 25 clients a week to 60+.
He had so many new bookings that he hired his cousin and gave him a weekly route.
He paid off nearly half his card balances within 4 months.

One weekend, while helping his mom fix her internet, she asked how he was doing.

"I'm great," he said, smiling. "I funded my own business expansion—no loans, no stress."

She looked confused. "How'd you do that?"

"Credit stacking," he said. "I used my good credit and a smart plan to get $90K in capital. Paid zero interest. Built everything faster than I thought possible."

She shook her head. "That's how the rich do it, huh?"

Anthony laughed. "That's how **we** do it now."

Today, Anthony earns three times what he did a year ago.
His credit score? **Still above 740.**
His cards? All current, paid down, and being used strategically.

He's mentoring two friends on how to stack credit for their own businesses. One wants to open a food truck. The other, a mobile pet grooming service.

Because now, Anthony understands:

"You don't need investors. You don't need loans.
You just need to know how to use the system smarter than it was designed for."

Credit stacking didn't just fund his business—it funded his future.

Chapter 7: Rewards Mastery – How to Turn Points, Perks, and Cashback into Wealth and Lifestyle Upgrades

"Most people chase money. The wealthy chase value—and squeeze every dollar for more than it's worth."
— Joe Correa

The Real Value of Credit Card Rewards

When most people think of credit card rewards, they think small: 2% cashback here, 1.5 points per dollar there. But when used strategically, **rewards can save or earn you thousands of dollars per year**—without changing your spending.

There are **three primary types of credit card rewards**:

1. **Cashback** – Direct money back into your pocket

2. **Points** – Flexible reward currencies redeemable for travel, gift cards, or statement credits

3. **Miles** – Airline or hotel-specific rewards, ideal for luxury travel

The key isn't just earning rewards—it's **maximizing their value**. You can earn:

- Free flights worth $1,000+

- Hotel stays that cost $0 out of pocket

- Business class upgrades
- Free insurance, elite status, and lifestyle perks
- Cashback that can fund investments or pay down debt

How to Choose the Right Rewards Strategy for Your Life

Your goals determine your rewards game plan.

Here's how to align your strategy with your lifestyle:

If you want to travel for free:

✓ Focus on **flexible points cards** like:

Chase Sapphire Preferred / Reserve

Amex Gold or Platinum

✓ Transfer points to airline or hotel partners

✓ Book during off-peak dates for maximum value

If you want to earn cash:

✓ Use **flat-rate cashback cards** like:

Citi Double Cash (2%)

Wells Fargo Active Cash

✓ Or rotating category cards like:

Chase Freedom Flex (5% rotating)

Discover It

If you travel for business or with family:

✓ Use cards with perks:

Free checked bags

Priority boarding

Travel insurance

Global Entry/TSA PreCheck reimbursement

Tip: Pick **2–3 core cards** and use them consistently for specific categories: travel, dining, groceries, ads, subscriptions, etc.

How to Redeem Points and Miles for Maximum Value

One of the biggest mistakes people make is redeeming points for **low-value options** like merchandise or low-rate gift cards.

Here's how to **stretch your points for maximum return**:

Best Redemptions (High Value):

- **Transfer to travel partners** (e.g., Hyatt, United, JetBlue)
- **Book through travel portals** with bonus value (Chase Ultimate Rewards adds 25–50%)
- **Upgrade flights or hotels** to business class or suites

Moderate Redemptions (Okay Value):

- **Cashback or statement credits** (usually $0.01 per point)
- **Gift cards** only when discounted

Poor Redemptions (Low Value):

- Shopping on Amazon or with PayPal
- Merchandise via reward portals

- Donating or cashing out below $0.01 per point

Real Example:
50,000 Chase points =
→ $500 in cash
→ $625 in travel (through portal)
→ $900+ when transferred to Hyatt for a 3-night luxury stay

Hidden Perks That Save You Thousands

Beyond points and miles, many credit cards come with **built-in benefits** that most users never claim:

Travel & Purchase Protection

✓ Trip delay/cancellation reimbursement (save $300–$500 per incident)

✓ Lost luggage reimbursement

✓ Rental car insurance

✓ Extended warranty on electronics and appliances

Everyday Use Perks

✓ Cell phone protection (up to $600 if you pay your bill with the card)

✓ Return protection (return denied items)

✓ Purchase protection (covers stolen/damaged items within 90–120 days)

Business Perks

✓ Free employee cards

✓ Spending tracking by category

✓ Discounts through Visa SavingsEdge, Amex Offers, and more

Make a habit of visiting your card's **benefits page** every quarter to remind yourself what's available—and use it.

How to Automate and Multiply Rewards

Once your strategy is in place, **automation** helps you maximize without stress:

Step 1: Set Category Triggers

- Groceries: Use Amex Blue Cash Preferred
- Dining: Use Chase Sapphire
- Gas: Use rotating 5% cards

Step 2: Use Portals to Stack Bonuses

- Use Rakuten, Capital One Shopping, or your card's shopping portal
- Earn up to **10–15% extra cashback** or points

Step 3: Set Up Autopay

- Avoid interest by setting auto-pay to pay in full each month
- Avoid missing out on perks by keeping accounts active

Step 4: Monitor and Reallocate

- Check usage and rewards earned quarterly
- Move low-performing spend to higher-earning cards

Advanced Tip: Pair **multiple cards from the same ecosystem** (e.g., Chase Freedom + Chase Sapphire) to pool points for better redemptions.

Action Plan: Turn Rewards into a Wealth-Boosting System

1. **Pick your goal**: travel, cash, or perks

2. **Select 2–3 main cards** to fit that goal

3. **Assign categories** to each card: food, gas, subscriptions, etc.

4. **Join reward portals** like Rakuten or your issuer's site

5. **Redeem wisely**: Points = travel, cashback = savings or investing

6. **Use perks** to replace insurance or protection you'd otherwise pay for

7. **Review your rewards strategy every 90 days**

Real-World Application

Let's say you spend $2,500/month using three optimized cards. That's $30,000/year. If you average just 3% in combined rewards (points, cash, bonuses), that's **$900–$1,200/year back into your pocket**—with no extra work or spending.

Multiply that over 5 years, and that's $5,000–$6,000 earned passively. Add in travel redemptions, protections, and card perks? Easily worth **$10,000+.**

"Points for Possibility: How Rachel Traveled the World Without Touching Her Savings"

Rachel Perez didn't travel. Not because she didn't want to—but because, as a single mom and full-time nurse in Dallas, vacations always felt like a luxury she simply couldn't afford.

Her budget was tight. Between rent, daycare, groceries, and student loans, anything left over went into an emergency fund—or didn't go anywhere at all.

So, when her friend Kim invited her on a girls' trip to Puerto Rico, she hesitated.

"I can't drop $1,200 on a vacation," Rachel said.

Kim smiled. "You don't have to. I booked the whole trip using credit card points."

Rachel blinked. "What do you mean? Like miles?"

Kim nodded. "Yup. I haven't paid for a flight in over a year. And I'm not rich—I'm just strategic."

That night, after putting her daughter to bed, Rachel stayed up late reading everything she could about credit card rewards. By 1:30 a.m., she had opened four browser tabs, downloaded three PDFs, and had a notebook full of scribbled phrases like "transfer partners," "5/24 rule," and "travel portals."

She couldn't believe what she had discovered.

Over the next week, Rachel built her first credit rewards plan.

She applied for the **Chase Sapphire Preferred** card, was approved for $9,000, and earned **60,000 bonus points** after meeting the spending requirement over the next three months—on things she already paid for: daycare, groceries, and gas.

Then she paired it with the **Chase Freedom Flex**, which offered 5% rotating categories and another bonus.

She spent intentionally, tracked her rewards, and watched her points grow.

Three months later, she logged into the Chase travel portal and found **roundtrip flights to Puerto Rico for 22,000 points** and a **4-night beachfront hotel for 34,000 points**.

Out-of-pocket cost?
$67 total in taxes and fees.

Rachel cried when she hit "book now."

The trip wasn't just a getaway—it was a life-changer.

She walked barefoot on white sand beaches, drank coffee on a balcony overlooking the ocean, and danced with strangers under the stars. For once, she didn't feel like she was scraping by—she felt free.

When she got home, she doubled down.

She opened an **American Express Gold Card**, this time focusing on dining rewards and grocery spend. She added **Rakuten**, **Southwest Rapid Rewards Dining**, and a few shopping portals to her arsenal.

Soon, every dollar she spent—on school supplies, gas, food—was earning her something back. But she never spent more than she planned. She paid in full. Every. Single. Month.

Over the next 18 months, Rachel used rewards to:

- Visit her sister in Chicago (flights covered with points)
- Take her daughter to Disney World (hotel 100% booked with points)
- Fly to Denver for a nursing conference (paid for with a sign-up bonus)
- Stay in a 4-star hotel in New York for a weekend girls' trip—completely on points

She even used cashback to cover unexpected car repairs and Amazon gift cards to help with holiday shopping.

One afternoon, while helping her daughter with homework, Rachel smiled as she checked her rewards balance:
112,000 points, $147 in cashback, two free hotel nights pending.

She wasn't just earning back money. She was building **a new lifestyle.**

At her next nursing staff meeting, her coworkers joked about needing a break.

Rachel pulled out her phone and said, "You know you can fly roundtrip to San Diego for 12,000 points and stay at the Hyatt downtown for free, right?"

They looked at her like she had just revealed a magic trick.

One of them whispered, "Rachel… you travel more than anyone I know. How do you afford all that?"

She replied with a smile, "Points. I make my money work twice."

Today, Rachel is still a full-time nurse. Still a single mom. But she's also a **travel hacker**, a rewards strategist, and a low-key credit card expert among her friends.

She pays zero interest. Carries no debt. And treats every purchase like an investment—because it is.

"It's not about spending more," she says. "It's about getting more from what I already spend."

And what started as a reluctant "no" to a Puerto Rico trip turned into a five-country travel streak—powered entirely by rewards, discipline, and knowledge.

Chapter 8: Wealth Cycling: How to Rotate, Reinvest, and Grow Using Credit Rewards, Cashback, and Credit Lines

"The secret to long-term financial success isn't making one big move—it's cycling small, smart moves over and over."
— Joe Correa

What Is Wealth Cycling?

Wealth cycling is the process of using credit cards, rewards, cashback, and 0% APR opportunities in a continuous loop to:

✓ Access capital

✓ Fund income-generating activities

✓ Redeem rewards or profits

✓ Pay back credit

✓ Repeat—on a higher level

This is how people build wealth without loans, venture capital, or massive savings. It's a system that reinvests itself. When done correctly, wealth cycling becomes **a reliable rhythm of building and scaling** using tools you already have.

The 5-Part Wealth Cycling Formula

Let's break down the core cycle step by step:

Step 1: Fund with Credit

Use 0% APR cards or available credit lines to:

- Start or scale a business
- Run an ad campaign
- Purchase high-demand inventory
- Pay for a course or mentorship

Use only **intentional credit**—not emotional spending.

Step 2: Build Income or Asset Value

Convert the borrowed capital into something productive:

- A digital product that sells passively
- A flipping hustle that returns profit
- Rental setup or service equipment

Track every dollar. Know what your capital is earning.

Step 3: Reap Rewards or Revenue

As income rolls in or rewards build up:

- Redeem points for travel or cashback
- Collect payments from clients
- Receive affiliate, ad, or platform payouts

This is where cash flow or value is realized.

Step 4: Pay Down Card & Recycle Limit

Start paying back the credit card(s) used:

- Set auto-pay for minimums
- Aggressively pay down principal with profit
- Free up available credit for the next round

As you reduce debt and maintain payment history, your score increases and your limits rise.

Step 5: Repeat at a Higher Level

Now that your cards are paid down, rewards earned, and profits made—do it again:

- Apply for another 0% APR offer
- Invest in a larger project
- Stack multiple cards
- Redeem bigger bonuses

Each cycle builds more momentum than the last.

Real-World Wealth Cycling Examples

Let's see this in action:

Example 1 – Digital Course Launch

1. Use $2,500 from a 0% APR card to build a course (camera, hosting, software)
2. Launch the course and earn $6,000 over 6 months
3. Pay off the card with $3,000, keeping $3,000 profit
4. Points earned = 2,500+ (used for free travel)
5. Repeat with upgraded materials or a second course

Example 2 – Inventory Flipping

1. Spend $4,000 on liquidation pallets or sneaker resale

2. Flip items for $7,000 in revenue

3. Pay off card, keep $3,000+ profit

4. Cashback: 2% = $80 bonus

5. Reinvest into larger or multiple orders

Example 3 – Service Business Scaling

1. Use $3,000 to set up website, branding, and ads for a cleaning business

2. Secure $1,200/month in recurring contracts

3. Break even in 90 days, then use cash flow to expand

4. Points from ad spend used for a hotel stay or cashback to fund insurance

5. Repeat for another local service niche

Tools to Automate and Track Wealth Cycles

Smart cycling requires smart tracking. Use these tools:

Spreadsheets:

✓ Create a master "cycle dashboard"

✓ Track spend, repayment dates, ROI, rewards earned

Apps:

- **Credit Karma / Experian:** Monitor score & utilization
- **Mint or Monarch Money:** Track spend by card
- **AwardWallet or CardPointers:** Manage card benefits & expirations
- **Google Calendar:** Set reminders for due dates and 0% expiration periods

Journaling:

Keep a simple "Wealth Log" where you record:

What you used credit for

What came of it

What you learned

What to do next cycle

Pitfalls to Avoid When Cycling Credit for Wealth

Wealth cycling is powerful—but only with **discipline**.

Avoid these common traps:

✘ **Spending for lifestyle, not leverage**

✘ **Missing minimum payments** (which cancels 0% offers)

✘ **Overestimating profits before they're earned**

✘ **Not tracking results, leading to waste**

✘ **Mixing business and personal transactions blindly**

Stay focused. This is a strategy, not a shortcut.

ACTION PLAN TO BEGIN WEALTH CYCLING TODAY

Here's how to get started:

1. **Review your credit limits and 0% offers**—what capital is currently available?

2. **Decide on one income-producing use**: course, resale, content, service, etc.

3. **Create a simple plan**: total cost, ROI goal, timeframe

4. **Use credit to fund only that plan**, nothing else

5. **Track your results and payments weekly**

6. **Set a "cycle close date"** (when your goal ends and credit is repaid)

7. **Assess results, redeem rewards**, and begin again

Final Thought

"Wealth is built in cycles. The faster and smarter you cycle, the faster you grow."

Credit doesn't just buy time—it buys possibility. When you use it wisely and repeat your success rhythm, you're no longer playing defense with money.

You're building offense—with every swipe.

"The Cycle That Built a Business: How Eli Turned Credit Into Compounding Wealth"

Eli Washington didn't look like someone who used credit cards to build wealth. He didn't wear expensive clothes or drive a flashy car. Most days, he wore a hoodie, jeans, and sneakers worn thin from walking.

But ask anyone in his Atlanta neighborhood, and they'd tell you: Eli had one of the most quietly successful landscaping businesses around. He didn't come from money. He didn't have investors. And he sure didn't take out a loan from the bank.

Instead, Eli built his business with something most people overlook: **a simple credit card.**

It started three years ago.

He was tired of living paycheck to paycheck working at a warehouse, always watching other people win. One night, scrolling through Instagram, he came across a story: a woman who launched a six-figure business using **a 0% APR credit card**.

"Build first, pay later," she said. "Credit is capital—if you respect it."

That sentence stuck in his head.

Eli pulled his credit report. His score was 702—not bad. He'd never missed a payment, but he'd also never used credit to do anything meaningful.

He applied for a **Wells Fargo Reflect Card**—18 months 0% APR on purchases. Approved for $7,500.

He stared at the screen for 10 minutes, realizing what just happened.

"This is it," he whispered. "Seed money."

Eli didn't blow the limit. He had a plan:

1. Buy second-hand landscaping equipment
2. Register his LLC and get business cards printed
3. Build a basic website and run $200 in local Facebook ads
4. Offer neighbors a discounted service to build testimonials

He used $3,200 of the card. Then set up auto-pay for $200 a month, knowing he had 18 months to pay it off interest-free.

Within 60 days, he had 14 paying clients.

By month three, he'd brought in $4,000 in revenue and already made two early payments toward the card balance. But he wasn't done.

Eli started what he later called his **"wealth cycle."**

As money came in, he paid off the card and **reused the available credit** for growth:

☑ He reinvested in better tools

☑ Bought branded uniforms

☑ Launched a referral rewards program

Every dollar borrowed had a purpose. Every payment had a plan.

Once that card was 80% paid off, he applied for a **Chase Ink Business Unlimited** card and got approved for $20,000—at 0% APR for 12 months.

This time, he used it to:

- Hire part-time help
- Add gutter cleaning and pressure washing to his services
- Pay for SEO and Google Ads

His income doubled.

By the end of year one, Eli had:

✓ Paid off his first credit card in full

✓ Used two cards to rotate funds and scale faster

✓ Built a client base of 80+ homes

✓ Maintained a personal credit score of 735

✓ Traveled to Miami on points for a much-needed break

✓ Saved over $1,200 using cashback and rewards

One night, sitting on his porch with his cousin Marcus, Eli explained his system.

"I just keep cycling," he said. "I borrow, I build, I earn, I repay—and then I repeat. I don't take on debt. I use credit as a temporary tool to level up. No interest. No pressure."

Marcus asked, "But don't you get stressed borrowing like that?"

Eli shook his head. "Not when you've got a plan and the income to back it. It's not about debt—it's about **discipline**."

Today, Eli runs a six-figure landscaping and property maintenance business with four part-time employees. His personal and business credit are both strong. He teaches workshops on how to responsibly use credit to scale small businesses.

He still tracks every card in a spreadsheet. He still sets calendar alerts for payment due dates and 0% promo expirations. And he still follows the same cycle:

1. Fund a goal
2. Grow with intention
3. Collect and reinvest
4. Pay down and prepare for the next level

He calls it **"rotating responsibility."**

"Most people see credit as a trap," he says. "But if you build with it—if you respect it—it becomes the most consistent investor you'll ever have."

And it all started with a $7,500 card… and a belief that credit could be something more.

Chapter 9: Business Credit Mastery – Build Business Credit Fast and Separate It from Your Personal Profile

"Personal credit gets you started. Business credit scales you—quietly, powerfully, and without personal risk."
— Joe Correa

Why Business Credit Matters

Most people run their businesses on **personal credit cards**, personal loans, or their own savings. But the truly scalable path to wealth?
It's **business credit.**

When you build business credit the right way, you can:

✓ Access higher credit limits

✓ Protect your personal credit score

✓ Qualify for funding regardless of personal income

✓ Secure 0% APR business cards that don't report to personal bureaus

✓ Position your company for loans, lines of credit, equipment financing, and vendor terms

The key is **separating your personal identity from your business profile**—while using your good credit to get the ball rolling.

How Business Credit Works (and Why It's Different)

Business credit has its **own ecosystem**, built on these core principles:

1. **EIN (Employer Identification Number)** – Your business's SSN

2. **Business credit bureaus** – Experian Business, Equifax Business, Dun & Bradstreet

3. **Trade lines (vendor accounts)** – Establish payment history and creditworthiness

4. **Paydex Score (D&B)** – A 0–100 score based on how fast your business pays its bills

Unlike personal credit, business credit:

- Doesn't require a social security number to build
- Can be grown much faster (in 3–6 months)
- Isn't tied to your personal utilization or inquiries

And the best part? Some business cards (like those from Amex, Chase, and Capital One) **don't report to your personal credit**—even if you carry a balance.

STEP-BY-STEP PLAN TO BUILD BUSINESS CREDIT FROM SCRATCH

Step 1: Set Up Your Business Properly

Lenders want to see that your business is **legit** and established.

➔ Register your business as an **LLC or Corporation**

➔ Get an **EIN** from the IRS (free)

➔ Open a **business checking account**

➔ Get a **professional phone number and business address** (even virtual)

➔ List your business with **411 Directory Assistance**

Make sure your business name, phone, and address match **exactly** across all documents and websites.

Step 2: Open 3–5 Net 30 Vendor Accounts

These vendors extend credit to your business and report payment history to business credit bureaus. You buy products and pay **within 30 days** (Net 30 terms).

Recommended starter vendors:

Uline (office and shipping supplies)

Grainger (tools and hardware)

Summa Office Supplies

Nav (business credit monitoring)

Crown Office Supplies

Place small orders (e.g., $50–100), pay early, and let them report to D&B or Experian.

Step 3: Get Your D-U-N-S Number

This is your **Dun & Bradstreet ID**. Required to build a Paydex score.

- Go to dnb.com and apply for your D-U-N-S number (free for business credit building)
- Use your exact business information
- Link your Net 30 accounts to your DUNS once they start reporting

After 2–3 on-time payments, your **Paydex score** will begin to form. Aim for 80 or higher.

Step 4: Apply for Business Credit Cards

After you've opened 3–5 vendor accounts and used them responsibly for 60–90 days, you're ready to apply for **true revolving business credit.**

Recommended business credit cards:

- **Chase Ink Business Unlimited** – High limit, 0% APR, no annual fee
- **Amex Blue Business Plus** – 2x points on all purchases
- **Capital One Spark Cash** – Great for cashback
- **Divvy or Brex** – Fintech cards with flexible underwriting

Use your EIN and business info. Some may ask for your SSN for a **personal guarantee**—this is fine during the early stages.

Bonus: Many business cards don't show up on your personal report, even if approved using your SSN.

How to Use Business Credit Without Hurting Personal Credit

Here's how you keep personal credit clean and business credit growing:

Use Business Cards Exclusively for Business

✓ Separate business and personal expenses

✓ Don't mix grocery or gas purchases with your business ad spend

Avoid Maxing Out Business Cards

✓ Keep usage under 50% unless it's temporary

✓ Business utilization isn't scored the same—but lenders still see it

Pay Vendors and Creditors Early

- Paying Net 30 vendors 10–15 days early boosts your Paydex score
- Auto-pay your minimums to avoid late payments

Track Your Credit Separately

- Use **Nav** to monitor your business scores
- Use your personal apps (e.g., Credit Karma) for your FICO and utilization

Business Credit Expansion Plan (for 6–12 Months)

Month 1–2:

- Form LLC, get EIN, open business bank account
- Apply for 3 Net 30 accounts and make small purchases
- Get a D-U-N-S number

Month 3–4:

- Add 2 more vendor accounts
- Begin monitoring your business credit on Nav
- Ensure payment history is being reported

Month 5–6:

- Apply for 1–2 business credit cards
- Use cards only for business expenses
- Begin rotating rewards and building credit lines

Month 7–12:

- Apply for higher-tier business cards or lines of credit

- Leverage rewards or 0% APR for business growth
- Pay off balances with business revenue
- Separate personal credit from operations

By month 12, you'll be positioned to:

- Apply for larger credit limits
- Qualify for SBA funding, equipment leases, or real estate
- Scale your company without touching personal resources

Final Thought

"You can hustle your way to a few thousand. But if you want to scale, you need structure—and credit gives you that structure."

Business credit is not just a tool—it's a shield. It protects your personal profile, expands your funding options, and gives your business the identity it needs to grow.

Start small. Build smart. And let your business earn the right to grow—without dragging your personal credit down with it.

"The Invisible Ladder: How Darnell Built Business Credit and Stopped Risking His Personal Score"

Darnell Hayes had ambition. What he didn't have—yet—was capital.

He ran a small media business out of his garage in Charlotte, North Carolina. He filmed promotional videos for barbershops, fitness trainers, and real estate agents. He was talented, hungry, and resourceful.

But his biggest problem? Every time he upgraded his gear or ran a Facebook ad campaign, he put it on his **personal credit cards**.

The result?

A personal credit score that hovered in the low 600s, nearly maxed-out cards, and zero room to grow.

"I'm building a business," he told himself. But what he was really doing… was burying his own financial foundation.

Then one day, while filming a podcast interview for a startup founder, something clicked.

The guest said, "I never use my personal credit for business. I built everything using business credit—separate cards, separate lines, even a DUNS number."

Darnell paused mid-recording. "Wait… what's a DUNS number?"

The guest laughed. "It's like a credit score for your business. And once you build it, you don't have to touch your personal profile again."

After the session, Darnell stayed up past midnight watching YouTube videos and reading blog posts. The next morning, he printed a checklist titled:

"How to Build Business Credit Without Using Personal Credit."

Step one? **Form an LLC.**

He'd been operating as a sole proprietor for two years. It was easy, but it had no credibility. Within a week, he filed his LLC papers for "Hayes Media Co." and applied for an EIN with the IRS.

Step two? **Get a business checking account.**

He walked into his credit union, opened the account, and deposited $1,000 he'd been saving for a new drone. From now on, every dollar earned by Hayes Media would go through this account.

Step three? **Set up Net 30 vendor accounts.**

He signed up with Uline and Grainger—vendors that let him buy supplies now and pay within 30 days. He ordered a few things he needed anyway: gloves, extension cords, portable lighting kits. Then he paid early.

He added two more vendors: Summa Office Supplies and Nav, which also let him track his new business credit profile.

A few weeks later, he got an email from Dun & Bradstreet:
Your D-U-N-S Number Has Been Created.

That same day, he checked Nav again—**his business Paydex score was now live.**

He had officially entered the world of business credit.

Two months later, with three vendor accounts reporting and his LLC showing consistent deposits, he applied for the **Chase Ink Business Unlimited** card.

Approved. $15,000 limit. 0% APR for 12 months.
And best of all? **It didn't show up on his personal credit report.**

He used it to upgrade his editing laptop and prepay ad campaigns. He paid it back in chunks, using client payments that came in weekly.

A month later, he applied for the **Amex Blue Business Plus** card. Approved again—$20,000 limit.

His confidence soared.

One weekend, at a BBQ with his cousins, they started talking money.

"You still putting all that business stuff on your own credit cards?" one asked.

Darnell shook his head. "Nope. I've got three business cards now. None of them touch my personal report."

His cousin frowned. "How'd you do that?"

"I stopped acting like a freelancer. I built a real business. I've got an LLC, an EIN, and a DUNS number. Now the banks lend to my *business*, not me."

They looked at him like he had just cracked the cheat code. And he had.

Because for the first time ever, Darnell had:

✓ $50,000 in business credit access

✓ A 90-day buffer to grow before paying interest

✓ A healthy personal credit score again

✓ A system to separate his business from his name

Today, Hayes Media is no longer just a side hustle—it's a growing brand.

Darnell uses business cards to travel to film conferences, book last-minute rentals, and run split-test ads for clients. He's hired an intern. He's bidding on larger contracts.

And most importantly, his personal credit is clean. Protected. Safe.

"I used to feel like I was growing my business on quicksand," he says. "Now? I've got a foundation."

And it all started with a checklist, a late-night research binge… and a decision to treat his business like one.

Chapter 10: The Lifetime Credit Strategy: How to Maintain, Multiply, and Pass On Credit Wealth

"Credit mastery isn't a one-time win—it's a lifelong strategy that creates stability, freedom, and legacy."
— Joe Correa

The Big Picture – Why Credit Is a Long-Term Game

You've now learned how to:

☑ Build and protect personal credit

☑ Stack credit for capital and business

☑ Use 0% APR and high limits strategically

☑ Earn and multiply rewards

☑ Build business credit separate from your personal profile

Create wealth cycles that reinvest and grow

Now, in this final chapter, we shift focus from tactics to longevity.

This is your **lifetime credit strategy**—a practical plan for:

- Maintaining elite credit
- Repeating growth without risk
- Preparing for high-level funding
- Protecting your financial identity
- Teaching the next generation

Build, Rotate, and Rest

The most successful credit users rotate through 3 phases every year:

Phase 1: Build

✓ Apply for 1–2 new cards (business or personal) with strong rewards or 0% offers

✓ Increase credit limits with existing cards

✓ Open new trade lines for your business

✓ Set up automation tools (autopay, trackers, calendar alerts)

Phase 2: Rotate

✓ Use credit to fund profitable activity (business launch, ad campaign, travel, equipment)

✓ Earn rewards and cashback

✓ Pay back balances systematically

✓ Monitor score weekly for changes

Phase 3: Rest and Reflect

✓ Stop applying for new credit for 3–6 months

✓ Focus on increasing income and savings

✓ Audit your reward redemptions and ROI

✓ Decide what worked and what didn't before the next build cycle

This cycle creates **rhythm without pressure**—and allows your credit to grow predictably over time.

Protecting Your Credit and Financial Identity

As your credit access grows, **so does your exposure**. Here's how to protect yourself:

Credit Protection Tools

- Freeze your credit reports when not applying (Equifax, Experian, TransUnion)

- Use identity theft protection apps like **Aura**, **LifeLock**, or **Credit Karma**

- Set **2FA (two-factor authentication)** on every financial account

- Use different, strong passwords for each bank and credit app

Smart Monitoring Habits

✓ Check reports every 30 days

✓ Dispute incorrect items immediately

✓ Get notifications for new accounts or credit pulls

✓ Track your credit utilization by individual card

Remember: One stolen identity or one reporting error can wipe out years of good standing if you're not monitoring.

Advanced Credit Moves as You Grow

As your income and business expand, you'll want to level up your credit strategy:

Set Up a Holding Company

- Use an LLC or Corporation to hold properties, digital assets, or brands
- Apply for credit under that entity once it builds business credit

Establish Banking Relationships

→ Open accounts with local and regional banks

→ Build trust with business bankers and ask about:

◆ Business lines of credit

◆ Equipment or fleet financing

◆ Real estate or investment lending

Leverage Personal and Business Credit Together

✓ Use 0% APR business cards for working capital

✓ Use personal rewards cards for high-category spend (groceries, travel)

✓ Use cashback to fund tax payments or reinvest into new ventures

Pro Tip: Credit is just the first layer. With good credit and business history, you unlock **private funding, real estate leverage, and strategic capital partnerships.**

Building Credit Legacy

Credit mastery isn't just for you—it's something you can pass on.

Teach Your Kids or Family

➔ Add a child as an **authorized user** on a card (age 13+ for many banks)

➔ Help them build a score before they even turn 18

➔ Teach them to pay in full and use rewards wisely

➔ Show them how business credit works and how to build it early

Share With Your Community

➔ Host a credit education night for your church, school, or group

➔ Create a workbook or checklist based on your journey

➔ Help others rise without judgment

This multiplies your impact and turns what you've learned into **generational wisdom**.

Lifetime Credit Success Plan (Use Annually)

1. **Review** personal and business credit reports quarterly
2. **Apply** for 1–2 strategic cards each year with purpose
3. **Rotate** spending and rewards based on current business goals
4. **Use** credit for building assets, never lifestyle inflation
5. **Redeem** points or cashback efficiently
6. **Pay off** high balances before promotional periods end
7. **Teach** at least one person per year what you've learned

Over a decade, this system adds up to:

- Hundreds of thousands in accessible capital
- Tens of thousands in saved interest
- Five- or six-figure value in points, perks, and cashback
- A legacy of knowledge and smart credit behavior

Final Thought

"Credit doesn't just buy you what you want—it unlocks who you can become."

You now hold the tools that most people never take the time to learn. With discipline, intention, and strategic rotation, you can turn credit into income, rewards into wealth, and knowledge into legacy.

This is not the end. It's the beginning of a lifetime of financial control.

Go build something great—with the credit you now command.

"Legacy in Motion: How One Man Turned Credit Mastery Into Generational Wealth"

Marcus Fulton never considered himself a "money guy." He worked hard, paid his bills on time, and made sure his kids had what they needed. He wasn't flashy—just focused.

But in his early 40s, after back-to-back layoffs and rising credit card debt, he realized something chilling:

"I'm not building anything they can inherit."

He meant his children. His wife, Denise, reassured him. "We've always gotten by," she said.

But Marcus didn't want to "get by" anymore. He wanted to leave behind more than stories—he wanted to leave behind structure.

It started with a podcast episode he listened to on a late-night drive home. The guest was a retired entrepreneur who said:

"The first time I felt wealthy wasn't when I made six figures—it was when I had $150,000 in available credit and zero balances. That's when I could breathe."

That sentence flipped a switch.

Marcus had never thought of credit that way. He always saw it as a trap. Something to be feared, not leveraged. But that night, he made a commitment:

He would **learn everything about credit**. Not just how to fix his score, but how to use it—for cash flow, rewards, growth, and eventually, legacy.

He started simply: pulling his credit report and watching YouTube videos after the kids went to bed.

What he found shocked him.

He'd been carrying a 665 score for years, all because of high utilization on two cards and an old medical collection he didn't even know about. He paid off balances strategically, disputed the error, and within three months, his score was 734.

He felt powerful.

He then applied for his first **0% APR card** with Chase. Approved. $11,500 limit. He used it to pay off a high-interest balance from another card and immediately began planning a rotation strategy.

By year's end, he had:

- Three personal cards with over $40,000 in available credit

- Paid $0 in interest

- Collected over 78,000 points—used to take the kids to Disney for the first time

But he didn't stop there.

In year two, Marcus launched a side business with his son: **a vending machine company**.

They formed an LLC, got an EIN, and opened a business checking account. He used vendor accounts to start building business credit. Then, applied for the **Amex Blue Business Cash** card.

Approved. $20,000 limit.

The vending machines turned $2,000 in startup costs into $7,800 in the first year—and every cent earned ran through their business credit profile.

His son, just 17 at the time, was added as an **authorized user** on one of Marcus's oldest cards. By the time he turned 18, he had a credit score of 765.

Marcus smiled every time he saw it.

"My son started life with what I didn't have until I was 45."

By year three, Marcus had a system:

- ➔ One personal card for groceries and gas
- ➔ One travel card for family trips
- ➔ One business card for expenses
- ➔ Cashback was reinvested into a stock portfolio
- ➔ Points paid for flights and hotels
- ➔ A digital tracker with all payment due dates and APR periods
- ➔ Biweekly credit check reminders
- ➔ Annual credit "audits" in January and July

He even hosted a family meeting once a year to review credit goals—like most families would plan a vacation.

Denise started calling it **"the Fulton Family Credit Summit."**

The real reward came the day his daughter came home from college orientation and said, "Dad, my roommate just maxed out her card buying a TV. I told her about how we rotate spending and pay in full every time."

Marcus laughed. "You teaching the class now?"

"No," she said, "just paying the knowledge forward."

He walked away quietly, tears forming.

Because it wasn't about the score. Or the credit lines. Or the travel perks.

It was about **changing the default**—so that his children would never again see credit as survival. They would see it as a strategy. A tool. A launchpad.

Today, Marcus teaches financial literacy at a local youth center. He helps young adults understand credit, build responsibly, and avoid common traps.

His legacy isn't a mansion or a massive inheritance.

It's something stronger:

A working system they can use. A mindset they can trust. A future they can fund—one swipe, one cycle, one decision at a time.

"I may not leave behind millions," he says, "but I left behind the map."

And for his family, that map is worth more than gold.

VOLUME 6: CREDIT CARD HACKING FOR SMART BORROWERS

Chapter 1: The miles and points Wake-Up Call

Carlos had never flown first class before. In fact, he'd never flown without paying for checked luggage, fighting for armrest space, or worrying about the mounting credit card bills waiting at home. But there he was—seat 2A, sipping sparkling water, being offered a warm towel on his way to Hawaii—all thanks to a credit card welcome bonus he hadn't even known existed a year earlier.

Just twelve months ago, Carlos had been deep in debt, swiping cards for groceries and minimum payments. He had a decent job, sure, but every dollar seemed to vanish into rent, bills, and gas. Then, while watching a YouTube video on budgeting, he saw someone casually mention "credit card hacking." At first, he scoffed. "Another scam," he thought.

But curiosity got the best of him. He spent that evening learning everything he could about points, sign-up bonuses, and how some people flew around the world for nearly free. The key? Strategic use of credit—not abuse. No debt. No gimmicks. Just leveraging what he already spent on bills and food to earn value back.

Carlos started with a basic cashback card—nothing fancy. Just 1.5% back on all purchases. But it was a win. He paid it off every two weeks, just like the tutorials recommended. No interest. No surprises.

Then he applied for a card offering 60,000 points after spending $4,000 in three months. At first, it seemed like a lot—but when he added his rent (paid via a fee-free rent portal), groceries, insurance, and utilities, he realized he already spent that much anyway. He just had to shift the payments to the card, without spending more.

That's when things changed.

With 60,000 points, Carlos booked two roundtrip flights to Mexico. He felt like he'd cracked some secret code. One that bankers don't teach you. One that your broke cousin doesn't know. One that most people use incorrectly—or not at all.

But Carlos wasn't done. He began learning about travel protections, free hotel nights, price protections, extended warranties, and rental car insurance—all included just for holding the right cards.

Now, Carlos teaches others. Friends, co-workers, even his parents. And he makes one rule very clear: **"If you can't pay the balance in full every month, don't play this game."**

This book is about unlocking the hidden wealth that credit cards offer. Not by getting into debt—but by playing smart, spending intentionally, and paying it all off.

Chapter 2: Choosing the right cards for your goals

If you want to master credit card hacking, you need to start with the right foundation. That means choosing cards that align with your **financial behavior**, **credit score**, and personal goals. The mistake most people make? Chasing shiny rewards without a strategy—leading to unnecessary debt or underused perks. In this chapter, you'll learn how to select the ideal card for your unique goals and situation.

Step 1: Know Your Credit Score First

Before you apply for any credit card, pull your credit report and check your FICO score. You can do this for free using:

- AnnualCreditReport.com (for your full report from all three bureaus)
- Credit Karma or Credit Sesame (for educational scores and monitoring)
- Or your bank's built-in credit tracker

Why it matters: Each credit card has a recommended score range. If your score is too low, you'll get denied—and each denial can temporarily lower your score further due to the hard inquiry.

Target Ranges:

- Excellent Credit (750+): Access to premium travel cards, elite cashback cards, and business cards

- Good Credit (700–749): Solid travel and cashback options with decent bonuses

- Fair Credit (640–699): Consider starter cards or secured cards with rewards

- Poor Credit (<640): Focus first on rebuilding your credit before chasing rewards

Step 2: Define Your Reward Strategy

Ask yourself: *What do I want from this card?* Your answer should shape the type of card you apply for. The three main categories are:

1. **Travel Rewards**

    - Earn points or miles you can redeem for flights, hotels, car rentals, or upgrades.

    - Ideal for people who travel a few times a year or want to plan free vacations.

2. **Cashback**

   - Earn a percentage of your purchases back in cash (usually 1.5%–5%).
   - Best for people who want simple, flexible rewards they can use on anything.

3. **Balance Transfers or Low-Interest Intro Offers**
   - Useful for those who need to pay off existing debt and avoid interest.

Example:

- If you spend heavily on groceries and gas: look for a **card with 3%–6% cashback in those categories.**
- If you travel frequently: look for a **card with airline partners, free checked bags, and airport lounge access.**

Step 3: Understand the Fees and Interest Rates

Even great rewards cards can have hidden downsides. Always check the **Annual Percentage Rate (APR)** and **fees** before applying.

Key fees to look for:

- **Annual Fee:** Some travel and cashback cards charge $95–$695 per year. Make sure your rewards exceed this.

- **Foreign Transaction Fees:** If you travel abroad, look for a card with *0% foreign transaction fees.*

- **Balance Transfer Fees:** If transferring debt, check for a **0% APR promo** and **3% or lower transfer fee.**

Warning: If you **don't pay your balance in full**, your interest charges can wipe out all rewards. Credit card hacking only works when you're paying off the card **monthly, in full.**

Step 4: Find the Best Welcome Bonuses

One of the fastest ways to earn travel and cashback value is through **welcome bonuses**, sometimes called **sign-up bonuses**.

Typical Offer: Spend $3,000 in the first 3 months and get 60,000 points or $500 cash back.

This can be worth hundreds—or even thousands—when redeemed for flights or hotels.

Pro Tip: Make sure the **minimum spend requirement** matches your normal spending. Never spend more just to meet a bonus—it defeats the purpose.

Step 5: Consider Long-Term Value

Beyond the initial bonus, consider the **ongoing rewards** and perks that fit your lifestyle:

- **Rotating Categories:** Cards like the Chase Freedom Flex offer 5% cashback on changing categories each quarter.
- **Flat Rate Cards:** Like the Citi Double Cash (2% on everything).
- **Premium Travel Cards:** Like the Chase Sapphire Preferred or Amex Gold, which come with travel insurance, priority boarding, and more.

Additional Perks to Look For:

- Cell phone protection
- Extended warranties
- Price protection
- Return protection
- Rental car insurance

If these perks match your habits, they add even more value.

Step 6: Apply Smart—One Card at a Time

Space out your applications. Too many at once can:

- Lower your score due to multiple hard inquiries
- Get you denied for appearing "credit hungry"

Rule of Thumb: Apply for **one new card every 3–6 months**, unless you're following an advanced strategy like the "Chase 5/24 Rule" (which we'll cover later in the book).

Summary Action Plan

1. **Check your credit score and reports**
2. **Define your goals: travel, cashback, or balance transfer**
3. **Compare cards by rewards, fees, and long-term benefits**
4. **Plan for the welcome bonus by aligning it with normal expenses**
5. **Apply when your score is ready and your spending aligns**

By choosing the right card with strategy, not impulse, you set yourself up for long-term financial wins—whether it's free flights, cashback, or smarter credit building.

The Story of Maya's Financial Transformation

Maya had always been careful with her money. As a middle school teacher in Georgia, she lived modestly, saved when she could, and avoided credit cards like they were traps. She'd grown up watching her parents struggle with debt—late-night calls from collectors, overdraft notices on the fridge, and holidays filled with stress instead of joy. To Maya, credit cards represented everything she didn't want to become.

But things changed when Maya turned 30. She wanted more freedom—to travel, to see her family in California without draining her savings, to stop feeling like she had to choose between an oil change and a weekend getaway. That's when she heard about "credit card hacking" on a podcast while grading essays. At first, she rolled her eyes. But something about the guest's story caught her attention.

This woman, also a teacher, had flown to Europe twice in one year—just by using points. No gimmicks. No interest. Just strategic credit use. Maya paused the podcast and started searching. "Is credit card hacking legit?" "How do I start travel hacking?" She stayed up until 2 a.m. reading blogs, YouTube guides, and Reddit threads.

By the next morning, she was ready to try. But Maya didn't just jump in. She made a list of her goals:

1. Fly to California twice a year to visit her parents

2. Stay in hotels without breaking her budget

3. Get cashback on groceries and school supplies

She realized she wasn't looking for luxury—she just wanted value. So she started with her credit score: 728. Not bad. She qualified for most cards, which meant she had options. But that also made the decision harder.

Maya made a spreadsheet and categorized cards into three groups: travel, cashback, and balance transfer. She narrowed it down to two choices:

- **The Chase Sapphire Preferred**, offering 60,000 points after $4,000 in spending
- **The Amex Blue Cash Preferred**, offering 6% cashback on groceries and streaming

She hesitated. The Sapphire card came with a $95 annual fee and seemed focused on serious travelers. The Amex had more practical benefits for her daily life.

Then she had an idea: why not plan a strategy that combined both? She'd start with the cashback card to earn rewards on her daily spending, and later, once she had a rhythm, she'd go for the travel card.

Maya applied for the Amex Blue Cash Preferred. She was approved instantly. Limit: $5,000. She took a deep breath. "Okay," she told herself. "I'm going to use this the right way."

She automated her bill payments and groceries onto the card. Every Sunday night, she paid off the balance with the money she had already set aside. No stress. No temptation. Just a system.

Three months later, she had earned over $300 in cashback and had paid **zero** in interest. That summer, she used her rewards to cover a hotel for a three-night stay in Savannah. Her first "free" vacation. She was hooked.

By the next year, she added the Chase Sapphire Preferred to her wallet. She put her annual insurance, back-to-school expenses, and holiday travel on the card—all things she already planned to buy. She hit the $4,000 bonus mark with ease and used the points to fly to San Diego in December.

On that flight, window seat, headphones in, Maya smiled. She wasn't rich. She hadn't gotten a raise. But she felt powerful.

She had learned how to use credit on her terms. No fear. No shame. Just strategy.

Now she teaches others. Her friends at work, her brother, even a few of her students' parents. "The trick isn't just using credit," she says. "It's choosing the right card for your life—not someone else's."

Maya now reviews her cards every six months. She cancels ones she no longer uses, applies for new ones when the bonuses make sense, and always—always—pays in full.

And the best part? She finally bought her parents flights to come visit her for Thanksgiving. She used her points to cover everything. No debt. No guilt. Just joy.

Chapter 3: Earning and Maximizing Rewards Daily

Once you've chosen the right credit card, the next step is learning how to use it **strategically and consistently** to earn maximum rewards. This chapter will teach you exactly how to turn everyday spending into free flights, hotel stays, cashback, and more—**without spending a penny more than you already do.**

If you do this right, your credit cards become **income-producing tools**, not expenses.

Step 1: Organize Your Spending Into Reward Categories

Every credit card offers different rewards depending on where and how you spend money. Start by creating a **spending map** of your top 5 expense categories. Here's how:

Example: Maya's Monthly Spending Map

- Groceries: $450
- Gas: $150
- Streaming Subscriptions: $60
- Dining Out: $200
- Utilities and Insurance: $300

- Other: $100

Once you know where your money goes, **match those categories** to the right card. For example:

- Use a card with 6% cashback on groceries for your supermarket purchases.
- Use a card with 3x or 5x points on dining for restaurants.
- Use a flat-rate 2% cashback card for non-category purchases.

This matching process is called **"category alignment."** Most people never do it, and they leave hundreds—if not thousands—of dollars in rewards on the table.

Step 2: Stack Bonuses with Portals, Offers, and Extensions

Now that your categories are matched, you can **stack rewards** to increase earnings without changing what you buy.

Three Easy Ways to Stack:

1. **Online Shopping Portals** – Use portals like Rakuten, TopCashback, or your credit card issuer's portal (e.g., Chase Ultimate Rewards or Amex Offers). You click through the portal before buying from major retailers like Nike, Walmart, or Best Buy and earn **additional cashback or points.**

2. **Card-linked Offers** – Activate targeted offers through your bank. For example, Amex Offers might give you $20 back for spending $100 at a certain store.

3. **Browser Extensions** – Install tools like *Honey*, *Capital One Shopping*, or *Rakuten* that alert you to coupon codes and cash bonuses while browsing.

Example: Maya buys a $100 pair of running shoes from Nike:

- Uses Chase Sapphire Preferred (3x points on travel & certain online purchases)
- Clicks through Rakuten for 8% cashback
- Activates a $10 cashback offer through her card's app

Result: $8 cashback + 300 Chase points + $10 bonus = triple-stacked rewards

Step 3: Automate and Optimize Your Bill Payments

Bills are a credit card hacker's secret weapon. Most people pay them through their bank account and earn **nothing**. But when possible, pay bills through your credit card to:

- Hit spending thresholds for welcome bonuses

- Earn rewards on regular fixed costs

Bills You Can Often Put on Credit Cards:

- Phone, internet, and streaming
- Insurance (home, auto, life)
- Utilities (with payment processors like Plastiq)
- Subscriptions (software, gym, cloud storage)

Warning: Never pay rent, mortgage, or taxes with a credit card unless:

- The fee is under 2.5% AND
- You're hitting a big bonus AND
- You'll pay it off in full the same month

Step 4: Take Advantage of Monthly Perks and Credits

Premium cards often offer **credits and protections** most cardholders forget to use. These are automatic money-savers.

Examples of Common Credits:

- Amex Gold: $10/month dining credit (Uber Eats, Grubhub)

- Chase Sapphire Reserve: $300 annual travel credit
- Hilton Aspire: $250 airline fee credit + free hotel night

How to Maximize: Set a **monthly reminder** to use credits. Consider keeping a running list in your Notes app or calendar for:

- Monthly statement credits
- Free shipping perks
- Priority access or reservations

If you're not using these perks, you're not getting the full value of the card—and in most cases, you're losing money on the annual fee.

Step 5: Track, Review, and Adjust Every Quarter

Every three months, conduct a **card performance review**. Ask:

- Which cards gave me the most rewards?
- Did I use them in the right categories?
- Did I miss any bonus offers or credits?
- Are there better options I should consider switching to?

Use tools like:

- **Mint** or **YNAB** to track expenses by category
- **AwardWallet** or **MaxRewards** to track points and offers
- **Google Sheets** for a custom tracker of all your card benefits, bonuses, and due dates

Example Review Summary:

- Amex Blue Cash: $72 in grocery cashback (6%)
- Chase Freedom Flex: $54 from Q1 rotating category (gas)
- Amex Offers: $20 from Staples credit
- Rakuten: $45 cashback from portal stacking

Total reward value this quarter: $191

Final Tips for Everyday Reward Mastery

1. **Never use a debit card unless absolutely necessary.** Debit gives you zero rewards and less protection.
2. **Pay your balance every week, not just every month.** It keeps your credit utilization low and protects your score.
3. **Avoid carrying more than 2–3 active cards** if you're just starting. Focus on what you can manage easily and responsibly.

4. **Treat points and cashback like real money.** Because they are—when used wisely.

Chapter Recap:

- Match your credit cards to your top spending categories
- Stack rewards through portals, offers, and apps
- Put recurring bills on your cards to boost passive points
- Use every monthly perk and credit you're entitled to
- Review your usage every quarter to optimize earnings

This chapter is about building habits. You don't need to chase the next shiny card—you just need to **use what you have smartly and consistently.**

The Story of Derek, the Daily Hacker

Derek Alvarez had never considered himself the "organized" type. He was a freelance graphic designer in Austin, Texas, juggling multiple clients, chasing down invoices, and keeping up with software subscriptions, groceries, and bills. His finances were more like organized chaos—until a random YouTube rabbit hole one evening introduced him to the world of credit card rewards.

At first, it sounded like a rich person's game—first class flights, airport lounges, luxury hotels. "Must be nice," he thought. But as he dug deeper, he discovered people like him—regular folks—who were earning hundreds, even thousands of dollars in travel and cashback every year just by using their credit cards **intentionally**.

He didn't need luxury. What he wanted was **efficiency**. To stop feeling like every dollar disappeared the second he earned it. To use the spending he already had to his advantage.

So he took a deep breath and decided to try. One rule: he would never carry a balance. Not a penny.

Derek started by mapping out his expenses. He opened up his budgeting app and looked at the last 3 months:

- Food delivery and dining out: $600/month
- Subscriptions and software: $300/month
- Gas and rideshares: $200/month
- Groceries: $250/month
- Miscellaneous (client gifts, office supplies, and tech): $150/month

"Okay," he thought. "Now what?"

He read that the **Amex Gold Card** offered 4x points on dining and supermarkets. That seemed perfect. He applied—and got approved. Next, he picked up the **Chase Freedom Flex**, which offered 5% cashback in rotating categories, and the **Citi Double Cash** for a flat 2% back on everything else.

For the first time in his adult life, Derek felt like he had a **system**.

He color-coded his cards with tiny stickers—red for Amex (dining and groceries), green for Citi (everything else), and blue for Chase (rotating categories). He even created a digital cheat sheet on his phone labeled "What Card to Use Where."

Soon, things got fun.

One morning, he ordered lunch through Uber Eats using his Amex Gold. He remembered he had activated an Amex Offer for $10 back on a $25 Uber Eats purchase. The food cost $28. He got 112 points for the purchase—**and** $10 instantly credited back to his account.

Another time, while buying software for a client project, he checked the Rakuten portal. Adobe was offering **8% cashback** if you clicked through Rakuten first. He did, made the $100 purchase, and got $8 back in his Rakuten account—on top of the 2% he'd earn with his Citi card.

His favorite moment came three months in. Derek looked at his Chase and Amex accounts and saw:

- **Amex Membership Rewards points: 34,000**
- **Chase Ultimate Rewards: 16,200**
- **Cashback earned on Citi: $92**

That was over **$600 in travel or cash**—earned without changing his lifestyle at all.

He hadn't spent more. He hadn't done anything complicated. He'd just aligned his spending to the right cards.

Then came the big test: Derek planned a weekend trip to Denver with friends. He checked his points, transferred Amex rewards to Delta, and booked a roundtrip flight worth $362. The cost to him? $0.

He sat on the plane, boarding group one, sipping coffee. "This is nuts," he said to himself. "I'm flying for free because I bought groceries and paid for Netflix."

Now, he was obsessed—in a good way.

He created a spreadsheet that tracked every card's category bonuses, expiration dates, credit limits, and perks. He scheduled a monthly 15-minute "reward check-in" on the first Sunday of each month.

He made it a game: **How much free value can I squeeze from the money I already spend?**

But Derek was also smart. He never used his cards to buy things he couldn't afford. He never paid interest. He used autopay, reminders, and set all his cards to alert him when his balance reached 50%.

It wasn't just about the points anymore. It was about control. Clarity. Ownership of his financial life.

By the end of the year, Derek had earned:

- Two roundtrip flights
- Three hotel nights at a Marriott
- $200 in cashback
- A year's worth of Adobe Creative Cloud for free using Amex Offers
- And his credit score? It jumped from 712 to 761.

All because he used the **same money he'd always spent**—but ran it through a smarter system.

Now, his friends come to him for advice. He teaches them how to pick the right card, how to use browser extensions, and how to review their cards quarterly.

But his advice always starts the same:

> "Don't start with travel. Start with groceries, gas, and Netflix. Start with what you're already doing. Master that. And never carry a balance."

Derek may not have been organized at first, but now he's a **daily hacker**—someone who earns while they live, saves while they spend, and travels while others say, "I wish I could afford that."

Chapter 4: Redeeming Rewards the Smart Way

Earning points, miles, or cashback is only half the game. The real value of credit card hacking comes when you **redeem those rewards wisely**. Redeeming without a strategy can cut their value in half—or worse, waste them entirely. This chapter will show you how to turn your hard-earned points into real value for **travel, cashback, gift cards, or experiences**, all while avoiding common redemption traps.

Step 1: Understand Reward Values and Their Hidden Math

Each reward system works differently, and not all points are created equal. Let's look at three types:

1. **Cashback** – Usually fixed value:
    - 1% = $0.01 per dollar spent
    - 5% = $0.05 per dollar spent This is the most straightforward redemption.
2. **Travel Points (Flexible Programs)** – Such as Chase Ultimate Rewards, Amex Membership Rewards, and Citi ThankYou Points:
    - Value can vary: **$0.01 to $0.025** per point

- Better redemptions come from **transfer partners** (airlines, hotels)

3. **Airline Miles or Hotel Points** – Each has its own system:
    - Delta SkyMiles: ~$0.012 per mile (but varies)
    - Marriott Bonvoy: ~$0.007 per point The key is finding **sweet spots**, which we'll explain shortly.

Step 2: Avoid Low-Value Redemption Traps

Credit card issuers often tempt users with easy options that sound good—but offer **poor value**. Examples:

- **Gift cards**: Often redeem at 0.8 to 1 cent per point
- **Merchandise or shopping portals**: Extremely poor value (0.5 to 0.8 cents per point)
- **"Pay With Points" at checkout (e.g., Amazon)**: Usually gives the **worst** rate—sometimes less than 0.7 cents per point

Rule of Thumb: If it's convenient, it probably comes with **less value**. Take the extra step to transfer or redeem your points properly—it can **double or triple your reward value**.

Step 3: Redeem Travel Rewards the Right Way

The best value often comes from transferring your flexible points (Chase, Amex, Citi) to airline or hotel partners.

Examples:

- **Chase Ultimate Rewards → Hyatt**: Book luxury hotels for a fraction of the points compared to using the Chase portal.
- **Amex Membership Rewards → ANA or Air Canada**: Fly roundtrip to Europe or Asia for 60k–80k points, when direct purchases would cost $1,000+.
- **Citi ThankYou Points → Turkish Airlines**: Fly U.S. to Hawaii for 15k miles roundtrip—an incredible deal.

These are called **sweet spots**, and they make your points go much further.

Steps to Transfer:

1. Log into your credit card rewards portal.
2. Choose your airline/hotel transfer partner.
3. Link your loyalty account (e.g., Marriott Bonvoy, Delta SkyMiles).
4. Transfer the required number of points.

5. Book through the airline or hotel's platform, not your card issuer's site.

Warning: Transfers are often **non-reversible** and can take 1–5 days, so always confirm availability before initiating a transfer.

Step 4: Use Travel Portals for Simplicity and Solid Value

If transferring points feels overwhelming, don't worry—you can still get decent value through your card's travel portal.

Chase Example:

- Chase Sapphire Preferred gives you **25% more value** when booking through the Chase Travel Portal.
    - 60,000 points = $750 in travel (instead of $600 cash)

How to Use It:

- Search for flights, hotels, or rental cars through your bank's travel portal (like Expedia or Priceline).
- Use your points at a fixed enhanced rate (e.g., 1.25 cents or 1.5 cents per point).
- You often earn miles and elite credits on these bookings, unlike with point transfers.

This is a great middle-ground for people who want **simplicity** with **above-average value**.

Step 5: Combine Points, Pool Rewards, and Redeem as a Team

Most people don't know that you can often combine or share points with spouses, business partners, or family members.

Chase:

- Combine points from all your Chase cards to maximize value (e.g., Freedom + Sapphire Preferred = higher redemption power)
- Transfer points to one household member per policy

Amex & Citi:

- Allow transfers to authorized users or linked loyalty accounts

Pro Tip: Designate one person as the "redemption strategist" in your household. Pool points into that account for large bookings or high-value redemptions.

Step 6: Redeem Cashback the Right Way

Cashback cards don't offer travel transfers, but they still need strategy.

Best Practices:

- **Redeem for statement credits or direct deposit**, not gift cards
- **Wait until larger balances** to avoid friction or fees
- Use cashback for **specific goals** like emergency funds, debt payoffs, or reinvestment in other tools (like paying for your next course or software)

Stack Your Strategy:

- Use cashback from one card to pay an annual fee on a travel card
- Use your rewards to offset costs of side hustle investments
- Combine with bank bonuses or referral rewards for extra income

Chapter Summary and Action Plan

To redeem rewards the smart way:

1. **Know the true value** of your points, miles, or cashback.
2. **Avoid poor redemption options** like gift cards or Amazon checkouts.

3. **Transfer points to airline/hotel partners** when seeking maximum value.

4. **Use portals like Chase Travel or Amex Travel** when seeking simplicity and decent value.

5. **Combine points within households or among your own cards** to boost redemption power.

6. **Cashback works best when used with intention**, not for impulse spending.

Redemption is the **payoff** phase of credit card hacking. The smarter you are here, the higher your return on every dollar you spend.

The Story of Amanda's Upgrade

Amanda Douglas had always been the type to collect things—coins, postcards, airline miles. But collecting points from credit cards? That was something she'd been doing for years without actually using them. Like digital trophies, they sat untouched in her account, gathering virtual dust.

She'd opened her first travel rewards card, the Chase Sapphire Preferred, three years ago when she got a promotion as a marketing coordinator. She earned the welcome bonus—60,000 points—and told herself she'd use them for a dream vacation someday. Then life happened.

Someday became next year. Next year became never.

By the time Amanda turned 35, she had **over 210,000 points** across Chase, Amex, and Citi cards. She had no idea what they were worth, how to use them, or where to start. She'd redeemed some for gift cards here and there—$50 to Amazon, $100 to Target—but it never felt exciting. It felt… average.

Then, her younger brother Jason booked a $4,000 roundtrip flight to Japan using just 70,000 points. First class. Private suite. Free meals and drinks. No cash. Amanda stared at the photos he sent from the ANA lounge in Tokyo and felt a wave of regret.

"You used points for that?" she asked, shocked.

"Of course," he laughed. "What else are they for?"

That was her wake-up call.

Amanda opened her laptop that night and logged into her Chase account. She clicked "Redeem Points," and sure enough, the first thing she saw was "$0.01 per point" for gift cards. A $100 Visa card would cost her 10,000 points.

"But Jason booked a first-class ticket for 70,000 points," she thought. "That's worth four grand. That's like… 6 cents per point?"

She did the math again. Her stomach dropped. She'd traded her valuable points for store credit. Over and over.

"I've been doing this all wrong."

She dove headfirst into travel hacking forums, YouTube guides, and Reddit posts. She learned about **sweet spots**—those rare redemptions where your points stretch farther than you'd think. Like booking Hyatt hotels through Chase, or transferring Amex points to Air Canada for flights to Europe.

She learned how **gift cards and Amazon checkouts are the worst redemptions**, how **travel portals give better value**, and how **airline transfers can explode the value of her points—if she plays it right.**

And she was ready to play.

Her next trip was to New York for a marketing conference. She found a Hyatt hotel near the venue: $480 per night. But through Chase's portal? Just 18,000 points per night. Four nights. 72,000 points total.

She clicked "Book." Boom. $1,920 in hotel value—redeemed for points.

Then came the flight. Delta was charging $350 one way. But she remembered Amex points could transfer to Air France and book Delta flights through their SkyTeam partnership.

After a few searches, she found it: JFK to ATL, roundtrip, 24,000 Amex points + $11 in taxes.

She transferred the points instantly. Five minutes later, the flight was booked.

"Okay," she whispered to herself. "That's $2,270 in travel for less than 100,000 points."

And she still had over 100,000 points left.

Amanda kept going. She made a chart in Google Sheets with each of her cards, their point balances, and the best transfer partners. She learned that her **Chase Freedom Flex points could be moved to her Sapphire account**, giving them more power when redeemed through the Chase Travel Portal. She even taught her coworker how to book a honeymoon using only points.

But the real reward came in April.

Amanda had always dreamed of going to Italy. But she'd assumed it was too expensive. With her new skills, she searched award travel sites and found a roundtrip business-class ticket from Boston to Rome on United—through a Chase transfer partner—for 80,000 points.

She booked it.

The day she boarded, sipping champagne in the Polaris Lounge, she smiled.

She had spent the same money she always did—on groceries, business lunches, software subscriptions—but this time, she'd **redeemed it with intention**.

She now saw her credit cards not as bills, but as tools. Tools that paid her to live her life smarter.

As the flight attendant offered her a hot towel, Amanda thought back to those $50 gift cards. She almost laughed. Those were scraps.

This… this was the **real** value of credit.

And she'd only just begun.

Chapter 5: Managing Multiple Cards Like a Pro

Once you've mastered earning and redeeming rewards from a single card, the natural next step is expanding your strategy. But with more cards comes more complexity—and more opportunity. This chapter teaches you how to manage multiple credit cards **without missing payments, damaging your credit, or getting overwhelmed**—all while maximizing every dollar you spend.

Step 1: Know Why You're Adding a New Card

Before you add a second, third, or fourth card, be clear about your goal. Each card in your wallet should serve a **specific purpose**.

Here are smart reasons to open a new card:

- To **earn a welcome bonus**
- To **unlock category-specific rewards** (like 5% on groceries or gas)
- To **access travel perks** (airport lounges, free hotel nights, priority boarding)
- To **increase your available credit** and lower your credit utilization ratio

Avoid applying out of FOMO or to cover emergency expenses. Cards are tools—not crutches.

Step 2: Build a System to Keep Track of Everything

As you add cards, staying organized becomes essential. A forgotten payment or misunderstood benefit can wipe out months of progress.

Create a Credit Card Tracker that includes:

- **Card name and issuer**
- **Open date**
- **Credit limit**
- **Due date**
- **Current balance**
- **Rewards type** (points, miles, cashback)
- **Annual fee and when it's due**
- **Category bonuses and perks**
- **Welcome bonus and spend deadline (if new)**

You can use:

- A simple spreadsheet (Google Sheets works well)
- Free apps like **MaxRewards**, **AwardWallet**, or **Travel Freely**
- Reminder apps or calendar alerts for payment due dates

Pro Tip: Color-code your categories and rotate your focus every 90 days based on new promotions, limited-time offers, or bonus categories.

Step 3: Set Up Autopay—and Check Weekly Anyway

The golden rule of credit card hacking: **never carry a balance**.

Set up **autopay** for the full statement balance for every card. That way, even if you forget, you won't pay interest.

However, don't just "set and forget."

Instead:

- **Check your balances weekly** to ensure no fraudulent charges have appeared
- Pay off your balance **early** if you want to keep your credit utilization ratio low

- Log expenses into your budget so you don't overspend just to chase rewards

Even experienced users get tripped up when they don't monitor closely.

Step 4: Use the Right Card in the Right Place

This is where the magic happens: aligning your spending with the **highest-earning card** for that specific purchase.

Here's a breakdown of how a 3-card user might do it:

Expense Type	**Best Card Example**	**Why Use It?**
Dining & Takeout	Amex Gold (4x points)	Highest rate for restaurants
Groceries	Blue Cash Preferred (6% cashback)	Best return on food
Gas & Transit	Chase Freedom Flex (5% quarterly)	Rotating bonus category
Streaming Services	Citi Custom Cash (5% in top category)	Matches top spend category monthly
Online Shopping	Rakuten Portal + any rewards card	Stack cashback and card points
Travel	Chase Sapphire Preferred (2x travel)	Plus 25% bonus when redeemed

Pro Tip: Use stickers, digital wallet notes, or custom card names on Apple Pay/Google Pay to remind yourself of the card's category bonuses.

Step 5: Review Cards and Benefits Quarterly

Every 3 months, do a credit card checkup:

- Are you still using the card enough to justify the **annual fee**?
- Are you using all the included **credits and benefits**?
- Are any **bonus categories changing** soon?
- Are there new **welcome offers** you could qualify for?

If a card no longer serves a purpose:

- **Call the issuer** and ask if you can **product change** to a no-fee version
- Downgrade instead of closing the card to preserve your credit history

Why this matters: Length of credit history and total available credit are major factors in your credit score. Don't lose years of progress just because you're not using a card daily.

Step 6: Protect Yourself from Fraud and Identity Theft

The more cards you have, the more vigilant you must be.

Best Practices:

- Set up **text or email alerts** for every transaction
- Use **virtual card numbers** when shopping online (offered by Capital One, Citi, and others)
- Freeze cards you don't use often through your bank's app
- Check your **credit reports monthly** with services like Credit Karma or Experian

If fraud is detected:

- Report it immediately to your card issuer
- File a report with the FTC at **identitytheft.gov**
- Monitor your credit for new inquiries or accounts

Staying proactive keeps your financial identity secure while you build wealth through smart credit use.

Chapter 5 Recap: Your Multi-Card Management Plan

1. **Add cards with a specific strategy**—don't collect them aimlessly.

2. **Track all your cards** with a spreadsheet or app—know your limits, bonuses, and due dates.

3. **Set up autopay** but still monitor activity weekly.

4. **Match spending to the right card**—use every card where it earns the most.

5. **Review your lineup quarterly**—maximize value or downgrade dead weight.

6. **Stay secure**—enable alerts, use virtual cards, and monitor credit reports regularly.

With a little structure and strategy, managing multiple cards isn't stressful—it's empowering. It transforms you from a passive consumer into an intentional earner. The more cards you manage well, the more free flights, cashback, and opportunities flow your way.

The Story of Malik's Card Control

Malik Summers had a system for everything—his calendar, his fitness goals, even the order of spices in his kitchen. But when it came to credit cards, his system was chaos.

He had seven cards. One in his wallet, two in a drawer, one in his glove compartment for gas, and three more that he couldn't even remember applying for. Malik was good with money—he never missed a payment—but he was **leaving thousands of dollars in rewards on the table** every year.

It hit him one afternoon at his favorite coffee shop. He swiped a card for his $5 flat white, and his friend Chris shook his head.

"Dude… you just used a 1% cashback card at a restaurant. Why not 4x points?"

Malik laughed it off, but when he got home, he pulled out all his cards and laid them on the dining table like a poker hand. Chase Sapphire Preferred, Amex Blue Cash, Citi Double Cash, Target REDcard, an Amazon Visa, Discover It, and something called the HSBC Platinum Rewards that he hadn't touched since college.

He felt like a magician who didn't know his own tricks.

That night, Malik made a promise to himself: **no more wasted potential**. He would create a real system. Something scalable. Something that fit his brain the way his gym split or his Google Calendar did.

Step one: a spreadsheet.

He opened Excel and built a table:

- Card name
- Issuer
- Category bonuses
- Credit limit
- Payment due date
- Annual fee
- Notes and perks

As he filled in the columns, patterns emerged. He realized his Chase Sapphire gave him 2x points on dining and travel—but he'd been using his Citi Double Cash (2% flat rate) for everything out of habit. His Amex gave him 6% cashback at grocery stores, but he never brought it to Publix. And the Amazon card? Great for Amazon. But he rarely shopped there anymore.

He color-coded each card by category:

- **Green for groceries**
- **Blue for travel and dining**

- **Yellow for gas and transit**
- **Red for online shopping**
- **Gray for storage or backup**

Then came the real challenge: **payment dates**. They were all over the place. One was due on the 2nd, another on the 11th, two on the 20th, and one randomly on the 27th.

Malik called each bank and requested the same due date: the 15th. Most of them agreed. Now, instead of chasing bills all month, he had a single "credit card check-in" day—set on the second Sunday of every month. It was sacred.

Step two: automation.

He set every card to **autopay the full statement balance**. No interest. No surprises. But he didn't stop there. He added weekly calendar reminders to:

- Check balances
- Log any unexpected charges
- Adjust his spending if a card was getting too close to the limit

Step three: practice.

He started small. For one week, he made it a game: use only the card that earned the **most** rewards for that specific purchase. Groceries? Amex. Dining? Sapphire. Gas? Discover It's 5% category for Q2. Everything else? Citi Double Cash.

By day three, it was second nature. He even renamed the cards in his Apple Wallet to say **"Dining Only," "Groceries Only,"** and **"Everything Else."**

Soon, he wasn't just managing his cards—he was **mastering them.**

But the real payoff came six months later.

Malik had been tracking his rewards in the same spreadsheet. He tallied up the results:

- $122 in cashback from Amex
- $134 in Ultimate Rewards from Chase, worth $167 in travel
- $84 from Discover's quarterly bonuses
- $220 in cashback from Citi
- A $100 Amazon gift card from his Visa

Total reward value: **$727.**

He hadn't changed his income. He hadn't bought anything he wouldn't have bought anyway. He just used the right card in the right place, and he never paid a cent in interest.

It felt like getting a raise—quietly, automatically, without asking.

Later that year, Malik took a trip to San Diego. Flights and hotel? Booked with points. Rental car? Paid with cashback. Dinner with friends on the beach? Chase Sapphire. Double points, thank you.

Now, when his friends ask about his system, he pulls up the spreadsheet with a grin. "I treat my credit cards like employees," he says. "Each one has a role. If it's not doing its job, it gets demoted."

Malik didn't just learn how to manage multiple cards—he turned them into a **money-making machine**. And like everything else in his life, it runs on a system.

Chapter 6: The Secrets to Building Credit While Hacking Rewards

If you want to master credit card hacking long-term, you must understand how to **build and protect your credit score** while earning rewards. Many people focus on points and cashback but forget the foundational system that makes this strategy possible: a strong credit profile.

This chapter will teach you how to **boost your score, avoid damaging mistakes, and use credit cards to your advantage without hurting your future borrowing power**.

Step 1: Understand What Makes Up Your Credit Score

There are five key factors that affect your FICO score, which most lenders use to evaluate your creditworthiness:

1. **Payment History (35%)**
    - Do you pay on time? Every time?
    - Missing a payment can stay on your report for **7 years**.
2. **Credit Utilization (30%)**
    - This is the percentage of your available credit that you're using.

- Aim to use **under 30%**, and ideally under **10%** on each card and overall.

3. **Length of Credit History (15%)**
    - Older accounts = stronger score. Don't close your oldest cards unless absolutely necessary.
4. **New Credit Inquiries (10%)**
    - Every hard inquiry can drop your score a few points temporarily. Apply for new cards strategically.
5. **Credit Mix (10%)**
    - A mix of credit types (credit cards, loans, auto financing, etc.) shows you can manage different forms of debt responsibly.

Pro Tip: Focus most on **payment history** and **utilization**—together, they make up 65% of your score.

Step 2: Use Credit Cards to Build Positive Credit Habits

Every time you use a card and pay it off responsibly, you're reinforcing a strong credit profile. Here's how to build habits that boost your score while hacking rewards:

- **Pay your balance weekly** (not just monthly). This keeps your utilization low and prevents forgotten bills.
- **Keep utilization under 10%** of each card's limit—even if you plan to pay in full later.
- **Don't close old accounts** unless the fee outweighs the benefit.
- **Open new cards only when needed**, and space them out every 3–6 months.

Example: If you have a $10,000 credit limit across all cards, try to keep your total balance **under $1,000 at all times**.

Step 3: Increase Your Credit Limit Without Increasing Your Spending

One of the fastest ways to improve your score is to **increase your credit limit** while keeping your spending the same. This lowers your credit utilization ratio.

You can do this by:

- Requesting a credit limit increase from your card issuer (usually available in the app or online)
- Getting approved for a new card with a high limit

- Allowing automatic increases (some banks offer this every 6–12 months if you pay on time)

Important: Do **not** see a higher limit as permission to spend more. Treat it like a safety net that boosts your score.

Step 4: Monitor Your Credit and Dispute Errors

Just like you check your bank account or budget, you should **monitor your credit report** regularly. Mistakes happen, and they can hurt your score if left unchecked.

Here's what to do:

- Use **AnnualCreditReport.com** to get your free reports from Experian, TransUnion, and Equifax once a year.
- Use free credit monitoring apps like **Credit Karma**, **Credit Sesame**, or **Experian** to stay on top of changes.
- Look for:
    - Late payments reported in error
    - Accounts you don't recognize
    - Incorrect balances

- Accounts not updated after payoff

If you find an error:

- File a dispute online through the credit bureau's website.
- Provide documentation (e.g., payment confirmations).
- The bureau has 30–45 days to respond.

Step 5: Avoid the Most Common Credit Card Mistakes

To build credit while hacking rewards, you must avoid these common traps:

1. **Carrying a balance to "build credit"**
   - **MYTH.** You do NOT need to carry a balance or pay interest to build credit. Just use the card and pay it off in full.
2. **Applying for too many cards too quickly**
   - Space out your applications. Too many inquiries in a short time can lower your score and scare lenders.
3. **Using over 30% of your credit limit**
   - Even temporarily. Utilization is often calculated based

on **statement balances**, so keep them low before the statement closes.

4. **Ignoring due dates**
    - Set **autopay** for the full amount due. Late payments hurt more than almost any other factor.
5. **Closing old cards without checking the impact**
    - If it's your oldest account or a card with a high limit, consider **downgrading** it instead of closing.

Step 6: Build Toward Your Long-Term Credit Goals

Credit hacking isn't just about points—it's about positioning yourself for **bigger opportunities**:

- Qualifying for **low mortgage rates**
- Getting **higher credit limits**
- Accessing **premium travel and business credit cards**
- Being approved for **business loans or HELOCs**

Set these goals:

- Credit score target: 750+

- Credit limit goal: $50,000+ total available
- Length of credit: Maintain accounts for 7+ years
- Payment history: 100% on-time

Chapter Summary and Action Plan

1. **Know your FICO score factors**, and focus on payment history and utilization.
2. **Use your cards like a credit-building tool**—low balances, on-time payments, and strategic spending.
3. **Increase your limits gradually**, and treat them as leverage, not temptation.
4. **Monitor your credit reports regularly**, and dispute any errors immediately.
5. **Avoid common traps** like carrying a balance or closing old cards.
6. **Think long-term**—your future borrowing power is shaped by the habits you start today.

When done right, building credit while hacking rewards becomes a win-win. You enjoy the perks now—and open doors to bigger opportunities later.

The Story of Janelle's Credit Comeback

Janelle Thompson stared at the email on her laptop screen. It was another denial.

She had applied for a mid-tier travel rewards card—a basic one, nothing flashy—and yet again, the message was the same: *"We regret to inform you…"* She sighed, closed the tab, and pushed her coffee aside. It wasn't just about the card. It was about what the denial represented.

Janelle had been through a rough stretch. A messy divorce, job loss during the pandemic, and a medical emergency had thrown her finances into chaos. She hadn't filed for bankruptcy, but her credit score had plummeted into the low 600s. She was rebuilding now—steady job, stable income—but her credit history told a story she was no longer living.

She'd recently discovered credit card hacking and was fascinated. Free flights? Cashback? Hotel upgrades? It sounded like a dream. But as she dug deeper, she realized something crucial: **before she could play the game, she had to repair the board.**

So she made a decision. No more impulse applications. No more guessing games. She would **rebuild her credit strategically**—and do it while laying the groundwork for future rewards.

Step one: she pulled her credit reports from all three bureaus using AnnualCreditReport.com. It was overwhelming at first. Old accounts, a couple of late payments, and some credit cards she hadn't used in years. But she took notes.

She opened a spreadsheet and listed everything:

- Open accounts
- Payment histories
- Utilization rates
- Derogatory marks

It wasn't pretty—but it was honest.

Step two: she set up **autopay** for every bill she had—utilities, insurance, and her remaining credit card. She made a rule: **every Friday was "Money Check-In Day."** She'd review her balances, update her spreadsheet, and make early payments. It became a habit. Like brushing her teeth. It gave her control.

Then she found out about **secured credit cards**. She applied for one with a $300 deposit and was approved. It was a small step—but for her, it was huge. She used it for gas and groceries only. Never more than $100 at a time. Paid it off **twice a month**.

After four months, her score ticked up—632 to 658.

Then she called her bank and requested a **credit limit increase** on her older card. She had paid on time for over a year. To her surprise, they doubled her limit.

Her utilization dropped. Her score went up again.

She was building.

Janelle also signed up for **Experian Boost**, adding her phone and utility payments to her credit file. It gave her a 15-point jump overnight. Not magic—just momentum.

Six months in, she was back in the 700s. For the first time in years, she smiled when she checked her credit score.

Then came the moment she'd been waiting for: she applied for a **real rewards card**—the Amex Blue Cash Everyday. No annual fee, decent cashback, and a modest welcome bonus. She was approved. Limit: $2,000.

She used it only for groceries and streaming subscriptions. Set autopay. Never carried a balance. After three months, she'd earned $78 in cashback—and another credit limit increase.

By the end of the year, Janelle had:

- Three open cards
- Over $6,000 in total credit
- 100% on-time payments
- Utilization under 8%
- A credit score of 742

But more than numbers, she had confidence. She no longer feared credit. She understood it. She used it intentionally—not just to earn rewards, but to secure her future.

She started mentoring her younger cousin who was just getting started with credit. Taught her how to track spending, check reports, avoid minimum payments, and keep balances low. She told her:

> "Credit isn't the problem. How we use it is."

Janelle booked her first reward flight to Chicago that fall—paid entirely with cashback. As she boarded the plane, she thought about the journey. Not the flight. The **real** journey.

From denied… to approved. From stressed… to empowered. From buried in credit fear… to building credit freedom.

And she knew this was just the beginning.

CREDIT TO CAPITAL

Chapter 7: How to Travel for Free Using Points and Miles

One of the biggest motivators for credit card hackers is the dream of **traveling for free**—flights, hotels, rental cars, upgrades, even luxury experiences. What sounds like a fantasy is actually possible when you learn how to **accumulate and redeem points and miles effectively**.

In this chapter, you'll learn the core strategy behind booking **free or deeply discounted travel**, and how to plan trips using your rewards like a pro.

Step 1: Choose a Flexible Travel Rewards Ecosystem

Not all points are created equal. To travel for free consistently, focus on cards that earn **flexible points** that can transfer to multiple airlines or hotel partners.

Top ecosystems include:

- **Chase Ultimate Rewards**
    - Transfer partners: United, Hyatt, Southwest, British Airways, etc.
    - Cards: Chase Sapphire Preferred, Sapphire Reserve, Ink Business Preferred
- **American Express Membership Rewards**

    - Transfer partners: Delta, Air Canada, Hilton, ANA, etc.
    - Cards: Amex Gold, Amex Platinum, Amex Business Platinum

- **Citi ThankYou Points**
    - Transfer partners: Turkish Airlines, Avianca, Choice Hotels, etc.
    - Cards: Citi Premier, Citi Rewards+
- **Capital One Miles**
    - Transfer partners: Air France/KLM, Emirates, Wyndham, etc.
    - Cards: Capital One Venture, Venture X

Why it matters: Flexibility gives you the best chance to find **award availability** and **maximize point value**, especially when booking international or peak-season travel.

Step 2: Understand the Booking Value of Your Points

Before booking anything, understand how much value you're getting for your points. You want to aim for **at least 1.5 cents per point**, and ideally **2+ cents** with travel redemptions.

Example:

- A flight costs $500.
- It requires 25,000 points.
- $500 ÷ 25,000 = **2 cents per point (cpp)** — that's excellent value.

Use calculators on sites like:

- The Points Guy (TPG)
- AwardWallet
- NerdWallet

If the value is below **1 cent per point**, consider paying with cash and saving your points for a better redemption.

Step 3: Transfer Points to Airline or Hotel Partners

Transferring your points from your credit card account to a travel partner can **more than double their value**. But it takes planning.

Here's how to do it:

1. Search for availability directly on the airline or hotel website (not your credit card's portal).

2. Create a loyalty account with that airline or hotel.
3. Log in to your credit card rewards dashboard.
4. Select "Transfer Points" and choose the partner.
5. Enter your loyalty account info and the number of points.
6. Confirm the transfer (note: most transfers are **one-way and non-reversible**).

Pro Tip: Always confirm the seat or room is available **before** transferring.

Step 4: Know the Sweet Spots and Award Charts

Sweet spots are redemptions where the value of your points is disproportionately high.

Here are examples:

- **Hyatt Hotels via Chase Ultimate Rewards**
    - Park Hyatt NYC: $1,200/night or 30,000 points = **4 cpp**
- **ANA Roundtrip Business Class via Amex**
    - U.S. to Japan for 75,000 points roundtrip

- **Turkish Airlines via Citi ThankYou Points**
  - U.S. to Hawaii roundtrip for 15,000 points in economy
- **British Airways Avios**
  - Short-haul flights in the U.S. (under 650 miles) for 7,500 points + $5.60

Always check for **low surcharges** and **partner availability**, as some programs have better deals for specific routes.

Step 5: Use Travel Portals When Simplicity Matters

If you don't want to transfer points or deal with loyalty programs, use your card's **travel portal** to book directly. Some portals even **boost the value** of your points.

Examples:

- Chase Sapphire Preferred: Points worth **1.25x**
- Chase Sapphire Reserve: Points worth **1.5x**
- Amex Travel: Sometimes offers exclusive rates and upgrades

This is a great option when:

- You want to book a flight on a low-cost carrier (like JetBlue or Spirit)
- You're booking a hotel that's not part of a major chain
- You don't want to worry about blackout dates or reward availability

Downside: You may not earn frequent flyer miles or elite status benefits.

Step 6: Maximize Hotel Stays Using Points

Hotel rewards can be just as valuable—if not more—than flights. With hotel points, you can often stay multiple nights for free, especially at mid-tier properties.

Top hotel programs include:

- **Hyatt** (via Chase)
- **Hilton Honors** (via Amex)
- **Marriott Bonvoy** (via Chase or Amex)
- **Choice Privileges** (via Citi)

Tips to Maximize Hotel Points:

- Look for **5th night free** promos (Hilton and Marriott)
- Use your co-branded hotel card for **free anniversary nights**
- Avoid luxury properties with inflated point requirements—focus on mid-tier hotels in great locations
- Book early for peak travel seasons

Chapter Summary and Action Plan

1. Focus on cards that earn **flexible points** for maximum travel value.
2. Always calculate your **cents-per-point value** before redeeming.
3. **Transfer points to travel partners** when you want to maximize value—but plan carefully.
4. Learn your program's **sweet spots** and use award charts when available.
5. Use **travel portals** for simplicity or when partner options don't fit.
6. Don't forget to **redeem points for hotel stays**, where long stays and fifth-night-free perks can stretch your value.

Travel hacking isn't just for jetsetters—it's for everyday people who spend smart, plan ahead, and use the right cards at the right time. With a few smart moves, you can start traveling better, more often—and sometimes, for free.

The Story of Luis's First-Class Surprise

Luis Rivera wasn't rich, but you wouldn't have guessed that from the way he strolled through the business class lounge at JFK, sipping ginger tea and staring out the window at the massive Airbus A350 that would soon carry him across the Atlantic.

In a few hours, he'd be in Paris—his first trip to Europe—and he'd paid less than $100 for the entire journey.

Only six months earlier, Luis had never heard the term "travel hacking." He worked as an elementary school teacher in Miami and had just finished paying off the last of his credit card debt from his twenties. Travel was always a dream, but one that felt just out of reach. Flights were expensive. Hotels even more so. He had never flown outside the U.S., let alone sat anywhere near the front of the plane.

It all changed when his friend Jamie invited him to a backyard barbecue and casually mentioned she had just booked a trip to Rome using credit card points.

Luis was floored. "Wait, like… you didn't pay anything?"

"Well," Jamie laughed, "I paid $52 in taxes, but yeah. First class. Entire thing booked with Amex points."

That night, Luis went home and typed *"how to fly for free using credit cards"* into YouTube. Three hours later, he had a notebook full of scribbles and a new obsession.

He started by applying for the **Chase Sapphire Preferred**, following the advice of every travel blog he could find. The sign-up bonus at the time was 60,000 points after spending $4,000 in three months. Luis knew he'd have to be smart—he didn't spend much—but he found ways to make it work. He used the card to pay his rent through a portal with a 1% fee, bought grocery store gift cards for gas and everyday purchases, and paid for his friend's wedding venue deposit (she reimbursed him right away).

He hit the bonus just in time.

With his points in hand, Luis did something different—he planned **backwards**. He didn't pick a destination and hope his points worked. He searched for **award availability** first. That's when he found it: a one-way business class ticket from New York to Paris on Air France. Retail price? $3,400. Points cost? 55,000 Chase points transferred to Flying Blue, plus $87 in taxes.

He transferred the points. Waited anxiously. And when the confirmation email came through, he sat back and smiled. He had done it.

Then came the hotel. Luis used the rest of his points to book three nights at a boutique Hyatt in the heart of the Marais district—22,000 points per night. If he'd paid cash, it would have been nearly $1,200.

The night before his flight, he could barely sleep. He kept checking the app, making sure the booking hadn't vanished. He packed carefully—passport, chargers, one pair of clean sneakers, and a notebook to journal the entire experience.

At the airport, he checked in at the Sky Priority counter. No line. No rush. He breezed through security and entered the Air France lounge, where soft jazz played and the espresso machine hissed in the background.

Sitting in a lounge chair, Luis looked around and chuckled. "I teach third grade," he thought. "How am I here?"

The answer, he knew, wasn't luck. It was knowledge. It was strategy. It was points.

The flight itself was everything he imagined. A lie-flat seat, a three-course meal, champagne at takeoff. He watched a French film, took a nap, and woke up just as they descended into Charles de Gaulle airport.

He took the train into the city. Walked along the Seine. Ate crepes from a street vendor and listened to street musicians play under golden streetlights.

The best part? Every time someone asked how much he paid for the trip, he just smiled.

Luis spent the next few days wandering museums and bookstores, journaling the entire journey. At night, he returned to his hotel, knowing it was all booked with points.

After he got home, he started planning his next trip—to Japan. He had already opened an Amex Gold card and started earning points for takeout and groceries.

For Luis, travel was no longer a dream. It was a system. A way of life. And it all started with a single card, a sign-up bonus, and a decision to stop saying, "I can't afford that."

Now, whenever someone asked him how he pulled it off, he didn't just give them tips—he handed them a pen and said,

Chapter 8: Advanced Strategies for Maximizing Every Dollar

Once you've built a strong foundation—earning points, redeeming for value, managing multiple cards, and building credit—what's next? This chapter dives into **advanced-level tactics** used by experienced credit card hackers to **amplify rewards**, **stretch redemptions**, and **turn everyday spending into extraordinary value.**

If you want to unlock elite travel, thousands in annual cashback, or even build a side income from your rewards system, these strategies are for you.

Step 1: Leverage Multipliers with Stackable Offers

The smartest hackers don't just earn 1–5% on purchases—they **stack offers** to earn 10% or more from the same transaction.

Here's how:

1. **Card Category Bonus** – Use a card that gives elevated points for the purchase type (e.g., 4x at restaurants).
2. **Shopping Portal Bonus** – Use sites like **Rakuten**, **TopCashback**, or **Chase/Amex shopping portals** for additional 1%–10%.
3. **Targeted Card Offers** – Activate targeted promotions (e.g., "Spend $50 at Best Buy, get $10 back").

4. **Coupon & Deal Extensions** – Tools like **Honey** or **Capital One Shopping** add auto-discounts and rebates.

Example: You buy $200 worth of shoes at Nike.com:

- Use a card that earns 3x on online purchases = 600 points
- Go through Rakuten portal for 10% cashback = $20
- Use an Amex Offer for $10 back on $100 spend
- Apply a 15% discount code via a browser extension

Total Value Earned: Over $50 in cashback and points

Stacking offers is **compound hacking**—a key trait of advanced users.

Step 2: Time Your Large Purchases for Maximum Bonus Returns

Big purchases—appliances, electronics, travel bookings, even taxes—can be timed to trigger massive value if aligned with:

- **Welcome bonuses** (e.g., spend $4,000 in 3 months)
- **Quarterly category activations** (e.g., 5% back on travel Q3)
- **New card spend thresholds** (e.g., spend $15,000 in a year for bonus points)

Advanced Tip: If you know you'll be spending a large sum (wedding, renovations, medical bills), **plan ahead and open a card 30–60 days before the expense.**

Then:

- Use the purchase to hit the bonus
- Stack it with shopping portals and offers
- Redeem the bonus for a high-value trip or cashback

This method turns a one-time expense into a long-term reward.

Step 3: Use Multiple Cards as a Unified Ecosystem

Most beginners use cards in isolation. Advanced hackers treat their cards as a **team**.

The Ecosystem Strategy:

- Use **category cards** for their strengths (e.g., 5% on groceries, 3x on gas)
- Funnel those rewards into a **premium card** with a stronger redemption portal (e.g., Chase Freedom points transferred to Chase Sapphire Reserve)

- Combine **personal and business cards** to amplify points and keep categories separated

Example Setup:

- Chase Freedom Flex (5% rotating)
- Chase Ink Business Cash (5% on office supplies, internet)
- Chase Sapphire Preferred (hub card for travel redemption)

Result: You earn points at 3x–5x across multiple spend types, then redeem through one card's portal for **25–50% more value.**

Step 4: Optimize Authorized Users and Household Rewards

If you live with a spouse, partner, roommate, or family member, you can **maximize rewards as a unit.**

Options include:

- **Add authorized users** to cards to hit minimum spend faster and earn referral bonuses
- **Refer family members** to cards you already have (most issuers give $50–$200 per referral)

- **Pool points** from Chase, Amex, or Citi for a major travel redemption
- **Split spend across cards strategically** (e.g., one uses the 5% dining card, the other uses the 6% grocery card)

Pro Tip: Some cards (like Amex Platinum) offer **elite status** to both the primary and authorized users—great for hotel upgrades and lounge access.

Step 5: Use Rewards as Capital to Build Other Income Streams

Advanced credit card hackers often use rewards to:

- Travel to attend business conferences (points pay for flights and hotels)
- Use cashback to fund investments, courses, or business tools
- Open **business credit cards** and funnel their side hustle expenses to build even more points

Case Example: A freelancer opens the Amex Blue Business Plus (2x on all purchases). He uses it to pay for:

- Advertising
- Software

- Client gifts

He earns over 100,000 Membership Rewards in a year—worth $1,000–$2,000 in travel or more when transferred to partners.

That's **leveraged value**—earning while spending, then reinvesting rewards into business growth or personal freedom.

Chapter Summary and Action Plan

1. **Stack every purchase** using bonus categories, portals, and offers.
2. **Plan large purchases** around welcome bonuses or category promotions.
3. **Build a multi-card system** where rewards are pooled into one high-value portal.
4. **Coordinate with family** or partners to multiply earning potential.
5. **Think like an investor**—use rewards to support business, growth, or income-generating opportunities.

Advanced credit card hacking is about more than free flights—it's a mindset of **intelligent optimization**, turning every dollar you spend into a smarter version of itself. You don't need more money—you need to be more strategic with what you already spend.

The Story of Nia's Everyday Empire

Nia Jefferson wasn't flashy. She didn't post credit card selfies or humblebrag about lounge access on social media. She was a 39-year-old single mom from Charlotte, North Carolina, with two kids, a full-time job, and a growing photography side hustle. What set Nia apart wasn't how much she earned—it was **how strategically she spent.**

To most people, she looked like any busy professional. But to those who knew her system, Nia was a credit card hacker with **elite-level precision.**

Her journey started with a simple cashback card years ago, but once she paid off her debt and built her credit to a 760, she began to study how points and miles could change her financial trajectory—not just for travel, but for leverage.

Her first breakthrough came when she opened the **Chase Ink Business Cash** for her photography side gig. The welcome bonus was 75,000 points after $6,000 in three months. Nia timed it perfectly. She had a wedding shoot coming up and needed new lenses, lighting gear, and a second camera body. She bought everything with the new card—and hit the bonus in less than six weeks.

Next, she opened the **Amex Gold** and used it for groceries and dining, which accounted for nearly $1,200 a month between her family and client meals. That gave her 4x points on nearly $15,000 annually—**60,000 Amex points** on autopilot.

But Nia didn't stop there.

She started **stacking offers**. Before buying anything online—whether it was kids' school shoes, client albums, or holiday gifts—she checked shopping portals. She bookmarked **Rakuten**, **Chase Offers**, and **TopCashback**, and installed browser extensions that alerted her to cash bonuses. Every purchase became a puzzle. Which card? Which portal? Which offer?

Then came the strategy that changed everything: **planned purchases.**

In February, she knew she'd be paying $2,000 in business insurance, annual software subscriptions, and tax prep fees. So in January, she applied for a **Citi Premier** card, offering 60,000 ThankYou Points after $4,000 in 3 months. She stacked the expenses, bought gift cards for future travel, and even paid her CPA through a low-fee payment portal to hit the bonus fast.

By April, she had enough points to cover a family trip to California—flights and hotels included.

But her proudest hack wasn't a free flight.

It was the **cycle she'd created**.

Every major bill or expense became an opportunity to:

- Earn a welcome bonus
- Stack category points
- Leverage rewards into travel, cashback, or business investments

She tracked everything in a color-coded spreadsheet:

- Card name, limit, bonus timeline
- Category strengths
- Current offers
- Statement due dates
- Redemption goals

Her Amex Gold had a sticky note: "Groceries + Dining Only." Her Sapphire card said: "Use for Travel Portal." Her Citi card? "Gift cards + Gas." Even her kids got involved. They would ask, "Which card do we use for Target this week?"

Over time, she layered in **authorized users**—adding her sister and her teen son, who was learning about credit. Every purchase they made was intentional and tracked. She earned referral bonuses for helping her best friend and sister get cards. One month, she earned **$500 in referral bonuses alone.**

Nia wasn't just hacking points. She was **building an everyday empire.**

The turning point came when her son, 17 at the time, asked how to earn points for his graduation trip to New York. She smiled and handed him a notebook.

"We'll build your first travel plan together," she said. "But you have to understand the system."

That night, they built a mock card ecosystem: one for groceries, one for gas, one for school expenses. They used real calculators, reward portals, and even printed boarding passes from mock redemptions.

Her son looked up, wide-eyed. "We can fly for free? Just from buying what we already buy?"

Nia nodded. "We don't spend more. We just spend smarter."

By the end of the year, Nia had earned:

- Over 350,000 total points across 4 programs
- $1,200 in cashback

- Two round-trip flights to Europe
- Four nights at a Hyatt in San Francisco
- And a new camera lens—paid entirely with points

But more than that, she had created something bigger: **financial freedom through intention.**

Every dollar had a job. Every purchase had a purpose.

And she didn't just hack credit cards—she taught others how to **leverage the life they already live** into one filled with options, opportunity, and adventure.

Chapter 9: Avoiding the Pitfalls of Credit Card Hacking

Credit card hacking can unlock thousands of dollars in free travel, cashback, and perks—but without careful management, it can also lead to overspending, debt, stress, and even a lower credit score. In this chapter, you'll learn the most common **mistakes to avoid**, how to recognize the **warning signs** of misuse, and how to **course-correct quickly** if things get out of control.

Advanced strategies are powerful—but only if you're protecting your financial foundation.

Step 1: Never Carry a Balance to Earn Rewards

One of the most damaging myths in credit is the idea that you should carry a balance to build your credit score or earn more rewards. This is **completely false**.

- You earn **rewards based on what you spend**, not on what you carry as a balance.
- Carrying a balance means you're paying **interest**, often at 18%–29%, which **erases any benefit** of your points or cashback.

Rule: Always pay off your statement balance in full. Set up **autopay** to prevent missing payments. If you can't afford to pay off a purchase by the end of the billing cycle, you shouldn't put it on the card.

Step 2: Don't Chase Bonuses Without a Plan

Welcome bonuses are one of the most exciting parts of credit card hacking—but chasing too many at once can backfire.

Here's what can go wrong:

- You miss a **minimum spend requirement**, losing the bonus and racking up unnecessary debt.
- You open too many cards in a short period, triggering a drop in your credit score due to multiple hard inquiries.
- You lose track of payment due dates, leading to late fees or missed payments.

Best Practices:

- Space out applications every **90–120 days**.
- Map out the spend you already expect before applying.
- Set a calendar reminder for the spend deadline and track your progress weekly.

Step 3: Watch Your Credit Utilization Like a Hawk

Even if you pay in full each month, your **credit utilization** can still hurt your score if you let your balances report too high on statement day.

Example:

- Credit limit: $5,000
- You spend: $3,000
- Utilization: 60%
- Even if paid off, this may hurt your score temporarily

Fixes:

- Make **mid-cycle payments** to lower your balance before the statement closes.
- Spread expenses across multiple cards to avoid high individual utilization.
- Ask for **credit limit increases** every 6–12 months to expand your cushion.

Goal: Keep overall utilization under 30%, and preferably under 10% for optimal scores.

Step 4: Don't Let Annual Fees Eat Your Rewards

Some premium cards come with high annual fees—sometimes $95, $250, or even $695. These can be **worth it** if you use the benefits… but many people forget and end up **losing money**.

What to watch for:

- Did you use all included credits (e.g., dining, Uber, travel, hotel night)?
- Are you getting more value in points than the fee costs?
- Are you holding a premium card **just because it looks good?**

Action Step: Every year, set a reminder 11 months after opening a card. Review your usage:

- If the value exceeds the fee, keep it.
- If not, **downgrade to a no-fee version** or cancel after redeeming your points.

Step 5: Avoid Account Clutter and Mental Overload

The average credit hacker manages 5–10 cards. That's doable—if you're organized. But adding cards without a system leads to:

- Missed payments
- Overlapping benefits
- Underutilized perks
- Decision fatigue

Solutions:

- Use a **credit card tracker** (spreadsheet or app like MaxRewards or Travel Freely)
- Rotate cards seasonally based on bonus categories
- Carry only 2–3 cards in your physical wallet—keep the rest for online or targeted spend
- Use calendar alerts for **renewal dates**, **credit anniversaries**, and **quarterly activations**

Step 6: Don't Let Credit Cards Replace a Budget

This is where many high earners fail: they assume rewards are a substitute for discipline. But the core rule remains—**spend only what you can afford**.

Make your cards work inside a real budget:

- Use a budgeting app like **YNAB**, **EveryDollar**, or **Mint** to track spending
- Set category limits—even on credit cards
- Check your rewards weekly and match them to your goals

Using cards without a budget is like flying a plane without instruments—you might stay in the air, but you're headed for turbulence.

Chapter Summary and Action Plan

1. **Never carry a balance** just to earn points—interest wipes out rewards.
2. **Don't chase cards too quickly**—strategize applications and spend wisely.
3. **Track your utilization** and avoid letting high balances report to the credit bureaus.

4. **Annual fees must be justified**—review benefits every 11 months.

5. **Keep your cards organized**—too many without a system will cause mistakes.

6. **Always spend within a budget**—your points should be a byproduct of control, not a replacement for it.

Hacking credit cards successfully isn't just about earning more—it's about protecting what you've built. Every reward should be a **bonus**, not a burden.

The Story of Tyler's Reset

Tyler Grant didn't start credit card hacking with bad intentions. Quite the opposite. He had read the blogs, watched the YouTube tutorials, and even downloaded a few apps to track his points. He'd opened his first travel rewards card just after landing his first remote marketing job. "Might as well get paid to live my life," he told himself.

And at first, everything went smoothly. He hit the sign-up bonus. He booked a free hotel stay. He transferred points to an airline and flew to visit friends in Chicago for just $28 in taxes. He was hooked.

But then… he got greedy.

One morning, he saw an email with the subject line: "Earn 80,000 Points—Limited Time Offer." It was a premium card with a $695 annual fee. He applied. Approved. Then another card caught his eye: 5% cashback on groceries and gas. "Makes sense," he thought. "I'll use that too."

Then came another. And another.

Within eight months, Tyler had **seven open cards**, five with annual fees, and three different points programs to manage. He had set up a spreadsheet—once. But it hadn't been updated in months. He had calendar reminders, but some were buried under work emails and ignored.

Then the due dates started to pile up.

Tyler forgot to pay one of his cards—just by a few days. He'd been traveling, didn't see the statement, and missed the payment. He paid it off right away, but the late fee hit—and worse, his credit score dropped 46 points.

That stung.

Next, he noticed his total balances creeping higher. He had promised himself he'd pay everything off in full, but somehow, he had racked up over $4,200 across his cards. Mostly small things: takeout, Amazon orders, Uber rides, a few impulse buys. It didn't feel like much when he swiped. But when the statements arrived, it hit hard.

He started only paying minimums. Then he stopped opening the statements.

The tipping point came when he tried to book a flight to Costa Rica using his points. He logged into the airline portal and… his balance was gone.

Confused, he called the issuer.

"Your account was closed due to inactivity and annual fee non-payment," the agent said. "Unfortunately, your points expired when the account closed."

That night, Tyler sat on his couch with his laptop, his credit report, and a pit in his stomach.

He had tried to hack the system… but the system had quietly taken control of him.

He was embarrassed—but determined not to let the story end there.

So he did what he should have done months ago.

He made a list of all his cards—balances, due dates, rewards types, annual fees. He created a new spreadsheet. Then he set **autopay** for every account.

Next, he transferred balances from his high-interest cards to a 0% APR card he still had open. He made a 6-month payoff plan.

He called the issuers of the cards he wasn't using and **downgraded** most of them to no-fee versions. He kept only three active cards: one for dining and groceries, one for travel, and one flat-rate cashback card.

He created a "Money Check-In" every Sunday night—30 minutes with his budget and his credit card tracker. He paid his cards **before** the statements closed to lower his reported utilization.

And the late payment? He wrote a goodwill letter and submitted it to the issuer. Two weeks later, the late mark was removed. His score rebounded.

In five months, Tyler:

- Paid off 80% of his balances
- Reclaimed his 740+ credit score
- Earned two small sign-up bonuses by planning spend strategically

- Booked a flight using points—**and actually got on the plane this time**

Sitting on that flight, journal in hand, Tyler wrote a note to himself:

> "This is how you do it. Controlled, clean, intentional. Never again will I let points be the reason I lose money."

He wasn't a beginner anymore. He'd fallen into the trap—and climbed out. Stronger. Smarter. More focused.

From that day on, Tyler didn't chase points. He **earned them**—on his terms.

Chapter 10: Building a Long-Term Credit Card Hacking Strategy

You've learned how to earn points, redeem them, manage multiple cards, and avoid common mistakes—but the real magic happens when you **build a long-term system** that runs on autopilot. A smart credit card hacking strategy isn't about chasing every bonus or opening the flashiest card—it's about creating a **repeatable, organized process** that works year after year.

In this chapter, you'll learn how to build a strategy that grows with you, protects your credit, and continues to generate free travel, cashback, and financial flexibility well into the future.

Step 1: Define Your Long-Term Goals

Before you add another card or redeem another point, define your "why." This keeps you focused and prevents distractions.

Ask yourself:

- Do I want to travel more? If so, where and how often?
- Do I want to earn passive cashback on regular expenses?
- Do I want to build credit for home or business financing?
- Do I want to use rewards to support my business or side hustle?

Your answers determine your card choices, redemption strategies, and spending patterns.

Examples:

- If you want to travel once per year to Europe: focus on points that transfer to international airline partners like Air France, ANA, or Turkish Airlines.
- If your priority is cash back for everyday savings: focus on 2% flat-rate cards and rotating bonus categories.

Step 2: Choose and Maintain a Core "Rewards Ecosystem"

Pick one or two rewards programs that match your goals, and build your strategy around them.

Top Ecosystems:

- **Chase Ultimate Rewards** – Best for beginners; flexible transfers to airlines and hotels; strong portal value.
- **Amex Membership Rewards** – Premium travel perks, high value for advanced users, lots of transfer partners.
- **Citi ThankYou Points** – Great for international travel; less intuitive but valuable for certain redemptions.

- **Capital One Miles** – Simple system with strong travel partners and decent redemption rates.

How to maintain your ecosystem:

- Pair a **core card** (like Sapphire Preferred or Amex Gold) with **category-specific or no-fee cards** to maximize earnings.
- Pool all points into your "hub" card to simplify redemptions.
- Review your point balances and upcoming trips quarterly.

Step 3: Create an Annual Card Review Schedule

Set a reminder every year—ideally one month before each card's annual fee is due—to review your card portfolio.

Checklist:

- Am I using the benefits of this card (credits, perks, insurance)?
- Did I earn enough rewards to justify the fee?
- Are better offers available from competitors?
- Can I **downgrade** or **product change** this card to a no-fee version?

This keeps your wallet lean and your strategy intentional. Don't hold onto cards just because you've had them a long time—unless they're helping your credit age or limit.

Step 4: Rotate New Cards Strategically

Add 1–3 new cards per year, spaced at least **90–120 days apart**. Each card should serve one of three purposes:

1. Earn a **new welcome bonus**
2. Cover a **category you're not currently maximizing**
3. Replace or upgrade an underperforming card

Advanced Tip: Align new card openings with planned expenses—like vacations, holidays, tax season, or business purchases—to meet minimum spend effortlessly.

Create a card planning calendar with:

- Application month
- Welcome bonus requirement
- Spend deadline
- Redemption goal

This reduces overwhelm and helps you maintain a sustainable pace.

Step 5: Build Redemption Plans in Advance

Don't wait until you're ready to travel to figure out how to use your points. Have 1–2 **target redemptions** in mind and reverse-engineer your card choices around them.

Example Goals:

- Book 2 roundtrip flights to Italy next summer using Chase points
- Stay 5 nights in a Hyatt hotel in Hawaii using a free night certificate + points
- Redeem $500 in cashback for end-of-year holiday expenses

Having a specific plan means:

- You'll avoid wasting points on low-value redemptions
- You can time redemptions during point transfer bonuses or award sales
- You can leverage cards with benefits that match your goals (e.g., travel insurance, elite status, transfer perks)

Step 6: Automate, Track, and Reinvest Your Rewards

Once your system is in place, **automate** as much as possible:

- Use autopay for all cards (full balance)
- Set up monthly reminders to check balances and reward balances
- Use spreadsheets or tools like **MaxRewards**, **AwardWallet**, or **Travel Freely** to track rewards and expiry dates

Then, use your rewards **intentionally**:

- Fund travel that aligns with your personal or business goals
- Use cashback to invest in courses, tools, or your side hustle
- Reinvest your value—don't let it sit unused

The smartest hackers don't just earn—they **redeem with purpose** and create systems that run themselves.

Chapter Summary and Long-Term Strategy Plan

1. **Start with your "why"**—define your travel, savings, or freedom goals.
2. **Choose a rewards ecosystem** that aligns with your lifestyle.

3. **Review your cards annually** and downgrade or cancel strategically.

4. **Apply for new cards intentionally**, aligned with planned spend.

5. **Plan redemptions in advance** so points go toward high-value experiences.

6. **Automate and track everything** to minimize stress and maximize value.

Credit card hacking isn't just a short-term game—it's a lifestyle upgrade. With a long-term plan in place, you'll enjoy **years of free travel, savings, and financial empowerment**—all by being intentional with the money you already spend.

Final Chapter: Living the Credit Card Hacker's Lifestyle

By now, you've learned how to master every major element of credit card hacking—from choosing the right cards and earning rewards to managing multiple accounts, avoiding debt traps, and building long-term strategies.

But the most important takeaway isn't the free flights, cashback, or lounge access—it's the mindset you've developed. A **credit card hacker's lifestyle** isn't about chasing perks—it's about controlling your financial choices, using systems to create freedom, and making your money work smarter, not harder.

This final chapter will help you lock in the habits, systems, and mindset that transform this strategy from a fun experiment into a **sustainable way of life.**

Step 1: See Credit as a Tool—Not a Crutch

Credit is not evil. It's not dangerous. It's not something to fear.

Used properly, it's one of the most powerful tools in your financial toolkit. But just like any tool, it must be handled with care, intention, and structure.

A credit card hacker:

- Spends only what they can afford
- Uses credit to **earn**, not to **escape**
- Treats points and cashback as a **bonus**, not a bailout
- Makes decisions based on **value**, not emotion

Your score, your limits, and your rewards are reflections of your behavior—not your identity. Own them. Direct them. Improve them.

Step 2: Make Smart Money Moves Automatic

The real key to success is consistency—and the best way to stay consistent is to **remove friction**.

Smart hackers automate:

- **Full-balance autopay** for every card
- **Monthly card check-ins** using calendar reminders
- **Quarterly ecosystem reviews** to spot gaps and opportunities
- **Goal-based redemptions**, so points are spent on things that matter

You shouldn't have to rely on memory or motivation. Your system should support you—quietly, efficiently, and every month.

Step 3: Use Points to Expand Your World

Points are more than currency—they're **permission**.

They give you permission to:

- Travel more
- See family more often

- Take a break without guilt
- Attend that conference you couldn't afford before
- Stay in places that were once "out of reach"

Credit card hackers don't hoard points—they **spend them wisely** on things that align with their purpose.

Use your rewards to invest in **yourself**, your **business**, your **family**, or your **freedom**. The value isn't just in the dollar amount—it's in what that dollar lets you do.

Step 4: Teach Others What You Know

You now have knowledge that most people never learn. The majority of credit card users either:

- Avoid credit entirely out of fear
- Abuse it out of desperation
- Or ignore the rewards they're entitled to

But not you.

Now that you've mastered this strategy, share it. Teach a family member how to build their credit. Help a friend earn their first free trip. Show your kids how to use credit responsibly from day one.

When you empower others, your wins multiply.

Step 5: Keep Learning and Evolving

Credit card programs change. Reward structures shift. New opportunities arise. Your life will evolve too—new goals, new expenses, new possibilities.

The best credit card hackers are lifelong learners.

Stay up to date with:

- Travel rewards blogs like The Points Guy, Doctor of Credit, and One Mile at a Time
- YouTube channels and podcasts that share current strategies
- Community forums and groups (Reddit's r/churning is a great example)

Every few months, ask yourself:

- What changed in my spending?

- Are there new bonuses I can earn?
- Can I get more value from the cards I already have?

This lifestyle isn't static—it's dynamic. And you're in control of every move.

Final Thoughts: The Hacker's Advantage

You don't need to spend more money.

You just need to spend with **intention**.

You don't need to work harder.

You just need to let your spending do some of the work **for you**.

You don't need to travel like a millionaire.

You just need to learn how to **travel like a credit card hacker**.

And now… you've done it.

You've joined a quiet revolution—one where your habits produce rewards, your credit opens doors, and your money works harder than it ever has before.

This is your system now. This is your power.

And your next free flight, hotel upgrade, or cashback win?

It's already on the way.

Congratulations. You're not just a credit card user anymore.

You're a credit card strategist. A reward earner. A financial hacker.

Now go live the life your points have earned.

VOLUME 7: HOW TO LEVERAGE BUSINESS CREDIT TO FUND REAL ESTATE PURCHASES

Welcome to *How to Leverage Business Credit to Fund Real Estate Purchases*. If you've ever dreamed of owning property but felt limited by your personal credit or lack of capital, this book is for you.

Over the next few chapters, you'll learn how to use business credit—completely separate from your personal credit—to secure funding for real estate investments. You'll discover how to build business credit profiles, access high-limit business credit cards and lines of credit, and strategically position yourself to qualify for business real estate loans.

Whether you're a first-time investor or an entrepreneur looking to expand your portfolio, this guide will help you understand how to control assets using credit that's not tied to your personal finances. And the best part? It's legal, scalable, and doable from anywhere.

Let's get started on your journey from credit to capital—one property at a time.

Chapter 1: Why Business Credit is a Game Changer for Real Estate

If you've ever tried to purchase real estate using your personal credit, you've likely faced some combination of the following: debt-to-income ratio limits, personal liability, hard credit pulls, and the emotional weight of tying up your name and finances in a high-risk investment. That's not just frustrating—it's limiting. The more real estate you try to buy, the more those limitations tighten around you like a vice.

That's where business credit comes in. Business credit doesn't just open new doors; it opens entirely new buildings—quite literally. It gives you access to funding that's not reported on your personal credit, allows you to separate your risk, and builds your business into a funding magnet for real estate opportunities that others can't touch.

But before we get into how to build and leverage business credit, let's talk about why it changes the game entirely for real estate investors like you.

The Personal Credit Trap

Imagine this scenario: You buy a single-family rental using a conventional mortgage tied to your personal credit. That mortgage shows up on your personal credit report, which affects your utilization and your debt-to-income ratio. Then you try to buy a second property, and suddenly lenders see you as higher risk—even if that first property is cash flowing and profitable.

This is one of the main frustrations for aspiring investors. They want to grow a portfolio, but personal credit limits how far and how fast they can go.

Now contrast that with someone using business credit. That same property—if financed through business credit lines or loans—would not show up on their personal credit report. This means they could continue building their business credit profile and qualify for more capital without it ever interfering with their personal score or credit capacity.

That's not just smarter—it's scalable.

Business Credit is Not Just for Corporations

Many people assume business credit is only for big companies or enterprises with employees, huge revenue, and long operating histories. That's false. You can start building business credit with a brand-new LLC or corporation—even as a solopreneur with zero revenue.

Lenders and vendors who report to commercial credit bureaus look at how your business is set up, whether you've established a credible foundation, and how you manage the credit you're given. In fact, many of the starter vendors we'll talk about in later chapters will extend net-30 terms to brand-new businesses without requiring personal guarantees.

And as you build those accounts and pay on time, you create a strong business credit profile that opens the door to higher-limit credit cards, lines of credit, and real estate-friendly funding tools like DSCR loans.

You don't need a huge business—you just need a properly set up business.

Real Estate Investors Who Use Business Credit Win Bigger

Let's take two real estate investors: Sarah and James.

Sarah is using her personal credit to fund everything. Her first rental was financed with a conventional loan under her name. Her credit score dropped slightly because of the new debt. Her DTI increased. And when she applied for a second loan, she had to jump through hoops to prove she could handle both mortgages.

Now take James. He formed an LLC, built a business credit profile, and got approved for a $50,000 business line of credit. He used that line of credit as a down payment for a fixer-upper duplex and financed the rest with a DSCR loan under his LLC. The property doesn't affect his personal credit. He didn't use his own money. And now he has a cash-flowing asset that increases his business creditworthiness for the next deal.

James can rinse and repeat. Sarah hits a wall.

Why Lenders Prefer Lending to Businesses

Here's a secret many new investors don't know: lenders actually prefer lending to businesses in many cases. Businesses can deduct interest. They can show higher income. They can separate assets. And when structured correctly, they pose less liability for the lender in terms of collections and asset recovery.

More importantly, lending to businesses is scalable. A business can take on multiple properties without the same constraints personal borrowers face. And businesses often seek more expensive, income-generating properties, which equals bigger deals and more profits for lenders.

That's why many lenders offer specialized products like business credit cards, working capital lines, DSCR mortgages, commercial loans, and SBA-backed financing—all of which can be used to fund or refinance real estate deals.

Real Leverage Comes From Separation

One of the most powerful aspects of using business credit for real estate is asset protection. When you buy real estate under your personal name and finance it with personal credit, you're liable. If someone sues, if the deal goes bad, or if you default, your name is on the line.

With business credit, and a property held under an LLC or corporation, you separate yourself from the asset. If structured and operated properly, that LLC takes on the debt, not you personally. You get the upside—cash flow, appreciation, tax advantages—while minimizing downside risk.

That separation is the foundation of real wealth. The wealthiest investors don't own everything under their personal name. They control assets through entities, funded by strategic credit, and protected by proper structures.

And it all starts with understanding how business credit works.

You're Not Just an Investor. You're a Funding Strategist.

If you walk away from this chapter with just one insight, let it be this: You're not just buying houses. You're building a business. You're leveraging capital. You're growing net worth by mastering the game of funding.

Think of real estate like a board game. Everyone's on the board trying to buy properties, collect rent, and increase their wealth. Some people play using personal money and credit, which limits the number of moves they can make. Others use business credit and financing strategies that give them more turns, more options, and more leverage.

The person with the most access to smart capital wins.

So if you've ever felt stuck because you didn't have the cash, or your credit wasn't perfect, or the banks said no—now you know. There's another way.

In the chapters ahead, I'll show you exactly how to build your business credit from scratch, unlock the right funding tools, and use them to buy real estate without relying on your personal credit. We'll talk about lenders, vendors, DSCR loans, credit stacking, and even exit strategies.

But before we do any of that, we need to start at the root: building the right foundation for your business credit.

That's what we'll cover next.

Chapter 2: Setting Up the Foundation for Business Credit

Before you can start leveraging business credit for real estate purchases, you need a rock-solid foundation. Think of your business like a house: you wouldn't build on sand, and you wouldn't finance property with a business that looks untrustworthy to lenders. This chapter is about getting everything in place so banks, credit bureaus, and vendors see you as a serious, fundable business.

We'll cover:

1. Choosing the right legal structure
2. Registering your business correctly
3. Creating a credible online and offline presence
4. Opening business banking and vendor accounts
5. Avoiding red flags that kill your creditworthiness

Follow each step closely, and you'll be ready to build real, usable credit fast.

Step 1: Choose the Right Legal Structure

To build business credit, your company must be a **separate legal entity**. That means:

- **Sole proprietors** do *not* qualify. Business credit built under your own name is tied to your personal Social Security number.

- You must form an **LLC (Limited Liability Company)** or a **Corporation (S-Corp or C-Corp)**.

LLCs are ideal for real estate investors. They're simple to create, flexible for taxes, and offer liability protection. Corporations work well for more complex business setups but come with more requirements.

Action Step: Register your LLC or corporation with your state's Division of Corporations. Make sure the business name is professional and ideally includes a neutral or finance-related term (e.g., "ClearPoint Acquisitions LLC" instead of "Joe Buys Houses Fast").

Step 2: Obtain Your EIN and Business Licenses

An **EIN (Employer Identification Number)** is like a Social Security number for your business. You'll use it to open bank accounts, file taxes, and apply for credit.

Action Step:

- Go to the IRS website and apply for your EIN online. It's free and instant.

Next, get any **local business licenses** required by your city or county. Even if you operate online, many jurisdictions require a business tax receipt or occupational license.

Why this matters: Lenders and credit bureaus cross-check your information. If anything is inconsistent or missing—like your EIN, licensing, or business address—your applications may be denied or flagged.

Step 3: Create a Fundable Business Profile

Lenders do online research. If your business can't be found—or what they find looks unprofessional—they assume you're high-risk. Here's how to fix that.

You need the following:

- A **dedicated business phone number** (can be a virtual service like Grasshopper or RingCentral)
- A **professional business email** (e.g., info@YourBusiness.com—not Gmail or Yahoo)
- A **real business address** (not a P.O. Box; virtual office addresses are okay if they meet lender requirements)
- A **simple website** that describes your services and contact info
- Your business listed on **Google My Business**, Yelp, and online directories

Action Step:

- Register your business on Google Maps.
- Set up your website with a domain matching your business name.

- Use a clean, modern layout and include basic pages: Home, About, Services, and Contact.

Pro Tip: Make sure your business name, address, and phone number are consistent *everywhere*. This includes your website, bank accounts, licenses, utility bills, and credit applications.

Step 4: Open a Business Bank Account

This step is required before you can apply for credit—and it shows you're operating as a real business. You'll also need your business bank account to receive funds, make payments, and track expenses for real estate purchases.

Action Step:

- Choose a bank that reports to business credit bureaus (e.g., Bank of America, Chase, Wells Fargo).
- Take your Articles of Organization, EIN, and business license to open the account.
- Deposit at least $100 to start.
- Never co-mingle personal and business funds. That's a legal and tax disaster waiting to happen.

Bonus Tip: Ask your banker about future credit products (lines of credit, credit cards, etc.) and what they look for. Starting a relationship early helps you qualify faster.

Step 5: Apply for a D-U-N-S Number

The **D-U-N-S Number** is issued by Dun & Bradstreet (D&B), one of the major business credit reporting bureaus. It's required to build your credit file and apply for funding with many lenders and vendors.

Action Step:

- Go to DNB.com and apply for a D-U-N-S Number. It's free.
- Register your business and verify your information.
- You'll receive your number within 1–2 weeks.

Why it matters: This is how D&B starts tracking your business credit. No D-U-N-S = no report = no credit score.

Step 6: Get Net-30 Vendor Accounts

"Net-30" vendors give you products or services with 30 days to pay. These accounts often report to business credit bureaus—helping you establish your first trade lines.

Top starter vendors:

- **Uline.com** – office and warehouse supplies
- **Grainger.com** – tools and industrial supplies
- **Quill.com** – office and cleaning products
- **Summa Office Supplies** – office goods with easy approvals

- **Nav.com** – credit monitoring that reports to D&B and Experian

Action Step:

- Apply for 3–5 of these accounts.
- Order small amounts and pay on time or early.
- Use your business name, EIN, business address, and bank info—no personal credit check required.

Pro Tip: Wait 30–60 days and then check your business credit reports. You'll start seeing trade lines appear, and your credit score will begin forming.

Step 7: Avoid These Common Fundability Killers

Many businesses never get approved for funding because of small, preventable mistakes. Avoid these:

- **P.O. Box as business address** – Most lenders reject it
- **Using a personal email (like Gmail)** – Looks unprofessional
- **No online presence** – Lenders can't verify your legitimacy
- **Inconsistent business info across platforms** – Raises red flags
- **Applying for credit too early** – Wait until you have 3–5 reporting accounts

- **Mixing personal and business finances** – Violates tax and legal rules

Remember: You are *creating the perception* of a stable, fundable business. Appearances matter as much as operations when it comes to credit approvals.

Final Checklist Before Moving Forward

Here's your business credit foundation checklist. Make sure each box is checked before proceeding:

- Formed LLC or Corporation
- Obtained EIN from IRS
- Secured required business licenses
- Set up a professional website and email
- Got a business phone number and physical address
- Opened a business bank account
- Registered with Dun & Bradstreet and received D-U-N-S
- Opened and used 3–5 Net-30 vendor accounts

Once you've completed these steps, you'll be ready to move to the next level—**building real business credit** that you can use to finance your real estate deals without personal guarantees or high interest rates.

In the next chapter, we'll talk about how to build your business credit profile the right way—from tier 1 to tier 3 vendors—and how to strategically qualify for high-limit credit cards and lines of credit.

Let's keep building.

From Hustler to CEO — Maya's Foundation

Maya sat at her kitchen table in a one-bedroom apartment in Phoenix, Arizona. Her laptop was open, not for browsing listings on Zillow like usual, but because today marked the day she was officially done hustling in the dark. For the past three years, she had been wholesaling properties—flipping contracts to investors—always using her personal cell phone, her Gmail, and her own name on every deal. She had closed a few good flips, made some decent money, but she always felt like she was stuck at the bottom of the ladder. Scraping by. Starting from scratch every time.

It hit her hardest when she tried to buy her first rental property. She was ready to scale—but the bank didn't see her as a business. They saw her as a freelancer with fluctuating income, no business assets, and a maxed-out credit card she'd been using to cover deal costs.

She was done playing small.

That morning, she poured her coffee and typed into Google: "How to build business credit for real estate." She didn't know what would come next—but she knew something had to change.

The Shift: Legitimizing the Hustle

She read for hours and found stories of other investors who built real estate portfolios by separating their personal finances from their business. They used LLCs, business credit, and DSCR loans. Maya had always thought she needed a perfect credit score or a big chunk of cash to get started. Turns out, what she really needed was structure.

That day, she registered "Keystone Acquisitions LLC" with the Arizona Corporation Commission. It cost her $85 and took less than an hour. It was surreal—finally seeing her business have a name, a structure, and a legal standing. This wasn't just a side hustle anymore. This was real.

By lunchtime, she applied for her EIN through the IRS website—free and instant. She opened a document to organize her new identity: business name, EIN, phone number, and a list of to-dos. She felt like a new version of herself. Focused. Confident.

Building a Fundable Identity

She quickly realized that just forming an LLC wasn't enough. To get funding, lenders had to see her business as legitimate. That meant no Gmail address, no P.O. Box, no random cash apps for payments. She set up a business email using her new domain, keystoneacquisitions.com, and ordered a virtual business address from a verified commercial provider downtown.

Then came the business phone line. For $29/month, she got a toll-free number routed to her cell. Now, when lenders called, she answered like a CEO—not like someone winging it from her living room.

She spent the next few days building a simple but clean website: "Helping Arizonans Sell Fast While We Build Stronger Communities." It had her story, her services, and a photo of her smiling in front of a property she helped renovate. It wasn't fancy—but it made her proud. It made her real.

The Bank Visit That Changed Everything

Two weeks later, she walked into a Chase Bank wearing her best blazer and a folder of her business documents. She had everything they needed: her Articles of Organization, her EIN letter, her new business address, and a $1,000 check to deposit.

"I'd like to open a business checking account," she said.

The banker smiled and walked her through the process. As they talked, Maya asked, "What kind of credit products do you offer for new businesses?"

The banker leaned in, impressed. "Most people don't ask that, but we do have a business credit card program and a line of credit option once your account is in good standing."

She left the branch with a business debit card, a printed checkbook with her LLC's name on it, and—most importantly—a foot in the door.

That night, she stared at her new check. *Pay to the order of: Keystone Acquisitions LLC.* She teared up a little. Not from sentimentality, but from clarity. This wasn't just an account—it was leverage.

Laying the First Bricks of Credit

With her business bank account open, Maya moved on to trade credit. She had read about Net-30 vendors—companies that give you 30 days to pay after you order, and more importantly, report to credit bureaus. She applied for Uline, Quill, and Grainger using only her EIN and business info.

At first, she ordered small: $60 in shipping supplies from Uline. A $40 pack of toner from Quill. Nothing major, but just enough to get her foot in the credit door. She paid them off early, tracked her payments, and followed up with each vendor to confirm that they reported to D&B.

She also applied for her D-U-N-S number and began monitoring her credit profile through Nav. Within 30 days, she started seeing trade lines appear under her business. Her Paydex score—the business version of a FICO—was born.

She was building her business's reputation the same way she had built her own: piece by piece, deal by deal.

The Confidence of Separation

One day, she got a call from a seller looking to unload a duplex. The numbers worked. The area was solid. And for the first time, Maya didn't panic about where she'd get the money.

Instead, she looked at her business checking balance. She looked at her credit lines. She called a DSCR lender she'd been researching and said, "Hi, I'm Maya from Keystone Acquisitions. We're interested in financing a buy-and-hold property under our company."

They didn't ask about her personal credit. They asked about the property's cash flow and her business bank statements. That deal ended up being her first true business-funded purchase.

It cash-flowed $500/month per unit. It appreciated within six months. And it built the confidence she never had when operating from her personal accounts.

Maya's story is real. Not because she's extraordinary—but because she chose to treat her business *like a business.*

You don't need perfect credit. You don't need a huge savings account. You need a strong foundation. An entity. An identity. A structure that lenders can trust and money can flow through.

Like Maya, the first step toward funding your real estate dreams is taking yourself seriously enough to build it right from the ground up.

Chapter 3: Building Your Business Credit Profile from Scratch

Now that your business foundation is solid—your LLC is formed, your business bank account is active, and you've established a professional presence—it's time to **build your actual business credit profile**.

This chapter will guide you step-by-step through:

1. Understanding business credit reporting agencies
2. Establishing your first tradelines
3. Creating a tiered credit-building plan (Tier 1 to Tier 3)
4. Monitoring your business credit
5. Optimizing your profile for faster access to higher limits

Step 1: Know the Business Credit Reporting Agencies

There are **three main credit bureaus** that track and score your business:

- **Dun & Bradstreet (D&B)**: Known for the Paydex score (0–100 scale). A score of 80+ indicates you pay on time or early.
- **Experian Business**: Provides an Intelliscore (1–100). 76+ is low risk.
- **Equifax Small Business**: Tracks business payment history and credit utilization.

Each bureau has different vendors reporting to them, so your strategy should include accounts that report to all three when possible.

Action Step:

- Register for a free Nav account (nav.com) to monitor your business credit scores and track tradeline reporting.

Step 2: Start with Tier 1 Net-30 Vendors

Tier 1 vendors are companies that:

- Approve brand-new businesses without requiring a personal guarantee
- Report to D&B, Experian, or Equifax
- Extend Net-30 terms (payment due in 30 days)

Top Tier 1 Vendors:

1. **Uline.com** – Reports to D&B. Office and shipping supplies.
2. **Quill.com** – Reports to D&B and Experian. Office supplies.
3. **Grainger.com** – Reports to D&B and Equifax. Industrial tools.
4. **Summa Office Supplies** – Reports to Equifax.
5. **Nav.com** – Monthly credit reporting subscription.

How to Apply:

- Use your EIN—not your SSN

- Ensure your business info matches your EIN, bank account, and website
- Start with small orders ($50–$100)
- Pay invoices early to boost your Paydex score

Important Note: Many vendors want to see that your business appears legitimate. If you're denied credit, it's often due to fundability issues—not creditworthiness. Double-check your online presence, business phone, and address consistency.

Step 3: Move to Tier 2 Credit Accounts

Once you have 3–5 positive tradelines reporting for 30–60 days, you can move up to Tier 2 credit accounts. These include more well-known brands and retail business cards that report to bureaus and may offer higher limits.

Tier 2 Accounts to Target:

- **Amazon Business Net-55** – Reports to D&B
- **Staples Business Credit** – Reports to D&B and Equifax
- **Home Depot Commercial Account** – Reports to Experian
- **Office Depot Business Credit** – Reports to D&B

These accounts typically don't require a personal guarantee if your business has tradelines and a strong Paydex score.

Action Step:

- Apply with your EIN
- Be prepared to show proof of revenue (bank statements or invoices)
- Avoid high balances—keep utilization under 30%

Step 4: Graduate to Tier 3 – Revolving Business Credit

After 60–90 days of responsible use, and at least 5–7 tradelines reporting, you can apply for **unsecured revolving credit**—including business credit cards and high-limit lines of credit.

Recommended Business Credit Cards:

- **Chase Ink Business Unlimited** – No annual fee, 0% APR intro
- **Amex Blue Business Plus** – 2x points, 0% APR intro
- **Capital One Spark Business** – Reports to all 3 bureaus

Credit lines and banks to consider:

- **Divvy** – Corporate expense card with credit-building reporting
- **Brex** – Offers high-limit cards with no personal guarantee
- **Fundbox or BlueVine** – Short-term working capital lines

Pro Tip: Some cards report to personal and business bureaus—so read the terms carefully. Focus on cards that report only to commercial bureaus to protect your personal credit.

Step 5: Monitor and Maintain Your Credit Profile

Once you've established credit, it's crucial to monitor and maintain it—just like you would with personal credit.

Here's how:

- Use Nav.com or CreditSignal (by D&B) for score alerts
- Pay all Net-30 and revolving accounts 5–10 days early
- Keep utilization low—under 30% if possible
- Add new accounts every 3–6 months to build depth
- Keep old accounts open to build history

What lenders look for:

- 5+ active tradelines
- Paydex score of 80+
- Low utilization
- At least 6 months of business banking activity
- Consistent EIN and business profile across all platforms

If your business meets these criteria, you'll qualify for higher credit limits, longer terms, and lender trust—opening the door to using this credit for real estate investments.

Common Pitfalls and How to Avoid Them

1. **Applying too soon:** Don't apply for Tier 2 or 3 credit before tradelines are reporting.
2. **Inconsistent business info:** Mismatched addresses, emails, or phone numbers will trigger red flags.
3. **Using personal credit by accident:** Make sure every application is EIN-based and doesn't require a PG (unless absolutely necessary).
4. **Late payments:** One late payment can drop your Paydex score dramatically.
5. **Vendor accounts that don't report:** Not all Net-30 vendors report—always confirm before applying.

Summary Action Plan

Week 1–2:

- Apply to 3–5 Tier 1 Net-30 vendors
- Order small and pay early

- Track payment due dates and receipts

Week 3–4:

- Register for a credit monitoring account on Nav.com
- Apply for your D-U-N-S number if you haven't already

Week 5–8:

- Begin applying for Tier 2 accounts
- Continue paying Tier 1 accounts early

Week 9–12:

- Apply for 1–2 business credit cards (Tier 3)
- Track your Paydex, Intelliscore, and Equifax scores monthly
- Keep all accounts active and utilization low

What's Next?

Now that you know how to build your business credit profile from scratch, you're ready to **access real capital**.

In the next chapter, we'll dive deep into accessing **high-limit business credit cards and lines of credit**—the kind of funding you can use to put down payments on properties, fund rehab work, or close deals that would otherwise require your own savings.

You've built the foundation and the profile—now let's start using it.

The Tradeline Blueprint

Three months had passed since Maya turned her hustle into a legitimate business. Keystone Acquisitions LLC now had a bank account, a business phone, a website, and even a small office suite downtown that she used for meetings and lender mail. But as she stared at her desk that Monday morning, something was still missing.

She needed funding—not promises, not spreadsheets, not another seminar—real capital. And she didn't want to use her personal credit ever again. Her eyes landed on a sticky note she had written in big, bold Sharpie weeks earlier: **"Business credit is the bridge."**

It was time to start building the bridge.

First Tradelines: Playing the Long Game

She started with the simplest, safest step: vendor credit. She remembered from her research that Net-30 accounts were the entry point. Maya pulled up Uline.com and created a business account using her EIN. She ordered $87 worth of shipping materials—bubble wrap, labels, and boxes—items she didn't even need yet, but knew she could store for later deals.

She wasn't sure they would approve her right away, but when the email came back that her order had shipped—and she had 30 days to pay—her heart jumped. It was working.

She did the same with Quill.com and Grainger. Each application took less than 10 minutes. Each used only her business information. Each reported to a credit bureau. Within a few days, she had nearly $400 in vendor credit available—no personal credit check, no personal guarantee.

And she paid every invoice on Day 5.

"I'm not here to float bills," she reminded herself. "I'm here to build a score."

The Waiting Game and the First Score

After 30 days, she signed into Nav.com to check her progress. At first, the reports showed "No data found." Maya was nervous. Had she done something wrong?

A week later, she checked again.

Boom. Three tradelines were now reporting under her EIN. Her D&B file had been activated. Her Paydex score was 80.

She felt like she had cracked a secret code. This was real. This was working.

She even got an email from Nav saying her profile was strong enough to qualify for her first true business credit card.

But Maya wasn't ready to jump too far ahead. She knew there were tiers to this.

Moving to Tier 2: The Retail Jump

At the 60-day mark, Maya had four solid tradelines. She decided to apply for the **Amazon Business Net-55** account. She filled out the form using only her EIN and business bank account. This time, the process felt smoother. Her business had history. It had payment behavior. It had proof.

She was approved instantly.

Next, she tried Staples. This one asked for additional documents, so she uploaded her Articles of Organization and bank statement. Two days later, the approval came through: $1,000 business credit line. Terms: Net-30.

Maya laughed. Just a few months ago, she couldn't get $300 from a lender without a hard pull. Now she was building a credit ecosystem—one that belonged to her business, not her name.

The confidence shift was massive.

She started thinking about how each of these accounts could be used for her next flip or rental. Boxes and office supplies from Uline. Paint and tools from Home Depot. Appliances from Amazon.

She wasn't spending just to spend. She was building access to cash flow tools. She was building credibility.

Tier 3: The Business Credit Card Play

After 90 days, Maya had seven tradelines reporting, an 82 Paydex score, and over $2,000 in vendor credit. She was ready for her first revolving business credit card.

She walked into her bank—Chase—and asked to apply for the **Ink Business Unlimited** card.

The banker pulled up her file and smiled. "Looks like your business has been active for a few months. Good deposits. Clean history. Let's see what we can do."

Maya waited in silence as the banker clicked through the screens. A minute later, he turned the monitor around and said, "You've been approved. $5,000 limit."

She didn't jump up and scream—but inside, she felt like she was flying.

This was the first time she'd been approved for a credit line that wasn't tied to her name or her personal FICO score. No personal guarantee. No personal liability. Just her business and its growing reputation.

She used the card to pay for staging furniture for an upcoming listing. The rewards alone covered her Nav subscription for the next six months.

The First Real Proof

The final confirmation came in the form of an unexpected email from a DSCR lender she'd spoken to months earlier. "Hey Maya, just circling back—do you have updated business credit data or any credit lines open?"

This time, she didn't hesitate.

She sent over her D&B report, her business credit card summary, and screenshots from her vendor accounts. Within 48 hours, the lender pre-approved her for a $150,000 line of credit—secured by a future property, backed by her business income.

She hadn't bought the property yet, but she had built something just as valuable: a real, fundable, scalable business credit profile.

Maya's journey is proof that anyone—from a solo wholesaler to a future property mogul—can create a credit infrastructure that fuels growth.

All it takes is a plan, consistency, and the willingness to play the long game.

In the next chapter, Maya—and you—will learn how to turn those credit profiles into **high-limit cards and powerful lines of credit** that can fund down payments, repairs, and even full real estate purchases.

The funding you want is already available. You just need to qualify the right way—and now you know how.

Chapter 4: Accessing High-Limit Business Credit Cards & Lines of Credit

At this point, you've set up your business the right way, created a fundable profile, and built a solid foundation of reporting trade lines. Now it's time to **move into the funding stage**—specifically, unlocking **high-limit business credit cards** and **lines of credit** that can be used to acquire, renovate, or scale your real estate investments.

This chapter will walk you through:

1. Understanding the power and flexibility of business credit cards
2. How to qualify for high-limit cards and lines of credit
3. How to apply for and use these credit tools properly
4. Smart strategies to avoid high interest and misuse
5. Tips for turning business credit into property funding

Step 1: Why Business Credit Cards and Lines Are Better for Investors

Unlike personal credit cards, **business credit cards:**

- Typically offer higher limits
- Don't affect your personal credit utilization
- Can be used solely for business purposes (tax deductible)
- Offer intro 0% APR offers for 6–18 months

- Are available even for newer businesses with established tradelines

Lines of credit (LOCs), whether revolving or term-based, provide cash you can draw from at any time, pay back, and reuse—ideal for down payments, repairs, or bridge funding between purchases and refinance events.

The key benefit? **These tools give you liquidity without using your own savings.** Used wisely, they become leverage machines for real estate acquisition and cash flow.

Step 2: Qualifying for High-Limit Business Credit Cards

Lenders and banks look at several key factors before issuing high-limit business credit. Here's what they want to see:

Minimum Requirements:

- At least **3–6 months in business**
- 5+ positive tradelines (vendor or retail accounts)
- Consistent revenue through a business bank account
- Strong Paydex or Intelliscore (80+ preferred)
- No red flags on business or personal credit (some lenders may soft pull personal credit to verify)

Bonus Factors:

- Having a relationship with the issuing bank
- Showing monthly cash flow of $3,000–$10,000+
- A business website, matching domain email, and online listings

Pro Tip: Even if a personal guarantee is required, these cards won't report to your personal credit as long as you pay on time—preserving your personal utilization.

Step 3: Best Business Credit Cards for Real Estate Investors

Below are some of the most popular and powerful business credit cards for investors:

1. Chase Ink Business Unlimited

- 0% APR for 12 months
- $750 sign-up bonus
- No annual fee
- Reports to business credit bureaus
- Great for: general spending, repairs, supplies

2. American Express Blue Business Plus

- 0% APR for 12 months
- 2x points on all purchases

- Soft pull application
- Flexible limits that scale with business growth
- Great for: large purchases, recurring costs

3. Capital One Spark 2% Cash Plus

- Unlimited 2% cash back
- May report to personal credit if not managed properly
- Great for: heavy spenders and high-volume operations

4. Divvy Business Card

- Expense tracking + built-in credit reporting
- No personal guarantee
- Works best for structured, recurring spend

Action Step:

- Apply for 1–2 of these cards after 90 days of building tradelines
- Use your EIN, not your SSN
- Start with smaller purchases and pay off before interest accrues

Step 4: Accessing Business Lines of Credit (LOCs)

Business lines of credit are more flexible than term loans or credit cards. They provide a **revolving cash limit**—often between $10,000 and $250,000—that you can use when needed.

Types of LOCs:

- **Traditional LOCs:** Issued by banks like Chase, Wells Fargo, or regional credit unions
- **Fintech LOCs:** Providers like BlueVine, Fundbox, and OnDeck offer faster approvals
- **Credit Union LOCs:** Local banks often offer better terms with lower interest

Requirements:

- 6+ months in business
- $5,000–$10,000+ in monthly revenue
- Business bank account
- Strong credit profile (some will check personal score)

Use Cases for Real Estate:

- Down payments on DSCR loans
- Covering renovation costs
- Short-term holding costs between financing events
- Appraisal fees, inspections, earnest money deposits

Pro Tip: Use lines of credit for cash flow timing—not long-term holding. The faster you repay, the more you can reuse.

Step 5: Avoiding Common Pitfalls

With great credit comes great responsibility. Misusing these tools can damage your business credit or create long-term debt problems.

Avoid These Mistakes:

- **Only making minimum payments:** Interest can balloon fast if you don't pay off in full before the 0% APR ends.
- **Using personal guarantees unnecessarily:** Some cards require it, but many don't—so check terms first.
- **Using business credit for personal expenses:** This can void protection and damage your business identity.
- **Not monitoring your utilization:** Even though cards don't show up on personal credit, utilization still impacts your business credit score.

Smart Practices:

- Pay early and often
- Use cards only for income-generating activities
- Track expenses clearly for tax deductions
- Limit open cards to what you can manage responsibly

Step 6: Turning Credit into Real Estate Capital

Once you've been approved for high-limit cards and credit lines, the question becomes: **How do you turn it into property?**

Real-World Scenarios:

- **$15,000 from a business credit card** covers a down payment on a $100,000 DSCR-financed property
- **$50,000 line of credit** funds a duplex rehab while you wait for refinance or flip sale
- **Multiple cards** (credit stacking) fund multiple acquisitions or fund one deal with diversified risk

Example Strategy:

1. Use $10,000 from Amex for down payment
2. Use $5,000 from Ink for inspection, title, and legal
3. Use LOC to cover 3 months of holding costs
4. Stabilize, refinance, and pay off credit with proceeds

By reinvesting profits and protecting credit utilization, you build a **repeatable funding engine**.

Summary Action Plan

1. Apply for 1–2 business credit cards with 0% intro APR

2. Open a business line of credit if revenue and tradelines allow
3. Only use funds for business-related, income-producing purposes
4. Repay early to maintain high credit scores
5. Track everything for tax and compliance purposes

Coming Up Next…

Now that you've unlocked access to high-limit cards and credit lines, the next step is to **use that funding to actually close on real estate**.

In the next chapter, we'll break down the entire **step-by-step process of funding and closing a real estate deal** using your business credit—from offer to keys.

Get ready. You're no longer just building credit—you're building an empire.

Credit is Capital

The sun hadn't even come up yet when Maya opened her laptop and logged into her business bank account. She was wired—not from caffeine, but from something deeper. The duplex she had her eye on was about to hit the market that morning, and she didn't want to lose it. But the question on her mind wasn't *can I afford it?*

It was *how do I fund it with business credit?*

For the first time in her life, Maya had options.

The Funding Game

Three months earlier, Maya had built her business credit profile with vendor accounts and a few retail tradelines. Today, she was ready to step into the big leagues.

She walked into her local Chase branch with her business checkbook in hand. The same banker who helped her open the account last quarter greeted her with a smile.

"How's Keystone Acquisitions doing?" he asked.

"Growing," Maya said. "I'd like to apply for a business credit card today."

The banker pulled up her file. "Looks like you're pre-qualified for the Chase Ink Business Unlimited. Want to go for that?"

She nodded. Ten minutes later, she walked out with a $7,000 approval—0% APR for 12 months.

It wasn't just the number that made her grin. It was the validation. Her business had earned this. No personal credit pulled. No co-signer. Just proof that she was playing the game right.

The Right Card at the Right Time

Back home, she reviewed her new credit dashboard. Her D&B Paydex score was 84. Experian Intelliscore? A respectable 78. More importantly, her limits were climbing.

In the last 30 days, she'd been approved for:

- The **Chase Ink card** for $7,000
- An **American Express Blue Business Plus** for $10,000
- A **Divvy expense account** that gave her weekly spending power of $2,500

All in her business's name. All built from scratch within six months.

She smiled as she remembered how it all started—with a few boxes from Uline and a pack of toner from Quill. Small moves. Big payoff.

Now it was time to level up again.

The Line of Credit Call

That afternoon, Maya jumped on a call with a lending advisor from BlueVine. They offered business lines of credit up to $250,000 based on banking activity and credit history.

The woman on the line, Amanda, sounded impressed. "Your business banking history is clean. Your revenue is steady. And your credit profile checks out. We can offer you a revolving line of $40,000 to start."

Maya paused. That was more than enough to make her duplex offer competitive.

Amanda continued, "You can draw as needed. Interest only applies to what you use. No early payoff penalties."

That night, Maya signed the offer letter digitally. She now had the power to move quickly on deals—and she didn't have to dip into her personal savings to do it.

She had become the bank.

Making the Offer

With her Chase Ink and BlueVine LOC active, Maya contacted her realtor and sent over the offer package: a full-price offer with a 15-day close, $10,000 earnest money deposit, and proof of funds from her business LOC.

Most investors would take 30–45 days. Maya was ready in 15.

The seller, a retired landlord with too many properties and not enough patience, accepted the offer that same night.

Maya had just secured her second property—without ever touching her personal bank account.

Credit in Action

The next week was a flurry of activity. She used:

- $7,200 from Amex to pay the inspection company, appraisal fee, and light plumbing repairs
- $5,000 from her BlueVine LOC for closing costs and earnest money
- $4,000 from Chase Ink for staging, listing photography, and utility deposits

Each card was paid down the moment rent checks hit her business account. And because they were all 0% APR for the first 12 months, she wasn't paying interest—just using leverage.

Her cash stayed in the bank. Her equity grew with every payment. Her business credit profile got even stronger with each transaction.

She wasn't worried about the balances because she had a plan—and predictable rental income.

Reflection: From Scrappy to Strategic

Sitting at her dining table a week later, Maya opened a spreadsheet. It wasn't full of dreams—it was full of reality:

- Two active properties
- Over $20,000 in usable business credit
- A $40,000 LOC
- Monthly cash flow of $1,700 after expenses

- A credit score on the rise

More importantly, she was in control.

What had once seemed impossible—buying property without savings or W-2 income—was now her business model.

She had built it, brick by brick, line by line.

Maya leaned back and smiled. She wasn't just buying properties anymore. She was building a business that funded itself.

The duplex would cash-flow in 30 days. The credit cards would be paid down in 60. And she already had her eye on a triplex across town.

Credit wasn't a crutch. It was a catapult.

Chapter 5: Business Loans & DSCR Mortgages

Now that you've accessed high-limit business credit cards and lines of credit, it's time to explore **longer-term funding options**—specifically, **business loans** and **DSCR (Debt Service Coverage Ratio) mortgages**. These tools allow you to finance entire properties without relying on personal tax returns or income documentation.

This chapter will guide you through:

1. Understanding business loans vs. DSCR mortgages
2. Preparing your business for loan underwriting
3. How DSCR mortgages work and when to use them
4. Choosing the right lenders
5. A step-by-step walkthrough of applying for each type

Step 1: Understanding Business Loans vs. DSCR Mortgages

These two types of financing serve different purposes in your real estate investing journey:

Business Loans:

- Offered based on your business income and credit profile
- Used for general business purposes, including real estate, renovations, and working capital
- Typically short to mid-term (1–5 years)

- Available from banks, credit unions, and online lenders
- May be unsecured or secured with assets

DSCR Mortgages:

- Designed specifically for real estate investors
- Based on the property's income—not your personal income or credit
- No tax returns or pay stubs required
- Loans range from 15–30 years
- Great for buy-and-hold rental properties

Both types can work together: for example, using a business LOC to fund a down payment, and a DSCR loan to fund the purchase.

Step 2: Preparing Your Business for a Loan

Before applying for either type of loan, your business should meet these criteria:

Basic Requirements:

- Business entity in good standing (LLC or Corp)
- EIN and business checking account
- 6+ months of revenue (for most fintech lenders; banks may require 1+ year)

- Strong business credit profile (Paydex 80+, low credit utilization)
- Clean online presence (website, domain email, Google listing)

Documents You May Need:

- Business bank statements (last 3–6 months)
- Articles of Incorporation/Organization
- Business license (if required by your state/county)
- Proof of business address (utility bill or lease)
- D-U-N-S number and credit report access

Pro Tip: Even if your business is new, strong vendor history and good banking activity can get you approved.

Step 3: Understanding DSCR Mortgages

A **DSCR loan** is a real estate investor's best friend. It allows you to borrow based on the **property's ability to pay for itself**, rather than your W-2 income or tax returns.

How It Works:

- DSCR is calculated by dividing the property's monthly income by its monthly mortgage payment.

- Example: A property rents for $2,000/month and the mortgage is $1,600/month = DSCR of 1.25.
- Most lenders want a DSCR of at least 1.0–1.25 to approve the loan.

Key Features:

- No personal income required
- Can close under your LLC
- 20–30% down payment typically required
- Available for single-family, duplex, triplex, and fourplex properties
- Loan terms of 30 years with interest-only options

Lenders will look at:

- Property rent estimates (based on appraiser or market rents)
- Your business credit profile
- Recent property taxes, insurance estimates, and HOA dues (if applicable)

Step 4: Finding the Right Lenders

Business Loans:

- **Traditional Banks:** Chase, Bank of America, Wells Fargo (slower, but lower rates)
- **Online Lenders:** BlueVine, Fundbox, OnDeck, Kabbage (fast approvals, higher rates)
- **Credit Unions:** Often offer lower fees and better customer service
- **SBA Loans:** 7(a) and 504 programs offer long-term financing, but have stricter requirements

DSCR Mortgage Lenders:

- **Specialized DSCR Lenders:** Kiavi, Visio, Lima One, CoreVest, Velocity Mortgage
- **Mortgage Brokers:** Can connect you with multiple DSCR lenders
- **Hard Money Lenders:** Can offer DSCR-style loans at higher rates, but faster closings

Pro Tip: Avoid lenders who try to pull your personal credit or require tax returns unless you're seeking a conventional loan.

Step 5: How to Apply — Step-by-Step

For a Business Loan or Line of Credit:

1. **Gather Documents:** EIN, Articles of Incorporation, last 3–6

months of business bank statements, business license

2. **Apply Online or In-Person:** Start with the bank you already use
3. **Wait for Underwriting:** May take 1–5 business days
4. **Get Funding:** If approved, funds may be available same-day for fintech lenders or within 1–2 weeks for banks

For a DSCR Loan:

1. **Find a Property:** Property must be income-producing or tenant-ready
2. **Submit Loan Application:** Include property address, rent estimate, and business info
3. **Provide Supporting Documents:** LLC docs, EIN, business bank statements, and property details
4. **Appraisal & Underwriting:** Property is appraised to determine rental value
5. **Close the Deal:** Funds are used for purchase; title and escrow handled by lender

Estimated Timeline:

- Business loan: 1–2 weeks
- DSCR loan: 2–4 weeks (can be faster with the right team)

Common Mistakes to Avoid

1. **Applying too soon:** Build business credit first and ensure revenue is consistent
2. **Mixing personal and business income:** This can disqualify you or cause tax problems
3. **Using personal guarantee unnecessarily:** Some lenders may sneak it in—read the fine print
4. **Choosing the wrong property for DSCR:** If rent is too low, the DSCR won't qualify
5. **Not negotiating rates or terms:** Many lenders will match or beat competing offers if asked

Summary Action Plan

Week 1:

- Evaluate your business credit and revenue history
- Choose which path to pursue first: business loan or DSCR mortgage

Week 2:

- Research lenders and gather necessary documents

- Apply to one business lender and one DSCR lender (if you have a property identified)

Week 3–4:

- Complete underwriting process
- Use approved funding to make offers, pay for inspections, or close deals

What's Next?

You now understand how to secure long-term capital for your real estate business—without touching your personal credit. In the next chapter, we'll walk through a **real deal scenario**: using business credit to fund a real estate purchase from offer to close.

You'll learn how to:

- Combine cards, LOCs, and DSCR funding
- Handle escrow, inspections, and rehab costs
- Protect your credit while scaling your portfolio

Let's put your knowledge into practice—and get the keys to your next property.

The Power of the Property That Pays for Itself

Maya stood across the street from a tan duplex with blue shutters in a quiet Orlando neighborhood. It wasn't glamorous, but it was solid—two units, long-term tenants, low maintenance. Her agent had called the night before and said, "This is the one. You can get it below market, and the numbers work."

She already knew the math: $1,900 rent per side, $3,800 total per month. Property taxes were low. The seller wanted $310,000. Maya checked her phone again—this one had potential.

But this time, she wasn't looking to patch funding together with credit cards or lines of credit. She wanted a 30-year play. A deal she could hold, cash flow, and scale off of. She wanted a **DSCR mortgage**.

The DSCR Discovery

Just three months earlier, Maya hadn't even heard the term "DSCR." Then she found an article explaining that investors could finance properties based on the **income the property generated—not their personal W-2 income**.

It clicked immediately. She didn't have years of tax returns showing a huge salary. But she had a business. She had credit. And she had properties that paid for themselves.

She looked back at her laptop notes:

> "DSCR = Rental Income / PITI (Principal, Interest, Taxes, Insurance)."

As long as that number was over 1.0, she could qualify. The higher, the better.

The duplex she just toured would rent for $3,800. With a 25% down payment and a DSCR mortgage, the projected mortgage was just under $2,600—including taxes and insurance. That gave her a DSCR of **1.46**. Solid.

The Business Loan Warm-Up

Before diving into DSCR, Maya wanted a financial cushion. She logged into her business bank account and uploaded her last 6 months of revenue to BlueVine.

Three days later, she was approved for a $50,000 **business line of credit**.

"Use what you need, when you need it," the approval email said.

That same afternoon, she applied with OnDeck and secured a **$30,000 working capital loan**, fixed at 12 months. The payments were high, but she didn't mind. It was bridge money—flexible, fast, and in her business name only.

These weren't investments. They were leverage. A way to move with speed while her DSCR lender processed the bigger loan.

Getting the DSCR Loan

Maya contacted a broker she found through a real estate investor podcast. His name was Leon, and he specialized in DSCR deals.

She emailed him everything:

- Property address
- LLC docs
- Rent comps
- Articles of Organization
- Business bank statements
- A screenshot of her business credit report

Within hours, he replied: "This will fly. You've got a great DSCR, and the area is landlord-friendly. I'll run it through underwriting."

The next week was a whirlwind. Appraisal. Title search. Rent estimates. Maya paid for it all using her business Amex. Every expense logged under Keystone Acquisitions. Clean. Professional. Separated from her personal life.

The appraisal came back at $325,000. Even better than expected.

Her down payment? $77,500. She pulled $30,000 from the OnDeck loan and the rest from her LOC and cash flow reserves.

The Close

Closing day was quiet. Maya sat across from the title agent, signed the documents, and smiled when she saw the lender's name: Velocity Mortgage, LLC—funded through a 30-year DSCR note with a 7.25% fixed interest rate.

No personal credit pulled. No tax returns. No employment verification. Just her business and the income the property produced.

The duplex was hers.

The tenants stayed. The cash flowed. Maya had done it again.

Scaling the Strategy

After the deal closed, Maya reflected on what had changed.

Just 10 months ago, she was stuck—running everything through her personal name, limited by banks that didn't understand her business.

Now, she had:

- Over $100,000 in business credit
- $80,000 in business loans and LOCs
- Two rental properties—one fully DSCR financed
- A cash-flowing business that was building real estate equity

The real secret? **She had become lendable—on the terms that worked for her.**

A New Kind of Leverage

That night, Maya opened her laptop and reviewed her next steps:

- Reinvest rental profits into paying down her LOC
- Apply for another DSCR mortgage next quarter
- Use her BlueVine LOC to fund the down payment on the next deal

She didn't feel stretched. She felt empowered.

Her goal wasn't to own 100 properties. Her goal was to own 10 free and clear—each one funded creatively, safely, and profitably through her business.

She turned off her laptop and poured a glass of wine. The duplex she'd just bought was already paying its own mortgage.

That was the magic of business credit and DSCR.

Not just getting funded—but **getting free**.

Chapter 6: Funding a Real Estate Purchase Step-by-Step

You've built your business credit, secured high-limit cards and credit lines, and explored loan options like DSCR mortgages. Now it's time to pull everything together and walk through the complete process of **funding a real estate deal using business credit**.

This chapter will guide you step-by-step through:

1. Sourcing the property
2. Structuring the funding
3. Managing the transaction from offer to close
4. Using business credit cards and LOCs for key costs
5. Keeping the purchase separate from your personal finances

Step 1: Sourcing a Deal That Qualifies

The first step is finding a **cash-flowing property** that meets the requirements of business-friendly lenders and DSCR loan programs.

What to look for:

- Single-family, duplex, triplex, or fourplex
- Long-term or short-term rental potential
- Low maintenance and minor repairs
- Strong local rental demand

- Price range that aligns with your available credit and funding options

DSCR Requirement: The property's gross monthly rent must be **equal to or greater** than the monthly mortgage payment (PITI). Aim for a **DSCR of 1.2+** for easier approval.

Pro Tip: Use rent estimation tools like Rentometer or Zillow Rental Manager to calculate local market rents. Then estimate your monthly mortgage using online DSCR calculators.

Step 2: Structuring Your Funding Strategy

Once you've identified a property, build your **funding stack**—a combination of business credit cards, business loans, LOCs, and mortgage financing.

Typical funding stack might include:

- **Business Credit Cards:** Used for inspections, appraisals, title fees, and contractor deposits
- **Business LOC:** Used for earnest money, down payment, or holding costs
- **DSCR Mortgage:** Used to fund 70–80% of the purchase price

Example:

- Purchase price: $250,000

- DSCR loan: $175,000 (70%)
- Down payment: $75,000
- Use $50,000 from business LOC, $10,000 from a working capital loan, and $15,000 from reserves

Pro Tip: Create a spreadsheet or project budget before making an offer so you know exactly where funds are coming from and how repayment will be managed.

Step 3: Making the Offer and Showing Proof of Funds

With your funding plan in place, make a competitive offer. If working with a DSCR lender, they may provide you with a **pre-approval letter**.

What you'll need to include with your offer:

- Pre-approval letter (DSCR lender or business loan provider)
- Proof of funds (screenshot or letter showing credit line availability)
- Earnest money deposit (typically 1–3% of purchase price)

Tip for using business credit: Transfer earnest money from your business LOC to your business bank account and write the check directly from the business. This keeps all expenses separate and shows professionalism to real estate agents and sellers.

Step 4: Managing the Transaction (Inspections, Appraisals, Title)

Once your offer is accepted, the transaction process begins. Here's how to use business credit strategically at each step:

1. Inspection Fees

- Pay using a business credit card for tax deductibility and easy tracking
- Cost: $300–$600 (depending on property type)

2. Appraisal

- DSCR lenders require an appraisal (cost: $450–$800)
- Use business credit card or line of credit to pay and ensure it's expensed to the LLC

3. Title, Insurance, & Closing Costs

- Work with a title company that can invoice your business
- Request a settlement statement early to plan your credit usage
- Use LOC or business card for closing costs not covered by loan

Tip: Ask your DSCR lender if you can roll some closing costs into the loan (many allow this).

Step 5: Closing the Deal Through Your Business

At closing, the property title should be transferred directly to your LLC or Corporation—not your personal name. This reinforces the business structure and ensures full asset separation.

Closing checklist:

- Title transferred to LLC
- Business name and EIN on all closing documents
- Funds wired from business bank account
- Mortgage closed under the LLC (for DSCR)

Important: Ensure all payments made during the deal—from inspections to earnest money—are made using your business credit sources and tracked via your accounting software or business expense tracker.

Step 6: Post-Close Management Using Business Credit

After closing, your business credit can continue working for you:

Use business credit for:

- Minor renovations and repairs
- Furniture, appliances, and landscaping
- Marketing and tenant screening services
- Property management software and automation tools

Set up automatic payments on your business cards and loans to build stronger credit and avoid interest.

Cash Flow Tip: Use rental income to pay off business credit lines as fast as possible, freeing up credit for the next deal.

Common Mistakes to Avoid

1. **Paying for expenses personally** – Co-mingling funds can ruin liability protection
2. **Overleveraging one source** – Diversify between cards, loans, and LOCs to manage risk
3. **Using credit without a cash flow plan** – Don't borrow if the deal won't cover the repayments
4. **Skipping inspections or appraisals** – Business-backed loans still require due diligence
5. **Failing to close in the business name** – This prevents you from using DSCR and asset protection benefits

Action Plan

Pre-Offer:

- Find a property with DSCR of 1.2+
- Build a funding stack using business credit sources

- Get DSCR pre-approval letter and proof of funds

Offer to Close:

- Submit offer with supporting docs
- Pay for inspection and appraisal using business cards
- Manage title and escrow using business LOC or cash
- Close in LLC name with DSCR loan

Post-Close:

- Use business credit to furnish, market, or renovate
- Set repayment strategy using rental income
- Monitor credit utilization and prepare for your next deal

Coming Up Next…

You've just completed a full real estate transaction using business credit and DSCR financing. In the next chapter, we'll talk about **scaling with multiple properties**, how to manage your growing credit stack, and how to get approved for higher limits as your portfolio grows.

Let's keep building.

The Deal That Paid Her Back

Maya stood outside the title company's office with a manila folder tucked under her arm and her laptop bag slung over her shoulder. She checked her phone one last time. Everything was ready—the funds had been wired from her business account, the DSCR lender had cleared the file, and the closing statement had her LLC's name at the top.

This wasn't her first deal—but it was the first she had funded entirely through business credit.

No personal money. No credit pulled. No explaining herself to bankers.

It had taken months of setup, but this moment—this building on the corner with two tenants paying rent—was the payoff.

Finding the Right Property

Two weeks earlier, Maya's agent sent her a pocket listing—a compact fourplex on the edge of a fast-growing college town. Three units were rented. The fourth just needed paint and a new appliance package. Asking price: $415,000. Monthly gross rent potential: $5,000. With some quick math, Maya realized the DSCR would be close to 1.35. Perfect.

But more important than the numbers was this: Maya had everything lined up.

She had already mapped her funding stack.

- $55,000 from her business LOC
- $12,000 on her Chase Ink business card
- $8,000 available on Amex

- DSCR pre-approval from CoreVest for up to 75% LTV

She wasn't just hoping the deal would work. She *knew* it could.

Making the Offer with Business Power

She emailed her agent the offer documents—LLC name, pre-approval letter, and proof of funds. Her earnest money, $5,000, came straight from her BlueVine line of credit into her business checking account. The check was printed under Keystone Acquisitions, LLC.

When the seller's agent called and said, "We have higher offers, but your buyer looks serious," Maya smiled. That's what good preparation does—it builds trust. Her offer was accepted in less than 24 hours.

Managing the Process Like a Business

The next 10 days were packed.

She scheduled the inspection and paid the $525 fee using her Amex Blue Business Plus. The inspector emailed the report to her business domain address, and Maya forwarded it directly to her DSCR lender.

Next came the appraisal, which cost $700 and was invoiced directly to her business. She paid early.

The appraised value came back at $435,000. That meant more equity than expected—and gave her extra negotiating power on the title side.

When the title company asked how she'd be handling closing costs, Maya pulled up her spreadsheet. She had $14,500 allocated from her LOC for closing, and $7,000 budgeted for repairs from her business card.

Everything was documented. Every dollar accounted for.

She didn't just feel like an investor—she felt like a CFO.

Closing in Control

On closing day, she double-checked the closing disclosure. The buyer was listed as "Keystone Acquisitions, LLC." The DSCR lender was CoreVest. The down payment had been wired from her BlueVine LOC. The repairs would be covered on her Ink card.

The tenants didn't even know a change had occurred. Rent would now be paid to a new property manager—contracted through Maya's LLC, paid via her business account, and tracked in her property management software.

She had gone from finding the deal to closing without once dipping into her personal funds or tying her name to the mortgage.

This wasn't just a real estate purchase—it was a credit-funded business acquisition.

After the Close

That weekend, Maya visited the vacant unit. She walked through with a contractor and showed him the list: paint, cabinet touch-up, new fridge and stove. $3,500 all-in.

She handed him a deposit via a business credit card, already labeled in her accounting app.

Two weeks later, a new tenant signed a lease.

The entire property was now cash flowing. The monthly mortgage was $3,150. Gross rent was $5,000. After expenses, she netted $1,200 per month—on a property she didn't personally fund.

And best of all?

She still had over $40,000 in credit availability to use for her next deal.

Reflecting on the Shift

Maya sat at her desk that night and opened her whiteboard app. She wrote in bold:

> "1 Deal Funded Entirely With Business Credit = Infinite Possibility."

She had learned how to use credit not just as a tool—but as a **system.** Business cards for inspections and appraisals. LOC for deposits and closing. DSCR for the big financing. Rental income to pay it all back.

It wasn't magic. It was method.

And she could do it again.

Chapter 7: Scaling with Multiple Properties

You've closed your first deal using business credit. Now the real question becomes: **how do you scale**?

The goal isn't just to use business credit once—it's to build a **repeatable, scalable system** that allows you to acquire multiple properties with minimal personal risk and increasing leverage. In this chapter, we'll cover exactly how to do that.

What You'll Learn in This Chapter:

1. How to build a scalable credit and lending system
2. How to increase your credit limits and access new funding
3. Managing multiple properties with credit protection
4. When and how to refinance or recycle credit
5. Tracking, automation, and reporting for ongoing scaling

Step 1: Build a Replicable Funding Blueprint

Every property you purchase should follow a consistent, proven system. Here's a sample framework that you can copy and adjust:

Your Scalable Property Funding Model:

- **Business Credit Cards** for initial costs (inspection, appraisal, earnest money)

- **Business LOCs or Term Loans** for down payments and closing costs
- **DSCR Mortgages** for 70–80% of the purchase price
- **Rental Income** to repay credit lines and cards
- **Property #1's profits** fund **Property #2's down payment**

By standardizing how you fund each deal, you reduce mental stress and increase your speed. Each property becomes a *project*, funded by tools your business already controls.

Step 2: Increase Credit Limits and Access More Capital

After 3–6 months of on-time payments and solid usage, most lenders will review your profile and offer limit increases. Here's how to approach this strategically:

Business Credit Cards:

- Call issuers and request soft-pull limit increases
- Show strong revenue and payment history
- Keep utilization below 30% for optimal increases

Lines of Credit:

- Ask for a credit limit review every 6–12 months
- Submit updated bank statements and rent roll

- Consider opening additional LOCs with new lenders (while keeping utilization low on existing accounts)

New Lenders to Explore:

- American Express (Business Gold/Plum)
- Truist and PNC for business LOCs
- Lendio, Credibly, and Fundbox for term loans

Pro Tip: Always keep one or two business credit lines completely unused—this gives you instant access to emergency funds and strengthens your DSCR loan applications.

Step 3: Managing Multiple Properties Without Financial Chaos

Once you own more than one property, systems and organization become your secret weapon.

Create the Following Systems:

- A **dedicated business checking account per property** (or at least per entity)
- **Monthly financial dashboard** tracking: income, expenses, debt usage, rent collection, and credit utilization
- **Automated expense tracking** using tools like QuickBooks, Xero, or Wave Accounting

- **A business email alias per property** to manage maintenance requests, tenant communication, and lender updates

Leverage Credit Safely:

- Never use 100% of your credit limits
- Avoid using short-term credit for long-term expenses (i.e., don't furnish rentals on a 12-month loan unless the ROI is immediate)
- Repay high-interest accounts first—even if balances are smaller

Step 4: Recycling Capital with Refinance & Cash-Out Strategies

Once you've stabilized a rental property and proven its income, you can **refinance the property and pay off your business credit**—freeing up your limits to repeat the process.

Types of Refinancing Options:

- **DSCR Refinance**: Based on rental income, no tax returns needed
- **Cash-Out Refinance**: Pull out equity to repay debt or fund next purchase
- **HELOCs on Business-Owned Properties** (available through certain lenders)

Timing Your Refinance:

- Wait 6–12 months after acquisition
- Show clean payment history and full occupancy
- Prepare updated rent rolls, business bank statements, and credit reports

Why This Works: You're essentially using the **BRRRR method** (Buy, Rehab, Rent, Refinance, Repeat), but powered by business credit instead of personal savings.

Step 5: Monitor, Automate, and Prepare to Scale Again

To keep growing, you must monitor both your properties and your credit profiles.

Weekly Tasks:

- Review credit card usage and payments
- Monitor new trade lines and reports via Nav or CreditSignal
- Check rent collection and expense ratios

Monthly Tasks:

- Update your profit and loss sheet per property
- Request credit limit increases from vendors or banks
- Reevaluate your current funding stack and liquidity buffer

Quarterly Tasks:

- Evaluate performance of each property
- Meet with your lender(s) to discuss pre-approvals for the next purchase
- Conduct a soft credit check on your business to ensure no negative marks

Tools to Use:

- **Nav.com** – for credit monitoring
- **QuickBooks or Wave** – for cash flow tracking
- **Stessa or Rentec Direct** – for property-specific accounting
- **Gusto or Bench** – for business financial reporting and payroll (if applicable)

Common Mistakes to Avoid While Scaling

1. **Over-leveraging credit without rental coverage**
2. **Ignoring credit utilization and score drops**
3. **Using personal funds out of habit or emotion**
4. **Closing credit accounts after paying them off** – this can hurt your business credit
5. **Buying properties too quickly without stabilizing previous ones**

Remember: speed is not the goal—**sustainability and predictability are**.

Summary Action Plan

Immediately:

- Standardize your property funding model
- Create a checklist for each new acquisition
- Request credit limit increases where eligible

Next 30 Days:

- Open a new business LOC or card if needed
- Systematize tracking of each property's cash flow and expenses
- Analyze at least one refinance opportunity

Next 60–90 Days:

- Refinance or pay down current credit
- Begin the acquisition process for your next deal
- Track results and repeat your proven system

Coming Up Next…

You now have the framework to scale your real estate business using business credit. In the next chapter, we'll go into **avoiding legal,**

financial, and credit-related mistakes that can ruin your progress—and show you how to protect your business and personal assets while continuing to grow.

Let's keep building smart, sustainable wealth.

One Property at a Time, Forever

Maya's phone buzzed with a calendar reminder: "Property #3 rent due." She smiled—not because she needed the reminder, but because it was the third property she had acquired in under a year. And this time, she didn't feel overwhelmed.

She felt organized. She felt powerful.

Because Maya had figured out something most investors miss—**it wasn't about owning the most properties, it was about building the most sustainable system**.

The Turning Point

It started two months ago, right after the closing on her DSCR-financed fourplex. The success of that deal gave her momentum, but it also came with new responsibility—four units, eight tenants, and multiple payment due dates.

She realized if she wanted to keep going, she needed a **scaling plan**—something repeatable, organized, and efficient.

She opened her laptop and created a simple note titled: **"Maya's Repeatable Funding System"**

At the top, she listed her resources:

- Two business credit cards with $10,000+ limits
- A $50,000 business line of credit
- A DSCR lender who trusted her
- Two rental properties with full occupancy
- One strong business credit profile

The question became: *How do I use this same model again and again?*

A Repeatable Process

The first step was documenting every phase of her previous deal: sourcing, funding, closing, and management. She broke it down into stages and listed exactly which tools she used for what:

- **Chase Ink card** for inspections and appraisals
- **Amex Blue** for renovations and contractor deposits
- **BlueVine LOC** for down payments and closing costs
- **DSCR mortgage** for 75% LTV funding
- **Rental income** to repay credit lines within 90 days

It was like solving her own puzzle, and the pieces fit perfectly.

She turned it into a template. The next deal would follow this path—and so would every one after.

Growing Smarter, Not Faster

As new deals came in, Maya made a critical decision: she would not pursue multiple closings at once. Instead, she would use a **"one-in-one-out" model**.

She'd fund and stabilize one property, **then refinance or repay**, and only then would she begin the next acquisition.

This rhythm helped her avoid burnout. And it made her smarter. With each property, she learned what worked, what didn't, and how to improve.

Her second duplex? Funded in 30 days using a mix of a $15,000 business credit card draw and a DSCR loan. After 90 days of full occupancy, she refinanced, paid off the card, and restored her credit capacity.

Three months later, she was ready for deal number four.

Tools, Teams, and Automation

By the time she owned three properties, Maya knew she needed to build systems. She signed up for **Stessa** to track rental income and expenses. She opened **QuickBooks Online** to link her business cards and automate bookkeeping.

Each property had its own nickname and bank account:

- "Lincoln" – her first single-family rental
- "Palms" – the fourplex with the best curb appeal
- "Willow" – her newest duplex with short-term rental potential

She even created a new business email alias for each property—willow@keystoneacquisitions.com—for maintenance requests and tenant communication.

Now, when a rent payment came in or a contractor needed to be paid, it was handled **by the system—not by Maya's memory**.

The Power of Credit Discipline

Maya was strict with her credit. She kept all utilization under 30%. She paid off balances twice a month. She rotated use across cards to keep them active and reporting.

Every quarter, she scheduled a 30-minute meeting with herself to request credit line increases, review property cash flow, and research new lenders.

Because of this discipline, her credit limits grew:

- Chase Ink: $10,000 → $18,000
- Amex Blue: $12,000 → $20,000
- BlueVine LOC: $50,000 → $75,000

She wasn't just growing a portfolio. She was growing her *credit ceiling*—the ability to fund bigger deals, faster, with less friction.

Scaling with Control

A year ago, Maya would've been anxious with three closings, thousands in monthly expenses, and multiple tenants calling. Now, she was at peace. Her business ran on structure. Her acquisitions ran on repeat.

She didn't rush. She didn't panic. She didn't overextend.

Each deal had a purpose. Each credit card swipe had a repayment plan.

By creating a process, Maya had done what most investors never do: **she had scaled without stress**.

The Vision Ahead

That night, she opened her notebook and wrote three goals:

1. Own 10 income-generating properties
2. Keep credit utilization below 20%
3. Have every property pay for the next one

Beneath it, she added a fourth:

> "Live off rental income. Let credit build the future."

Maya had started her journey with a single Uline account and a dream. Now, she owned three properties, had over $100,000 in available credit, and a growing list of pre-approved deals.

But more importantly, she had **a system that could scale forever**.

Chapter 8: Avoiding Common Mistakes and Legal Issues

As your business credit and real estate portfolio grow, so do the risks. While business credit offers power and flexibility, improper use or mismanagement can damage your credit profile, expose you to legal risk, or even jeopardize your business.

This chapter will walk you through:

1. The most common mistakes made by new investors using business credit
2. Legal risks you must avoid when using credit for real estate
3. Properly separating business and personal finances
4. Staying compliant with lenders, the IRS, and state regulations
5. Protecting your credit and reputation as you grow

Step 1: Recognize the Most Common Credit Mistakes

Let's start with the top business credit missteps that slow down—or ruin—growth:

1. Co-mingling business and personal funds

- Using personal cards for business expenses or vice versa can lead to legal liability and accounting issues
- Tip: Always use a business credit card and checking account, even for small purchases

2. Applying for credit too soon or too often

- Applying before your business is ready (no tradelines, low revenue, inconsistent data) often leads to denials
- Too many applications in a short period can trigger red flags and soft-pull denials

3. Over-leveraging business credit

- Just because you're approved for $100K doesn't mean you should use it all
- Use only what is needed for income-producing activity (like acquiring or improving real estate)

4. Failing to pay on time or not tracking due dates

- One late payment can hurt your business credit score for months
- Tip: Set up autopay or schedule bi-weekly checks of your accounts

5. Closing business credit accounts

- Closing a card after paying it off can hurt your business credit age and limit profile
- Keep accounts open and active with small monthly charges

Step 2: Avoid Legal Pitfalls with Proper Structuring

Many new investors make the mistake of treating their LLC like a nameplate instead of a legal entity. If your business isn't properly structured, you risk **piercing the corporate veil**—which means creditors or courts can come after you personally.

Avoid These Legal Pitfalls:

- Failing to separate business and personal assets
- Signing business credit agreements with personal guarantees (when not needed)
- Using your home address for business purposes without protection
- Not renewing your LLC or corporate registration annually
- Paying contractors or vendors from personal accounts for property expenses

Pro Tip: Keep all documentation organized. Lenders, auditors, and legal counsel may request:

- LLC or corporate formation docs
- Articles of Incorporation
- Business bank statements
- Business lease (if using a virtual or physical office)
- Operating agreement (especially if you have partners)

Step 3: Separate Business and Personal Finances—For Real

Separation isn't just for safety—it's for growth. Lenders are more likely to approve you when your business looks *legitimate, profitable, and independent.*

Here's how to separate the right way:

- Use your **EIN** for all credit and banking applications
- Open and maintain a **business checking account** (never use a personal one)
- Pay all business expenses using your **business cards and LOCs**
- Receive all rental income into your business account
- Pay yourself with a salary or owner's draw (instead of random transfers)

Accounting Best Practices:

- Use **QuickBooks**, **Wave**, or **Bench** to categorize income and expenses
- Hire a CPA familiar with real estate and small business credit
- Maintain clear records for all income, credit use, and property costs

Step 4: Stay Compliant with Lenders, the IRS, and State Agencies

Business credit is not a loophole—it's a professional tool. To keep it working in your favor, make sure your business is compliant at all times.

IRS Requirements:

- File taxes annually using your EIN and business structure (Schedule C, 1120S, etc.)
- Report all income, including rent, loan proceeds, and interest earned
- Maintain receipts and proof of credit card expenses for deductions

State Requirements:

- Renew your LLC or corporate status annually with your state
- Keep your registered agent and address current
- File annual reports or pay business privilege taxes (in some states)

Lender Compliance:

- Understand your loan covenants (minimum DSCR, occupancy rate, insurance)
- Respond to documentation requests in a timely fashion
- Avoid misrepresentation (e.g., saying a property is fully leased when it's not)

Step 5: Protect Your Business Credit and Reputation

Your business credit profile is one of your most valuable assets. Guard it like your personal credit score—or even more carefully.

How to Protect Your Profile:

- Monitor reports monthly using **Nav**, **CreditSignal**, or **Equifax Business**
- Use no more than 30% of available credit across all accounts
- Request removal of inaccurate negative items with dispute letters
- Avoid hard inquiries by asking lenders for soft pull options or pre-approval
- Build relationships with your lenders—relationship banking leads to better terms and higher limits

Reputation Tip: When working with DSCR lenders, brokers, contractors, or partners—your responsiveness, professionalism, and organization all matter. Keep clean records, communicate clearly, and follow through.

Summary: Action Checklist to Stay Safe

Daily/Weekly:

- Use only business accounts for real estate-related purchases

- Monitor credit card due dates
- Categorize new expenses in your accounting software

Monthly:

- Review credit reports and utilization
- Reconcile bank and credit card statements
- Evaluate whether any credit lines need to be repaid or increased

Quarterly:

- Review legal compliance (LLC renewal, filings)
- Meet with CPA or bookkeeper to review tax planning
- Submit updated income docs to lenders if needed

Annually:

- File taxes with all credit-related deductions properly documented
- Review and update business registration, website, licenses
- Evaluate your entire credit stack for optimization or consolidation

Coming Up Next…

Now that you know how to avoid costly credit and legal mistakes, you're ready for the next stage: designing your **long-term exit strategy** and building generational wealth. In the next chapter, we'll dive into refinancing, equity plays, and what to do once you've built your portfolio using business credit.

Let's start planning your freedom.

Chapter 9: Exit Strategies and Building Long-Term Wealth

Once you've used business credit to acquire and stabilize multiple properties, the next phase isn't just maintaining what you've built—it's using smart exit strategies to multiply your wealth.

In this chapter, we'll cover:

1. Why exit strategies matter—even if you never plan to sell
2. Refinancing and equity harvesting
3. Selling with maximum profit and tax efficiency
4. Leveraging your portfolio for wealth and credit expansion
5. Building a long-term plan for financial independence

Step 1: Understand Why Exit Strategies Are Essential

An **exit strategy** isn't just about selling—it's about knowing when, why, and how to reposition your capital for the next opportunity.

Without a clear exit plan:

- You may miss out on market timing opportunities
- You might overleverage or underutilize your equity
- Your credit lines may stay tied up longer than necessary
- You could face high taxes, lost profits, or poor cash flow

Common Real Estate Exit Strategies:

- **Refinance and hold** (long-term cash flow, equity harvesting)
- **Sell for profit** (at market peak or post-renovation)
- **Cash-out refinance** (extract equity for new deals)
- **1031 exchange** (defer taxes by trading up)
- **Seller financing or lease options** (creative exit structures)

Step 2: Refinance to Free Up Credit and Expand

One of the most powerful exit moves is **refinancing your real estate through a DSCR lender** or business-friendly bank to pay off initial credit lines and reposition the property for the long-term.

How to Structure a Refinance:

- Wait 6–12 months post-acquisition to show property income and stability
- Work with your existing DSCR lender or shop new ones
- Request a refinance quote based on current value and rental income
- Use proceeds to pay off business LOCs or credit cards used during acquisition

Benefits of Refinancing:

- Pay off higher-interest debt

- Free up credit for future deals
- Lock in long-term fixed-rate debt
- Potentially lower monthly payments
- Turn short-term leverage into long-term ownership

Pro Tip: Request cash-out refinance terms if the property has appreciated or been improved. Some lenders allow 75–80% LTV based on the new appraised value.

Step 3: Sell Strategically for Maximum ROI

Even if your plan is to build a rental empire, selling a property can sometimes be the best exit—especially if:

- The property has appreciated rapidly
- Market demand is high
- You want to reposition capital into a larger or more profitable asset

Steps for a Profitable Sale:

1. **Stabilize property**: Ensure occupancy, clean records, and curb appeal
2. **List with investor-savvy agents**: Especially those who understand cap rates and DSCR

3. **Minimize taxes**: Use a 1031 exchange to defer capital gains
4. **Time the market**: Sell during peak seasons or rising interest rate periods
5. **Show off cash flow**: Investors buy cash flow, not charm—highlight NOI and rent rolls

Example Exit: You purchase a fourplex using $30,000 in business credit and a DSCR mortgage. Two years later, you sell it for a $75,000 profit and pay off all business credit, then roll the gains into a larger 6-unit property.

Step 4: Leverage Your Portfolio to Multiply Credit and Wealth

The more properties you own and stabilize, the more powerful your financial profile becomes—not just in terms of cash flow, but **business credibility and lendability**.

Here's how to use that leverage:

- Use rental income history and DSCR strength to qualify for larger loans
- Request higher credit card and LOC limits based on business performance
- Create a portfolio summary to show banks and private lenders

- Use refinanced equity to fund down payments without personal savings
- Partner or syndicate deals using your established track record

Bonus Strategy: Open a holding company (e.g., Keystone Holdings, LLC) to own multiple property LLCs. This makes it easier to consolidate accounting, secure portfolio-level credit, and eventually sell or refinance multiple assets under one umbrella.

Step 5: Build a Long-Term Wealth Plan with Business Credit

You didn't start this journey just to get one or two deals done. You're building a life of freedom, control, and passive income. The final step is **turning this system into a long-term wealth machine**.

Design Your Plan:

- Determine how many doors you want to own
- Decide whether to hold forever, refinance in phases, or sell at milestones
- Use business credit not just for purchases—but for tax strategy, maintenance, marketing, and expansion
- Set annual financial goals: revenue, equity, and debt limits
- Build a team: CPA, attorney, property manager, bookkeeper, credit strategist

Legacy Building Tip: Real wealth isn't just about what you earn—it's about what you **own**, what you can **pass on**, and how you **structure it to last**.

Start small, scale responsibly, and reinvest intelligently. In 5–10 years, your real estate holdings and business credit profile can become a self-sustaining empire.

Summary Action Plan

Short-Term (0–6 months):

- Refinance one property to repay credit
- List one property for strategic sale if market timing is optimal
- Build a portfolio overview document to present to lenders

Mid-Term (6–12 months):

- Apply for higher credit limits using updated financials
- Set a goal for number of new doors to acquire
- Plan a 1031 exchange for a cash-out exit

Long-Term (1–3 years):

- Open a holding company for asset protection and tax savings
- Scale to 5–10 stabilized properties
- Build passive income to replace active work

- Consider estate planning, trusts, or private lending

Coming Up Next…

In the final chapter, we'll help you map out a **90-day action plan** that ties everything together—from building your foundation to closing your first (or next) business-credit-backed real estate deal.

Let's turn your knowledge into motion and your credit into capital.

Chapter 10: Your 90-Day Action Plan

You now have the complete blueprint for leveraging business credit to fund real estate deals—from structuring your business and building credit to acquiring and scaling properties. But none of it matters without execution.

This chapter gives you a clear, practical **90-day roadmap** to take action. Whether you're starting from scratch or optimizing an existing business, this plan helps you move forward with speed and clarity—using the exact steps outlined throughout this book.

What You'll Accomplish in 90 Days:

- Build or optimize your fundable business structure
- Establish strong business credit with vendor and tradeline accounts
- Get approved for business credit cards and lines of credit
- Fund and close your first—or next—real estate deal
- Prepare to scale with confidence and consistency

Phase 1: Week 1–4 | Foundation Building

Primary Goal: Set up your business entity and fundability profile.

Tasks:

1. **Form a Legal Entity**
    - Register your LLC or corporation with your state
    - Obtain your EIN from the IRS
    - Apply for a business license if required in your locality
2. **Establish a Professional Business Presence**
    - Set up a dedicated business phone number
    - Purchase a professional domain and email (e.g., info@yourcompany.com)
    - Create a simple, clean website outlining your services and mission
    - List your business on Google, Yelp, and local directories
3. **Open Financial Accounts**
    - Business checking account with a bank that supports commercial credit
    - Consider digital banks that integrate with credit apps (e.g., BlueVine, Mercury)
    - Open a basic accounting software account (QuickBooks, Wave, Xero)
4. **Apply for a D-U-N-S Number**

- Go to dnb.com and apply for your free number
- Ensure your business info is 100% consistent across all registrations

Outcome by Week 4:

- Fully formed and fundable business entity
- Online presence established
- Financial infrastructure ready for credit applications

Phase 2: Week 5–8 | Credit Building and Access

Primary Goal: Build credit history and secure business credit products.

Tasks:

1. **Apply for Tier 1 Net-30 Vendor Accounts**
   - Choose 3–5 vendors (Uline, Quill, Grainger, Summa, Nav)
   - Place small orders ($50–$100) and pay within 10–15 days
   - Track due dates and follow up to confirm reporting
2. **Set Up Business Credit Monitoring**
   - Use Nav.com or CreditSignal for weekly score updates

  - Track Paydex (D&B), Intelliscore (Experian), and Equifax Business reports

3. **Apply for Business Credit Cards**
   - Use your EIN for application (avoid PG if possible)
   - Target cards with 0% APR for 6–12 months
   - Examples: Chase Ink, Amex Blue Business Plus, Capital One Spark
4. **Apply for a Business Line of Credit (LOC)**
   - Submit financials (3–6 months bank statements)
   - Start with online lenders like BlueVine or Fundbox for faster approval

Outcome by Week 8:

- 3–5 trade lines reporting
- Business credit scores active
- $5,000–$50,000 in total business credit access

Phase 3: Week 9–12 | Deal Execution

Primary Goal: Acquire or fund your first property using business credit.

Tasks:

1. **Find a DSCR-Qualifying Property**
    - Use real estate agents, wholesalers, or MLS
    - Target properties with strong rental income and light rehab needs
    - Calculate DSCR using projected rent / PITI (aim for DSCR 1.2+)
2. **Get Pre-Approved for a DSCR Loan**
    - Choose a lender (CoreVest, Kiavi, Lima One, Visio, etc.)
    - Submit property details, rent estimates, and business docs
    - Obtain a conditional approval letter
3. **Fund Deal Costs with Business Credit**
    - Use cards for inspection, appraisal, and earnest money
    - Use LOC or working capital loan for down payment and closing costs
    - Track all expenses through your business accounts
4. **Close in Your LLC's Name**
    - Title, insurance, and deed under your business

    - Secure the property with long-term DSCR financing
    - Begin tenant placement or management onboarding

Outcome by Week 12:

- First business credit–backed deal completed
- Systems in place to manage cash flow and expenses
- Credit lines intact and ready to recycle

Bonus: Optimization Tasks (Ongoing)

To further accelerate results:

- Request credit limit increases every 90–120 days
- Apply for additional vendor accounts for diversity
- Refinance stabilized property to pay off initial credit
- Set up automated payments and tracking for all cards
- Create a repeatable checklist for your next deal

Avoid These Common 90-Day Pitfalls

- **Skipping steps:** Don't rush to funding without a complete foundation
- **Mixing personal funds:** Keep all business expenses separate

- **Overapplying:** Too many credit applications early on can hurt approval odds
- **Failing to follow up:** Confirm vendors are reporting and credit scores are updating

Your First Milestone

At the end of these 90 days, you should:

- Own a fully funded real estate deal through your business
- Have over $20,000–$100,000 in available business credit
- Be positioned to scale into your second deal within 30–60 days
- Have the confidence and knowledge to repeat this process

Final Thoughts

This action plan isn't theory—it's a playbook you can use for the rest of your investing career. Whether you buy one property a year or ten, the principles don't change. Structure smart. Build business credit. Leverage it wisely. Reinvest profit. Protect your assets.

You now have the keys. The only thing left to do is drive.

The Next 90 Days

Maya opened her notebook and turned to a fresh page. At the top, she wrote in bold: **"90-Day Plan: From Property #3 to Financial Freedom."**

She took a breath and smiled. It was the first time in years that she felt totally in control—not just of her money, but her direction.

She had used business credit to fund three properties in less than a year. No personal debt. No stress. Just systems, strategy, and one bold decision after another.

But now, it was time to go from *capable* to *unstoppable*. Time to turn momentum into mastery.

Week 1–4: Starting Again, Smarter

Maya had already created her first LLC. But this time, she wasn't setting up just a company—she was building a **real estate group**. A brand. A system.

She formed a new LLC: **Keystone Equity Holdings, LLC**. This would be her parent company. Underneath it, she planned to create a new LLC for each new property or cluster of rentals.

She registered it with the state. Got her EIN from the IRS. Set up a virtual office address in downtown Orlando. She opened a new bank account. Ordered new business cards. Her website was live within a week.

She even went a step further: she created a branded Google Business profile, set up a professional email domain, and scheduled a monthly newsletter to document her journey.

It wasn't just about making deals anymore. It was about **building a business** that could run without her.

Week 5–8: Fueling the Fire

Next came credit. Maya already had some powerful tools: her Chase Ink, Amex Blue, and a $75,000 BlueVine line of credit.

But she wasn't done.

She logged into Uline, Quill, and Grainger—her old Net-30 accounts—and placed small orders to keep the trade lines active.

Then she applied for three new vendor accounts using her new LLC.

Within two weeks, they were approved. Reporting would begin shortly. She was already rebuilding credit on a brand-new entity.

Her monitoring dashboard showed new Paydex activity. She knew it wouldn't be long before she could request larger limits.

Then came her newest tool: a **Fundbox working capital line**—approved for $20,000 within 48 hours based on her new LLC's EIN and revenue projections.

By the end of week eight, Maya had over **$130,000 in available business credit** across two entities. She was playing chess while everyone else played checkers.

Week 9–12: Closing Property #4

The email came from her broker on a rainy Monday morning:

> "Small multifamily just hit the market. Seller wants quick close. Three units, all occupied, clean inspection history. Asking $320K."

Maya ran the numbers.

Rental income: $3,200/month Estimated PITI: $2,150 DSCR: 1.49

Perfect.

She emailed CoreVest and requested a new DSCR pre-approval using her new LLC. Within two days, they issued a letter.

She wired $6,000 in earnest money from her new Fundbox line. Paid the inspection fee on her Amex. Covered the appraisal with her Chase Ink.

The closing costs and down payment—$70,000—were structured from a mix of business LOCs and reserves from her previous refinanced property.

When she closed 22 days later, it was **entirely funded by business credit and previous real estate income.**

Not one personal dollar touched the transaction.

Building Her Empire—One Quarter at a Time

By day 90, Maya had:

- A holding company
- Two active LLCs with separate banking and credit
- Four properties cash flowing
- Over $130K in business credit
- A checklist and calendar she followed like gospel

But it wasn't just about what she owned. It was about what she now *expected* of herself.

Every Friday, she reviewed her weekly numbers. Every month, she checked credit utilization and rent roll.

Every quarter, she requested credit limit increases, applied for a new line of credit, and evaluated refinance or 1031 options.

She had built a flywheel. Her business credit opened doors. Her rentals repaid the credit. Her credit grew with her cash flow. And her wealth scaled while she worked less.

The Bigger Vision

That night, Maya sat by her window as the Florida rain came down in slow waves. She flipped back to the first page of her old notebook—the one where she had scribbled goals she wasn't even sure were possible.

- Replace active income with passive? Done.
- Own five doors? She had eight.
- Build a business backed by credit, not cash? Fully operational.

But now, her vision had grown.

She wasn't just building wealth for herself. She was building something that her future family, her community, and maybe even students she hadn't met yet—could learn from.

She wrote one final line on the last page of the notebook:

> "The next 90 days won't change everything. But they will change me."

And with that, Maya closed the book, turned off the light, and rested—knowing the next chapter of her business and her life was just beginning.

VOLUME 8: BUSINESS CREDIT ECOSYSTEM

Welcome to Book Eight in the *Credit to Capital* series. If you've made it this far, you're not just interested in improving your credit—you're ready to master it. This book is where everything comes together. The knowledge you've gained from previous books is about to evolve into a real-world system for creating wealth, security, and true financial independence. Whether you're an entrepreneur, a side hustler, a real estate investor, or someone just trying to get ahead, this book is your blueprint for turning credit into capital that works for you.

Credit is not just a score. It's not just a card in your wallet. It's a form of leverage—a silent partner in every financial decision you make. When used correctly, credit unlocks time, opportunity, and exponential growth. But to get there, you need more than tips and tricks. You need a strategy. And that's exactly what this book will deliver. From stacking business credit lines to leveraging high-limit vendor accounts, you'll learn how to organize, apply, and multiply credit into actual cash flow.

I've seen too many people waste years chasing savings, hustling endlessly, or trying to bootstrap every idea without any financial backing. What they didn't realize is that the capital they needed was already available to them—it just wasn't visible. Why? Because no one taught them how to access it. That changes now. I'm going to teach you how to access credit the right way, use it to fund real opportunities, and protect yourself from unnecessary risk.

You'll hear detailed strategies and walkthroughs on building multi-tiered business credit profiles, securing funding without a personal guarantee, and negotiating with lenders and vendors like a pro. We'll go deep into the psychology of underwriters, the structure of credit scoring systems, and the timing it takes to execute each move successfully. No fluff. No theory. Just proven steps.

Throughout this book, I'll also share personal experiences—mistakes I made, lessons I learned, and the exact moves that helped me go from having $36 in my bank account to building a multi-six-figure business portfolio. These aren't just financial wins. These are freedom wins. I've helped single moms become property investors, immigrants build successful companies, and college dropouts get access to capital that changed their lives. You don't need a degree, rich parents, or perfect credit to do this. You need the right information and the willingness to act.

By the end of this book, you will understand how to build credit that works for you—not against you. You will know how to separate personal and business credit, how to legally maximize funding, and how to create a system that continues to build capital even while you sleep.

This book is not just a continuation—it's an acceleration. If you're ready to turn potential into performance and ideas into income, let's begin.

Chapter 1: Unlocking the Hidden Power of Business Credit

Most people think credit is about borrowing money you don't have. But true financial builders know that credit—especially business credit—is about unlocking resources that multiply what you already have. In this chapter, we'll strip away the confusion around business credit and reveal how to start building it from the ground up—even if your personal credit isn't perfect.

The first thing you need to understand is that business credit is not tied to your Social Security number. It's tied to your business identity—your EIN, your DUNS number, and the profile your business builds over time. This separation allows you to build a financial engine that can access capital, buy assets, and scale without putting your personal credit or assets on the line. But just like a child doesn't go from crawling to sprinting in one day, your business credit profile needs time, attention, and the right steps in the right order.

Start by legitimizing your business. That means forming an LLC or corporation, getting a professional website and business email, and making sure your business phone number, address, and details are consistent across every platform. This step alone can make or break your ability to get approved for basic net-30 vendor accounts. Banks and credit issuers will check your credibility—online and offline. If your business looks sloppy or inconsistent, you're signaling risk.

Once your business foundation is solid, it's time to start reporting credit activity. This is where net-30 accounts come in. These are vendors that allow you to purchase supplies and pay in 30 days—building a credit history with Dun & Bradstreet and other reporting agencies. Good examples include Uline, Quill, Summa Office Supplies, and Strategic Network Solutions. But here's the trick—don't just open accounts. Use them. Order something small and pay it off early. This activity creates a payment history that opens doors to bigger lines later.

After three to five vendors report positively for at least two billing cycles, you'll begin to see your Paydex score rise. A Paydex score of 80 means you're paying early or on time—a green light for lenders. This is the stage where you can start applying for store credit cards from companies like Lowe's, Home Depot, Staples, or Amazon—in your business name only. Again, use them smartly. Buy only what you need, and always pay before the due date. These accounts will boost your business credit file dramatically.

With positive activity and a few months of history, the next level becomes available—revolving credit cards and cash credit. Cards like the Chase Ink Business, Amex Blue Business Plus, or Capital One Spark start opening up, many with no personal guarantee if your profile is strong enough. These are powerful tools. Used properly, they provide zero percent introductory rates, huge limits, and even reward points that reduce your business costs.

Now here's where it gets interesting. As your business matures, you can start applying for loans, lines of credit, and vehicle or equipment financing—all in your business name. But remember: The key to all of this is **strategy**. Don't apply blindly. Don't stack credit just to stack it. Plan your next 12 months of expenses. Know what you want to fund—whether it's inventory, marketing, real estate, or digital product development. Then align your credit lines to support those goals.

And never forget the value of relationships. Visit local banks and credit unions. Build rapport with small business bankers. Ask them what they're looking for in a strong business credit file. Many times, these conversations unlock insider knowledge you'll never find online. Once they trust you and see your profile, they'll often guide you to the right product—even helping push your application through the approval process.

In the next chapter, we'll explore how to **stack** this credit, combining funding sources for maximum power while minimizing your risk. You'll learn how to time your applications, layer approvals, and create a waterfall strategy that floods your business with capital at exactly the right moment. But remember—it all starts with credibility, structure, and intention. Build smart now, and you'll have the financial freedom to execute any plan you dream up.

Unlocking the Hidden Power of Business Credit

Jasmine sat in her car outside the bank, gripping the steering wheel tightly. She had just walked out of her third loan appointment in two months, and once again, the answer had been no. "You've got great ideas," the banker had said. "But without collateral or stronger personal credit, we can't approve you." Jasmine was frustrated—not because she was unqualified, but because she knew there had to be another way. Her online boutique was picking up traction, and she was turning a small profit, but she needed capital to expand. Inventory, marketing, shipping software—it all cost money. And she had none.

That evening, she vented to her friend Marcus, a real estate investor who had built his business from nothing. "You ever feel like no matter how hard you work, the door stays closed?" she asked. Marcus smiled. "You're knocking on the wrong door," he said. "You're asking for money as a person when you should be asking as a business. Jasmine, have you built your business credit yet?" She stared at him blankly. "Business credit? I thought that was for huge companies." He shook his head. "That's the biggest myth out there. I started with zero. Let me show you something."

Over the next hour, Marcus walked her through the exact steps he had taken. He told her about how he set up his LLC, got an EIN, and registered for a DUNS number—all free. He explained how important it was to have a real business phone number, not a personal cell. A professional email, not Gmail. A business address, even if it was virtual. "They check everything," he said. "If your business looks legit, they'll start trusting it. It's just like building personal credit—but smarter."

Inspired, Jasmine went home and restructured everything. She updated her website, got her DUNS number, and applied for her first net-30 accounts. She ordered basic packaging supplies from Uline and paper goods from Quill. When the invoices came in, she paid them early—every time. "You're building history," Marcus had told her. "Early payments make you golden." Within 60 days, two accounts started reporting to Dun & Bradstreet. Her Paydex score popped up. It wasn't perfect yet—but it was active. That was everything.

Three months later, Jasmine got approved for her first business credit card: a $2,500 limit from Office Depot. She almost cried when the email came through. "This is real," she whispered to herself. "This is finally happening." She bought a label printer, shipping supplies, and marketing materials. She sold more. Reinvested. Then came her approval for a Sam's Club card. Then an Amazon business line. Then, the big one—a Chase Ink Business card with a $15,000 limit and zero percent APR for 12 months. It felt like a dream.

But she didn't spend recklessly. She followed the plan. She used each card for a specific purpose—inventory, shipping, ad spend. She tracked every dollar. She stacked approvals by waiting 30 days between applications, letting each new line boost her score and her fundability. Her confidence grew with every approval. By month eight, she wasn't chasing banks anymore. They were reaching out to her. Credit unions, fintech lenders, even local banks offering business lines of credit.

One day, she went back to the bank that had first denied her. This time, she brought her business credit report, revenue history, and credit card approvals. The same banker who had once told her no leaned back in his chair and smiled. "Wow," he said. "You've built quite the profile. We can work with this."

Jasmine walked out of the bank with a $40,000 business line of credit—unsecured and without a personal guarantee. She had cracked the code. And it all started with consistency, education, and understanding the power of business credit. She now teaches others how to do the same.

Her story isn't rare. It's happening all over the country—people who take ownership of their financial future, not by chasing money, but by learning how to position themselves properly. Jasmine wasn't rich, connected, or lucky. She was determined. And in a world full of closed doors, business credit had become the master key.

Chapter 2: Credit Stacking for Maximum Leverage

Credit stacking is the practice of applying for multiple lines of business credit strategically within a short time window to maximize approvals and funding potential—while minimizing hard inquiries and delays. Done right, it gives you a powerful burst of capital. Done wrong, it can tank your profile and limit your future options. In this chapter, we'll break down the exact strategy I teach entrepreneurs and investors who want fast results without the long-term damage.

To begin, you need to understand the mechanics of credit applications. When you apply for business credit, lenders often perform a soft pull or hard pull on your personal credit if your business profile isn't strong enough on its own. That's why stacking must be timed carefully. By applying for several accounts within a short window—typically 7 to 10 days—you reduce the chance of additional inquiries being seen by other lenders. This is similar to how mortgage or auto loan inquiries are grouped when shopping for rates. The key is applying before the new accounts report to your credit file.

Before you begin stacking, ensure your business foundation is flawless. Your business should have at least 5 vendor accounts reporting positively to Dun & Bradstreet, Equifax Business, and Experian Business. Your Paydex score should be 80 or higher, and you should already have one or two revolving store credit cards—like a Home

Depot or Amazon business card—showing healthy usage. Lenders want to see a history of responsible usage before granting higher limits.

Next, prepare your application bundle. Choose lenders known for fast decisions and high limits. These often include Amex Business, Capital One Spark, Chase Ink Business, Divvy, and newer fintech players like Ramp, Brex, or Fundbox. Each of these has slightly different requirements, so prepare your documents ahead of time. Have your EIN, legal business name, business address, gross revenues (real or projected), and time in business ready. If you've been in business less than a year, focus on lenders that cater to startups or no-PG (no personal guarantee) cards.

Timing is everything. Start with lenders that perform soft pulls or use alternative underwriting methods. For example, Amex is known for soft pulls if you already have a relationship with them. Brex uses cash flow and bank account data, not personal credit. Fundbox and Divvy use business banking data and invoices. Start with these before applying to traditional banks that will run a hard inquiry, such as Chase or Capital One.

Once your first approval hits, don't wait. Move to the next lender on your list. The goal is to apply to 3–5 credit sources over a 7-day window. As the approvals roll in, your funding pool increases rapidly. You might get a $10K card from Chase, $15K from Amex, $5K from

Office Depot, and a $25K line from Fundbox. You're now looking at $50K+ in business credit—without touching your personal limit.

But stacking doesn't stop at credit cards. The next level includes business lines of credit, equipment financing, trade credit with suppliers, and short-term capital loans. Each of these requires a similar strategy: demonstrate business activity, show a clean file, and apply in logical sequences. Don't apply to five banks back-to-back—mix it up with fintechs, credit unions, and B2B vendors. Diversity is critical.

One overlooked tactic is "tier stacking." This means grouping lenders based on their approval difficulty and structuring your applications accordingly. Tier 1 includes vendors and low-risk store cards. Tier 2 includes major cards like Amex or Capital One. Tier 3 includes lines of credit and large working capital accounts. Never jump to Tier 3 before building credibility with Tier 1 and 2. You'll waste inquiries and burn your chances.

Finally, protect your progress. Don't overuse your new lines. Keep utilization under 30%, make early payments, and set up autopay to avoid missed payments. You want lenders to see you as a low-risk, high-activity business. That's how you get limit increases, better terms, and future approvals.

Credit stacking is like climbing a ladder. Each rung gets you closer to funding independence, but you have to climb strategically. With every account you add, you're not just getting money—you're building momentum. And with momentum, you can fund opportunities most people never get to touch.

Credit Stacking for Maximum Leverage

The sun hadn't even risen yet when Luis sat down at his kitchen table, laptop open, coffee steaming, and a list of business credit card applications in front of him. After a year of building his landscaping company from scratch—hauling mulch in a borrowed truck, taking cash jobs, and grinding every weekend—he was finally ready to level up. He didn't need a loan. He needed leverage. And today, he was going to stack business credit like a pro.

His mentor, Celeste, had warned him: "If you don't plan this right, you'll get denied, leave inquiry footprints everywhere, and blow your chances. But if you time it—really time it—you'll walk away with more funding than you thought possible."

Luis had listened. For six months, he'd done everything she told him. He set up an LLC. Got his EIN. Created a business email and phone number. Even rented a virtual address so he wasn't using his apartment address anymore. Then came the vendor accounts—Uline, Summa Office Supplies, Grainger, Quill. He didn't need everything he ordered, but he used them to buy what he could—gloves, packaging tape, work boots. Every invoice was paid early.

At first, it felt silly. Like he was buying his own reputation. But slowly, the reports started showing up. His Paydex score hit 80. His Equifax business file activated. That was the moment he knew it was time.

He called Celeste that night. "I'm ready," he said. She laughed. "Then let's stack."

Together, they mapped it out. First on the list: Divvy. It was a soft pull, connected to his business bank account, and didn't require a personal guarantee. Approval came within 24 hours—$6,000 in revolving credit. No interest if he paid on time. Next came Brex. Another fintech, another soft pull. Approved for $10,000, based on his cash flow. He used it to cover gas, supplies, and team uniforms.

Luis took a breath. The real test was next—traditional banks.

He applied for the Chase Ink Business card at 6:15 a.m. before business hours kicked in. Hard pull—but he was ready. Approved: $12,000 with zero percent interest for 12 months. He almost shouted. He took a short break, then applied for Capital One Spark. Another hard pull. Approved: $8,000. This one he would use strictly for marketing—website redesign, Google ads, and uniforms with his company logo.

In less than 72 hours, Luis had stacked nearly $40,000 in usable business credit. No collateral. No cosigner. No personal savings at risk.

He couldn't believe it.

But he wasn't done.

The following week, he visited a local credit union. Instead of asking for a loan, he showed them his new business credit cards, his Paydex score, and three months of clean bank statements. The loan officer was impressed. "You've built a really solid profile," she said. "We can offer you a $15,000 line of credit with interest-only payments for the first year." He accepted it on the spot.

A week later, Luis used part of that funding to buy two gently used trucks. He hired a second crew. His weekend business became a full-time operation. His income doubled within 90 days.

He never forgot the power of planning. The key, Celeste had told him, was timing and trust. "They trust you when you look prepared," she said. "And when you stack correctly, you build that trust faster than most people ever will."

Luis became known in his circle as the guy who knew how to get funding without loans, debt stress, or asking family for help. When new entrepreneurs asked how he did it, he'd smile and say, "I didn't chase money. I built a plan and let the money come to me."

CREDIT TO CAPITAL

Chapter 3: Building a Business Credit Ecosystem

Creating real, lasting financial power through business credit requires more than just stacking accounts—it requires building a full **credit ecosystem**. This means structuring your business to maintain a healthy credit profile across all tiers of credit: vendor accounts, revolving credit, fleet cards, installment loans, and lines of credit. Each type of credit has a purpose, and together, they create a system that fuels long-term business growth while protecting your personal finances.

Let's start with **the foundation: vendor credit**. This is Tier 1. These net-30 or net-60 accounts are critical because they establish your credit history with Dun & Bradstreet, Experian Business, and Equifax Business. Companies like Uline, Grainger, Quill, and Strategic Network Solutions are standard starting points. Their real power is not in how much credit they give you—but in what they report. Pay these invoices early, and your Paydex score will climb. This foundation tells lenders you're responsible, reliable, and ready for more.

Next comes Tier 2: revolving store credit. These are cards for retailers and suppliers like Home Depot, Lowe's, Amazon, Staples, and Office Depot. These cards usually don't offer cash access, but they are great for business expenses. They show creditors that you know how to use credit limits and repay them without maxing out. Your goal here is to maintain utilization under 30% and pay in full or early. These cards typically report to business credit bureaus and help build depth in your credit file.

Now we move to **Tier 3: fleet cards and specialized vendor credit.** These include fuel cards like Shell, WEX, or BP, as well as specialized business cards for trucking, construction, or medical supplies. Fleet cards are particularly useful for service-based businesses with travel needs. They not only provide revolving credit but also track expenses per vehicle, which is a bonus during tax season. Apply for fleet cards once your Paydex score is over 80 and you have 3–5 tradelines reporting.

Tier 4 is where funding gets serious: business credit cards with major lenders. These are the Amex Blue Business Plus, Chase Ink Business, Capital One Spark, and more. At this stage, you'll want to leverage your business profile to avoid or reduce personal guarantees. Many of these cards offer 0% interest periods, points rewards, and high limits. Always apply with a strong file—established business, solid vendor history, and low existing utilization. These cards are the heartbeat of your spending power.

Then we reach Tier 5: business loans and lines of credit. These include short-term loans, equipment financing, and revolving lines of credit from banks or online lenders like Fundbox, Bluevine, or your local credit union. These require documentation—revenue reports, bank statements, possibly tax returns. These are relationship-driven. Build rapport with local bankers and keep all business funds flowing through a dedicated business checking account. When your income, credit score, and business history align, you'll qualify for significant funding.

The goal isn't just to get these accounts—it's to **layer them**, use them responsibly, and rotate usage to keep everything active. Use vendor accounts monthly. Rotate usage on business credit cards every 60 days. Keep utilization low but visible. Pay early. And track it all in a spreadsheet or credit monitoring software like Nav.

A healthy ecosystem also includes protecting your profile. That means separating personal and business finances, avoiding late payments at all costs, and freezing your personal credit between application rounds. When you apply for no-PG credit, you don't want unnecessary hard pulls that damage your personal score.

Think of your business credit ecosystem like a garden. Vendor accounts are your soil. Store credit and fleet cards are your roots. Major cards and loans are your branches. With time, care, and discipline, this system grows into something that can fund anything—real estate, equipment, staff, marketing, or new ventures.

In the next chapter, we'll talk about **automation**—how to put parts of your ecosystem on autopilot so your credit grows while you sleep.

Building a Business Credit Ecosystem

Darren stood at the edge of his small warehouse, watching two workers load pallets of bottled health supplements into the back of a delivery truck. It was a scene he used to dream about—his own branded product, moving out to real customers, fulfilling real orders. But behind the scenes, what made it all possible wasn't just his hustle or his product. It was the ecosystem he had quietly built over the past year—his business credit ecosystem.

Twelve months earlier, Darren was a freelance health coach trying to turn his private label supplements into a full-time business. He had a website, a logo, and a loyal following, but he didn't have capital. A few rejections from banks had left him cautious. He was also determined not to max out his personal credit cards again like he did with his first business attempt. That's when he stumbled upon a late-night YouTube interview with a business credit expert.

"Build the system before you need it," the man said. "And it will support your growth when the time is right."

Darren took that to heart. The next day, he set up a spreadsheet and mapped out five tiers. At the top, he wrote in bold: *Business Credit Ecosystem.* This wasn't going to be a series of random applications. It was going to be a coordinated plan.

He started with vendors—Uline, Quill, Summa Office Supplies. He bought boxes, cleaning supplies, office paper. Nothing flashy. He paid every invoice early and watched as the first trade lines showed up on his business credit reports. His Paydex score inched up. Equifax Business started tracking him. It felt like planting seeds.

Then came Tier 2. He applied for an Office Depot card and was approved for $2,000. Two weeks later, Staples gave him $3,000. He used the cards sparingly—ordering printed inserts for his product packaging and tracking every transaction in his spreadsheet. He noticed his score climbed every month. He was growing credit roots.

By month four, Darren felt ready for fleet cards. He didn't have a delivery truck yet, but he planned to lease one within the year. Still, he applied for a Shell card and a WEX fleet card and was approved for both. He used them to fill up his car while meeting vendors and suppliers. To the credit bureaus, it looked like business was booming.

With his ecosystem forming, Darren tackled Tier 4—major business credit cards. He applied for the Amex Blue Business Plus and was approved for $10,000. Two weeks later, Capital One Spark approved him for $8,500. With his vendor, store, and fleet credit active, his profile was rock-solid. He now had enough revolving credit to cover raw materials, packaging, shipping, and marketing.

What made the difference was how intentional he was. He rotated card usage, never going above 30% utilization. Every payment was automated and early. His business bank account was active and clean. No overdrafts. No NSF fees. He treated the account like it belonged to a million-dollar company, even though it barely had five figures in it.

By month nine, Darren was ready for Tier 5: the big leagues. He walked into a local credit union with a binder—business plan, credit report summaries, bank statements, proof of revenue. The loan officer, impressed with his preparation, offered him a $25,000 line of credit with interest-only payments for the first six months.

Darren used that line to lease a delivery truck, outsource fulfillment, and fund a regional ad campaign. Within three months, his revenue doubled. His warehouse had real movement. His part-time helper became a full-time employee. And his confidence? Sky-high.

One night over dinner, a friend asked him, "How did you manage to grow so fast without borrowing money from friends or family?" Darren smiled. "I built a system," he said. "Like a financial ecosystem that fed itself. Credit isn't something you chase when you're desperate. It's something you grow when you're focused."

That night, he updated his spreadsheet with new accounts, fresh limits, and upcoming credit reviews. He wasn't done growing. His ecosystem was alive now—and it was only the beginning.

CREDIT TO CAPITAL

Chapter 4: Automating and Protecting Your Credit System

Building business credit is only the beginning. To truly benefit from your credit ecosystem, you need to **automate and protect** it. Think of your credit as a living system—one that needs regular maintenance, smart management, and strong security. Without these, even a solid credit foundation can collapse from missed payments, fraud, or neglect.

The first step is **automation**. Automation ensures that your credit activity continues—even when you're distracted, overwhelmed, or out of the country. It starts with setting up **automatic payments** on all your accounts. Whether it's net-30 vendor invoices or business credit card minimums, set up autopay to avoid late fees or negative marks on your credit profile. Lenders want to see consistency. One missed payment can tank your Paydex score or disqualify you from high-tier funding for months.

Use business accounting software—like QuickBooks, Wave, or Zoho Books—to link all your credit cards and vendor accounts. This helps you track due dates, spending patterns, and available credit. Many tools will also send alerts when a bill is due or your utilization crosses a set threshold. If you're managing five or more accounts (which you should be), this is critical to keeping everything under control.

Next, **schedule your credit usage** like a routine. Rotate your accounts every 30–60 days. For example, use your Office Depot card one month, your Amazon card the next, and your fleet card for all fuel purchases every other week. This activity keeps accounts active, which helps your credit profile grow. Inactive accounts can be closed by the issuer or stop reporting, which weakens your overall file.

Beyond automation, your credit system needs **protection**—from both internal errors and external threats. Start by **separating your personal and business finances** completely. Never use personal cards for business expenses, and avoid putting personal guarantees on business loans unless absolutely necessary. This separation limits your risk and protects your personal credit from business-related turbulence.

Next, use **business credit monitoring tools**. Services like Nav, CreditSignal by Dun & Bradstreet, or Experian Business Credit Advantage allow you to track your business credit in real-time. Set alerts for score changes, inquiries, and new accounts. These tools are especially important if you're stacking credit or applying frequently—you'll be able to see how each new account affects your file.

You should also **freeze your personal credit** when you're not applying for funding. This protects you from identity theft and stops unauthorized credit checks. It also prevents credit bureaus from handing out your information without permission. A personal credit freeze can be temporarily lifted when you're planning to apply for personal or PG-backed business credit.

An often overlooked part of credit protection is **fraud prevention**. Make sure your business address, phone number, and email are secure and consistent. If your information changes, update all vendors and bureaus immediately. Use two-factor authentication on every financial login. Install monitoring software on your business devices to prevent cyber threats. The most damaging credit problems often come from fraud that could have been prevented with basic precautions.

Finally, set up a **monthly review routine**. Block one hour per month to review your credit profile, balances, usage percentages, and upcoming renewals. Look for errors on reports, inactive cards, or any duplicate accounts that may cause confusion. Many entrepreneurs ignore this and end up with ghost accounts or inaccurate reports that cost them funding opportunities.

Here's your action checklist for this chapter:

- Turn on autopay for every credit account.
- Use accounting software to track and categorize spending.
- Monitor all three business credit bureaus monthly.
- Freeze your personal credit when not applying.

- Rotate usage of cards every 30–60 days.
- Review reports monthly for errors and inactivity.
- Secure all login information and activate 2FA.
- Back up financial records on a secure, encrypted cloud platform.

When your system is automated and protected, you gain time, peace of mind, and trust from lenders. You stop reacting and start managing. That's what separates people who "have credit" from those who **control credit**.

In the next chapter, we'll dive into **funding real assets with business credit**—how to use your ecosystem to acquire real estate, equipment, and digital properties that generate income.

Camila's story

Camila paced her apartment, laptop in one hand, cell phone in the other, her forehead creased with stress. "I swear I paid that bill," she muttered, pulling up her account. But there it was—her Amazon Business card showed a late payment. Not only had it dropped her Paydex score by 12 points, but it had triggered a warning from a bank where she had just applied for a $20,000 working capital line. All because she got too busy to click "pay."

That mistake cost her the opportunity—and reminded her of something her mentor had once said: "If you don't automate your success, chaos will handle it for you."

Camila had launched her home staging business just over a year ago. At first, she was on top of everything—emails, invoices, vendor orders, credit cards, inventory. But as her business grew, so did the complexity. She had five credit accounts, three vendor lines, and was trying to juggle two upcoming property projects. Things started slipping. That one missed payment? It wasn't about the money. It was about the message it sent: this business can't manage its obligations.

She called her mentor, Glenn, that night.

"You're ready to grow," Glenn said, "but your system isn't. You need automation—not just to save time, but to protect everything you've built."

So Camila took a full weekend to rebuild her financial workflow. She started with autopay. Every single card, vendor account, and software subscription was updated with her business checking account and set to pay either the full balance or minimum due—automatically. She even set reminders a few days before each due date to double-check.

Then, she subscribed to a credit monitoring service that pulled reports from Dun & Bradstreet, Experian Business, and Equifax Business.

Each week, she received alerts about score changes, account activity, and payment reporting. No more surprises.

But automation was only one part of the fix—she needed protection too.

She separated her finances completely. She opened a new business checking account for operations and a second one for taxes and reserves. She destroyed her old spreadsheet that mixed personal and business expenses and created a new one—simple, clear, color-coded. She stopped using her personal credit cards entirely for business purchases. If the business couldn't pay for it, it didn't need it—yet.

To protect herself further, she froze her personal credit through all three bureaus. That way, any unauthorized pulls or identity theft attempts would hit a wall. When she applied for new business credit, she could temporarily lift the freeze for a day, then refreeze it afterward.

Her next step was rotating credit usage. She made a list of every account she had and created a two-month calendar: one week was Amazon, the next was Office Depot, the next was Sam's Club. Every card would be used at least once every 60 days to keep it active, visible, and contributing to her credit profile. No more dormant accounts. No more surprise closures.

By the end of the month, Camila had also set up a monthly "money meeting" with herself. One hour, the last Sunday of every month, was dedicated to reviewing her credit reports, checking account activity, and making adjustments. She created a folder in the cloud with all her passwords stored securely using two-factor authentication. She scanned and saved all her EIN, LLC documents, and bank account info, so she never had to dig through drawers again.

It didn't take long to see the results.

Her Paydex score climbed back to 85. The bank that once declined her approved her for a $25,000 line of credit. A new vendor offered her net-60 terms, and her credit limits increased across three different business cards—all without her asking. She wasn't just building anymore. She was maintaining and protecting what she had built like a pro.

Six months later, Camila was managing five staging projects at once and had hired her first assistant. When a new entrepreneur asked how she kept everything running so smoothly, she smiled and replied, "It's not about doing more—it's about building systems that don't let you fail."

She learned that automation wasn't about being lazy. It was about being **ready**. And protection wasn't about paranoia—it was about **preserving freedom**. With every automated payment, every monthly review, and every secure login, she was no longer just building credit. She was building a fortress.

Chapter 5: Funding Real Assets with Business Credit

At this stage in your business credit journey, you've built a strong foundation, stacked strategic credit lines, and automated your system for long-term growth. Now it's time to shift into the next phase: **turning credit into cash-flowing assets**. In this chapter, you'll learn how to strategically use your business credit to acquire **real estate, digital products, vehicles, and other appreciating or income-generating assets**—without using your personal credit or draining your cash reserves.

Let's start with **real estate**, one of the most common and effective ways to use business credit to generate wealth. Contrary to popular belief, you don't need massive cash reserves or perfect personal credit to get started. If your business has a solid credit profile and some cash flow, you can qualify for short-term bridge loans, fix-and-flip funding, or DSCR (Debt Service Coverage Ratio) loans that are underwritten based on the property's income—not your personal income.

Many business owners start by using a business credit card or line of credit to fund earnest money deposits, appraisals, inspections, or light renovations. For example, a $15,000 Amex card at 0% interest for 12 months can cover the upfront costs of a $200K investment property that's being funded by a hard money lender. If you flip or refinance within 6–12 months, the credit card gets paid off—and you keep the profits.

Next, consider **vehicle and equipment financing** using your business name. With an established Paydex score and 5+ active tradelines, you can qualify for vehicle leases or purchases without a personal guarantee. This is especially useful if your business involves deliveries, service calls, or logistics. Companies like Ford Commercial, GM Financial, and Ally Business offer programs where the vehicle is titled in the business name and reported to business credit bureaus. Always ask lenders if they report to D&B, Equifax Business, or Experian Business—this ensures your payments help grow your profile even further.

If you're building an online brand, **digital assets**—like websites, e-commerce stores, and courses—can be funded with business credit cards and vendor lines. For instance, use business credit to pay for ad campaigns, web design, copywriting, SEO, and digital product creation. Tools like Kajabi, Shopify, and Google Ads often allow business accounts, making it easy to track and separate your spending. Once your funnel is built and profitable, you've created an asset that runs on autopilot and generates recurring revenue.

You can also invest in **automated income sources**—like vending machines, ATMs, car rental fleets, or even AI-powered SaaS tools. Most of these can be acquired for under $10K and financed entirely with business credit if you have the right partners. You don't need to be an expert in each asset class—just treat them like a business acquisition. Ask: will this asset produce income that can pay down the credit line and produce profit beyond the minimum payments?

As you grow, you'll want to **layer your assets** with funding from multiple sources. For example:

- Use a $20K line of credit to renovate a short-term rental.
- Use a $10K card to advertise your online course.
- Use vendor credit to buy product inventory for e-commerce.
- Use a no-PG vehicle lease to build a delivery fleet for your logistics brand.

All of this can be done simultaneously, provided your automation, utilization, and payment systems are in place. You are no longer funding your ideas with your own cash. You are using OPM—Other People's Money—strategically and responsibly.

But never forget the golden rule: **credit should fund assets, not liabilities**. Don't use business credit to buy gadgets, vacations, or lifestyle upgrades unless they're connected to your income-generating system. Each dollar borrowed should have a job. That job is to either make more money or increase your capacity to do so.

Finally, as you acquire real assets, make sure to track their performance. Create a simple spreadsheet or dashboard to monitor:

- Cash flow generated by each asset
- Outstanding credit balance used to fund it
- ROI and breakeven timeline
- Which credit product was used and terms

This helps you understand which types of assets perform best, which funding sources are most efficient, and when it's time to reinvest or pivot.

In the next chapter, we'll explore how to **leverage business credit to scale income streams** across multiple verticals—so you're not just building one business but building a portfolio of automated, credit-fueled income machines.

Funding Real Assets with Business Credit

Tyrell stood in front of a two-bedroom bungalow in a quiet part of Tampa, squinting against the morning sun. The house needed work—the paint was peeling, the landscaping overgrown—but the bones were good. "This place has potential," he whispered. He wasn't a real estate agent, contractor, or even an investor—at least not officially.

He was a graphic designer who had just unlocked $50,000 in business credit lines.

Three weeks earlier, Tyrell had never considered buying a property. But after hearing a podcast about using business credit to fund income-producing assets, something clicked. "You can't save your way to wealth," the host had said. "But you can build the right systems to buy it."

That same day, Tyrell reached out to his cousin Maya, a real estate agent. "What if I found a small property I could fix up and rent on Airbnb?" he asked. Maya was skeptical—until Tyrell showed her his newly approved Amex Business card, a line of credit from Bluevine, and three vendor accounts that had helped him build a solid Paydex score.

"That's actually doable," she admitted. "If we find the right deal, you could use that credit to fund the renovation—and even part of the purchase."

Tyrell dove in. He spent a week learning about DSCR loans, which base approvals on the property's projected income instead of his personal income. Maya helped him find the Tampa bungalow. The price was right, and the rental income potential looked strong. The lender approved the loan with 20% down, and Tyrell used his business credit to cover the $10,000 earnest deposit, the appraisal, and inspection fees.

Once under contract, he used his Amex to purchase appliances and paint. His Staples Business card covered furniture, and he ordered linens and small electronics through vendor accounts that offered net-30 terms. He didn't spend a dollar of his own savings.

As contractors got to work, Tyrell was already planning his next move.

He called a leasing company to inquire about vehicles for a mobile branding service—a side hustle he'd dreamed about for years. With his Paydex score sitting at 85 and multiple tradelines reporting, the company approved a commercial van lease in his business name, no personal guarantee required. "I didn't know I could do that," he said, stunned.

Within weeks, he had a second income stream—offering mobile design services to small businesses, delivering signage, and even branding event booths on-site. The van was covered in his company logo, doubling as a rolling advertisement.

At night, Tyrell worked on his third asset: a digital course teaching creative entrepreneurs how to turn branding skills into service packages. He paid a virtual assistant through his Divvy card, ran Facebook ads using a no-interest business credit card, and hosted the course on Kajabi—all funded with credit, not cash.

By the time the Airbnb went live, Tyrell had created three income-producing assets: a short-term rental, a branded service vehicle, and a digital product. All funded through business credit. All generating revenue.

He set up a spreadsheet to track every dollar:

- The Airbnb cleared $2,400/month net.
- The mobile branding van brought in $3,000/month.
- The digital course had sold 112 copies at $97 each.

He called it "The Credit-Paid Portfolio."

When friends asked how he managed to launch so many things at once, he'd smile. "I stopped thinking of credit as debt—and started seeing it as fuel."

Tyrell understood something most people never figure out: when you use business credit to fund **assets**, not expenses, it becomes a tool for multiplication, not subtraction. The cards were paid on time. The utilization stayed low. The income streams covered more than the minimums. He was building wealth, not just running a business.

And the best part? His savings account was still full.

Chapter 6: Scaling Your Income Streams Using Credit-Fueled Multipliers

Once your business credit ecosystem is in place and you're using it to acquire real assets, the next level is **scaling**. Scaling means multiplying your income streams without multiplying your time or risk. In this chapter, we'll cover how to use your established business credit to **launch or grow multiple income-generating projects**, expand operations, and build systems that work even when you don't.

The key to scaling is simple: **invest in things that produce income without constant input**. Business credit lets you test and launch these income multipliers without sacrificing your cash reserves or relying on personal credit. The formula is to start small, use borrowed capital efficiently, validate the income stream, and then double down.

Let's begin with **digital income streams**—the easiest to scale using credit. Once you've created a profitable online product like a course, ebook, coaching program, or digital template, you can use business credit to scale its reach:

- Use 0% APR business credit cards to fund Facebook, YouTube, or Google Ads.
- Hire virtual assistants with revolving credit lines to manage customer service, scheduling, or lead generation.

- Use business software subscriptions (billed monthly or annually) to automate delivery, email marketing, and upselling.

The goal is to reinvest borrowed capital into systems that grow the business—automated emails, sales funnels, affiliate partnerships, and paid traffic. Once you break even from your first round of ad spend, you're using other people's money to create your customer base and generate recurring sales.

Next, consider **physical product businesses**—especially drop shipping, Amazon FBA, or white-labeling. Business credit can fund:

- Inventory purchases from suppliers using net-30 or net-60 terms.

- Branding, packaging, and photography using cards with cash-back or points rewards.

- Warehouse, shipping, or 3PL services using trade credit accounts.

By staging your operations to match payment cycles, you can delay actual cash outflow for 30–60 days, giving you time to sell the product and use revenue to pay off the credit—creating a near self-funding loop.

Another multiplier is **real estate services or property management**. If you already own rental property or manage short-term rentals, use business credit to scale:

- Pay for professional cleaning, furnishings, and digital lock systems.
- Automate guest check-ins, marketing, and listings with platforms like Guesty or Hostaway.
- Offer add-on services like guided tours, airport pickups, or catered meals using outsourced contractors—all funded through business credit.

Every improvement you make boosts your property value, revenue, or efficiency, creating an outsized return from relatively small credit-funded investments.

Now let's talk **outsourcing and hiring**. Scaling means eventually doing less yourself. That's where smart credit use can multiply your time. Use business credit to:

- Hire part-time help on Upwork or Fiverr to handle design, admin, editing, or writing.
- Use credit-funded payroll solutions for part-time contractors.

- Pay for specialized consulting or mentorship that accelerates your growth.

This is not a cost—it's an investment that frees you to focus on your highest-value tasks. A $1,000 investment into a part-time video editor can generate $10,000 in sales from better content. That's a 10x multiplier funded entirely by credit.

If you're in services—coaching, consulting, or freelancing—credit can fund the creation of **scalable productized offers**. Record your process, package it into a paid course, and run ads to a funnel. You're no longer trading hours for dollars—you're selling knowledge at scale.

Here are a few scaling ideas by category, all of which can be funded with business credit:

- **Courses or Membership Sites:** Use credit for video production, ad campaigns, and email automation tools.

- **Airbnb Management:** Fund cleaner schedules, staging furniture, lockboxes, and automation tools.

- **YouTube Channels:** Use credit to buy royalty-free music, thumbnail design, editing tools, and ads to boost views.

- **Mobile Services:** Lease equipment or vehicles using business credit to expand geographic coverage.

Important: track every new stream. For each one, ask:

- What's the upfront investment?
- How fast can it start generating income?
- What systems or people are needed to automate it?
- How can I scale it without scaling my stress?

Scaling is about **leveraging credit into controlled expansion**. You don't have to explode your business overnight. Grow deliberately. Test every income stream with credit-funded micro-launches. If it works, reinvest. If it fails, learn fast and pivot—without draining your savings.

In the next chapter, we'll dive into **protecting your assets and income streams with the right legal and financial frameworks**, so the wealth you build is secure and positioned for long-term freedom.

Scaling Your Income Streams Using Credit-Fueled Multipliers: Malika's story

Malika leaned back in her chair, watching the sales dashboard on her screen refresh every few seconds. $197. $197. $197. The payments kept coming in. What started as an experiment—a $1,000 investment on her Amex Business card to launch a mini-course—had just made her over

$10,000 in less than a month. And she hadn't recorded a single new video since launch day.

Just a few months earlier, Malika was a freelance photographer barely keeping up with client work. Every week was another shoot, another round of edits, another check that barely covered rent. She had talent, no doubt—but no time, no freedom, and no cushion. Then she took a course on business credit and heard one phrase that stuck: *"Credit is a tool, not a trap—if you use it to multiply income, not inflate lifestyle."*

That night, Malika stayed up mapping out her first digital product—a mini-course on "DIY Branding for Small Businesses." She already had the content from previous client trainings. She used her business credit card to pay for a logo redesign, course platform subscription, and an editor to polish her videos. Total cost? $1,000. She uploaded everything to a clean Kajabi site, set up a payment page, and launched with no email list—just organic Instagram traffic and a few Facebook ads.

Sales trickled in the first week, then picked up. The course broke even in 10 days. By the end of the first month, she was in profit—and for the first time in years, she wasn't chasing clients. She was attracting them.

But she didn't stop there.

With new confidence and a growing Paydex score, Malika applied for a second business card—Capital One Spark—and used it to outsource lead generation to a virtual assistant. She hired a part-time content writer and doubled down on paid traffic. Then, she used vendor credit to print branded workbooks she could sell as part of a premium bundle. Her ecosystem expanded—without increasing her workload.

Then came her second multiplier: YouTube. She used her Divvy card to hire a video editor and purchase music licensing. Her assistant repurposed content from the course into short, punchy videos. By month three, her channel had 2,000 subscribers and was sending traffic to her course every day. More sales. More reach. No extra effort.

Malika was hooked.

She created a second course—this time on smartphone photography for online entrepreneurs—and followed the same formula. Recorded in two days. Edited in one. Funded entirely by business credit. She now had two evergreen products, both selling while she slept.

To diversify, she leased a small studio using a local bank line of credit under her business name. She rented it to other creators by the hour—photographers, YouTubers, content coaches—and turned it into an asset. Her business was no longer just service-based. It was scalable.

By month six, Malika had five active income streams:

- Two online courses
- YouTube ad revenue
- Studio rental income
- Affiliate commissions from business tools
- A small coaching program funded through paid ads

All of them had one thing in common: they started with a **credit-funded micro-investment** and turned into income-producing systems.

When a fellow photographer asked how she found the time to do all of this, she smiled. "I stopped working harder and started funding smarter. My credit does more work than I do now."

She wasn't overwhelmed. She had systems. She didn't feel like she was taking risks. She felt like she was **strategically multiplying her efforts**—using business credit to validate ideas, then automate what worked.

Scaling didn't mean stress. It meant structure. She had built something that grew without her having to constantly be in the room. Credit, wisely used, became her most powerful business partner.

And it all started the day she stopped seeing credit as a last resort—and started seeing it as a launch pad.

Chapter 7: Creating Long-Term Financial Control with Business Credit

At this stage, you've learned how to build, stack, and use business credit to acquire assets and scale your income. But there's one crucial concept we haven't fully explored—**control**. Long-term financial freedom doesn't come from just having access to credit or cash flow. It comes from **controlling the flow of money, credit, risk, and reinvestment** across your business ecosystem. This chapter is all about how to use business credit not just as leverage—but as a system for ongoing control.

Let's start with **credit utilization strategy**. One of the most overlooked factors in business credit health is how you manage your available credit. Even if you have $100K in credit lines, maxing them out—even for business purposes—can reduce your scores, signal financial distress to lenders, and make you ineligible for the next tier of funding. You must treat your utilization as a strategic tool. Keep revolving balances under 30% whenever possible, and rotate spending across multiple cards instead of stacking usage on one.

This allows you to operate from a position of strength. You want lenders to see you as someone who could take on more credit—but doesn't need to. That's power.

Next, let's talk about **reporting behavior**. Not all business credit accounts report to all bureaus. Some only report to D&B, some to

Experian, and others to Equifax. Know which accounts are improving which reports, and balance your activity accordingly. You should aim for **a minimum of five active tradelines reporting across all three bureaus**. This gives you full-spectrum strength and increases your chances of approval across all types of lenders.

Now consider your **banking relationships**. As your business grows, you'll want to form a relationship with a bank or credit union that understands your long-term goals. Open a business savings account. Ask about pre-approval programs. Find out what their underwriting guidelines are for higher credit lines, SBA loans, or commercial real estate loans. When your banker knows your story, your numbers, and your credit usage habits, they can become an advocate—not a gatekeeper.

The next layer of control is your **cash flow strategy**. Use your credit to float expenses and time your payments for maximum efficiency. Here's an example:

- Use a net-30 vendor account to buy inventory.
- Sell that inventory within 15 days.
- Use proceeds to pay off the invoice before it's due.
- Profit while preserving your working capital.

This method creates a zero-debt growth model—especially powerful when your sales cycles are shorter than your payment terms.

Another advanced strategy is **credit cycling**—where you use short-term 0% APR cards to fund projects that return profit before the promo period ends. Let's say you get a card with a $20K limit and 12 months no interest. You invest in a small real estate rehab, use the funds for materials and contractors, and sell or refinance the property within six months. You pay off the card with the profits, and your credit profile improves without ever incurring interest.

That's financial control. But control also means **knowing when to say no**.

Not every opportunity is credit-worthy. Avoid using business credit for liabilities like luxury vehicles, personal vacations, or high-risk, untested business models. These won't pay you back. Every credit decision should be tied to a measurable ROI. Ask yourself: Will this use of credit grow my revenue, increase my efficiency, or add long-term value?

Let's talk about **reinvestment discipline**. Once you build income streams with business credit, use part of the profits to reinvest back into your ecosystem. Increase your ad spend if it's working. Hire better staff. Automate more processes. And build a reserve account that allows you to make your minimum payments—even during slow months—without relying on new debt.

Set guidelines for yourself:

- Always pay more than the minimum.
- Never carry more than 30% utilization unless you're in a controlled short-term cycle.
- Reinvest at least 25% of profits into growth or debt reduction.
- Review your business credit reports monthly.

Finally, make time for **quarterly audits**. Review:

- Which credit lines are underused and can be increased
- Which assets are performing or underperforming
- What new funding sources are available based on your improved profile
- Where you can negotiate terms or convert vendor accounts into revolving lines

Financial control is about predictability. It's about creating systems where your revenue, credit, and reinvestment strategy align to build a stable, expanding business.

In the final chapter, we'll look at **designing a complete wealth system with business credit at the core**, and how to turn your growing business into a legacy asset.

Creating Long-Term Financial Control with Business Credit: Eli's story

Eli poured a second cup of coffee and sat down at his desk, staring at the neatly organized dashboard he'd built over the past year. It tracked everything—business income, credit utilization, interest-free cycles, asset ROI, and upcoming application dates. To anyone else, it looked like overkill. To Eli, it was freedom on a spreadsheet.

He hadn't always been this way.

When he first started his online fitness brand, Eli operated in survival mode. He used personal credit cards to run Facebook ads. He mixed business and personal expenses. He didn't even know what a Paydex score was. "Revenue was good," he recalled, "but everything felt unstable."

That changed when a failed credit card payment tanked his personal score—and cost him a loan he was counting on. "That was my wake-up call," he said. "I realized I didn't have a business. I had chaos."

That week, Eli made a commitment: no more guesswork. He dove into the world of business credit—not just how to get it, but how to **control it**.

He started by mapping out his **credit utilization**. He stopped maxing out single cards and started spreading his purchases across four different accounts. He kept each one under 25%, even if he had to split a $2,000 ad campaign between three cards. It wasn't efficient—but it was strategic. Within 60 days, his business credit scores climbed. His lenders increased his limits—without him asking.

Then he learned about **credit reporting behavior**. He realized some of his cards only reported to D&B, while others went to Experian or Equifax Business. So he built a tracker. He wanted at least two active tradelines reporting to each bureau. That way, no matter who pulled his file—he looked solid.

He also made it a point to **build real banking relationships**. Eli didn't just open a business account—he started visiting his local credit union every two weeks, asking questions, updating them on his growth, and showing them how his credit profile had evolved. By month five, they offered him a pre-approved line of credit—no application required.

But what really changed his game was learning how to **cycle credit to control cash flow**. One of his product launches brought in $12K in 30 days. Instead of dipping into that for business expenses, he used a vendor account to buy $3K in branded gear and gave himself 30 days to pay it. He used customer payments to clear the invoice and kept his cash untouched.

He repeated the same process for marketing. When he had a 0% APR business card, he funded a limited campaign to test a new service. The results? A $9K return on a $3K spend—all paid back before the promotional period ended.

Every dollar had a purpose. Every card had a plan.

But perhaps the most important thing Eli did was develop **discipline around his decisions**. He stopped using credit for things that didn't make money. He had a rule: if it doesn't produce revenue, or reduce future expenses, it doesn't go on a business card.

That meant skipping the flashy office, the overpriced ads, and the unnecessary software tools. Instead, he doubled down on what worked—sales funnels, ads with proven ROI, and smart reinvestment.

He reinvested 30% of profits into automation, hired two virtual assistants, and created a small financial reserve account. For the first time, he wasn't afraid of a slow month. He had a cushion—and control.

Every quarter, Eli sat down for what he called his "Money CEO Meeting." He reviewed credit reports, utilization ratios, spending efficiency, and asset performance. If a card had been underused, he'd schedule a cycle. If a product wasn't converting, he'd pause it. He even reviewed lender offers to see if he could renegotiate terms.

People began to ask him how he stayed so calm when others were stressed about debt. His answer was simple: "Debt isn't dangerous. Uncontrolled debt is. I don't just have access to credit—I manage it like a business partner."

Eli had come full circle. From a freelancer hustling to stay ahead, to a business owner with systems, control, and true financial peace. And it all started when he stopped chasing money—and started mastering the game.

Chapter 8: Turning Business Credit Into a Legacy Wealth System

You've built credit. You've stacked funding. You've automated your systems and even begun acquiring income-producing assets. Now it's time to take the final step—**turning business credit into a long-term legacy**. This chapter is about designing a financial framework that outlasts your work hours, your active income years, and even your physical presence. It's about using credit as the foundation of wealth you can **own, grow, and eventually pass on**.

Let's begin by reframing how you see your business credit profile. It's not just a tool to borrow money. It's a **business asset**—a form of financial reputation that, once mature, can be transferred, leveraged, and even sold as part of a company valuation. When your business has a high Paydex score, multiple trade lines, strong revenue history, and well-managed liabilities, it becomes a **fundable, investable entity**. Banks, buyers, and partners will all treat it as a serious business—not just a side hustle.

Step one in creating a legacy system is **entity structure**. If you haven't already, consider forming a corporation (C-Corp or S-Corp) and assigning ownership properly through bylaws and share structure. This makes your business easier to sell, partner with, or pass on. LLCs can work, too—especially if you add an operating agreement that clearly outlines roles, profit distribution, and succession rules.

The next step is building your **asset portfolio inside the business**. This includes:

- Intellectual property (courses, ebooks, licenses)
- Digital products with recurring revenue
- Rental properties or managed Airbnbs
- Equipment, vehicles, or infrastructure
- Active trade accounts and revolving credit lines

All of these become part of your business valuation. The stronger your credit, the more assets you can acquire using OPM—Other People's Money—and the more powerful your balance sheet becomes. Over time, your business can own properties, lease vehicles, license content, and even fund other ventures—all while continuing to grow its own credit profile.

Now let's talk about **credit-based business flipping**. One of the most scalable ways to build long-term wealth is by launching automated or semi-automated businesses, growing their cash flow and creditworthiness, and then **selling them for a multiple**. Whether it's a digital brand, a small service-based business, or an Amazon FBA store, your credit can provide the startup capital to get it running, and your systems can increase its value.

Let's say you use $10,000 in business credit to launch a course business. Within six months, you're generating $3,000/month in profit. With a clean brand, automated systems, and transferable assets, that business could sell for 20x–36x monthly profit—$60K to $100K. Your credit gave you a profitable exit.

That's legacy play number one: **credit-fueled business building and selling**.

The second strategy is **credit-to-capital-to-holding model**. This means using business credit to buy cash-flowing assets that you never plan to sell—properties, revenue-generating websites, dividend-yielding stocks through a business brokerage account, or equity in other people's businesses. Instead of flipping, you hold. You keep cash flow. You minimize taxes. And you pass those assets on to your kids, your trust, or your foundation.

To protect this legacy system, you'll want to form a **holding company**—an LLC or corporation that owns your cash-flowing businesses. This gives you better liability protection, easier tax planning, and the ability to raise capital, bring on partners, or leave behind a full empire instead of disconnected projects.

Once you have your holding structure, begin separating accounts. Create dedicated business checking and credit accounts for each business or stream. This ensures clean books, clear tracking, and less confusion during scaling or exit events.

Let's break it down into a repeatable legacy formula:

1. **Build a strong credit profile** With vendor accounts, cards, and revolving lines under a business EIN.

2. **Use credit to launch income streams** Courses, rentals, online brands, vending, mobile services, etc.

3. **Scale and automate those streams** Use credit again to fund systems, hiring, and marketing.

4. **Organize under a holding structure** For liability protection and future flexibility.

5. **Sell or hold depending on your goal** Flip for cash, or keep for passive income.

6. **Reinvest profits strategically** Into new credit-funded ventures or legacy assets.

This is how credit becomes a **machine**, not just a card. It's how people go from side hustles to full portfolios. From $10K cards to $1M valuations. From hustle to legacy.

And that's what you're building now.

In the final section of this book, we'll bring everything together—with final words on execution, resilience, and the mindset that separates those who **use credit** from those who master it.

Turning Business Credit Into a Legacy Wealth System: Miriam's story

Miriam stood under the shade of a large oak tree, watching her son kick a soccer ball across the backyard of the duplex she had bought just eight months ago. The sound of laughter filled the air, blending with the hum of a lawnmower in the distance. On the surface, this looked like a typical Saturday. But to Miriam, it was the sound of legacy being built—one that started with a few vendor accounts and a dream no one else saw.

Two years ago, she was working as an administrative assistant at a law firm, raising her son on a modest salary, and living paycheck to paycheck. She had always wanted more—but not just for herself. She wanted something she could **pass on**. Something that would give her son options, stability, and freedom. When she discovered the world of business credit, she didn't just see a financial opportunity—she saw a foundation.

She started small. A vendor account here, a business credit card there. She learned how to build her business credit file without ever touching her personal credit. It wasn't fast. It wasn't flashy. But it was steady.

Within a year, she had seven trade lines reporting, a Paydex score of 85, and multiple revolving credit accounts in her company's name.

That's when she made a bold move: she formed a holding company, "Legacy Living LLC." Instead of using her name, she used the business as the face of every future project. She wanted the credit history, the revenue, and the assets to belong to something bigger than her. Something transferable. Something that could outlive her.

The first property she bought was a small duplex in a working-class neighborhood. It needed paint, plumbing, and new appliances. Miriam didn't panic. She used her Amex Business card—at 0% for 12 months—to pay for the renovations. She used her Uline and Home Depot vendor accounts for fixtures and supplies. She even paid the electrician with a card that earned points. All of it was tracked, automated, and assigned to Legacy Living LLC.

She rented one side. Moved into the other.

Her monthly mortgage was fully covered—and she still had her full-time income. She called it her first "legacy asset."

Then she built an online course on property investing for single moms. She recorded it using credit-funded software and a borrowed camera. It sold. Not millions—but enough to cover utilities and groceries.

As her confidence grew, she started a second project: a short-term rental in the nearby city. This time, she didn't touch savings. She used business credit to stage it, automate the guest experience, and launch a small ad campaign. Within three months, it was booked out. The cash flow was consistent. Her son's college fund—once empty—was now filling month by month.

But it wasn't just about cash. Miriam had built **a system**. Her holding company owned the assets. Each property had its own bank account and credit card. Her digital products were sold through a business Stripe account. Her credit profile was monitored weekly. Her payments were automated. Every dollar worked for her—even when she wasn't working.

And then came the moment that made it all real.

During a routine financial planning session, her accountant looked at the books and said, "Miriam, this isn't just side income. You've built something real here. If you ever wanted to sell the business, it's worth six figures—and that's without touching the properties."

She didn't flinch. "I'm not selling," she said. "I'm preparing to hand it down."

She had already started teaching her son about credit, leverage, and business. She showed him how the duplex paid for itself. How to check a credit score. How to make money while you sleep. To Miriam, her greatest legacy wasn't the money—it was the mindset she was passing on.

On paper, she was just another small business owner with a few properties. But in reality, she had become what she once thought was impossible—a first-generation wealth builder, using business credit as her launch pad.

She smiled as her son ran up to her, sweaty and breathless. "Can we build a treehouse?" he asked. She looked at the house, the yard, and the life she had created.

"Of course," she said. "We'll build it together."

Chapter 9: Advanced Business Credit Strategies for Scaling Beyond Six Figures

By now, you've mastered the essentials of business credit—how to build it, protect it, and use it to fund assets. But if your goal is to go beyond just covering expenses and build a multiple six-figure or even seven-figure empire, you'll need to level up your strategy. This chapter covers advanced business credit tactics that top entrepreneurs use to increase credit limits, secure better terms, unlock new funding tiers, and expand credit across multiple entities.

The first advanced strategy is credit stacking across multiple businesses. Once you've successfully built credit under one LLC, you can apply that knowledge to additional businesses. Each EIN is treated as a separate financial identity. This means you can create multiple funding channels by strategically opening and building credit lines under separate LLCs or DBAs (doing business as). You'll want to stagger these to avoid overlap in reporting and inquiries—but once each one is established, you can use it to fund different verticals (e.g., real estate, ecommerce, content production) without cross-risk.

Start by using the same foundational playbook:

1. Register your new LLC or DBA.
2. Set up a dedicated EIN, business phone, email, address, and domain.
3. Open a business checking account.
4. Apply for Tier 1 vendor accounts.
5. Build 3–5 tradelines, and grow from there.

This multiplies your funding power while keeping your operations segmented and protected.

The next advanced move is credit recycling with float periods. This means timing your purchases and payoffs to get the most out of 0% APR promotions and grace periods. Let's say you get approved for a card with a $20K limit and a 0% promo for 12 months. You use $10K to fund an ad campaign or real estate renovation, generate income in 60–90 days, and pay off the card. Then you repeat the process with a new promo card before the first one expires.

By stacking float periods (especially with cards that don't report to your personal credit), you essentially create interest-free capital rotation, which accelerates growth while minimizing repayment stress.

Another advanced tactic is relationship-based funding. While fintech lenders rely on algorithms, traditional banks rely on relationships. Once your business is generating steady revenue, you can schedule quarterly or semiannual meetings with a dedicated business banker. Come prepared with updated P&Ls, credit reports, and plans for expansion. These meetings often lead to pre-approved lines of credit, SBA options, and larger limits—with little to no hard pulls.

Banks reward predictability. If they see regular deposits, strong cash flow, and low utilization across existing business accounts, they're more likely to offer unsecured funding or increase your limits without additional underwriting. This is how you gain soft leverage—where opportunities come to you without you chasing them.

Next, focus on strategic limit increases. Every 3–6 months, contact your card issuers and request limit increases. If you've maintained low utilization, paid early, and added revenue to your business profile, many will approve your request with no hard inquiry. Higher limits improve your credit utilization ratio, which boosts your credit scores and opens the door to even larger funding tiers.

One often-overlooked move is credit diversification. Aim to have a mix of:

- Vendor credit (Uline, Grainger)
- Store credit (Amazon, Home Depot)
- Fuel/fleet cards (WEX, Shell)
- Revolving credit cards (Amex, Chase)
- Installment loans (term loans or equipment financing)
- Lines of credit (revolving access to capital)

This mix improves your business credit "depth," which is similar to personal credit's credit mix factor. The more diverse your file, the more attractive you are to higher-tier lenders and credit unions.

Finally, you'll want to integrate credit into your overall business architecture. That means:

- Building out dashboards to track balances, billing cycles, and ROI
- Separating credit lines by project or product for easier tax accounting
- Using credit to hedge cash flow while investing in automation or expansion
- Setting up recurring audits to review interest costs, renewal dates, and reporting

Remember: the goal is no longer survival. It's scalable sustainability.

Credit isn't just for solving short-term problems. When used with discipline, it becomes a predictable source of working capital, a tool for exponential growth, and a gateway to building serious business valuation.

In the final chapter, we'll wrap everything together—explaining how to turn your credit system into a self-sustaining wealth engine and prepare it for long-term handoff, sale, or succession.

Advanced Business Credit Strategies for Scaling Beyond Six Figures: Devin's story

The first time Devin got approved for a $10,000 business credit card, he thought he had reached the top. It felt like a miracle. He had spent years bootstrapping his small media agency—editing videos at 3 a.m., juggling invoices, and scraping by on inconsistent client work. But over time, as he learned how to properly build and use business credit, he started thinking differently.

That $10K card was just the beginning. The question that kept repeating in his mind now wasn't "Can I get credit?"—it was, "How far can I scale this?"

One morning, while sipping coffee and reviewing his business dashboard, Devin realized that most of his agency income came from just three services. But what if he could use the same business credit system to launch spin-off brands under separate business names, each targeting a specific niche?

He decided to test the idea. Within two weeks, he formed a new LLC called "Social Scope Media." It focused solely on TikTok growth packages for influencers. He followed the same blueprint—EIN, virtual business address, business phone, domain, business checking. Then came the vendor accounts—Uline, Quill, and Summa Office

Supplies—all approved. By month two, he had a functioning website and three tradelines reporting.

But here's where it got interesting.

Devin didn't use his personal savings. He used credit stacking. With his strong file on his first LLC, he got approved for an Amex Blue Business card with a $15,000 limit. He used $3,000 to run ad campaigns and outsource short-form content creation. Then he applied for a Capital One Spark card under the new LLC—approved for $8,000. With two businesses running independently, both generating revenue, his total available credit more than doubled.

"I wasn't just growing," he realized. "I was multiplying."

His next move was bold. He applied for a 0% APR card with a 12-month promotion and used it to lease new camera gear. Not just for his own work, but to rent out to other creators in his network. That side business brought in an extra $800/month and allowed him to test the waters of credit-funded asset acquisition.

Around this time, Devin began scheduling quarterly check-ins with his business banker at a local credit union. During one meeting, he brought a printed report showing his cash flow, credit usage, and accounts across both LLCs. Impressed, the banker offered him a $25,000 line of credit—unsecured. "Most clients never come in this prepared," the banker said. "We want to help you grow."

Devin smiled. He already had a plan.

He used the LOC to fund a new training platform called "Creator School Pro"—a subscription-based course for content creators, hosted entirely online. He funded the initial build-out, marketing, and team support entirely on credit—while carefully managing utilization across five cards and two entities.

To avoid mixing funds, he created project-based budgets: each income stream had its own business credit card, billing cycle, and reporting dashboard. By now, he had eight open tradelines, revolving credit, and a blended Paydex score that made him attractive to top-tier lenders.

He wasn't just managing a business—he was managing a credit-powered portfolio.

One night, he sat with a mentor and said, "It feels like I'm doing a hundred things. But I've never been more in control." His mentor replied, "That's the shift—you're not chasing opportunities anymore. You're engineering them."

Devin didn't stop at two LLCs. By the end of the year, he had formed a third focused on digital tools and AI content services. Each business had its own EIN, website, structure, and stack of credit. By layering his accounts and rotating through float periods, he kept utilization low and approval rates high.

As his brands grew, so did his confidence. He no longer feared rejection, risk, or expansion. He understood the power of systems, timing, and visibility. He had become a builder—someone who used credit not as a crutch, but as a catalyst.

And the best part?

None of this touched his personal credit. His FICO score remained untouched while his businesses funded growth, built assets, and multiplied income.

Devin looked at the whiteboard in his office, now filled with arrows, charts, and revenue projections. At the top, he had written in bold red letters:

"I don't need more money—I need more structure."

And credit was the structure he had mastered.

Chapter 10: Building a Self-Sustaining Credit Wealth Engine

After learning how to build, protect, stack, scale, and optimize business credit across multiple entities, the final piece of your journey is transforming everything into a self-sustaining credit wealth engine. This chapter will walk you through how to turn your credit ecosystem into a repeatable, automated machine that generates capital, funds assets, and preserves your wealth—without relying on your constant time and attention.

Let's start with a core principle: consistency beats intensity. You don't need 100 credit lines, 5 LLCs, or wild income spikes to build long-term wealth. You need a system that works, can be managed in a few hours a month, and compounds value over time. A credit wealth engine does exactly that—it runs on clear rules, disciplined reinvestment, and smart delegation.

Step 1: Automate Everything That Matters

The first requirement for a sustainable engine is automation. You should no longer be manually logging into each vendor portal or remembering due dates. By this stage, your business credit system should include:

- Auto-payments for every card, loan, and vendor account

- Accounting software (like QuickBooks, Zoho, or Wave) connected to all business accounts
- Scheduled calendar alerts for statement closing dates and reporting cycles
- Credit monitoring via services like Nav, D&B CreditSignal, or Experian Business

This keeps your system error-free and trustworthy in the eyes of lenders. Missed payments or forgotten balances are no longer acceptable at this level. Automation gives you peace of mind and maximizes your reputation.

Step 2: Build Credit Cycles Into Your Business Model

Next, start engineering credit usage into your normal business flow. For example:

- Use specific business credit cards to cover recurring ad spend
- Assign a fuel or fleet card to each contractor or delivery vehicle
- Use vendor accounts for inventory restocks on a 30- or 60-day float

- Use 0% APR cards for short-term projects, and repay before interest accrues

Every dollar borrowed should have a mapped-out repayment plan, ROI expectation, and purpose. This discipline builds momentum and allows you to forecast future capital needs and approvals based on your business goals.

Step 3: Document and Delegate

A true wealth engine must operate independently of you. That starts with documentation.

Create an SOP (Standard Operating Procedure) that outlines:

- Your credit-building timeline and active tradelines
- Which bureaus report each account
- When each card was opened and when to request limit increases
- Float strategy for ad campaigns, product launches, or seasonal needs
- Your banking contacts and relationship notes
- Login credentials secured via a password manager

- Guidelines for team members using cards (limits, usage types, etc.)

This becomes the credit playbook—your business's funding DNA. If you ever sell, scale, or step away from the company, this system remains intact.

Step 4: Reinvest the Profits Wisely

At this level, you're generating revenue from multiple income streams: digital products, rentals, services, reselling, or content creation. You must now shift your focus from just earning to allocating.

A healthy self-sustaining engine allocates profits like this:

- 25% for debt payoff or credit cycling
- 25% for reinvestment in growth or automation
- 25% for reserves and cash flow protection
- 25% for owner profit or future acquisitions

This balanced approach ensures that you reduce risk, remain flexible, and always have capital to take advantage of new opportunities.

Step 5: Evolve Your Structure Into a Legacy System

If you've followed the framework from earlier chapters, now is the time to take it even further. Consolidate your businesses under a holding company structure. This simplifies taxation, streamlines credit management, and enhances your valuation if you ever seek investors or buyers.

Use this central entity to:

- Own the LLCs or DBAs where revenue flows
- Centralize vendor and banking relationships
- Apply for higher-tier credit based on consolidated income
- Create family succession plans or asset protection strategies

You now have a legal and financial infrastructure that can be handed off, expanded, or protected—regardless of your personal involvement.

Step 6: Expand Only With a System

Growth should now be systematic, not emotional. Don't launch new ventures just because they're trendy. Use a checklist:

- Does this venture fit within my credit ecosystem?
- Can it be funded with current limits or recycled capital?

- Can it be delegated or automated within 90 days?
- Will it require personal guarantees or disrupt my credit utilization?

If it checks the boxes, test it with a credit-funded MVP (minimum viable product). If it works, scale. If not, shut it down without damage to your core engine.

Building a Self-Sustaining Credit Wealth Engine: Nina's story

Nina stood barefoot on the deck of her vacation rental in Sedona, a steaming mug of chai in her hands, watching the sun climb over the red rock cliffs. It was 7:00 a.m., and her phone buzzed with a notification: "$997 payment received – Digital Strategy Blueprint." She didn't flinch. Didn't scramble. She simply smiled.

Because this wasn't luck. This was the result of something she had spent the last 18 months building—a credit-powered system that now worked harder than she did.

Nina had once worked in corporate marketing, commuting two hours a day, trading her ideas for a paycheck. When she discovered business credit, she wasn't just looking for capital—she was looking for control. Not just over her time, but over the flow of money, risk, and possibility.

She started simple: one LLC, one EIN, and a mission to create a digital course she could sell on autopilot. Using her business credit card, she funded her initial content creation, a Kajabi subscription, and paid a designer on Fiverr. She didn't overcomplicate it. She focused on results. Within three months, her first sale came in. Then another. Then ten.

But she didn't stop there.

She built an ecosystem. She set every bill—credit cards, vendor accounts, software tools—on autopay from her business checking account. She connected everything to QuickBooks and had a weekly report sent to her inbox. She didn't want to manage it manually. She wanted a machine.

Then, she expanded.

Nina opened a second business account under a new brand—this time a boutique social media agency that hired VAs from the Philippines. She used her 0% business credit cards to fund team training, ad campaigns, and a new website. She mapped out every billing cycle and used one card per campaign, paying it off with incoming revenue before the promo expired.

Each card had a job. Each account had a purpose. Nothing was random.

She even created a "Credit Playbook"—a shared Google Drive folder with SOPs that included login info, credit reporting cycles, banking contacts, and a project plan for each stream. If she ever got sick, her team could keep things running. If she ever sold a piece of her brand, the buyer would get a turnkey funding system.

At that point, Nina realized she wasn't building a business anymore. She was building a self-sustaining wealth engine.

The engine paid her monthly. It paid her team. It funded new experiments—like the AI tools she was developing or the real estate retreat she was planning to host. And it did all this without ever touching her personal credit.

Every quarter, Nina reviewed her dashboard: available credit, current utilization, income per project, interest-free periods left. She didn't guess anymore. She guided the machine.

When a friend asked her how she managed to work so little but grow so fast, she replied, "I don't run a business. I run a system. Credit is just the fuel."

Eventually, she formed a holding company—Legacy Works Inc.—and moved all her brands under it. This gave her better tax strategy, made it easier to apply for higher credit limits, and allowed her to eventually begin estate planning. She even wrote a letter to her niece, who she planned to mentor, explaining the entire system. Her true legacy wasn't just money—it was the ability to print possibility from a blueprint.

That morning in Sedona, as the desert air warmed and her inbox pinged with two more sales, Nina opened her journal and wrote:

> "I don't hustle anymore. I just adjust the engine. Credit gave me power. Structure gave me peace. Now I can pass it on."

Chapter 11: Credit-Conscious Exit Strategies and Wealth Transfer

Most entrepreneurs build with excitement—but few build with an exit in mind. In this final instructional chapter, we'll explore how to exit or transfer a credit-powered business the right way. Whether your goal is to sell, retire, delegate, or pass your company to the next generation, credit plays a central role in how well you transfer not just income—but wealth, structure, and stability.

Let's start by redefining what an "exit" really is.

An exit doesn't have to mean selling your company for millions and walking away. It can also mean:

- Handing operations to a team while retaining ownership
- Licensing your business model or content
- Selling a portion of your income streams
- Consolidating brands under a holding company
- Transferring ownership to family
- Creating a sellable asset using credit infrastructure

Regardless of your exit path, the goal is always the same: extract value without destroying the engine you built.

Step 1: Prepare Your Credit Profile for Sale or Transfer

Your business credit history is a major asset—especially when clean, active, and well-structured. To prepare for a future exit, you need to:

- Ensure all credit lines are tied to your EIN and not your SSN
- Remove personal guarantees wherever possible
- Keep utilization below 30% for at least 6 months before a sale
- Maintain on-time payments across all tradelines
- Diversify your credit profile with vendor, revolving, and installment credit

Buyers and successors will look at how fundable the business is. The stronger your credit structure, the more leverage you—and they—have.

Step 2: Clean and Document Your Financial Systems

Just like when selling a home, the cleaner the presentation, the higher the perceived value. Clean your financials by:

- Reconciling accounts
- Eliminating unnecessary subscriptions or unused credit lines
- Clearly labeling accounts by project, department, or stream

- Preparing a 12-month report of credit usage, payment history, and available funding
- Creating an SOP manual for your credit and cash flow systems

You should be able to show a prospective buyer or successor how your business uses credit to create growth, manage expenses, and preserve profit—without relying on your personal involvement.

Step 3: Convert Credit-Fueled Income Streams Into Sellable Assets

You may not sell the business itself—but you can sell parts of it. A course brand, a rental property, a YouTube channel, or an ecommerce store—all funded with credit—can be packaged and sold.

To do this:

- Isolate the income stream under a separate LLC or DBA
- Open dedicated accounts and credit cards for that stream
- Document expenses and ROI
- Create a repeatable growth plan using existing credit tools
- Determine the monthly net profit and multiply it by 24–36x (typical valuation range)

This creates "mini exits" that allow you to liquidate and reinvest—without walking away from your core business.

Step 4: Structure for Succession or Inheritance

If your goal is to pass your business to a child, spouse, or partner, credit must be integrated into your succession plan.

Steps include:

- Adding successors as authorized users on business credit cards
- Introducing them to your bankers, vendors, and account reps
- Teaching them your credit management system
- Creating legal documents (LLC operating agreement, family trust, will) outlining the transfer of ownership and credit responsibility
- Keeping all business credit activity isolated from your personal credit to avoid confusion during the transition

The smoother and clearer your systems, the easier it is for someone else to take over without stress or decline in credit performance.

Step 5: Protect and Preserve Your Credit Legacy

Even if you never plan to sell, you should protect what you've built. That means:

- Forming a holding company to consolidate and insulate assets
- Monitoring credit reports monthly
- Setting alerts for unusual activity
- Using a CPA or financial advisor to review credit usage and tax implications
- Continuously documenting systems in case of sudden illness, relocation, or opportunity

Lastly, pass on the knowledge. Whether to your children, mentees, or community, teach the blueprint. Your credit system isn't just for you—it's a framework others can benefit from, long after you stop using it.

A smart entrepreneur knows how to use credit. A legacy builder knows how to pass it on.

In the next and final section, we'll wrap this book with a powerful closing reflection and guide you toward the next book in the *Credit to Capital* series.

Credit-Conscious Exit Strategies and Wealth Transfer: Jason's story

Jason stood in front of a small group of real estate investors at a local networking event, clicking through the final slides of his presentation. Behind him, on the projector screen, was a breakdown of his last 12 months: three income-producing properties, one online course generating consistent sales, and a short-term rental business—all funded and scaled using business credit. The room was impressed. But what caught everyone's attention was his final slide: "Preparing Your Business Credit for Exit or Transfer."

After the Q&A, one attendee approached him. "Jason, I've heard hundreds of talks on real estate and funding," she said. "But I've never heard anyone talk about how to exit from it. Why now?"

Jason smiled. "Because I didn't build all this to die with it. I built it to pass on."

Just two years earlier, Jason had been working a full-time job while managing one rental on the side. Business credit changed everything. He used a single $15,000 card to renovate a short-term rental, paid it off with bookings, then duplicated the model under two new LLCs. With his credit built across three entities, he rotated projects, timed his float periods, and reinvested profits into automation. He called it his credit-powered flywheel.

But after his son was born, Jason began thinking differently.

"I don't want my son to inherit keys," he told his wife one night. "I want him to inherit a system."

So Jason began his exit prep—not because he was leaving, but because he wanted options. He opened a holding company, transferred ownership of his three LLCs to it, and restructured every bank account, credit card, and vendor relationship under that umbrella. He created SOPs for each: what card paid for what, when payments were due, how to apply for new lines, and how to track usage.

He brought his virtual assistant in for training. "If anything ever happens to me," he said, "you'll help my wife manage this until she's ready."

Next, he taught his younger brother—who was in college—how to build credit the right way. "I'm not just giving you a credit card," Jason said. "I'm giving you a blueprint." Together, they created a content channel teaching others how to build business credit responsibly. It became another stream—built entirely on the same system.

Jason also started thinking about selling one of his course brands. It was fully automated, had its own credit lines, and brought in $4,000/month in passive income. He cleaned up the reports, removed himself as a personal guarantor, and listed the brand on a digital marketplace with documentation of how the business used credit to scale.

Three months later, he sold it for $98,000.

But Jason didn't spend it. He reinvested—into a legacy.

He met with a business attorney and created a family trust. He listed Legacy Holdings LLC as a beneficiary and named his wife and son as successors. Inside the trust were the rental properties, the holding company, the remaining businesses, and all associated credit systems.

One evening, he walked his wife through the entire structure.

"This card handles the ad spend," he explained. "These two are vendor lines. This account is tied to property maintenance. This binder?" He tapped it gently. "That's everything you need to know."

She looked overwhelmed, but grateful.

"Why are you doing all this now?" she asked.

Jason paused. "Because the best legacy isn't the money we leave behind. It's the systems that keep feeding the family after we're gone."

Years later, when his son was older, Jason handed him a binder titled *"The Credit Engine Blueprint."* Inside were years of documentation, lessons, passwords, strategies, and a letter:

> "You don't have to hustle like I did. You just have to learn the system. Credit gave me access. Systems gave me peace. Now I give both to you."

And that's how Jason exited—not from business, but from the stress of not knowing how to preserve it.

Final Words from the Author — Joe Correa

If you've made it to the end of this book, I want to start with something simple, but important: I'm proud of you. Not because you've just listened to hours of strategy, tips, and real-world applications—but because you're clearly serious about building something that most people never even attempt: **financial control powered by leverage, discipline, and vision**.

This journey isn't easy. It takes patience, and it requires you to unlearn a lot of what you were taught about credit, money, and risk. Most people are trained to fear credit. To avoid it. To treat it like a trap instead of a tool. But now, you know better.

Credit, when used with strategy and purpose, is **one of the most powerful tools in the world**. It doesn't just give you access to money—it gives you access to momentum. To opportunities. To scalable systems. Credit allows you to fund what matters before you've saved the money to do so—and to profit in ways that compound over time.

Throughout this series, I've shared with you not just tactics, but frameworks—how to build, how to protect, how to scale, and how to structure credit for real wealth. What you choose to do next is up to you. You could take one strategy from this book and change your life. You could take five and build a thriving business. Or, you could take everything and build a system that frees you completely.

My hope is that you never again look at credit as something that controls you. Instead, see yourself as the **orchestrator of a financial engine**. You now have the blueprint to create money when you need it, expand income when you want it, and reduce risk as you grow.

Let me tell you this: I've seen credit change lives. I've watched people go from underbanked and overlooked to owning property, launching digital products, and flipping businesses they built with no money down. I've helped immigrants, single parents, young professionals, and retirees all use the same system you've just learned to create options they never had before.

I've also seen what happens when this knowledge is passed on—when children grow up watching their parents use credit responsibly, build companies, and talk about business and ownership at the dinner table.

That's legacy. That's the kind of impact that doesn't just last a lifetime—it echoes through generations.

And that's what I want for you.

Here's my final advice to you, from someone who started with a $500 credit card and turned it into a global business:

- **Always be a student.** The world of credit evolves. Laws change. Tools improve. Keep learning, keep testing, and keep adjusting.
- **Use credit for assets, not indulgence.** If it doesn't pay you back in time, don't swipe for it.
- **Track everything.** Wealth loves clarity. The more you track, the faster you'll grow.
- **Don't rush.** Build your credit ecosystem the right way. Slow is smooth. Smooth is fast.
- **Teach what you learn.** Show your kids. Show your community. Be the example.

Most people never get access to this kind of knowledge. You do. That means you have the responsibility—and the opportunity—to use it wisely.

Whether your next move is launching a new income stream, buying your first investment property, or selling a credit-funded business for six figures, know this: you're no longer starting from scratch. You're starting with **strategy**.

And if no one has told you lately—you are fully capable of building wealth, protecting your future, and creating something that matters.

Thank you for trusting me with your time, your attention, and your financial journey. I look forward to hearing your success story. And remember, this is just the beginning.

With respect and belief in your potential,

Joe Correa

Epilogue: Where to Go From Here — Your Next Financial Evolution

You've come a long way.

You started with a simple concept—using business credit to grow your financial potential—and ended up with a system that can transform your income, your business, and your future. But now that you've reached the end of this book, the real question is: **What's next?**

The truth is, there's no one-size-fits-all answer. Some of you will finish this book and immediately launch your first credit-funded business. Others will restructure existing operations, improve their financial discipline, or begin building a legacy from the ground up. And a few of you may need to go back and re-listen to certain chapters to solidify your foundation before moving forward. That's all part of the process.

Because credit mastery isn't a race. It's a **financial evolution**.

You've learned how to build your credit profile from scratch, how to stack and time funding opportunities, how to automate and protect your ecosystem, and how to use business credit to acquire income-producing assets. You now understand how to scale without stress and how to convert credit into capital that funds not just ideas—but freedom.

But there's one more level, and it starts here.

Leveling Up: From Operator to Architect

In the early stages of business, you're the operator—doing, managing, building from the ground up. But as your credit and income grow, your role needs to evolve. You must become the **architect**—the one who builds the blueprint, hires the right people, installs automation, and steps away from the day-to-day.

That's when true wealth begins—not just income, but time, ownership, and peace of mind.

Think about this: the wealthiest people in the world don't just run businesses. They design businesses that **run without them**. They use credit to acquire, scale, and systematize. They focus on structure. And you can too.

That's why the next stage in your journey might not be another credit card or business—it might be building **teams**, expanding into **multiple entities**, or creating a **holding company** that allows you to protect everything you've built under one umbrella.

Shifting to Portfolio Thinking

Once you've proven you can build one income stream, the question becomes: how do I build five? Ten?

This is where **portfolio thinking** becomes crucial. Your goal should no longer be just to grow one business—but to develop a diversified collection of revenue-producing assets across different markets. Some digital. Some physical. Some passive. Some active.

The engine behind it all? Business credit.

You can use it to:

- Launch new ventures without risking savings
- Buy into profitable businesses or partnerships
- Acquire undervalued assets and improve them
- Flip credit-funded businesses or brands for lump-sum exits
- Invest in income-generating systems for long-term holding

Start thinking like an investor. Use credit to **control**, not consume. The more streams you control, the less dependent you are on any single one. And the more confident you'll feel about the future.

Reinforcing Your Financial Legacy

Building wealth is only half the equation. The other half is protecting it—and **passing it on**.

That's where estate planning, trusts, family LLCs, and documented systems come into play. Begin writing down your processes. Teach your children, your spouse, your team. Create documentation that explains how your credit lines work, when payments are due, where to apply, and how to manage usage.

It may feel early—but creating **continuity** ensures that what you've built doesn't disappear if you're ever absent. That's not morbid—it's smart. It's what true wealth builders do.

And if you're thinking, "But I'm not there yet," remember: you weren't here either when you started Book One.

You've grown. And your next chapter is already writing itself.

VOLUME 9: HOW TO GET $1M IN CREDIT AND KEEP IT

Building a Million in Credit Isn't a Dream — It's a Strategy

When most people hear "$1 million in credit," they picture private jets, luxury cars, and high-risk lifestyles. But the truth is, building seven figures in credit isn't about showing off—it's about unlocking control. Control over your finances. Control over your business. Control over your future.

In this audiobook, you'll learn the step-by-step blueprint for how I—and thousands of others—built well over a million in total available credit. Not just personal credit, but business credit too. You'll learn how to get it, how to manage it, how to avoid common traps, and most importantly, how to keep it working for you long-term.

This isn't just theory. You'll get real examples, real numbers, and practical steps that you can follow whether you're just getting started or already have strong credit and want to go to the next level.

Why This Book Matters Now More Than Ever

Banks are tightening. Lenders are cautious. And AI is starting to make credit decisions faster and more data-driven than ever. That's both an opportunity and a threat. If you understand how the system works, you can use it to scale—responsibly and sustainably. If you don't, one bad move can cost you everything you've built.

This book is about longevity and leverage. You'll learn how to position yourself to:

- Get $100,000 in new credit every 3–6 months
- Maintain lender trust and avoid shutdowns
- Turn credit into income-producing assets
- Build business credit that doesn't rely on your personal guarantee
- Monitor and protect your credit profile like a pro

Whether you're a real estate investor, business owner, or entrepreneur looking to scale, this audiobook will give you the full roadmap to hit the $1M mark—and stay there.

The Structure of This Audiobook

Each chapter is designed to be easy to follow, starting with a step-by-step instructional format followed by a real-world story that shows the lessons in action. At the end, you'll find a complete checklist and strategy summary to help you implement what you've learned.

If you've made it to Book 9 of this series, you're already ahead of 99% of the population. Let's keep going. Let's break the barrier. And let's do it smart.

Welcome to **"How to Get $1M in Credit and Keep It."** Let's begin.

Chapter 1: Understanding the $1M Credit Blueprint

What Does $1M in Credit Actually Mean?

Before we begin chasing numbers, let's define them. Getting to $1 million in credit doesn't mean holding a million in debt. It means having access to credit—secured or unsecured—that adds up to a seven-figure total.

This includes:

- Personal credit cards with high limits
- Business credit cards and lines of credit
- Personal and business loans
- Revolving credit lines like HELOCs
- Equipment and vendor financing

The key difference between amateurs and experts is **control**. Professionals build access to large credit limits without maxing them out. They use credit strategically, not emotionally.

❖ **Rule #1:** Getting $1M in credit is not a one-time event—it's a layered strategy of approvals, management, and growth over time.

The Four Pillars of Million-Dollar Credit

To reach this level, you need to build on these four pillars:

1. **Strong Personal Credit Foundation**
   - 720+ FICO score
   - At least 3–5 primary accounts over 3+ years
   - Low credit utilization (<10%)
   - No recent derogatory marks
2. **Established Business Credit Profile**
   - Active LLC or Corporation
   - D-U-N-S Number with strong Paydex score
   - Vendor trade lines reporting to business credit bureaus
   - Separate EIN and business bank account
3. **Strategic Credit Applications**
   - Applying for cards and credit in batches (credit stacking)

    - Targeting lenders that pull from different credit bureaus
    - Leveraging 0% intro APR and balance transfer offers to fuel growth

4. **Responsible Credit Behavior**
    - Never carry high balances on personal cards
    - Pay early or on time, every time
    - Keep a strong mix of credit (revolving and installment)

Building in Phases — From $0 to $1M

Most people fail because they try to jump from $10K in credit to $1M in one leap. Here's a phased approach that works:

Phase 1: The First $100K

- Personal cards from high-limit lenders (Amex, Chase, Navy Federal)
- Business credit cards from your existing bank (e.g., Capital One Spark, Chase Ink)
- 2–3 vendor tradelines reporting to D&B and Experian Business

Phase 2: The $250K Tier

- Add LOCs (Lines of Credit) and credit union cards
- Apply for business fuel cards, fleet cards, and store credit
- Establish 6+ tradelines and 3+ personal cards with low balances

Phase 3: The $500K+ Leap

- Leverage relationship banking for large LOCs and term loans
- Request credit limit increases every 6 months
- Use personal credit as a guarantor if needed to secure initial large lines

Phase 4: The $1M Positioning

- Access 5–7 business credit cards with limits above $30K
- Use high-limit personal cards as a foundation for asset purchases
- Add strategic financing tools: equipment financing, invoice factoring, HELOCs on investment properties

The Hidden Traps That Kill Long-Term Credit

It's not just about getting the credit. It's about keeping it. These traps destroy long-term access:

1. **Over-utilization** – Carrying high balances will trigger lender concern, even if you're paying on time.

2. **Inactivity** – Accounts can be closed for inactivity, especially business cards.

3. **Hard pull stacking without strategy** – Applying randomly can get you blacklisted.

4. **Mixing personal and business expenses** – Especially on business cards—this raises red flags.

5. **Cross-default clauses** – Missing one payment on a bank product can cause other accounts to be closed.

6. **Unreported changes** – Change in income, business structure, or address can invalidate your terms.

Your 90-Day Action Plan to Start

Let's set some real-world goals you can accomplish in the next 90 days:

Week 1–2

- Check your personal credit report from all 3 bureaus

- Open a business bank account
- Get your D-U-N-S Number (free from Dun & Bradstreet)

Week 3–4

- Apply for 2–3 net 30 vendor accounts
- Apply for a business credit card (e.g., Chase Ink or Amex Blue Business)
- Ask for a credit limit increase on one personal card

Month 2

- Make on-time payments to vendor accounts
- Use less than 10% of your personal credit limit
- Open a credit union account and explore LOC options

Month 3

- Apply for 1–2 more business cards with different banks
- Begin tracking your business Paydex and Experian Business score
- Schedule your next round of credit limit increases

- ❖ **Pro Tip:** Stay consistent. Credit growth is exponential, but only if you master the fundamentals.

The Wake-Up Call

Michael Reynolds sat in his small home office in Tampa, Florida, sipping his coffee while staring at his laptop screen. The same spreadsheet he'd looked at for weeks taunted him: $42,000 in total available credit, maxed-out cards, and a business idea going nowhere fast.

He had good intentions. Two years ago, he started a mobile detailing business, funded by a single personal credit card. No business account. No LLC. Just hustle.

Now, he was burned out, behind on payments, and terrified that one more late fee would tank his credit score. He'd never even heard of business credit—until one YouTube video changed everything.

In that video, the speaker said something Michael couldn't forget: **"You can get $1 million in credit if you follow the process—but only if you treat credit like a business asset, not a lifeline."**

Something clicked.

That night, Michael stayed up until 2 a.m. Googling terms like "business tradelines," "DUNS number," and "credit stacking." By the time he closed his laptop, he had a new goal: rebuild his credit the right way and build $1 million in total credit across personal and business lines.

Rebuilding the Foundation

Michael started with the basics.

He pulled all three of his personal credit reports, identified the high utilization that was killing his score, and called each creditor to negotiate better terms. He applied for a secured card with a credit union and committed to paying it off weekly.

Next, he formed **Reynolds Auto Solutions LLC** and opened a business bank account with Navy Federal. It was a simple step—but it changed everything. Suddenly, he was being treated like a business, not just a broke guy with a side hustle.

He applied for a **D-U-N-S number**, ordered a virtual office address, and signed up with Uline and Grainger—two vendor accounts that reported to Dun & Bradstreet. Within 30 days, those accounts showed up on his business credit profile.

When he checked his Paydex score 60 days later, it was 80.

"Now I can build," he thought.

The Credit Stacking Strategy

With his personal credit utilization down to 9% and three business tradelines reporting positively, Michael moved into what he called "Phase 2"—strategic applications.

He learned to group his credit applications in **batches**, targeting lenders that pulled from different bureaus. He applied for a **Chase Ink Preferred** (approved for $15,000), an **Amex Blue Business Plus** (approved for $20,000), and a **Capital One Spark Cash** (approved for $10,000).

In just 30 days, his total credit jumped from $42,000 to **$87,000**.

Three months later, he repeated the process. He requested credit limit increases, opened new business lines with Sam's Club and Shell Fleet, and kept usage low.

When he hit $150K, it finally sank in—he was playing a different game now.

But the real test was coming.

Temptation and Discipline

Success was intoxicating. With over $200K in available credit, Michael got offers for everything—loans, credit cards, even luxury car financing. He almost said yes to a Tesla Model Y he didn't need.

But he remembered the rule: **"Just because you have credit, doesn't mean you use it recklessly."**

Instead, he invested $50K into building an online detailing course, set up an ad campaign, and hired a VA to help run the business backend. Within 6 months, the course brought in $6,000/month in passive income.

With that income, he was never late on payments. He kept utilization under 7%, paid off his balances weekly, and requested increases every 6 months like clockwork.

By year two, he had six business cards, five vendor tradelines, two business LOCs, and four personal cards—totaling **$1.1 million in available credit**.

Legacy Over Leverage

Now 37, Michael mentors other entrepreneurs. He teaches them that million-dollar credit isn't about racking up debt. It's about leverage, discipline, and building long-term trust with banks and institutions.

He tells his students:

> "If you chase credit like cash, it'll ruin you. But if you build credit as a tool—strategically, intentionally—you'll have more power than most people ever imagine."

Michael didn't become a millionaire overnight. But with a solid plan, disciplined execution, and long-term thinking, he earned what most people only dream about: control, freedom, and legacy.

And it all started with a late night, a spreadsheet, and a decision to take credit seriously.

Chapter 2: The Personal Credit Foundation – Your First Million Starts Here

Why Personal Credit Is Still King

Even if your end goal is to build massive business credit, your personal credit score will always play a key role—especially in the early stages. Lenders use your personal FICO score to gauge your overall risk. A weak personal score can disqualify you from high-limit cards, lower your business credit approvals, and block you from crucial funding opportunities.

To put it simply: **If your personal credit isn't solid, your $1M credit strategy will crumble.**

Here's why personal credit matters:

- It's often required to **personally guarantee** business credit cards or loans
- It reflects your **financial habits** to lenders and partners
- It's the foundation for **mortgages, car loans, and HELOCs**
- It can **fast-track approvals** when applying for large lines of credit

If you're starting below 700, this chapter is your game plan to get to 740+ and stay there.

Anatomy of a High FICO Score

FICO scores range from 300 to 850, and you need to be at **720 or higher** to access the best rates and limits. Here's how your score is calculated:

FICO Score Breakdown:

1. **35% – Payment History:** Late payments are credit killers. Even one can drop your score by 50+ points.

2. **30% – Credit Utilization:** Try to stay below 10% of your total credit limit across all cards. Below 30% is okay, but <10% is optimal.

3. **15% – Length of Credit History:** The longer your accounts are open, the better. Don't close old accounts unless absolutely necessary.

4. **10% – New Credit Inquiries:** Limit hard inquiries to 2–3 every six months. Too many can trigger denials or lower scores.

5. **10% – Credit Mix:** A healthy mix includes revolving credit (credit cards) and installment loans (car loans, student loans, etc.).

- ❖ **Action Step:** Pull your credit report from all 3 bureaus (Experian, TransUnion, Equifax) and dispute any inaccurate items.

Repair, Rebuild, and Optimize

Whether your score is 650 or 800, there are always ways to improve or optimize it for strategic growth.

If Your Score Is Below 700:

- **Dispute inaccuracies** on your credit report using tools like Credit Karma or Experian Boost.
- Apply for **secured credit cards** or credit-builder loans.
- Ask family or friends with good history to **add you as an authorized user** on their cards.
- Pay off collections and negotiate for **"pay-for-delete"** arrangements when possible.

If Your Score Is 700–750:

- Keep utilization low and begin requesting **credit limit increases** every 6 months.
- Open a **new high-limit card** from a top-tier bank (e.g., Amex, Chase).
- Maintain perfect payment history.

If Your Score Is 750+:

- Use your strong credit to **apply for large business credit lines** with a PG (personal guarantee).
- Begin leveraging your credit to fund **income-producing assets** (real estate, digital products, etc.).

❖ Pro Tip: Keep your total personal card balances below $1,000—even if you have $50K in available credit. It's not about how much you're allowed to spend, it's how little you actually use.

Credit Habits of Million-Dollar Borrowers

Building a strong credit foundation isn't just about what you do once—it's about the habits you build and repeat every month. High-limit borrowers and wealth builders tend to follow these rules:

❖ Golden Credit Habits:

- **Pay in full** before the statement date (not just due date)
- **Avoid carrying balances** into the next month unless using a 0% promo offer
- **Check scores monthly** using free services or paid monitoring
- **Never co-sign** for others—it's a shortcut to disaster
- **Use autopay** to prevent accidental missed payments
- **Negotiate annual fees or request waivers** on premium cards
- **Track due dates and utilization** with apps like Credit Karma, Mint, or MyFICO

If you want to keep $1M in credit, you have to look like someone the banks can trust with $10M. That means discipline, transparency, and precision.

Build Personal Credit with These Tools

Now that you understand the habits and structure, here are powerful tools and resources to help speed up your credit journey:

- Tools That Work:

- **Experian Boost** – Instantly adds on-time utility and phone payments to your Experian report
- **Self (formerly Self Lender)** – Credit-builder loan that adds installment credit history
- **Navy Federal Credit Union** – High-limit cards for members with strong internal scores
- **Amex EveryDay Preferred** – Good for long-term usage and limit growth
- **Capital One Venture X** – Premium card with business applications and strong limit growth potential

30-Day Checklist:

1. Pull all 3 credit reports and fix errors
2. Set up autopay for every card or loan
3. Keep balances <10% (ideally 1–3%)
4. Request 1–2 credit limit increases
5. Apply for 1 strong personal card if ready

- Warning: Do NOT apply for multiple cards unless you've checked which bureaus they pull from. Spread applications to avoid excessive hard pulls on one report.

Next Step: Now that your personal credit foundation is solid, it's time to build **business credit without a personal guarantee** — that's the topic for Chapter 3.

The Credit Denial That Changed Everything

Ava Morales stood in line at her local bank, nervous but excited. After three years of running her mobile notary business in Orlando, she was finally applying for a small business line of credit. She had built a loyal client base, maintained decent income, and wanted to scale.

But when the banker returned, he didn't have good news.

"I'm sorry, Ava. You were denied. Your FICO score is a 612, and there are some red flags."

Her stomach dropped. She'd paid her bills—mostly. But she'd made the classic mistakes: maxed out two cards during a slow season, paid one credit card 32 days late, and ignored a $58 medical bill that went to collections.

She felt humiliated—but determined.

That night, she made a decision: she was going to fix her personal credit no matter what. And not just fix it—she was going to build a bulletproof score so no lender could deny her again.

The Repair Begins

Ava spent the weekend researching everything she could on credit repair. She signed up for **Credit Karma** and ordered her **three full credit reports**.

She found:

- One late payment (Capital One, 32 days late)
- A $58 collection (a lab bill she never received)
- Two cards maxed out: $3,000 limit with a $2,950 balance, and a $1,500 card at $1,400

She didn't panic. She made a plan.

First, she **called the collection agency**, paid the $58 in full, and got them to agree to a "pay-for-delete." Next, she called Capital One, explained the late payment, and politely asked if they'd remove the late mark as a courtesy. They said no—but she added a consumer statement explaining the one-time issue.

Then she **cut her spending by 40%**, used her side income to pay down the high balances, and set up **autopay on every single account**.

By the end of Month 1, her score jumped to **662**.

Rebuilding Strategically

In Month 2, Ava opened a **Self credit-builder loan** and added herself as an **authorized user** on her cousin's long-standing Amex card with a $10,000 limit and perfect payment history.

That one move gave her an instant credit age boost, raised her available credit, and pushed her score to **693**.

Excited, she reached out to **Navy Federal Credit Union** and opened an account. Because she had a military spouse, she qualified for membership. She applied for their **CashRewards card**—and was approved for **$5,000**.

It was the first time she had a card approved over $2,000. It felt like a turning point.

Her mindset shifted. She started treating her credit like a business asset, not a reactive tool. She paid off every card **before the statement date**, used no more than 3% of her limit, and checked her score weekly.

By Month 5, her FICO score hit **737**.

Unlocking Real Leverage

With her credit now in the 700s, Ava finally felt ready to try again.

She applied for:

- **Amex Blue Cash Preferred** (approved: $8,000)
- **Discover It** (approved: $6,500)
- **Capital One Quicksilver** (approved: $7,000)

Instead of celebrating by spending, she focused on preserving the gains. She rotated small recurring bills across her cards—Spotify, her phone bill, and monthly software. Everything else went through her business account.

By Month 8, she'd built:

- A 790 FICO score
- $28,500 in total personal credit limits
- Zero late payments
- Zero balances carried forward

She was now in a position to apply for **$25K–$50K business cards** with a personal guarantee—and she was ready.

A Whole New Game

Ava walked back into that same bank 10 months later. This time, she brought her new business tax ID, proof of income, and her pristine credit report.

She wasn't just applying for a loan—she was **positioning her business** for growth.

The banker reviewed her file, nodded, and smiled.

"You've really turned things around. We can offer you a $40,000 business line to start, backed by your personal credit."

Ava grinned. This was just the beginning.

From 612 to 790, from denied to approved, from reactive to strategic—Ava had proven that anyone with the right mindset, the right tools, and enough discipline could build a foundation strong enough to hold **$1 million in credit**.

Her motto became simple: **"Credit is power. But only when you control it."**

Chapter 3: Building Business Credit Without a Personal Guarantee

Why Business Credit is the Fast Lane to $1M

While personal credit is the foundation, **business credit is the acceleration**. It allows you to access funding that doesn't report to your personal credit report, avoids damaging your debt-to-income ratio, and—most importantly—**can grow much faster** than personal credit.

And here's the key: you can build business credit **without using your Social Security Number or a personal guarantee (PG).**

This is what separates high-level credit users from everyone else. Business credit is reported to commercial bureaus like:

- **Dun & Bradstreet**
- **Experian Business**
- **Equifax Business**

Your goal is to build a strong business profile that lenders trust—so they approve large limits without tying it to your personal credit.

Setting Up Your Business for Credit Success

Before you apply for a single business card or vendor account, your business must be "credit ready." Lenders look at several factors to determine if your company looks legitimate and fundable.

Fundable Business Checklist:

- **LLC or Corporation** – Sole proprietors are high-risk. Form an LLC or Inc. through your state's website.
- **EIN from IRS** – Free from the IRS website. Do not use your SSN.
- **Business Bank Account** – Open this right after forming your business. All expenses must run through this.
- **D-U-N-S Number** – Register for free at Dun & Bradstreet. This is your business credit identity.
- **Business Phone Number** – Get a dedicated number (e.g., Grasshopper or Google Voice).
- **Professional Email & Website** – Use a domain-branded email (e.g., info@YourCompany.com) and basic website.
- **Business Address** – Use a virtual business address if you work from home (e.g., Regus, Opus, or iPostal1).

- ❖ Warning: Mismatched addresses, phone numbers, or inconsistent business info across credit apps will trigger red flags.

The Tier System of Business Credit

Think of business credit like climbing stairs. You can't jump to the top tier overnight. You build your profile by progressing through **credit tiers**, each one unlocking more powerful funding opportunities.

Tier 1: Net-30 Vendor Accounts

These accounts give you supplies or services on credit and report to business bureaus. Start with:

- **Uline** (office supplies)
- **Grainger** (tools and industrial supplies)
- **Quill** (cleaning and office items)
- **Summa Office Supplies**
- **Nav.com** (business credit monitoring)

Buy something small, pay within 30 days, and repeat for 3–6 months. These tradelines will begin reporting.

Tier 2: Store Cards (PG Optional)

Once 3–5 tradelines are reporting, apply for store credit cards like:

- **Amazon Business**
- **Sam's Club**
- **Office Depot**
- **Staples Business Advantage**

Some may ask for a personal guarantee, but others don't if your business credit file is strong.

Tier 3: Fleet Cards

Used for fuel and auto maintenance:

- **WEX Fleet**
- **Shell Business**
- **Fuelman**

These are often no-PG with a strong business profile.

Tier 4: Business Credit Cards & LOCs

With 6–8 tradelines, solid payment history, and revenue proof, you can qualify for:

- **Amex Blue Business Cash**
- **Chase Ink Business Unlimited**
- **Divvy or Brex** (modern no-PG fintech cards)

Keep It Separate and Clean

Many entrepreneurs ruin their business credit by **mixing it with personal spending** or by skipping essential business practices.

Rules for Using Business Credit Responsibly:

- **Never use personal credit for business expenses** (especially if trying to get non-PG cards)
- **Keep business purchases consistent and necessary** (supplies, software, marketing—not personal vacations)
- **Pay off business accounts early**—even earlier than net terms
- **Track all purchases and categories** in your bookkeeping software (e.g., QuickBooks or Wave)

Also, make sure to **monitor your business credit reports** regularly. Errors are common, and they can destroy your credibility without notice.

- ❖ Pro Tip: Sign up for **Nav.com** or **CreditSignal** by Dun & Bradstreet to track your Paydex and Experian Business scores for free.

90-Day Business Credit Building Blueprint

Month 1: Foundation

- Form LLC and apply for EIN
- Get business phone, email, and address
- Open a business checking account
- Register with Dun & Bradstreet and get your D-U-N-S number

Month 2: Tradelines

- Open 3–4 Net-30 accounts (Uline, Quill, Summa)
- Make small purchases and pay invoices in full before due date
- Monitor for when tradelines start reporting

Month 3: Growth

- Apply for 1–2 Tier 2 store cards (Amazon Business, Office Depot)
- Request business credit limit increases if available
- Apply for a business monitoring service to track your Paydex and Experian Business score

Once these steps are complete, you'll be positioned to apply for your **first $10K–$50K in real business credit**—without ever tying it to your personal credit score.

- ❖ Remember: This process takes consistency. Business credit grows faster than personal credit—but only if you respect the structure.

Darren's Business Credit Playbook

Rock Bottom and a New Beginning

Darren Price had been a high school economics teacher for over a decade. He loved teaching but hated the paycheck. Every year, inflation crept up, and his salary barely moved. He dreamed of starting a financial literacy company for teens—but he had one major problem.

His credit score was okay. Not amazing—just okay. But more importantly, he didn't want to risk his personal credit or co-sign anything. With a family of four, he wasn't willing to bet their future on a business that hadn't proven itself yet.

So instead of applying for loans or personal credit cards to fund his dream, Darren went down a different path: **business credit without a personal guarantee.**

He didn't know anyone else who'd done it. But after months of reading, watching, and obsessing over credit-building strategies, he decided: if this is real, I'm going to make it work.

Making His Business "Lender Ready"

The first thing Darren did was legitimize his business.

He created **SmartStart Youth, LLC**, applied for an **EIN**, and opened a **business checking account** with a local credit union. He made sure the business had:

- A virtual address (not his home)
- A dedicated business phone line
- A branded domain email (info@smartstartyouth.com)
- A basic website outlining his services

He then registered for a **D-U-N-S number** on Dun & Bradstreet and created a free account on **Nav.com** to monitor his business credit activity.

No one had ever taught him this in his finance degree. But within two weeks, he had what looked—on paper—like a 10-year-old company.

The First Credit Moves

Darren started by ordering $40 worth of printer paper and markers from **Uline**. He paid the invoice five days early.

Then he ordered light cleaning supplies from **Quill**, followed by office accessories from **Grainger**. He repeated the same process: buy small, pay early, let it report.

He made sure **nothing was purchased personally**. Every order was logged in a spreadsheet and paid through the business account.

After three months, he saw it: three tradelines were reporting to Dun & Bradstreet and Experian Business. His Paydex score was 80.

It felt like a win.

By Month 4, he applied for his first non-PG store credit card—**Office Depot Business**. He was approved for $2,500.

Then came **Amazon Business**, **Staples Advantage**, and **Shell Fleet**. Approvals started coming more easily, and his confidence grew.

> "I was finally building something that didn't depend on my personal name," he later said. "It was like watching a separate version of myself grow financially."

Growth Without Guarantees

At Month 6, Darren's small curriculum packs were selling on TeachersPayTeachers and Shopify. Revenue was modest—$1,000/month—but his business profile was strong.

That's when he decided to apply for his first big leap: the **Divvy Business Card**—a modern fintech card that didn't require a PG.

Approved. $6,000 limit.

Then came **Brex**, followed by an offer from a local bank for a $15,000 line of credit—all approved based solely on his business performance and tradeline strength.

He was now at **$42,500 in business credit**, with **zero ties to his personal credit report**.

His personal score never dropped. No hard pulls. No risk to his family's finances. And every single account was paid in full, early, and tracked meticulously.

Darren's Business Credit Philosophy

Today, Darren speaks at school board conferences and parent associations across the Southeast. His company, SmartStart Youth, is now making over **$8,000/month**, and his business credit limit sits at **$126,000**—with more applications in the pipeline.

His advice to new entrepreneurs is simple:

> "Don't think of credit as a backup plan. Think of it as a growth engine. And never, ever confuse your personal credit with your business ambitions."

He continues to use vendor accounts, Tier 2 cards, and business-only loans to fund expansions—still without any personal guarantees.

From teacher salary to six-figure business credit, Darren proved that building wealth through credit doesn't require risk—it just requires **structure, patience, and professionalism.**

His personal goal? "$1 million in business credit. No shortcuts. No personal guarantees. Just smart, disciplined growth."

Chapter 4: Credit Stacking — How to Build Credit Fast Without Getting Shut Down

What Is Credit Stacking?

Credit stacking is the strategy of applying for multiple high-limit credit cards or lines of credit **in a short window of time** across different lenders, **without triggering red flags** or damaging your score. The goal is to maximize approvals before the new accounts or inquiries show up on your reports.

Used correctly, this strategy can unlock $50K–$250K in new credit within 90 days. Used recklessly, it can get you flagged, denied, or blacklisted.

Why It Works:

- Most lenders only see **their own inquiry in real time**
- There's a **24–72 hour lag** before new applications or approvals hit the credit bureaus
- Strategic planning allows you to take advantage of this lag and build fast, without panic

❖ Key Principle: You're not "gaming" the system—you're simply **understanding timing, bureau pulls, and risk**

management.

Timing and the 48-Hour Rule

The biggest risk in credit stacking is spreading out your applications. If you apply for Card A today and Card B next week, B may see A's new inquiry—and deny you.

To avoid that, apply within a **tight 24–48 hour window**, using this sequence:

1. Personal credit cards first (if needed)
2. Business credit cards next
3. Lines of credit and high-limit business funding last

Why this order? Because business cards often don't show up on personal credit, and LOCs are more conservative with approvals.

- Pro Tip: Use tools like **CreditBoards.com** or **Doctor of Credit** to find out which bureaus each lender pulls from, and plan accordingly.

Bureau Diversification — The Smart Stacking Advantage

Not all lenders pull from the same credit bureaus. This is a key element of smart stacking.

Example Breakdown:

- **Chase**: Typically pulls **Experian**
- **Amex**: Often pulls **Experian**
- **Navy Federal**: Usually pulls **TransUnion**
- **Capital One**: Pulls from **all 3 bureaus**
- **Discover**: Often pulls **Equifax**

By choosing lenders that pull from **different bureaus,** you can:

- Avoid multiple hard pulls on the same report
- Protect your score from sudden drops
- Spread inquiries evenly across your profile

This allows you to stack 3–6 approvals with minimal impact on any single bureau.

How to Prepare for a Stacking Round

Pre-Stack Checklist:

- Credit score above 720 (ideally 740+)

- Utilization under 10% (ideally under 5%)
- No new inquiries in the past 60 days
- Business is credit-ready with 3+ tradelines reporting
- All recent payments made early or on time

Application Flow:

1. Day 1 AM: Apply for 2 personal cards (e.g., Amex Platinum, Chase Sapphire)
2. Day 1 PM: Apply for 2 business cards (e.g., Amex Blue Business, Chase Ink)
3. Day 2 AM: Apply for 1–2 more business cards or LOCs (Divvy, Brex, regional banks)

Keep a spreadsheet to track:

- Application date
- Lender and product
- Approved/denied status
- Credit bureau pulled

- Credit limit received

❖ Tip: Request **credit limit increases** on your existing cards 2 weeks prior to stacking. This boosts your total available credit and score.

After the Stack — Protecting Your Profile

The stacking round is done—but your work isn't.

Here's how to protect your new approvals and ensure long-term growth:

Post-Stack Action Plan:

- **Freeze new applications** for 3–6 months to avoid suspicion
- **Keep utilization under 10%** on each card and under 5% total
- Set **autopay for all new accounts**
- Call lenders to request **monthly reporting**
- After 90 days, **request credit limit increases** on all new cards

Avoid applying for more credit too soon. Lenders monitor new accounts and will shut down cards if they see excessive growth that looks risky.

- Red Flag Behaviors:
  - Applying for 10+ cards in 2 weeks
  - Maxing out newly opened cards
  - Missing first payments or making only minimums
  - Shuffling balances aggressively between cards

Used correctly, credit stacking can help you leap from $25K to $150K in credit **without harming your score**. Used carelessly, it can destroy your credibility overnight.

Stack smart. Stack small. Stack intentionally.

Naomi's 3-Day Credit Leap

A Bold Goal with No Room for Error

Naomi Carter was no stranger to hard work. She'd built her online nutrition coaching business from scratch, working nights and weekends while raising two kids as a single mom in Atlanta. But now, her business was ready to scale—and she needed funding.

Her plan? Launch a digital course series, run ads, and hire a VA. The challenge? She didn't want outside investors or personal loans. She wanted to use credit—but **do it without compromising her score or**

triggering red flags.

So she turned to something she'd heard in an obscure podcast: **credit stacking**.

The host claimed he got over $100K in new credit in 3 days. Naomi was skeptical—but intrigued. If this worked, it could change everything.

Prepping for the Stack

Naomi wasn't going in blind.

She spent two weeks preparing her personal and business credit:

- Her **FICO score** was 752
- Credit utilization was down to **3%**
- She had **3 tradelines reporting** to D&B
- Her LLC, website, and EIN were set up properly
- She reviewed her reports on **Credit Karma** and **Nav.com**

Next, she mapped out which lenders pulled from which bureaus:

- **Amex** – Experian
- **Chase** – Experian

- **Navy Federal** – TransUnion
- **Capital One** – All 3
- **Discover** – Equifax

She created a spreadsheet. Her goal: **apply to six cards in 48 hours across three bureaus**, to avoid stacking hard inquiries on one.

The clock was ticking.

The 48-Hour Execution

Day 1, 8:00 AM Naomi applied for the **Amex Business Gold**. She got instant approval for **$20,000**.

Day 1, 9:30 AM Next was **Chase Ink Unlimited**. Approved for **$15,000**.

Day 1, 12:00 PM She submitted her **Capital One Spark Business** application. This one wasn't instant—it went to manual review. She moved on.

Day 1, 3:00 PM She hit submit on the **Navy Federal Business Rewards card**. Approved—**$12,000** limit.

Day 2, 9:00 AM She applied for **Divvy**. Instant approval for **$10,000**.

Day 2, 11:00 AM Final card: **Brex**, based on business performance. She linked her business account, showed consistent revenue, and got approved for **$8,000**.

By 5:00 PM, the Capital One manual review came back—approved, **$10,000** limit.

In just two days, Naomi secured **$75,000 in business credit**—and none of it appeared on her personal credit report.

She didn't just beat the system. She used it the way it was designed to work—if you understood it.

Strategic Use, Not Flashy Moves

Temptation hit quickly. Naomi got ads in the mail for business equipment leasing, travel cards, and startup loans. She ignored them.

Instead, she:

- Spent $2,500 on course design and production
- Paid a graphic designer and VA through her business Amex
- Used Divvy to run Facebook and YouTube ads
- Left the other cards untouched for now

Her goal wasn't to spend all the credit. It was to **build trust** with each lender by using small amounts and paying them back early.

She added every card to her project tracker. Due dates, statement dates, utilization goals—all mapped out.

Her score didn't drop. Her business didn't stall. And within 60 days, she was generating **$6,500/month in new revenue**.

Naomi's Rules for Credit Stacking

Naomi now teaches other women how to build and fund online businesses through smart credit use. Her core rules:

> "If you're stacking credit to spend, you'll fail. If you're stacking credit to build systems, you'll win."

She tells her students:

- Stack across bureaus, not in one place
- Don't apply for too many cards in one day—spread it over 48 hours
- Only stack when you're fully prepared—no rushed decisions
- Track everything like a CFO, not a shopper

- Don't brag about how much credit you have—prove it by how you use it

Within 6 months, Naomi's business had crossed **$100K in annual revenue**, and she had access to over **$110,000 in credit**—without hurting her personal credit at all.

And it all started with a spreadsheet, a deadline, and a strategy most people never learn.

Chapter 5: Keeping the Credit — How to Protect, Grow, and Never Lose What You Built

The Reality of Losing Credit Overnight

Getting to $1M in credit is impressive—but keeping it long-term is where true mastery lies. Many people build large credit lines only to **lose them within a year** due to poor management, risky behavior, or lender crackdowns.

- A single misstep—like a late payment, sharp credit score drop, or sudden cash advance—can trigger **automatic limit reductions or account closures**.

So while earlier chapters taught you how to build and stack credit, this chapter is about how to **protect** it, **grow it safely**, and **ensure it works for you long-term.**

Red Flags That Get Accounts Shut Down

Banks and lenders don't always give you a warning. They monitor your behavior behind the scenes using risk algorithms, AI tools, and internal scoring.

Here are the biggest credit-killing behaviors:

1. High Utilization Across Cards

Even if you pay on time, using 80–90% of your credit line consistently is a red flag. It signals financial distress.

2. Late Payments

Just one 30-day late payment can drop your score 50–100 points and lead to automatic closures.

3. Opening Too Many Accounts Too Fast

If you continue applying aggressively after a stacking round, it looks like desperation and raises risk scores.

4. Cash Advances

Lenders see cash advances as a signal that you're short on funds. Avoid them unless absolutely necessary.

5. Mixing Personal and Business Funds

Using your business card for personal purchases can violate terms of service and result in a sudden closure.

- ❖ Pro Tip: Set up **alerts** for due dates, keep utilization below 10%, and monitor your reports monthly.

Strategies to Keep and Grow Your Credit

Keeping your credit is about routine, discipline, and communication. Here's how high-limit users protect and expand their credit long-term:

1. Request Credit Limit Increases (CLIs) Every 6 Months

Many lenders allow "soft pull" increases online. Increasing limits boosts your total available credit and lowers your utilization ratio.

2. Use All Cards Lightly

Don't let any account go unused for more than 6 months. Lenders close inactive accounts.

3. Build Relationships with Bankers

Local or regional banks still rely on relationships. Get to know your banker. Ask what they need to extend new credit.

4. Schedule Recurring Payments

Use small recurring charges (like subscriptions) on each card to maintain activity and payment history.

5. Create a Credit Calendar

Track statement dates, reporting dates, and due dates for all accounts. This prevents payment overlap and late reporting.

Monitoring Tools and Automation

As your credit empire grows, manual tracking becomes inefficient. Smart credit users rely on tools to stay ahead.

Recommended Tools:

- **Nav.com**: Monitors both business and personal credit
- **Experian Business**: Tracks business credit score changes
- **Credit Karma & MyFICO**: For alerts on personal credit activity
- **Tiller or YNAB**: Budgeting tools that sync with accounts
- **Google Calendar**: For payment reminders and statement tracking

You can even use tools like **Plaid** or **Zapier** to automate data collection for business reporting.

❖ Review your full credit report every 90 days. Catch errors, unexpected inquiries, or any signs of identity fraud early.

Future-Proofing Your Credit

If your goal is $1M+ in credit, you'll eventually attract attention from underwriters, fraud prevention teams, and relationship managers. Here's how to future-proof yourself:

Smart Habits:

- **Keep business and personal finances completely separate**
- **Avoid any sign of financial instability**—large cash advances, missed payments, or over-leveraging
- **Diversify across institutions**—don't let one bank control too much of your credit
- **Build assets, not liabilities**—use credit to buy income-generating tools, not luxury items
- **Reassess every 90 days**—what can you increase, renegotiate, or shift?

Legal and Strategic Considerations:

- Use **LLCs and holding companies** to manage risk and separate ventures
- Consult with a CPA to ensure you're reporting correctly for tax and credit purposes

- Consider forming a relationship with a **business banker or advisor** once your credit exceeds $500K

The end game isn't just access to credit—it's using credit to build **real, lasting wealth.**

How Jordan Almost Lost Everything

Jordan Lyles had done the impossible. At just 29 years old, he'd built over **$200,000 in personal and business credit** in less than a year. A former retail manager turned e-commerce entrepreneur, Jordan had leveraged credit stacking, built a sleek Shopify store selling sustainable pet products, and landed a viral moment on TikTok.

Sales hit $20,000 in a single week. He celebrated with a trip to Tulum, upgraded his laptop, and booked a branding coach.

For the first time in his life, **he felt like he'd made it.**

But three months later, he logged into his Capital One dashboard and froze.

> "Credit limit reduced from $15,000 to $3,000."

Then Amex followed suit. Then Chase. One by one, the limits dropped—without warning.

His business hadn't failed. His products still sold. So what happened?

Missteps That Cost Him Dearly

When Jordan retraced his steps, the red flags became obvious:

1. He'd used **80–90%** of his Amex limit to pay for product inventory.
2. He made **two minimum payments** during a slower sales month.
3. He pulled **cash advances** from his Chase card to cover emergency shipping fees.
4. His new ads hadn't performed, leading to a negative cash cycle.
5. He'd opened **four new business cards** right after a stacking round—within 30 days.

To him, it felt like smart scaling. To lenders, it looked like he was panicking. His behavior triggered **automated risk alerts** across multiple accounts.

They didn't care about his TikTok success. They cared about **risk**—and his profile suddenly screamed it.

Damage Control and Humility

Jordan spent the next month in triage mode. He paused all ad spend. Canceled unnecessary subscriptions. Paid down $15,000 in balances using reserve funds he hadn't touched in months.

Then he did something most people never consider: **He picked up the phone.**

He called every bank and asked to speak to an account manager—not to complain, but to take responsibility.

He told them:

> "I scaled too fast, didn't manage my limits properly, and I understand the reduction. I'm taking steps to stabilize and would like to rebuild our relationship."

Some were cold. A few were kind. Most thanked him for calling—something they rarely heard.

One banker even said:

> "We usually only hear from people after they've defaulted. You're ahead of the curve."

Learning to Protect the Castle

Jordan turned the experience into a lesson in **credit protection**.

He created a "Credit Castle" board in his office with five pillars:

1. **Utilization Below 10%** at all times
2. **No Cash Advances — Ever**
3. **Limit Increases Every 6 Months**
4. **No New Applications Within 90 Days of a Stack**
5. **Separate Funds for Emergencies**—credit is for scaling, not survival

He set **alerts for every card's due date**, used **Nav.com** to track his business credit, and reviewed all reports monthly.

Three months later, Amex restored his original limit. Then Chase did. Then Capital One.

The lesson was clear: building credit was only part of the journey—**maintaining it was the mission**.

Legacy Over Leverage

A year after the scare, Jordan's Shopify business had grown past $500K in revenue. He now had over **$300,000 in total credit**, but only used about 4% monthly—and paid it off weekly.

He had four bank relationships, two business credit lines, and a rock-solid personal score of 786.

When asked by a podcast host what he'd tell entrepreneurs chasing high credit limits, Jordan didn't talk about cards or points.

He said:

> "Protect it like your home. Don't spend credit like cash. Respect it like capital. If you don't, the banks will remind you who's really in charge."

Jordan had come dangerously close to losing everything—but emerged wiser.

Now, every new credit approval came with a sticky note he kept above his desk:

"Getting credit is temporary. Keeping it is forever."

Chapter 6: Using Credit to Build Income, Not Just Buy Things

The Most Dangerous Misuse of Credit

Once you've secured access to tens or even hundreds of thousands of dollars in credit, one of two things will happen:

- You use it to **buy income-producing assets**, or
- You use it to **buy things that lose value** and trap you in debt

Most people choose the second. They buy vacations, luxury items, or non-essential upgrades under the illusion that having credit equals having cash.

But million-dollar credit users don't think that way. They know:

- ❖ **"Credit is capital. Capital should create income, not expenses."**

In this chapter, we shift from building credit to **leveraging credit**—without getting burned. You'll learn how to use credit as a **tool to create cash flow**, so your payments are always covered and your wealth grows while your risk shrinks.

What Makes an Asset vs. a Liability?

It starts with redefining what credit should fund. Ask one simple question:

Does this purchase bring money in every month—or take money out?

Credit-Worthy Income-Producing Assets:

- **Digital Products**: Online courses, ebooks, templates
- **Rental Real Estate**: Airbnbs, long-term units, multifamily properties
- **Audiobooks & KDP Publishing**: Scalable intellectual property
- **Automated E-commerce**: Dropshipping or branded products with proven demand
- **Marketing for Proven Offers**: Running paid ads with high conversion
- **Licensing & Software Tools**: For businesses that use tech to scale revenue

Risky or Non-Recoverable Purchases:

- Cars or equipment that doesn't earn

- Inventory without market research
- Personal items bought on business cards
- Vacations, weddings, gifts
- Paid ads with no validated product or offer

Rule: Use credit to buy **scalable cash flow**, not consumable satisfaction.

Core Credit-Funded Business Models

Let's walk through **three proven business models** where people routinely use credit to build scalable income.

1. Digital Product Business

- Cost to create: $500–$3,000
- Funded by: Business cards, 0% APR offers
- ROI potential: $1K–$15K/month Use credit to create and market ebooks, courses, templates, or bundles. You build once, earn forever.

2. Real Estate Investment

- Cost to enter: $10K–$100K (down payment, rehab)

- Funded by: Personal/business cards, HELOCs, LOCs
- ROI: $500–$5,000/month per property Use business credit or HELOC to fund down payments or renovations on short-term rentals, then refinance or rent for profit.

3. Ad-Funded Online Sales

- Cost to launch: $2K–$10K (ads + inventory)
- Funded by: Business cards, fintech lines
- ROI: $2K–$20K+/month Use cards to launch paid ads on proven product funnels. Track ROAS (Return on Ad Spend) and scale only if profitable.

❖ Remember: Always have a repayment plan before you charge your card. Credit is only leverage when used responsibly.

Pay-Down Strategies That Keep You Safe

Using credit for business growth only works if you **manage your repayment strategy.** Here's how to structure your cash flow.

Strategy 1: The Float Method

Use 0% APR credit cards to fund a product or campaign. Repay before the intro period ends (usually 12–18 months).

Strategy 2: Weekly Auto-Pay from Revenue

Set your Stripe, PayPal, or other revenue processors to auto-transfer weekly to pay off cards.

Strategy 3: Rolling Profits into Payments

Split every dollar earned:

- 50% to credit repayment
- 30% to reinvest in marketing
- 20% to personal savings

This structure allows you to **grow your business without growing your debt.**

Also, track **credit card billing cycles** and pay strategically **before the statement date**, not just the due date, to keep reported balances low.

Final Tips for Using Credit to Create Wealth

Start with a Small Win

Use $1,000–$2,000 in credit to create a micro-product or a small ad campaign. Build confidence before scaling.

Stack Capital, Not Purchases

Use your access to build repeatable income, not just cover expenses.

Separate Growth & Maintenance Accounts

Have one card for recurring business expenses and another for scaling projects. This prevents overuse on a single account.

Track ROI Like a CFO

Use tools like Google Sheets, QuickBooks, or YNAB to know exactly how much every dollar of credit earns—or loses—you.

Never Bet the House

Never use personal credit to fund risky experiments without validation or proof of concept.

- ❖ Your mindset shift: "Credit isn't money to spend—it's a weapon to multiply results."

Lina's Digital Empire

The First Swipe That Changed Everything

Lina Morales had always dreamed of building something of her own. Working as a paralegal by day and raising two kids at night left little time—but plenty of motivation.

She wasn't trying to get rich quick. She just wanted to create income that didn't rely on 40-hour weeks. That's when she came across a YouTube video on digital products. The idea of making money from ebooks, templates, and downloadable planners sounded too good to be true—until she realized people were doing it every day.

There was only one problem: she had **no savings**.

But she did have a **$4,000 business credit card** with a 0% APR for 12 months.

After weeks of hesitation, she swiped it. $1,700 went to a course on digital marketing and Canva design. Another $800 went to hiring a Fiverr freelancer for her product mockups and logo.

With just $1,500 left on her card and zero room for mistakes, Lina pressed "Publish" on her first Etsy shop.

First Sales, First Panic

For two weeks, nothing happened. No clicks. No sales. She second-guessed everything.

Then came the first sale. A $7.99 downloadable wedding planner. Then another. Then a $27 bundle pack. Within 30 days, she had made $412—small, but real.

Encouraged, she reinvested $400 from her next paycheck into Etsy ads and expanded her product line. This time she stayed lean—designing everything herself.

By Month 2, her total credit usage was down to $800. Sales for the month hit $2,300. She began to understand something she'd never been taught:

> "If I use credit to build something that pays me back monthly, I never have to go into real debt."

Scaling Smart

Lina kept her expenses disciplined. She never touched the card for groceries or bills—only for tools that moved the business forward.

She used $300 to buy a course on SEO and $200 on upgraded listing photography. Slowly, she improved her store's visibility. By Month 3, she was profiting $1,100/month after ad costs.

She started paying off her card **weekly**, sometimes even **daily**, using the float strategy.

A few months later, she launched a second store with niche digital content for teachers. She funded the launch with another business card—this time from Chase, approved for $12,000.

She used only $1,500 of it and built that store to $3,000/month in revenue by Month 6.

She didn't just grow a business. She learned to use credit as **a tool for expansion, not consumption.**

Risk, Reinvestment, and Control

Lina knew she couldn't stay small forever. She wanted to hit $10,000/month, but not by working 16-hour days. So she hired a virtual assistant using credit, trained her over Zoom, and handed off order processing and customer service.

Then, she invested in **Facebook and Pinterest ads**—but slowly. She tested $5–$10/day using her Amex Blue Business card. Her rule was simple: if an ad didn't return at least 2X within 5 days, she cut it.

Her business never owed more than $3,000 across $30K+ in credit. Her **utilization stayed under 10%**, and her business Paydex score rose to 85.

She paid off her original $4,000 card in full by Month 8.

That same week, she crossed **$6,200 in monthly profit** across her two stores—and hadn't dipped into personal savings once.

The New Rulebook

Lina's friends were stunned. "Wait… you built all that on credit?"

She laughed, then explained: "No, I used credit. But I built it with discipline."

Her new rules were printed and taped above her desk:

1. **Credit only for cash-flow-producing expenses**
2. **Track ROI on every dollar spent**
3. **Never spend before a plan to repay**
4. **No emotional purchases on business cards**
5. **Scale what's working, pause what's not**

Today, Lina makes over **$100,000 a year in digital profit**, works from home, and has access to over **$75,000 in credit** across multiple business cards—with no debt.

Her final insight?

> "I didn't need funding. I needed a framework. Credit gave me the chance to build one—and income gave me the freedom to pay it off."

She turned plastic into profit—and made her dream of financial freedom real.

Chapter 7: Building Business Credit That Doesn't Rely on Your Personal Credit

The Power of True Business Credit

Most entrepreneurs never separate their personal and business finances—and it holds them back.

They max out personal cards to cover business expenses. They co-sign for every loan. They absorb all the risk. But smart credit users know: the real wealth is built when your **business stands on its own.**

- The ultimate goal: **No PG (Personal Guarantee)** required. That's when you know your business is truly fundable.

In this chapter, you'll learn how to:

- Build and grow credit under your business's EIN—not your SSN
- Qualify for lines and cards without risking your personal credit
- Create a credit profile that banks trust—even without years of history

Understanding No-PG Business Credit

What is No-PG Credit? It's a credit line, card, or loan issued to your business that's **not personally guaranteed by you.** This means:

- Your personal credit isn't pulled
- The debt won't show up on your credit report
- You're not personally liable if the business defaults (though default still hurts)

But No-PG isn't given out freely. Lenders want to see:

- A strong business credit file (Paydex score, Experian Business, Equifax Biz)
- Consistent revenue
- Industry stability
- Positive payment history from vendors or previous business accounts

How to Build a No-PG-Eligible Business Profile

Here's how to position your business to qualify:

Step 1: Business Legitimacy

- LLC or Corporation (not a sole prop)

- EIN from the IRS
- Business bank account with monthly activity
- Business phone number, website, and branded email
- Virtual or commercial business address

Step 2: Business Credit Profile

- Register for a **D-U-N-S Number** (free at DNB.com)
- Open 3–5 Net-30 vendor accounts that report (Uline, Quill, Summa Office)
- Pay vendors early to boost your Paydex score
- Monitor your business credit monthly via **Nav.com** or **CreditSignal**

Step 3: Add Tier 2 and Tier 3 Accounts

After 90 days of tradeline history:

- Apply for **store credit cards** (Amazon, Sam's Club, Office Depot)
- Apply for **fleet cards** (WEX, Shell, Fuelman)

- Use them lightly, pay in full

Step 4: Apply for No-PG Credit Cards

Once your business credit is established:

- Apply with fintech platforms like **Brex**, **Ramp**, or **Divvy**
- Explore banks like **Truist, Regions**, or local credit unions with no-PG business offers
- Avoid applying for cards that require your SSN unless necessary

Keys to Keeping Your No-PG Status

Even if you secure No-PG credit, lenders can revoke or change terms based on risk.

To protect it:

- Maintain **on-time payments** across all tradelines
- Keep balances low (under 30% utilization)
- Continue building your business credit file
- Avoid using personal cards for business
- Build revenue and cash flow that matches your credit usage

❖ Pro Tip: Never mix personal and business expenses—keep accounting, cards, and transactions fully separate to avoid legal and financial risk.

Tools and Platforms for No-PG Expansion

Here are some tools and platforms to fast-track your business's No-PG credit access:

Credit Monitoring

- **Nav.com** – Shows real-time Paydex, Experian Biz, and Equifax Biz scores
- **CreditSafe** – Business credit data reports for B2B lenders
- **Dun & Bradstreet CreditSignal** – Alerts you to changes in your D&B file

No-PG Lenders and Platforms

- **Brex** – Based on business revenue, not credit
- **Divvy** – Budget-based platform with real-time tracking
- **Ramp** – For funded or high-cash-flow businesses

- **Torro Funding**, **BlueVine**, **Fundbox** – For revenue-based lending
- Local banks and credit unions that issue corporate cards

❖ Final Word: When your business qualifies on its own, you're no longer dependent on your personal credit—and that's when the real freedom begins.

Daniel Journey to True Business Credit

Tired of the Risk

Daniel James had built a name for himself in the custom furniture space. What started in his garage grew into a profitable Shopify store with steady Instagram traffic and local word-of-mouth. But despite the growth, something kept bothering him:

> "Every loan I took. Every credit card I used. Every financing agreement—I was the one personally responsible."

He'd personally guaranteed over $80,000 in business debt. When the economy shifted and orders slowed, his personal credit score dropped, even though the business still had cash flow.

That was Daniel's wake-up call. If he was going to turn his company into a sustainable legacy, it couldn't be built **on his back alone.**

He needed **business credit that stood on its own.** No more using his Social. No more risking his personal credit every time he scaled.

Starting the No-PG Game

Daniel got serious about his company's structure.

He upgraded from a DBA to Daniel **James Designs, LLC.** He opened a new business bank account and applied for an **EIN**. He bought a virtual office address downtown and set up a business line through RingCentral.

He registered for his **D-U-N-S Number**, then opened accounts with **Uline, Quill, and Summa Office Supplies.**

Instead of large orders, he bought $50 to $100 in supplies—sandpaper, gloves, even paper towels—and paid early.

By Month 3, he had five tradelines reporting to Dun & Bradstreet. His **Paydex score hit 80.**

> "That was the first time a lender saw my business without asking for my personal credit," he said.

Doors Open Without a Signature

With his foundation in place, Daniel started applying for **No-PG credit options.**

First up: **Divvy.** Approved for $8,000.

Next: **Brex.** Approved for $12,000 based on revenue from Shopify and Square.

He applied for an **Amazon Business Card** through his LLC—no PG. Approved for $4,000.

He added a **Shell Fleet Card**, a **Sam's Club Business Card**, and even got a $5,000 **WEX Fleet** line to help with delivery vehicle expenses.

In less than 6 months, Daniel had secured **over $40,000 in business credit—without putting his Social Security number on a single application.**

He could finally breathe.

> "It was like building a wall between me and risk," he explained. "The business could grow—and I could sleep at night."

Smart Use and New Leverage

Daniel didn't go on a spending spree. He used his No-PG credit strategically.

- **Divvy** paid for ad testing
- **Amazon** stocked packaging materials
- **Brex** covered new website design
- **Fleet cards** fueled his delivery vans
- All payments were made **before** the statement date

His utilization never went above 20%. His business credit profile stayed clean. And most importantly, **his personal credit score went up**—because he wasn't over-leveraged anymore.

Soon, a banker from his credit union called him.

> "We noticed your business is growing. You may qualify for a $50K business LOC—no PG, since we've seen consistent deposits for 9 months."

He applied. Approved.

Legacy Without Liability

Today, Daniel has over **$120,000 in business credit**, all tied to his EIN—not his SSN.

He tells every new business owner he mentors the same thing:

> "If your business can't stand on its own credit legs, you're not building a business—you're just borrowing with a fancy name."

Daniel now uses credit to fund expansion, bring in contract workers, and finance inventory that earns him profit within 30–60 days. He hasn't needed a personal guarantee in over a year.

His dream of creating a sustainable, scalable brand is now rooted in smart financial architecture—not personal sacrifice.

And when his son asked him recently what it means to "own a business," Daniel replied:

> "It means I take the risk with a plan—and protect our future while I build it."

Chapter 8: How to Work with Banks and Lenders to Unlock Bigger Limits and Better Terms

Stop Hiding From Banks—Start Building Relationships

Most people avoid banks unless they need something. But the smartest credit users know that building relationships with banks is the **key to unlocking higher limits, better rates, and flexible approvals.**

- Relationship banking can unlock **$50K–$250K+** in credit and funding—even when automated systems say no.

The further you go in your credit journey, the more human relationships matter. Underwriters review large credit decisions. Commercial bankers recommend clients for loans. And business development reps often pre-qualify clients for exclusive offers.

If you want high-limit credit that grows with you, don't just build your credit profile—**build your lender profile** too.

Understanding the Bank's Perspective

Banks don't just lend money—they manage risk. To them, you're not just a score; you're a data profile made up of:

- Account activity and deposit history
- Average daily balances

- Business cash flow trends
- Past repayment behavior
- Account tenure and relationship strength

That's why people with "average" credit scores sometimes get approved for huge lines—because they've built trust with the bank over time.

- ❖ Relationship lending isn't about asking for money—it's about showing you're worth betting on.

Banks offer three levels of value:

1. **Consumer banking** – Personal accounts and cards
2. **Small business banking** – Business checking, business credit cards, merchant services
3. **Commercial banking** – High-level lines, equipment loans, real estate funding

As your credit access grows, you'll move through these tiers—and the relationships you build in each one matter.

How to Become a Bank's Ideal Client

Here's how to make banks want to lend to you:

1. Maintain High Average Balances

Even if it's short-term, keeping $5K–$10K in your business account shows you're managing cash wisely.

2. Make Frequent Deposits

Banks love activity. Weekly or biweekly deposits—even small ones—show consistent revenue.

3. Use Their Products

Use their merchant services, credit cards, or savings accounts. This strengthens your profile internally.

4. Ask About "Soft Pull" Pre-Approvals

Many banks offer pre-qualification that doesn't hurt your credit. This can fast-track access to large limits.

5. Get a Dedicated Business Banker

Having a single point of contact increases your chances of getting offers others never hear about.

- Example: Local and regional banks often offer $25K–$100K business lines of credit with low documentation—**if you already bank with them.**

Preparing for a Big Credit or Loan Ask

When you're ready to request a credit line increase or apply for a major business loan, come prepared:

The Lending Toolkit:

- Last 3–6 months of business bank statements
- Profit & loss statement (simple format using Wave or QuickBooks)
- Copy of your business license and EIN letter
- Personal credit report (only if PG is required)
- Business credit report (Paydex or Experian Biz)

Frame the conversation like this:

> "I'm planning to expand X and need flexible access to funding. Based on my account history, what would you recommend?"

Don't ask for a specific number. Let them guide you.

Also ask:

- What credit bureau do you pull from?
- Do you report to business credit bureaus?
- Can this be issued without a personal guarantee?

Long-Term Credit Growth Through Bank Relationships

The wealthiest credit users don't apply endlessly online—they build deep ties with 2–3 institutions.

Here's what that looks like over time:

Year 1–2:

- Open a business checking account
- Apply for an entry-level business credit card
- Maintain strong deposits and clean credit history

Year 3–4:

- Ask for larger lines of credit (LOCs or term loans)

- Leverage commercial banking offers for real estate or equipment
- Get assigned a relationship manager

Year 5+:

- Negotiate custom lending terms
- Qualify for private lending packages
- Access investment-grade funding backed by assets

❖ Final Tip: Relationships don't replace good credit—but they **multiply its value.**

When you're on a first-name basis with your banker and they know your growth plans, they stop seeing you as a number—and start seeing you as a partner.

How Camille Built a $250K Credit Relationship

The Door No One Told Her About

Camille Foster had always avoided banks. Not because she was irresponsible—just cautious. As the founder of a small but growing event planning business, she kept her money in a basic online checking account and used a few credit cards she'd found through blogs and forums.

She never missed payments. She had a 752 personal score. And yet, when she applied for a business line of credit online, she was denied.

> "Too little banking history."

That phrase haunted her. She realized she had strong credit—but no **relationship** with a lender who could actually fund her next level.

Camille didn't need to borrow $5,000. She needed access to **$50,000–$100,000** to expand her inventory, hire help, and say "yes" to the bigger, more lucrative events she kept turning down.

So she walked into her local credit union for the first time in years—and began what would become a game-changing journey.

The First Meeting That Changed Everything

Camille didn't know what to ask, so she kept it simple:

> "Hi. I run a growing event business and I'm looking to build a stronger relationship with a local bank. What kinds of business services do you offer?"

That question opened the floodgates.

Within 30 minutes, she had:

- A business checking account
- A meeting scheduled with a small business advisor
- A brochure of services she'd never even heard of: merchant services, SBA microloans, equipment financing, and internal pre-approvals

The business advisor, Karen, told her:

> "Honestly, people wait until they need money before they come to us. But it's smarter to start the relationship before the ask."

Camille made a promise to herself: she would show up—not just for the loan—but for the long-term.

Deposits, Discipline, and Data

Camille began depositing every client payment directly into her new business account—even the small ones. She automated transfers, maintained an average monthly balance over $5,000, and set alerts to track every transaction.

Karen checked in monthly. "Keep doing what you're doing," she said. "We're noticing."

Three months later, Camille applied for a business credit card. Approved: $15,000 limit.

She used it to pay vendors and suppliers, always paid it off before the statement closed, and kept usage under 10%.

After six months, she asked:

> "I'd like to explore a business line of credit for upcoming contracts. What do you recommend based on my account activity?"

This time, the answer wasn't no.

It was:

> "You're eligible for up to $50,000. No personal guarantee required."

From Denied to Pre-Approved

With her credit union line in place, Camille stopped applying for random online funding offers. Instead, she focused on growing deeper with two more institutions: a regional bank and a fintech lender her advisor recommended.

She repeated the process:

- Opened accounts
- Made consistent deposits
- Used their products wisely
- Asked about **soft pull pre-approvals**

Within 18 months, Camille had:

- $15K credit card at her credit union
- $50K line of credit (no PG)
- $35K equipment loan for event décor
- $100K revolving business line with her regional bank
- $50K Brex line for marketing and automation tools

Total credit: **$250,000**—all from **3 institutions**, built through relationships and smart behavior.

Teaching the Next Generation

Now earning over $30K/month in her business, Camille trains new event professionals in her city on how to scale responsibly.

She always includes one overlooked module in her curriculum: **How to build banking relationships.**

Her advice is simple:

> "Don't just open accounts. Introduce yourself. Ask how to grow. Treat your banker like your CFO."

She explains how relationships helped her secure funding, unlock better terms, and protect her business when a big client backed out of a $60K contract.

Because she had a history of trust, her lender extended a temporary working capital line—**within 48 hours.**

Her final piece of wisdom?

> "Your credit opens the door. But your reputation with a lender keeps it open—and sometimes, makes it automatic."

Chapter 9: Automate, Monitor, and Review — How to Maintain a Million in Credit with Less Stress

The Hidden Threat — Neglect

Most people assume the biggest risk to their credit is misusing it. In reality, the biggest threat is **neglect.**

- Forgetting due dates
- Ignoring changes in your credit profile
- Letting business tradelines go inactive
- Missing subtle signs of fraud or account errors

❖ Your credit doesn't collapse from one big mistake—it erodes slowly when you stop paying attention.

That's why top-tier credit users automate 80% of their management. This chapter is about building a **credit maintenance system** so you don't have to manually track everything while still protecting—and growing—your million-dollar access.

Set It and Forget It — Smart Automation Strategies

Autopay for All Cards

- Set **autopay to minimum** on all credit cards to avoid missed payments
- Then, manually pay full statement balances **before** the due date
- This double layer ensures you never miss a due date—even if distracted

Scheduled Weekly or Biweekly Payments

For revolving accounts (especially high-limit cards), set recurring payments from your business account every Friday or biweekly to lower utilization throughout the month.

Expense Rules

Use tools like **Divvy, Ramp, or QuickBooks** to categorize and limit employee spending on business cards.

- ❖ Bonus: These tools also sync with your accounting software and flag overspending in real-time.

Credit Monitoring — Stay Alert, Stay Safe

Monitoring your credit is non-negotiable if you have over $100K in open credit.

Monitor Your Personal Credit:

- **MyFICO.com** – Real FICO score updates from all 3 bureaus
- **Experian Premium** – Offers alerts, score simulations, and identity protection
- **Credit Karma** – Free and good for soft monitoring, especially TransUnion/Equifax

Monitor Your Business Credit:

- **Nav.com** – Shows your Paydex score, Experian Biz, and Equifax Biz in one place
- **Dun & Bradstreet CreditSignal** – Free alerts when changes happen
- **CreditSafe** – Detailed risk scoring used by lenders

Set **monthly reminders** to check your reports—even if everything is automated.

❖ Remember: Catching a single error, data breach, or misreport can save you thousands.

Monthly and Quarterly Reviews

Even if most of your system is automated, you should do **a short review every month** and a **deep review every 90 days**.

Monthly Review Checklist:

- Check balances and due dates
- Look for unexpected charges or account changes
- Ensure no utilization spikes
- Request credit limit increases if eligible
- Confirm new tradelines are reporting

Quarterly Review Checklist:

- Pull personal credit reports from all 3 bureaus
- Pull business credit reports (Nav or D&B)
- Evaluate which cards or accounts are inactive
- Consider consolidating or replacing underperforming cards
- Update your strategy based on new revenue, expenses, or goals

❖ Pro Tip: Set Google Calendar events or use apps like Notion or Trello to create a recurring credit review workflow.

Protecting the Fortress You Built

Once you've built a seven-figure credit structure, your mindset must shift from **builder to protector**.

Ongoing Credit Habits:

- Never co-sign or let others use your credit
- Use 5–10% of each account monthly to keep it active
- Avoid large spikes in spending unless you have the cash on hand
- Keep cards diversified across issuers (Amex, Chase, FNBO, regional banks, etc.)
- Freeze inactive cards you don't want closed, and store card info securely

Also consider:

- **Setting up credit freeze/security alerts** with bureaus
- **Using a business VPN and password manager**
- Keeping a hard copy of key credit data in a secure location

❖ Your goal: Turn credit into a quiet, stable engine in the background—not a loud fire to constantly manage.

How One Mistake Almost Cost Elijah His Empire

A Silent Misstep

Elijah Benton was a systems guy. His tech consulting business had scaled to six figures in under 18 months, and he had built over **$220,000 in business and personal credit.**

He used credit like a pro—stacked it, leveraged it for growth, and maintained a solid 790+ score.

But there was one thing he hadn't set up: **a system for maintenance.**

One month, while traveling to speak at a fintech conference, Elijah missed a single payment on a $6,000 Amex card. Not because he didn't have the money—because he forgot.

The result?

- A 30-day late mark
- A drop from 792 to 718
- A sudden closure of two smaller cards
- A denied request for a $100K business line he'd been pre-approved for

> "It took 3 minutes to make the mistake," he said later, "and six months to rebuild the trust."

Cleaning Up the Mess

When Elijah returned, he did a full audit of his financial activity. What he found was shocking:

- Five cards hadn't been used in 3+ months
- Three due dates were within the same 2-day window
- Two vendor tradelines had stopped reporting due to inactivity

His system had worked—**when he had time to manage it.** But now that his business was growing, he realized he needed **automation and monitoring** that didn't rely on memory or spreadsheets.

He created what he now calls the "Credit Command Center."

Automating Everything

Step one was **autopay on every account**, with a backup alert for any payment over $500.

He separated his cards into categories:

- **Growth cards**: used for ad spend, marketing, and scaling

- **Maintenance cards**: used for recurring bills like software and subscriptions
- **Storage cards**: used once a quarter to keep them active

He used **Notion** to build a simple dashboard with due dates, statement dates, and credit limits. He linked it to his **Google Calendar** and set up:

- Weekly reviews on Fridays
- Monthly full balance checks
- Quarterly credit report pulls from all 3 bureaus

He signed up for **Nav.com**, **Experian Premium**, and **Dun & Bradstreet CreditSignal**.

Now, he got alerts for:

- Any change to his score
- Any new inquiry or account
- Any vendor that stopped reporting

System = Sanity

Within 90 days of setting up his system:

- His personal credit bounced back to 760
- He got re-approved for his $100K business line
- He requested and received **credit limit increases** on 4 of his cards
- He spotted a duplicate charge on a vendor account and resolved it before it hit his credit

His stress dropped. His confidence returned. And his team began using the system too—especially his VA, who could now manage credit activity without needing to guess or ask every time.

> "I went from credit being a checklist item to it being a controlled, living part of my business."

Teaching Others to Protect the Empire

Today, Elijah mentors other entrepreneurs who've built strong credit but struggle with **maintenance**.

He teaches one core belief:

> "If you treat credit like a project, it'll always fall apart. But if you treat it like a system, it'll protect you forever."

His "Credit Command Center" system is now used by over 300 of his consulting clients—and every one of them starts by answering the same question:

"If you stopped managing your credit for 30 days, would it survive or collapse?"

Elijah's story proves that having access to credit isn't enough. Protecting it with automation, structure, and monthly awareness is what keeps your million-dollar foundation intact.

Because at the highest level, **credit isn't about hustle—it's about systems.**

Chapter 10: From Credit to Capital — How to Turn Limits Into Leverage, and Leverage Into Legacy

Credit is the Starting Line, Not the Finish

Most people believe that getting access to large amounts of credit is the end goal. But in reality, that's just the beginning.

- **Credit is not wealth. Credit is leverage. Wealth is built when you use that leverage to create scalable, protected, and income-generating assets.**

In this final chapter, we shift focus from credit-building to **legacy creation**—using your credit profile to launch businesses, fund investments, and build a financial structure that serves your family and your future.

The same $100K in credit that destroys one person's life can generate lifelong income for someone with the right mindset and tools.

Leverage Defined

What is leverage? It's using borrowed money (in this case, credit) to earn a return that exceeds the cost of that money.

Good leverage grows your income and asset base without overstretching your risk. Bad leverage creates liabilities that collapse when the economy shifts or revenue dips.

Smart Credit Leverage:

- Funding digital products that earn passively
- Running profitable ad campaigns for services or e-commerce
- Investing in rental properties and using short-term credit to rehab
- Building businesses that can be sold (digital agencies, SaaS, etc.)

Risky or Toxic Leverage:

- Buying luxury items with no income attached
- Relying on debt to survive instead of grow
- Running expenses across personal cards with no business infrastructure
- Using cash advances to fund loss-heavy ideas

Rule: Only leverage when the outcome is **predictable, profitable, and protected.**

Protect the Downside, Multiply the Upside

If you're going to use $50K or $500K in credit, you need a **plan for both profit and protection**.

Protect the Downside:

- Keep 3–6 months of operating cash in reserve
- Never max out more than 40% of total available credit
- Diversify funding sources (use 4–6 different institutions)
- Always use business structures (LLC, S-Corp) to limit liability
- Insure physical and digital assets

Multiply the Upside:

- Build recurring revenue streams (subscriptions, rental income, memberships)
- Use credit to buy time: hire VAs, automate systems, free up your schedule
- Use your credit profile to qualify for **real estate, SBA loans, or acquisitions**

Strategy: Use credit to fund systems, not just sales. Systems scale. Hustle burns out.

Creating Long-Term Financial Independence

True wealth isn't just about having money—it's about building **financial infrastructure** that works without your daily effort.

Use Credit to Fund These Legacy Moves:

- **Buy properties** that can be passed to your kids
- **Create content-based businesses** that sell 24/7 (courses, audiobooks, publishing)
- **Fund a family trust or holding company** that separates wealth from personal risk
- **Start a credit repair, tax, or funding agency** to help others while generating cash flow

You can also use business credit to:

- Pay for **estate planning**
- Fund **retirement accounts through your LLC**
- Invest in your children's education or first businesses

Credit is temporary—but what you build with it can last for generations.

Exit Plan and Wealth Transfer

You didn't build your credit empire just to coast. You built it to exit smarter, freer, and more secure than when you started.

- Final Moves:

- Get your business or portfolio **valued**—know what it's worth
- Use credit to polish, market, or expand before selling
- Sell digital or physical assets for a lump sum
- Use proceeds to fund **real estate, trusts, or long-term investments**

If you're not planning your exit, you're just running in circles.

And when you're ready to pass the torch:

- Create a **step-by-step guide** for your heirs or partners
- List all credit accounts, banks, passwords, and automation flows
- Ensure your business and credit structures are legally transferable

Legacy = Leverage + Structure + Intention

The Final Move That Changed Marcus's Family Forever

More Than Just a Number

Marcus Tran had hit the number.

After three years of strategic credit building, stacking, vendor relationships, and disciplined business spending, he had **$1.2 million in combined personal and business credit.**

He'd built a successful logistics company and digital trucking academy, and his credit profile was flawless—scores above 780, $300K in revolving business cards, $250K in personal credit limits, and two $250K lines of credit from his banks.

But something felt unfinished.

One night, while reviewing his credit dashboard, he thought:

> "What happens if I'm not here tomorrow? Who knows how to run this? Who can access it? Who owns it?"

That was the moment Marcus shifted from **growth mode to legacy mode.**

From Builder to Architect

Marcus knew how to grow credit. But he hadn't prepared his family to inherit it—or the wealth it enabled.

His wife, a nurse, had no idea how the business cards worked or why one bank reported to Equifax and another to D&B.

His teenage daughter thought "business credit" was just a fancy way to get a car with no cosigner.

So Marcus got serious. He didn't just want to pass on his money—he wanted to pass on the **blueprint.**

He hired an estate planner. Created a **living trust**. Reorganized all credit cards under the business EIN. Transferred digital course ownership into an LLC holding company. Set up a family operating agreement.

Then he made a simple decision: **Every credit line would now fund income-producing assets only.**

No more shiny tools. No new gadgets. Just leverage turned into lasting value.

Turning Credit Into Capital

Marcus mapped out his next year of credit use differently.

He used $25,000 from a 0% Amex to fund:

- Audiobook production

- Facebook ads for a digital trucking mentorship
- A rebrand with a top-tier designer

That led to a **$12,000/month passive funnel** within 60 days.

Then he used $40,000 from his business LOC to:

- Purchase land in a growing city for a trucking lot
- Build a small pre-fab office
- Hire a VA to manage appointments

Six months later, he was leasing the space to a new trucking startup for **$4,000/month**, netting $2,800 after costs.

> "I realized I didn't need a million in cash. I just needed a million in credit I used with purpose."

Teaching the Next Generation

Marcus sat down with his daughter, now a high school senior, and showed her how credit really worked.

Not just how to swipe—but how to apply strategically, track utilization, build business credit, and keep a Paydex score above 80.

They set up her first LLC together. Helped her sell digital resume templates online. Got her a net-30 vendor account. Watched her first $500 come in—and paid it off from a Divvy business card.

> "My goal isn't to leave her a pile of money," he said. "It's to leave her a skill set and a system that will make her unstoppable."

He printed out a 12-page Credit Legacy Binder with all his accounts, passwords, strategies, and structures—just in case.

The Legacy Blueprint

Today, Marcus still runs his businesses—but with a new mission.

His credit is no longer just for growth. It's for **infrastructure.**

- He funds investment property rehabs
- He launches digital products with his kids
- He uses business credit to test ideas without risk
- He holds quarterly "Credit Meetings" with his family, just like profit reviews

And when he mentors other entrepreneurs, he always ends with this:

> "You didn't come this far just to get more cards. You came this far so that one day, someone else can say: I didn't have to start from scratch—because someone left me a path."

Marcus turned $1M in credit into **a permanent financial blueprint**—for himself, his children, and generations to come.

VOLUME 10: CREDIT FUNDED WEALTH FOR FAMILIES

Most people believe they must choose between living a good life today or saving everything for tomorrow. It's a dilemma many families face. You want to take that vacation, fix up your home, invest in your children's future—and still build wealth that lasts for generations. But how? How do you do both when your paycheck barely stretches far enough to cover the basics?

This book was written to show you that **you don't have to choose**. You can live well today **and** build a legacy that outlives you. The key is learning how to **use credit as a tool**, not a trap. You've probably heard horror stories about families buried in debt—but what you haven't heard enough about are the families who used credit wisely and strategically to **accelerate their income**, **acquire appreciating assets**, and **secure their children's futures**. That's who this book is for.

Why This Book Matters

Credit isn't just for emergencies or short-term spending. Used correctly, it can buy you time, resources, and leverage. It can fund your first rental property. It can pay for an online business that earns passive income while you sleep. It can even help you set up life insurance policies, trusts, or college plans that are backed by real assets. **Credit, when combined with discipline and knowledge, becomes capital.**

And when capital flows through the hands of an educated family, it multiplies.

Over the past decade, I've worked with thousands of individuals, couples, and families—many of whom were immigrants or first-generation Americans—who were starting from scratch. They didn't have inherited wealth. Some had bad credit or no credit. Others had no savings. But what they did have was a willingness to learn, and a desire to build a better life for their kids.

Through trial and error, they discovered how to access tens—even hundreds—of thousands in credit, and how to convert it into income-producing vehicles like real estate, businesses, and automated side hustles. I've watched families use credit cards and lines of credit—not for shopping sprees—but for flipping properties, investing in cash flow, and creating safety nets they never had growing up.

This book is a blueprint based on their successes—and my own.

Who This Is For

If you're a parent, a caregiver, or even a single adult thinking about your financial future, this book will walk you through every step to:

- Understand and build excellent credit
- Leverage credit to invest in real assets without going into unnecessary debt
- Fund experiences for your family that create joy and memories now
- Build a strong, protective structure around your wealth so it lasts

Even if you've made financial mistakes in the past—this book is for you. Even if you've been told that credit is dangerous or you don't trust it—this book is for you. Even if you think wealth is only for "rich people"—this book will change your perspective.

Because the truth is, **families are the most powerful financial units in the world** when they work together, educate themselves, and apply the right strategies.

What to Expect

Each chapter of this book will take you through a journey—from repairing and optimizing personal credit, to learning how to access and grow business credit, to using both for long-term wealth-building. We'll explore strategies like:

- Setting up your family LLC or trust
- Buying real estate without draining your savings
- Using life insurance policies as investment vehicles
- Teaching your children about money and credit early
- Creating emergency funds, vacation funds, and investment funds—all fueled by smart credit use

You'll also hear real-world stories of families just like yours who overcame financial limitations by rethinking how they used credit. These aren't fairytales—they're practical examples with numbers, tools, and templates.

A New Financial Legacy Starts Today

You don't need to be rich to start building wealth. You just need to start.

Chapter 1: Understanding Credit as a Wealth-Building Tool

Most people think of credit as a way to *buy now and pay later*. But in reality, credit is a financial instrument—one that, when managed properly, can **accelerate your ability to earn, invest, and grow**

wealth. This chapter will reframe the way you view credit and show you how to lay the foundation for building generational wealth using smart credit strategies.

The Two Types of Credit You Must Master

1. Personal Credit

Personal credit is tied to your Social Security number and tracked by the three major credit bureaus: Experian, TransUnion, and Equifax. It determines your ability to get mortgages, car loans, and personal credit cards.

Why it matters for families: A strong personal credit score can unlock:

- 0% interest promotional financing
- Higher limits on personal cards
- Low-interest HELOCs (Home Equity Lines of Credit)
- Better terms on student loans and home loans

2. Business Credit

Business credit is tied to your EIN (Employer Identification Number) and built through vendor relationships, business credit cards, and financing that doesn't report to your personal credit.

Why it matters for families: With strong business credit, you can:

- Access capital for real estate or online businesses
- Keep personal finances separate from investments
- Build a business as a family asset and legacy
- Use your LLC to write off certain expenses legally

The Wealthy Use Credit Differently

The wealthy don't fear credit—they understand it. They know that **debt tied to income-producing assets is not bad debt**. It's strategic debt. Let's compare two types of debt:

Type	Example	Result
Bad Debt	Maxing out a credit card on clothes	No ROI, long-term burden

Good Debt	Using a 0% APR card to flip a property	Asset appreciation, positive ROI

They also use credit to **free up cash**. For example:

- Use a 0% APR credit card to pay for everyday expenses, while investing your paycheck into an income-producing property.
- Get a personal line of credit to cover a down payment, then refinance after the property appreciates.

How to Use Credit Without Going Into Unmanageable Debt

Here's the key: **Credit is NOT free money—it's leveraged money.** You must treat it with the same care you would treat a business investment. Follow these principles:

1. **Only borrow with a repayment plan in place.** Never swipe unless you know how and when you'll pay it back.
2. **Use credit to buy or build assets, not liabilities.** Ask yourself: Will this make me money or lose me money?
3. **Avoid minimum payments.** Minimums keep you in debt longer. Set up auto-pay for full balances or large payments.

4. **Keep utilization under 30%.** Even if you have $50,000 in available credit, try not to carry more than $15,000 at a time on revolving accounts.

5. **Know your numbers.** Check your FICO score regularly and monitor your credit reports for errors. Use tools like Credit Karma, Experian, or MyFICO.

Start With a Family Credit Assessment

To build credit-funded wealth, you need a full picture of where you stand.

Action Plan:

1. Pull your **credit reports** from all three bureaus at AnnualCreditReport.com.

2. List your **current debts, interest rates, and limits**.

3. Identify any **collections, missed payments, or errors**.

4. Create a 90-day goal to **increase your credit score** by:

    - Paying down debt

    - Disputing errors

  - Opening new tradelines (secured cards, retail accounts)
  - Becoming an authorized user on a family member's seasoned card

Educating Your Household

Building family wealth means involving the whole family. Teach your spouse or children (age-appropriate) the basics of credit:

- Show them how a credit card works and what interest is.
- Let them see how much you save with good credit.
- Consider adding teens as authorized users to build their credit early.

Family Credit Tip: Create a "Credit Calendar" where your household tracks:

- When payments are due
- What's being paid off
- New cards or business lines added
- Family savings goals tied to credit use

Chapter Summary:

- Credit is a powerful tool for building family wealth when used with discipline.
- The wealthy use credit to generate income and acquire assets—not to buy liabilities.
- Start with a personal and family credit audit.
- Educate every household member on the role of credit in financial freedom.

In the next chapter, we'll dive into **how to build perfect personal credit from scratch—or repair it quickly—so you can qualify for high-limit cards, lines of credit, and real estate funding.** Stay with me—this is where your wealth journey begins.

"The Breakthrough"

It was 2:17 a.m. when Miguel sat upright in bed, drenched in sweat—not from the heat, but from panic.

He had just remembered that the mortgage was due in four days, the car needed new tires, and his daughter's braces payment had bounced last week. His wife, Carla, stirred beside him. She'd been taking extra shifts at the hospital just to keep them afloat. Their son needed a laptop for school, and their youngest had outgrown all her clothes again.

They were a good family. They worked hard. They loved each other. But it never seemed to be enough.

Miguel tiptoed out of bed, grabbed a worn-out notebook from the kitchen drawer, and sat at the table. He wrote at the top of the page in capital letters: **"WHERE IS ALL THE MONEY GOING?"**

He listed every bill—mortgage, electricity, gas, groceries, insurance, credit card minimums—and even the tiny subscription charges that crept in each month unnoticed. The numbers didn't lie. They were spending more than they earned.

He looked around the modest home they had built from scratch. His eyes landed on a family photo—Carla, himself, and the three kids laughing at the beach two summers ago. He remembered how hard they'd saved for that trip. It took them eight months to put aside enough for five days of joy. And now they were slipping behind again.

Miguel whispered to himself, "There has to be a better way."

The next morning, after dropping the kids off at school, he sat in his old pickup truck and opened YouTube. He searched: "How to get out of debt and build wealth with no money." One video caught his eye—"How Families Use Credit to Build Generational Wealth." He clicked.

The speaker, a man named Joe, said something that stopped Miguel cold:

> "Credit, when used right, is not for buying things—it's for building things."

He continued:

> "The wealthy don't use credit to survive. They use it to expand—buy assets, build businesses, acquire real estate. The problem isn't credit. It's how we use it."

Miguel leaned closer. Joe broke it down further:

- Separate personal and business credit
- Fix your personal credit first
- Only use credit for things that make money, not lose it
- Leverage 0% APR credit cards, business tradelines, and HELOCs with a plan

Miguel had never heard credit explained like this before. He had always seen it as the enemy. But now… it sounded like a tool. A strategy.

He took notes. That night, he shared everything with Carla. She was skeptical at first.

> "You think we can borrow our way out of debt?" she asked.
>
> "No," Miguel replied. "I think we can *build* our way out. If we use credit not to spend, but to *invest* in something that earns income."

They started small.

First, they pulled their credit reports from AnnualCreditReport.com. There were a few errors. A couple of missed payments from years ago. An old collection that wasn't even theirs. Miguel filed disputes immediately. Then he paid off two small balances and set up autopay for all recurring bills.

Next, he applied for a secured credit card to rebuild his payment history. He added Carla as an authorized user. Within three months, their scores jumped by 72 points.

Then came the bold step: Miguel used his improved credit to apply for a 0% APR credit card with a $12,000 limit. Instead of spending it, they followed Joe's advice and used $6,000 to buy a vending machine route. Two refurbished machines, placed in busy breakrooms, generated $1,200 a month.

The payments on the card? $200/month. Profit: $1,000.

Carla couldn't believe it. "This... is working?"

Miguel smiled. "One vending machine. Imagine what we can do with five."

A year later, Miguel and Carla had used business credit to expand the vending business. They had 12 machines in total. They used a personal line of credit to pay for an online course about rental real estate and bought a small duplex using a HELOC from their improved home equity.

Every credit move they made was strategic, calculated, and backed by income.

They weren't just surviving anymore. They were saving, investing, and even taking their kids on quarterly vacations without guilt.

And every Sunday night, they held a family finance meeting where they taught their children about credit, budgeting, and investing. The kids started helping run the vending business and learning how to track expenses.

Their oldest, 16-year-old Diego, was already building his credit through a teen banking app linked to Miguel's card. Their daughter, Sofia, had started reselling vintage clothes online. The family was turning into a financial machine.

Miguel still remembered that sleepless night.

The fear. The shame. The notebook.

But now, that same notebook was filled with a wealth plan, monthly projections, and handwritten goals in bright ink: **"Buy second duplex." "Start family LLC." "Teach kids to buy their first home by 20."**

They hadn't won the lottery. They didn't get a massive raise. They simply learned how to turn credit into capital.

And that changed everything.

Chapter 2: Building Perfect Personal Credit for Long-Term Leverage

Before you can use credit to create wealth for your family, you need to start with a **solid personal credit foundation**. Whether you're starting from scratch, recovering from past mistakes, or just trying to improve your score, this chapter will walk you through the **exact steps** to build, fix, and optimize your credit profile.

Understand What Makes Up Your Credit Score

Your FICO credit score is made up of **five main components**:

Factor	**Weight**	**What It Means**
Payment History	35%	Paying on time is the most important factor
Amounts Owed (Utilization)	30%	How much credit you're using vs. your available limit
Length of Credit History	15%	The age of your oldest and newest accounts
Credit Mix	10%	Types of credit (loans, cards, mortgage, etc.)

New Credit	10%	Recent inquiries and newly opened accounts

To build strong credit, focus first on **paying everything on time**, then **keep your balances low**—ideally under 30% of each card's limit.

Repair Your Credit File if Needed

If your credit has collections, charge-offs, or late payments, **don't ignore them. Fix them.**

Action Steps:

1. **Get Your Free Reports** Visit AnnualCreditReport.com to download all three bureau reports.
2. **Identify Errors and Negative Items** Look for:
    - Incorrect names or addresses
    - Accounts you don't recognize
    - Late payments you're sure were paid on time
    - Collections that should have aged off (7+ years)
3. **Dispute Inaccuracies** File online or via certified mail with supporting evidence. Each bureau must respond within 30 days.

4. **Negotiate Pay-for-Delete Deals** Some collectors will remove the negative item if you pay in full or settle the balance.

5. **Use the Goodwill Letter Strategy** If you have a solid history with a creditor, request that they remove a late payment out of goodwill.

Add Positive Tradelines to Boost Your Score

If you're lacking positive accounts, **you'll need to build new ones**. Here's how:

Credit-Building Tools:

- **Secured Credit Cards**: You deposit $200–$500 as collateral and build history with responsible use.

- **Retail Store Cards**: Easier to get approved for, even with average credit.

- **Authorized User Accounts**: Ask a family member with great credit to add you to one of their cards. Their history will reflect on your report.

- **Credit Builder Loans**: You "pay yourself" into a locked savings account while building payment history.

- **Rental Reporting Services**: Report on-time rent payments to bureaus through services like RentReporters or Experian Boost.

Use Credit Without Hurting Your Score

Here are the rules to **build and maintain high credit scores**:

- **Pay ON TIME—every time.** Even one 30-day late payment can drop your score 80+ points.
- **Keep utilization under 30% on each card.** Under 10% is ideal.
- **Don't close old accounts.** Length of history matters.
- **Only apply for new credit when you need it.** Too many inquiries can hurt your score short-term.
- **Set auto-pay on at least the minimum due.** Prevents late payments automatically.

Achieve a 700+ Score in 90–180 Days

With consistency, even someone recovering from bad credit can reach a strong credit score in just a few months.

Sample 90-Day Plan:

1. **Month 1**
   - Pull reports and dispute any errors
   - Get a secured credit card
   - Pay off past-due accounts
2. **Month 2**
   - Become an authorized user on a seasoned account
   - Use your card for small purchases and pay in full
   - Report rent and utility payments
3. **Month 3**
   - Apply for a retail card to diversify mix
   - Keep utilization under 10%
   - Track your score weekly (use Credit Karma or MyFICO)

By the end of this process, you'll be in a **position to qualify** for:

- High-limit credit cards

- Low-interest personal lines
- Mortgage pre-approvals
- Auto loans with no money down

Chapter Summary:

- Building personal credit is the **first major step** toward family wealth creation.
- Focus on **payment history** and **credit utilization** above all else.
- Use **positive tradelines** like secured cards and rental history to boost your file.
- A clean, high-scoring personal credit profile unlocks low-cost capital.

"Fixing Credit, Rebuilding Life"

April stood in the checkout line at Target, holding her breath as the cashier swiped her card.

Declined.

The cashier glanced up with an apologetic smile. April's heart sank. Her

9-year-old daughter, Ava, stood beside her, clutching a box of crayons and a pink backpack they had picked out for the first day of school.

April forced a calm voice. "Let me try another one."

Her second card worked—barely. The receipt showed she had less than $7 left in her account.

That night, after tucking Ava into bed, April sat in the kitchen with her laptop, a notepad, and a heavy heart. She hadn't always struggled this way. Five years earlier, she had a decent job, decent credit, and a small savings account. But then came the divorce, the medical bills, the missed payments, and the endless juggling of cards to stay afloat.

She was tired of living this way—tired of the anxiety, the late fees, the phone calls from creditors. And most of all, tired of telling Ava "not this time" when she asked for little things other kids seemed to take for granted.

April Googled "how to fix bad credit" and stumbled onto a podcast episode titled **"How a Single Mom Went from 480 to 780 Credit Score and Bought Her First Home."**

She clicked play.

The guest talked about pulling credit reports, finding errors, sending dispute letters, building new tradelines—even using rent and utility payments to boost her score. It all sounded... doable.

April grabbed her notepad and started writing a plan.

Step 1: Pull All Three Credit Reports

She visited AnnualCreditReport.com and downloaded her reports from Experian, Equifax, and TransUnion.

She stared at the pages, overwhelmed at first—but determined.

She saw a store card she never opened, a collection for a cable bill she didn't owe, and several late payments from a joint account her ex had stopped paying without telling her.

She circled them all.

Step 2: Dispute and Clean Up

April learned how to file disputes online and by certified mail. She created a simple spreadsheet to track each dispute, the bureau, the reason, and the response date.

A month later, **two accounts were removed** and one had the late payment updated to "paid on time." Her score jumped 46 points in just four weeks.

Step 3: Add Positive Credit

April applied for a **secured credit card** with a $300 deposit. She used it only for gas and groceries and paid it off every Friday.

She also signed up for **Experian Boost** to add her rent and utility payments to her credit report. Within two months, she had three new positive tradelines reporting.

Encouraged, she asked her older sister to add her as an **authorized user** on a long-standing credit card with a $10,000 limit and perfect history. Within a week, her score jumped another 32 points.

Step 4: Keep Building

By month four, April was approved for a retail store card and another unsecured credit card with a $1,000 limit. She kept utilization under 10%, never missed a payment, and watched her credit score cross 700 for the first time in her adult life.

With her improved credit, she applied for a **low-interest personal loan** to consolidate her remaining debts. Her monthly payments dropped by $120, and she paid off two high-interest cards.

Step 5: Family Goals

Ava noticed the difference. No more declined cards. Groceries paid on time.

A Saturday morning trip to the farmer's market where April let her pick out fresh fruit and flowers.

"Mommy, we rich now?" Ava asked with a big grin.

April laughed. "Not yet, sweetie. But we're getting smarter with our money."

They started a ritual: every Sunday, they sat together and wrote out their goals.

Ava's: "Get a dog." April's: "Buy a home."

12 Months Later…

April had done it. Her score was 756. She had three revolving accounts, two installment accounts, zero late payments, and a growing emergency fund.

She was pre-approved for a mortgage.

More importantly, she was confident. In control. And finally free from the shadow of bad credit.

She had turned a nightmare into a blueprint.

One step at a time.

And now she was helping other single moms do the same.

"Credit," she said at her local workshop, "is not a trap if you learn how to use it. It's a key. A key to everything you were told you couldn't have."

Chapter 3: Building Business Credit as a Family Asset

Most families focus only on personal credit—missing out on one of the **most powerful wealth tools available: business credit**. It doesn't rely on your Social Security number, doesn't impact your personal credit scores when used wisely, and can be scaled far beyond typical personal credit limits. In this chapter, you'll learn how to **establish, grow, and leverage business credit** to fund your family's long-term financial goals.

Why Business Credit Matters for Families

Business credit allows you to:

- Access higher limits with fewer personal guarantees
- Fund real estate, online businesses, and side hustles
- Protect your personal credit from overuse
- Turn your family into an income-producing "business unit"
- Pass down a real, cash-generating business to your children

Most importantly, **business credit is scalable**. A well-structured business can receive $50,000–$250,000 in credit within 12–18 months—even faster with the right strategies.

Set Up a Real, Fundable Business

Before applying for business credit, your company must look legitimate and meet lender standards—this is called being **"fundable"**.

Action Steps:

1. **Choose a Business Structure**
   - Register an **LLC** or **Corporation** (avoid sole proprietorships)
   - Use a state website or filing service to register
2. **Get an EIN**
   - Apply for free at the IRS website
3. **Open a Business Bank Account**
   - Use your EIN and formation documents to open an account
   - Deposit $100–$500 to get started
4. **Get a Professional Business Address & Phone Number**
   - Don't use a P.O. box or home address if avoidable

- Set up a virtual address (ex: iPostal1, Regus)
- Get a business phone number (Google Voice, RingCentral)

5. **List Your Business Online**

- Register with 411 directory
- Build a basic website and get a business email (yourname@yourcompany.com)

Lenders and vendors will research you. If your business looks unprofessional or incomplete, you won't get approved.

Start Building Vendor Credit (Net-30 Accounts)

Vendor credit, or **Net-30 accounts**, report to business credit bureaus and help you **build your business credit file from scratch**.

Start with 3–5 vendors that report:

Vendor	What They Offer	Reports To
Uline	Office and shipping supplies	D&B, Experian

Grainger	Industrial products	D&B, Equifax
Quill	Office and cleaning supplies	D&B
Crown Office Supplies	School & office items	Equifax, CreditSafe
NAV	Credit monitoring & reports	D&B, Experian

How to Use Them:

- Order $50–$100 of products you already need
- Pay the invoice early or on time
- Repeat monthly for 2–3 months

After 3–5 vendors report, you'll generate your **Paydex Score** (Dun & Bradstreet's version of a credit score).

Move to Tier 2 – Retail Business Credit Cards

Once your business has a few tradelines reporting, apply for **store credit cards** in your business's name. These do not require personal guarantees if your credit file is strong.

Examples:

- Amazon Business
- Lowe's Pro Business
- Shell, BP, or Chevron gas cards
- Dell Business Credit

Again, **only use what you can pay off monthly.** This is to grow your credit limits and build history—not to spend unnecessarily.

Graduate to Tier 3 – High-Limit Business Credit Cards and Loans

After 6–9 months of on-time payments with vendors and retail accounts, you'll be positioned to apply for:

- **Business credit cards** (Amex Blue Business Plus, Capital One Spark, Chase Ink)
- **Business lines of credit** ($10K–$100K)
- **Equipment financing, vehicle loans, and SBA funding**

You may still be asked for a **personal guarantee**, especially early on. But over time, as your business credit deepens, you'll access funding **with no PG**.

Pro Tip: Apply with **banks that you already have business accounts with**, as they're more likely to approve you.

Chapter Summary:

- Business credit can fuel your family's long-term wealth goals and protect your personal finances.
- Set up a **fundable business** with a legal structure, EIN, address, phone, website, and bank account.
- Start with **vendor accounts** to build your profile, then move up to **retail and high-limit credit**.
- Use business credit to fund **income-generating ventures**, not liabilities.

"The Family Business That Credit Built"

Victor Martinez stood in his garage, looking at a pile of used power tools stacked beside a half-built workbench. His 15-year-old son, Leo, was scrolling through his phone on the tailgate of Victor's dusty truck, bored.

"Dad," Leo said without looking up, "why don't you just sell them?"

Victor turned. "What, the tools?"

"Yeah. You've got, like, ten drills and four sanders. Sell 'em online."

Victor laughed. "People don't buy used tools like they used to."

Leo tapped his screen. "Actually… they do."

That conversation, as small and casual as it seemed, would change their family's life forever.

That night, Victor talked to his wife, Angela, over dinner. He'd been laid off from his warehouse job three months earlier. Angela was covering them with her nursing shifts, but they both knew they needed another source of income. Leo's comment stuck with him.

"What if we started a little tool resale business?" he asked. Angela raised an eyebrow. "With what money?"

Victor shrugged. "Maybe we could use some of our credit... but smart this time."

Angela was hesitant. Years ago, they had gotten into trouble with credit cards. But Victor had been reading about **business credit**—credit that wouldn't be tied to their personal names.

The Setup

Victor filed for an LLC that weekend—**"Tool Time Traders LLC."** He got an EIN for free on the IRS website and opened a business checking account with $250 from their tax return.

He registered a virtual business address and bought a simple domain name: *ToolTimeTraders.com.*

Then, he applied for Net-30 accounts with Uline, Quill, and Grainger. He ordered $60 worth of cleaning supplies and shipping tape, paid the invoices early, and watched his business credit profile come to life.

Every week, Victor taught Leo how to list items on Facebook Marketplace, eBay, and OfferUp. They posted pictures, wrote descriptions, and even learned how to bundle tools for higher profit margins. In just one month, they made over $1,000.

Angela noticed something different. They weren't just selling things—they were **working together as a family**.

The Climb

By month three, Victor had four vendors reporting on his business credit profile. His Paydex score showed up on Dun & Bradstreet.

He applied for an Amazon Business credit line and got approved for $4,000.

He bought a used lot of returned tools from a supplier in Georgia—paid with the Amazon Business account—and resold it locally for a 45% profit.

Then came the big milestone: approval for the **Chase Ink Business Cash** card with a $10,000 limit.

Angela was shocked. "Isn't that too much risk?"

Victor shook his head. "We're not using it to buy clothes or go on vacation. This card only touches things that make us money."

The Transformation

Within a year, Tool Time Traders was earning $4,000–$6,000 a month. Victor and Leo rented a small warehouse space with a delivery bay. Leo learned how to create simple video ads on TikTok, showing their "tool hauls," and built a following of 12,000 people.

Angela eventually cut back on her night shifts. She started managing the books and found more suppliers to negotiate with.

They added a service division—local tool repair and sharpening, run by a family friend who needed work. They even started teaching other families how to start their own credit-backed side businesses.

The Legacy

What started with a casual conversation turned into a **fully functional family business**, built on smart credit and fueled by unity.

Leo, now a high school junior, had a 760 credit score as an authorized user on one of the company's oldest cards. He planned to launch his own ecommerce store and major in business finance.

Victor had a vision board in his office. On it, three goals:

1. Buy a commercial property with business credit.
2. Fund Leo's college education without student loans.
3. Teach 100 other families how to do the same.

"I used to think credit was a trap," he said at a local seminar. "But now I know—it's a ladder. You just have to climb it the right way."

Chapter 4: Using Credit to Acquire Real Estate Without Draining Savings

For many families, owning real estate is the ultimate wealth-building goal. But with high prices, down payments, and closing costs, the dream can feel out of reach. The truth is, you can start acquiring properties using **credit strategically**—without draining your family's savings.

In this chapter, you'll learn exactly how to use personal and business credit to **fund down payments, cover rehab costs, and cash flow real estate**—all while protecting your financial foundation.

Why Real Estate Is Ideal for Credit-Backed Wealth

Real estate is one of the best investments to leverage credit because:

- It's a tangible, appreciating asset
- It produces monthly cash flow through rent
- It can be improved to increase value
- It offers tax deductions (mortgage interest, depreciation, etc.)
- Lenders allow **leverage**—you don't need to pay full price

Credit, when used correctly, can cover:

- Down payments
- Closing costs
- Renovations
- Furnishing for short-term rentals
- Bridge financing until long-term financing is secured

Funding Down Payments Using Credit

Important: Mortgage lenders typically don't allow **borrowed money** for down payments—unless it's from a **secured** source like a HELOC or business line of credit.

Strategies:

1. **Home Equity Line of Credit (HELOC)**
    - If you already own a home, use your equity to fund another property.
    - A $100K HELOC at 7% interest costs roughly $583/month interest-only.
    - Use HELOC to fund a down payment, then refinance or pay off quickly.

2. **Business Credit Card with 0% APR**
    - Use a 0% card to fund closing costs or small rehab projects.
    - Many business cards offer 12–18 months of no interest.
3. **Personal Line of Credit**
    - These can be used for down payments if you repay quickly.
    - Some banks offer $10K–$50K unsecured lines at competitive rates.
4. **Cash Advance to Purchase Options Contract**
    - Use credit to pay for a real estate option or earnest deposit.
    - Flip the contract (wholesale) or assign it to another investor.

Financing Property Repairs and Improvements with Credit

Real estate investors often fund renovations with **credit cards, business lines of credit**, or **vendor credit**.

Example:

- You purchase a fixer-upper for $180,000 with a 20% down payment ($36,000).
- You use a $15,000 business credit card at 0% APR to renovate.
- After repairs, the property appraises for $250,000.
- You refinance at the new value, pay off the card, and pull out equity.

This method is commonly known as the **BRRRR Method**: **Buy – Rehab – Rent – Refinance – Repeat.**

Create a Real Estate Investment Entity

To protect your personal assets and grow business credit:

1. Create an **LLC** specifically for real estate investing.
2. Use your LLC to:
    - Open business bank accounts
    - Apply for lines of credit and credit cards
    - Purchase insurance and services

   - Hold rental properties

3. Keep detailed records of income, expenses, and debt payments.

Having a formal business structure makes it easier to get funding, partner with investors, and pass properties on to heirs.

Risk Management and Smart Exit Planning

Credit can accelerate your wealth—but misused, it can create financial strain.

Tips to stay safe:

- **Use interest-free periods wisely.** Always have an exit strategy.
- **Avoid long-term balances on high-interest cards.**
- **Build multiple streams of income** from the property: long-term rental, Airbnb, storage space, etc.
- **Always have a reserve fund** for emergencies or vacancies.
- **Set up asset protection**: trusts, insurance, LLC layers.

If your plan is to flip the property, **have contractors, timelines, and resale strategies in place before swiping a card.**

If your plan is to hold and rent, **run cash flow numbers carefully**, including mortgage, taxes, insurance, utilities, and credit payments.

Chapter Summary:

- You can use credit to start building your real estate portfolio—without wiping out your savings.
- Use HELOCs, business cards, and lines of credit for down payments, repairs, and scaling.
- Create a real estate investment LLC to protect yourself and qualify for more funding.
- Always plan your exit, your refinance, or your repayment strategy in advance.

"From One Flip to Freedom"

The Thomas family didn't look like real estate investors.

Monica worked full-time as a 4th-grade teacher. Her husband, Darren, was a school bus mechanic who picked up extra shifts fixing cars on weekends. Their two daughters, Jade and Laila, were used to tagging along on trips to the hardware store—not for home projects, but because their parents were always fixing something for someone else.

The family had dreams—big ones. They wanted a second income. Monica had always wanted to travel. Darren dreamed of owning land. But with only a few thousand in savings and two maxed-out credit cards, those dreams seemed far off.

Until one day, while scrolling through YouTube videos about saving for retirement, Monica stumbled on a video titled: **"How I Flipped a House with Business Credit and Made $47K in 90 Days."**

She played the video on the TV.

Darren, half-listening while organizing his tools, perked up when the speaker said,

> "You don't need cash—you need credit and a plan."

That night, they stayed up talking.

Monica said, "What if we use our tax refund to start an LLC and get a business credit card?"

Darren raised an eyebrow. "To buy a house?"

"No," she said. "To flip a house. Or at least fix it up. Just one. If it works, we try again."

Getting Started

With $1,800 from their refund, Monica formed **T&L Property Solutions LLC**—named after their daughters, Thomas and Laila. She opened a business bank account, got a virtual address, and signed up for a business credit builder program online.

Within 60 days, they had:

- A business credit profile
- 4 vendor accounts reporting
- An 80 Paydex score with Dun & Bradstreet
- A $12,000 business credit card with 0% APR for 12 months

Then came the chance they were waiting for.

Darren's cousin, who had inherited a run-down home just outside Tampa, offered to sell it to them for $147,000—$30K under market value.

The catch? It needed repairs. Fast.

The Flip

The Thomases used $25,000 from the business card for:

- Roofing repairs

- Kitchen cabinets
- Paint, fixtures, and landscaping
- A handyman for plumbing work

Darren did the rest himself, using weekends and evenings to get the home ready for resale.

They kept every receipt, tracked every expense, and took photos of every improvement.

Monica handled the listings. Within three weeks of completion, they had three offers. They accepted one for **$219,000**.

Their profit after closing costs and fees? **$39,200.**

They paid off the business credit card. In full.

The Pivot

But something changed after the flip.

Instead of cashing out and spending the profits, they sat down at the kitchen table and asked themselves: **"What if we did this again? But this time... what if we held onto the property?"**

They started looking into BRRRR: Buy, Rehab, Rent, Refinance,

Repeat.

Using $10,000 of their profit, they found a small duplex in an up-and-coming area. They bought it using a hard money loan for purchase, then used their **business card again for repairs.**

After it was rented and refinanced, the cash-out allowed them to repay all debts and clear $450/month in cash flow.

The Family Shift

Jade, now 12, started helping Darren calculate renovation costs and watching Zillow to find "ugly houses" that could be next.

Laila asked if she could design the next Airbnb listing's room "so it looks cooler."

Monica created a Sunday ritual—real estate finance lessons around the dinner table. "How much did we spend?" "What's the rent?" "What's our monthly profit?"

Darren started teaching younger mechanics about how he used credit to fund tools, fix homes, and reinvest.

They weren't just flipping houses. They were **flipping their mindset**—from paycheck-to-paycheck to strategic, generational wealth.

One Year Later

T&L Property Solutions had:

- Completed 2 flips
- Held 3 rental units
- Received approval for a $50,000 line of credit from their local bank
- Created a family mission statement: "We don't borrow to survive. We borrow to grow."

They still lived modestly.

Still worked.

But now they had options.

And that was worth more than any raise they'd ever been promised.

Chapter 5: Creating Multiple Income Streams Using Credit

Relying on one paycheck is a risky strategy in today's economy. Families that build real wealth often do so by developing **multiple streams of income**—and many of them start by leveraging **credit** to launch, fund, or scale these income streams.

In this chapter, you'll learn how to use personal and business credit to **create diversified, family-friendly income sources** that can be managed part-time but produce long-term results.

Why Multiple Streams of Income Matter

Depending on one job or source of income makes your financial foundation fragile. But adding even **one or two supplemental income streams** can:

- Make you recession-resistant
- Provide security during emergencies
- Fund future investments
- Help pay off debt faster
- Create long-term family stability

Most wealthy families have 4 to 7 income streams, including:

- Rental income
- Online business income
- Dividend/interest income
- Royalties
- Freelance or consulting income
- Product sales
- Passive investments

Credit is the engine that can power the startup of these streams when cash is limited.

Credit-Backed Income Stream Ideas for Families

Here are proven income streams that can be launched or scaled using personal or business credit:

1. Ecommerce Business (Amazon, eBay, Shopify)

- Use credit to buy inventory, website setup, and product packaging.
- Business cards help fund order fulfillment and ad campaigns.

- ROI potential: 15–40% profit margin.

2. Short-Term Rentals (Airbnb)

- Use credit to furnish a rental, stage a home, or pay for digital marketing.
- Set up an LLC to manage the property.
- Use business credit for cleaning equipment, welcome kits, and insurance.

3. Online Course or Coaching Business

- Credit can cover course creation software, video tools, ads, and branding.
- Passive income potential once the product is complete.

4. Vending Machine or ATM Business

- Use business cards for initial machine purchase and placement fees.
- Ongoing cash flow once established.

5. Turo (Car Sharing) or Toro (Tool Sharing)

- Use credit to buy or lease a vehicle or high-value tools to rent.

- Market locally or through platforms.
- Write off expenses as business deductions.

Smart Use of Credit to Launch Your Income Stream

When launching an income stream with credit, follow these principles:

Do:

- Use **0% interest cards** for startup expenses.
- Have a **repayment plan** tied to projected income.
- Track **every dollar** you spend and earn.
- Open a **separate account** for the business side hustle.
- Limit use to **revenue-generating activities**.

Don't:

- Max out credit limits.
- Spend before validating your business model.
- Mix personal and business transactions.
- Use credit to fund lifestyle upgrades.

Example: If you use a $5,000 0% card to launch an online course, and it generates $1,500/month, you can pay off the balance in 4 months—leaving 8 months of pure profit before interest kicks in.

Involve the Family in the Income Stream

Turning your side income into a **family project** creates shared purpose and teaches financial skills early. Depending on age and interest, your children and spouse can help with:

- Product research
- Video editing
- Managing social media
- Shipping and packaging
- Bookkeeping
- Customer service

This builds financial literacy and generational wealth habits at home.

Scale and Stack Income Streams Over Time

Once you launch one income stream and it's stable, reinvest profits or reuse available credit to build **a second one**. This could look like:

1. Start with ecommerce using business credit
2. Use profits to fund a real estate down payment
3. Use rental income to support online course creation
4. Layer in passive income with affiliate marketing or royalty-based content

You'll move from **active effort** to **automated income** over time—freeing up hours and reducing financial pressure.

Chapter Summary:

- One income is risky. Smart families use credit to build **multiple income streams**.
- Start small with ecommerce, content creation, or vending—anything that can cash flow quickly.
- Always use **credit tied to revenue**, not spending.
- Involve your family and reinvest profits to stack streams.

"Weekends into Wealth"

The Reeds weren't rich. They weren't influencers. They weren't investors or trust fund kids. But they were **builders**—and not the kind that worked in construction.

Chris was a middle school science teacher. His wife, Yasmine, worked at the public library. Their three boys—Miles (13), Kian (10), and Noah (7)—kept them busy with soccer games, messy backpacks, and endless grocery runs. Most weekends, the Reeds just tried to survive.

But one Friday night, as they sat around the table reviewing bills and deciding whether to delay a car repair, Yasmine blurted out, "We have to stop depending on just these two checks."

Chris nodded, exhausted. "I know. But we don't exactly have a pile of cash to start something."

Yasmine grabbed her phone and pulled up a note labeled: **"Family Income Streams – Start with Credit."**

They had watched a webinar the week before about using **business credit to launch side hustles**. The speaker broke it down clearly:

> "You don't need capital. You need credit and a plan."

Yasmine had written down three ideas. They decided to start all of them—with credit.

Income Stream #1: Vending Machine Side Hustle

Using a $6,000 **business credit card with 0% APR for 12 months,** Chris bought two used vending machines and stocked them with snacks from Costco. He placed them in the breakroom of a local auto repair chain—after pitching the owner on a "no-maintenance, revenue-share" deal.

By month two, the machines were pulling in $600/month. After restocking costs and a small cut to the shop, they netted $350/month.

Chris had the boys help stock the machines on Saturday mornings. Kian handled the coins. Noah cleaned the glass. Miles tracked the sales on a spreadsheet.

It became a family ritual—and a business lesson rolled into one.

Income Stream #2: Digital Products Business

Yasmine had always created fun educational worksheets for her library's after-school program. Using a Canva Pro subscription (paid via a $120 business credit), she turned those worksheets into **downloadable activity bundles** for teachers and homeschoolers.

She listed them on Etsy and TeachersPayTeachers.

The initial $500 she spent on templates, branding, and a short Fiverr gig paid off in six weeks. Her bundles were earning $40–$60 a day in sales.

The boys helped name the bundles and even suggested themes: "Space Math," "Zombie Grammar," and "Fortnite Vocab."

By month four, she had created over 40 digital products—each one taking just 1–2 hours to build.

Income Stream #3: Car Rental (Turo)

Chris had recently paid off their second car. Rather than sell it, he listed it on **Turo**, a car-sharing platform. They used **business credit to purchase insurance, detailing, and a key safe** for self-check-in.

They rented it out on weekends and during school breaks—pulling in $400–$600 per month.

Chris and Miles made it a project—tracking mileage, cleaning, and handling customer hand-offs. It gave Miles real-world business exposure and something to be proud of.

One Year Later

The Reeds were earning **an extra $2,500/month** from their three side hustles.

- The vending machines grew to 5 units across 3 locations
- Yasmine's digital shop passed $20,000 in sales
- Their Turo car paid for itself and was upgraded with a newer, more fuel-efficient model—also credit-funded

They had **paid off all original credit balances** used to launch the projects. Their credit scores improved. They were pre-approved for a line of credit from their bank. And they started looking into a small Airbnb investment using the same principles they'd applied all year.

But the best part?

Their kids now knew what a "profit margin" was. They knew how to write a pitch email. And they understood the difference between **using credit to survive** and **using credit to grow.**

One Sunday morning, Noah asked, "Can we start a YouTube channel to show other families how to make money too?"

Yasmine smiled. "That's a fourth stream of income, baby."

Chapter 6: Protecting and Preserving Family Wealth with Credit-Funded Tools

Creating wealth is only half the equation. The other half is **protecting what you've built**. Without a plan, wealth can disappear as fast as it's created—from emergencies, lawsuits, economic downturns, or poor planning. This chapter focuses on using **credit-funded resources** to establish **legal, financial, and protective systems** that keep your family's income and assets safe for the long term.

Why Protection Matters

Here's the reality:

- 70% of families lose their wealth by the second generation.
- 90% lose it by the third.
- Most families don't lose it from bad decisions—they lose it from **no decisions**.

By using **credit strategically**, you can afford the tools and structures that preserve your legacy **now**, rather than waiting until you're "rich enough."

Credit-Funded Wealth Protection Tools

Let's explore the tools that help protect your income, property, and future—and how you can **fund them with credit** if necessary:

1. Insurance (Life, Property, and Liability)

- Life insurance protects your family if something happens to you.
- Umbrella policies protect you from lawsuits.
- Landlord or business insurance protects real estate and income streams.

Use 0% APR credit cards or business credit lines to prepay annual premiums at a discount.

2. LLCs and Legal Entities

- LLCs separate your personal assets from your business or rental properties.
- If you're sued, only the LLC's assets are at risk—not your family's home or savings.
- Series LLCs allow you to protect multiple assets under one structure.

Startup costs for LLCs ($150–$500) can be covered with business credit or reimbursement from side income.

3. Revocable Living Trusts

- Avoid probate, protect privacy, and ensure your wealth is passed on as you choose.
- You can name successors, guardians for children, and stipulate how wealth is distributed.

If legal fees are a barrier ($500–$2,000), fund it through a legal credit line or legal financing program.

4. Asset-Building Life Insurance (IUL or Whole Life)

- These policies **build cash value**, which you can **borrow against tax-free**.
- The policy protects your family and becomes a **credit-like wealth tool** over time.

Use a short-term credit strategy to afford early premiums while you build equity.

5. Emergency Funds and Credit Access

- Build a reserve for unexpected expenses using a **business credit card or line of credit**, only when needed.
- Keep personal credit intact for major life changes or backup funding.

Establish a credit-backed "family emergency account" as a line you don't use unless it's absolutely necessary.

Teach the Family to Protect What You've Built

Wealth is more easily protected when the whole family understands what's at stake and how to manage it.

Build a Family Wealth Protection Plan:

- Set up a monthly family financial review (even with young children).
- Share age-appropriate lessons about credit, risk, and responsibility.
- Document logins, passwords, asset accounts, and contacts in a secured file.
- Record a simple family video legacy explaining your financial decisions and values.

"Wealth without education disappears. But wealth with wisdom becomes legacy."

Affordable Protection Strategies Using Credit

Sometimes you're ready to build protection—but cash is tight. These options help bridge the gap:

Protection Tool	Average Cost	How to Use Credit
Life Insurance	$30–$200/month	Use 0% card for first year premiums
LLC Formation	$150–$500	Use business card or legal credit service
Estate Plan or Trust	$500–$2,000	Finance via legal firms or personal line
Emergency Fund Setup	$1,000–$5,000	Use business line or personal loan to establish backup
Legal Shield/Identity Theft	$30–$80/month	Use card with cashback or auto-pay setup

Start small if needed. Even **partial protection is better than none.**

Your Family Legacy Blueprint

By this point, you've already started creating wealth. Now it's time to **write your family legacy playbook**.

Include:

- Your values and vision
- What you want to pass on (assets, businesses, education)
- Instructions for property, passwords, and responsibilities
- How future generations should handle credit and debt
- A plan for each child to build credit early and avoid mistakes

This blueprint becomes a **living family financial manual**—one that can be printed, recorded, and passed on.

Chapter Summary:

- Protecting wealth is just as important as creating it.
- Use credit strategically to fund insurance, legal entities, and emergency resources.
- Teach your family how to preserve and expand what you've built.

- Create a formal plan that outlives you—and empowers your children.

"Guardians of the Legacy"

Camila adjusted the folders on her lap as the notary slid a packet of estate planning documents across the table. Her husband, Elijah, sat next to her, still in his work boots, a little out of place in the polished law office. Their kids—Ari (16) and Micah (13)—waited in the car, listening to music and texting friends.

Neither Camila nor Elijah had grown up with wealth. Elijah's father worked the fields in Central Florida. Camila's mother cleaned houses. They had learned to survive, not build.

But that was changing.

Ten years ago, they'd started a small mobile detailing business—Elijah cleaning cars while Camila handled marketing and scheduling. Over time, they added services, hired help, and eventually turned it into a thriving operation that brought in more money than their old 9-to-5s combined.

They used **business credit** to scale. They used **personal credit** to buy their first duplex. They used both to fund a real estate portfolio of four rentals and one Airbnb.

And now, they were doing something that no one in their family history had ever done: **Protecting it.**

A Wake-Up Call

Two months earlier, Elijah's childhood friend Rico had passed away unexpectedly at 39. No will. No trust. No insurance.

His wife was left scrambling to handle funeral costs, creditors, and three kids—without access to Rico's bank accounts, without knowledge of his business finances, and without any legal rights to his property.

It hit Elijah like a punch to the gut.

"We're building all this for the kids," he told Camila that night. "But what happens if I don't wake up tomorrow?"

Camila squeezed his hand. "We fix it. Now."

The Legacy Plan Begins

They started with life insurance.

Using a **business credit card with 0% APR**, they prepaid for both of their term policies for the first year—saving $200 by paying annually instead of monthly. The peace of mind was immediate.

Next, they booked a free consultation with a family attorney. The attorney suggested a **revocable living trust** to avoid probate, a **healthcare directive**, a **will**, and setting up each property in **separate LLCs** for asset protection.

The legal costs were $2,100.

Camila opened a **personal line of credit** they had been approved for months ago but never used. She used $2,000 from it to pay the legal retainer—then set up a six-month repayment plan from their Airbnb income.

"Why wait until we 'have the money,'" she said, "when we have **access** to money and a plan to pay it back?"

Bringing the Kids In

One Sunday, they sat Ari and Micah down and told them everything.

They explained:

- What a trust was
- Why they had life insurance
- What happens if something happened to Mom or Dad
- Why they weren't just leaving money—they were leaving a **map**

Ari, skeptical but intrigued, asked, "So... you guys are planning for when you're not here?"

"We're planning so you never have to scramble like we did," Camila said.

That afternoon, they drafted a simple **Family Wealth Legacy Book**—a binder with:

- Passwords
- Bank accounts
- Deeds and LLC documents
- Contact info for attorneys, CPAs, and insurance reps
- A one-page letter explaining their values and vision for the family

They even recorded a short video explaining it all—just in case.

Credit as a Shield

Their oldest rental property was in a rougher part of town. It brought in steady income, but also came with occasional drama—plumbing issues, noise complaints, a former tenant who had threatened to sue over "unsafe stairs."

That was when Elijah decided to restructure the property into its own **LLC** and purchase an **umbrella insurance policy** for extra liability protection.

The costs:

- LLC filing: $160
- Annual registered agent service: $99
- Insurance premium: $384/year

He charged it all to a **business cashback card**, set to auto-pay from the property's rent income.

"Credit isn't just for growth," he told Ari later. "It's also for defense."

The Breakthrough Moment

Weeks later, Elijah and Camila sat down for a review with their CPA. She was impressed.

"You two have a real structure now," she said. "A legacy plan."

She offered to help them set up **529 college savings plans** for the kids—using rental income or excess credit limits from business rewards cards to pre-fund tax-advantaged education accounts.

They agreed.

Even Micah, who hated math, leaned into the idea. "You mean… you're using credit cards to save for college?"

Elijah grinned. "The smart way. You'll learn."

More Than Money

One evening, Camila caught Ari rewatching the video they had recorded for the family legacy book.

"What are you doing?" she asked, surprised.

"I don't know," Ari shrugged. "It's just cool. You and Dad… built all this. Not just the houses. The plan."

Camila smiled.

That was the moment she knew this wasn't just about credit, or money, or paperwork.

It was about **intentionality**.

About **breaking cycles**.

About handing the next generation more than just keys and passwords—handing them the tools and wisdom to grow what was already planted.

CREDIT TO CAPITAL

Chapter 7: Teaching Children and Teens to Build Credit Early and Responsibly

Building wealth isn't just about you—it's about empowering your children with the skills, habits, and tools to make smart financial decisions. The earlier they learn how credit works, the sooner they can begin building a strong credit profile, avoid common mistakes, and create their own path to financial independence.

This chapter will guide you in teaching your children about credit in **practical, age-appropriate ways**, and show you how to help them **build real credit** before they turn 18—or right after.

Why Teaching Credit Early Changes Generations

Most young adults don't learn about credit until they're denied for an apartment, car loan, or credit card. By then, they're playing catch-up.

Teaching kids about credit while they're still under your roof can help them:

- Avoid debt traps and credit card misuse
- Qualify for better loans when they're ready to buy a car or home
- Build a foundation of financial responsibility

- Learn to use leverage wisely, not emotionally

By the time they're 21, they could have a **750+ credit score** and access to funding for their first business, education, or investment opportunity—**without needing a co-signer**.

Age-Appropriate Credit Lessons for Kids and Teens

You don't need a textbook. You need conversations and hands-on experiences.

Ages 6–10: Early Awareness

- Teach the difference between "buy now" and "pay later"
- Use a toy or game-based allowance system to show how earning and saving works
- Explain what a debit card is and how it's connected to real money

Ages 11–13: Introduction to Credit

- Introduce the idea of borrowing vs. owning
- Use a mock credit score game (ex: earn points for completing chores on time)

- Talk about good vs. bad uses of borrowing (investing vs. impulse buying)

Ages 14–17: Simulated Credit Experience

- Open a **youth checking account with a debit card**
- Use budgeting apps like Greenlight or Step that show spending habits
- Give them a prepaid card and let them "manage" their own monthly mini-budget
- Assign them to track a household bill (electricity, groceries, etc.) to understand budgeting

Helping Your Teen Build Real Credit Before Age 18

Yes—your teenager can begin building a real credit profile **with your help**.

Option 1: Add Them as an Authorized User

- Add them to a **seasoned credit card account** that:
    - Has been open for 2+ years
    - Has perfect payment history

    - Keeps utilization under 10%

- Most major card issuers report authorized user history to the credit bureaus

Within 60–90 days, your teen could have a FICO score of 700+ with no debt.

Option 2: Open a Secured Card in Their Name (18+)

- Once they turn 18, help them open a **secured credit card** with a $300–$500 deposit
- Teach them to use it only for small, predictable purchases (gas, groceries)
- Set up automatic payments to prevent late fees

Create a Family Credit Curriculum

Create a weekly or monthly "Money Talk" where your family sits down for 20–30 minutes to cover:

- What credit scores mean
- Why interest rates matter
- How to read a credit report

- How to use credit cards responsibly
- Real-life consequences of poor credit decisions

Bonus Project:

Assign your teen to research 3 credit cards, compare fees, APRs, and rewards—and present which one they would choose and why. Treat it like a credit "science fair."

Empower Their Credit Journey With a Purpose

The goal isn't just to give your teen access to credit—it's to give them a reason to use it responsibly. Help them:

- Set a goal: "Build 750 credit score by 21 to buy first car/home without a co-signer."
- Tie credit to opportunity: "Use my strong credit to get a business credit card and start my own online shop."
- Show the timeline: "Every payment builds your future. Every mistake sets it back."

Encourage them to track their credit with tools like:

- Credit Karma (free, educational)

- MyFICO (accurate for planning major purchases)
- Experian Boost (report utility bills for a score lift)

Chapter Summary:

- Teaching your kids about credit early prevents future mistakes and empowers them to succeed independently.
- Use age-appropriate tools and conversations to make credit a part of normal family life.
- Help them build actual credit with authorized user accounts or secured cards.
- Connect credit to real goals—college, car, business, or real estate—to make it meaningful.

"The Teen With a 740"

Marcus stood nervously in front of his high school's entrepreneurship club, holding a whiteboard with numbers scribbled in blue marker. "This month," he said, voice steady, "our sticker business cleared $1,204 in profit. We're reinvesting $400 into new designs and the rest… well, we're saving it to launch our Shopify store."

Applause broke out. One student raised a hand.

"How old are you again?"

"Sixteen."

A Different Kind of Talk

Marcus wasn't a typical teenager. He wasn't obsessed with shoes, gaming, or TikTok dances. He was obsessed with **credit**.

It all started when his dad, Jordan, handed him a printed credit score chart at the dinner table one evening.

"You can either learn about this now," Jordan said, "or wait until a bank denies you for something important later."

Marcus was confused. Credit? Wasn't that for grown-ups?

But Jordan explained: "How you use credit is how you build your future. We didn't grow up with this knowledge. You will."

The Authorized User Hack

That night, Jordan pulled up his credit card dashboard and added Marcus as an **authorized user** to his oldest card—15 years old, perfect payment history, and a low balance.

Within a few weeks, Marcus had a real credit file and a FICO score of 740.

He didn't even have a job yet. But he had a **track record**.

With that boost, they applied for a **student credit card** under Marcus's name, co-signed by Jordan. It had a $500 limit.

Marcus was instructed to only use it for:

- Gas
- School supplies
- One monthly streaming subscription

Each Sunday, they reviewed the charges. Marcus paid it off from his part-time tutoring gig.

By month three, his credit utilization was under 10%, and his payment history was perfect.

The Sticker Business

During summer break, Marcus came up with an idea: a custom motivational sticker brand for students and young athletes.

He used **$300 from his credit card** to buy a Cricut cutting machine and sticker paper. Jordan helped him register a **small LLC** for $150.

They built a simple Shopify site. His mom, Tanya, a part-time graphic designer, helped create the first sticker pack: "Grind Now, Chill Later."

Sales came in through TikTok and word of mouth at school.

The profits? Reinvested into bulk materials and shipping supplies—all managed through a **business debit card** tied to their LLC bank account.

Marcus handled:

- Order fulfillment
- Customer emails
- TikTok content

Jordan tracked the business credit file using NAV and added a Quill and Uline account to start building vendor credit under Marcus's new company.

Financial Confidence at 16

Marcus had a routine.

- Mondays: fulfill sticker orders
- Wednesdays: record new TikToks

- Sundays: review credit usage, spending, and income with his parents

He had:

- A 740 credit score
- A profitable side business
- A checking, savings, and business account
- A basic understanding of credit lines, APRs, and vendor accounts

But most importantly, he had **confidence**.

Confidence to say "no" when friends tried to convince him to max his card on designer shoes. Confidence to pitch his sticker packs to a local school supply store. Confidence to explain interest rates to a teacher who still used payday loans.

Looking Ahead

By 18, Marcus planned to:

- Apply for his first high-limit student business credit card
- Lease office space (a small garage) using business credit

- Expand into apparel
- Create an affiliate program for other teen entrepreneurs

His parents watched with quiet pride.

“We didn’t have this kind of start,” Jordan said. “But now our son does.”

Marcus smiled when people called him “disciplined” or “business-minded.” He knew the truth: He just had **access**, **education**, and a head start most teens never get.

And it all started with a dinner table talk about a credit score chart.

Chapter 8: Using Credit to Build or Buy Family-Owned Businesses

Owning a family business is one of the most powerful ways to generate wealth across generations. Whether you're **starting a new business from scratch** or **buying an existing one**, credit can give you the capital needed to launch, grow, or acquire income-generating operations—without waiting years to save.

This chapter will show you how to use personal and business credit to **start or purchase profitable family-owned businesses** and turn them into long-term assets that create income, employment, and legacy.

Why Family-Owned Businesses Create Lasting Wealth

When you own a business—especially one that involves your family—you're doing more than just making money:

- You're **controlling your income**
- You're **teaching your children entrepreneurial skills**
- You're building something that can be **passed down or sold**
- You're opening doors to tax advantages, funding, and flexibility

Unlike a job, which ends when you stop working, a business can pay you even while you sleep—or when your children take over.

Choosing the Right Business for Your Family

Your business doesn't have to be big—it just needs to be **scalable, manageable, and profitable**.

Start-from-scratch business ideas:

- **Mobile car wash/detailing**
- **Online store for handmade products**
- **Tutoring, coaching, or online courses**
- **Cleaning services (home or commercial)**
- **Airbnb or short-term rental management**
- **Lawn care and outdoor services**
- **Vending machine or ATM routes**

Buy-an-existing-business ideas:

- **Cash-flowing eCommerce websites**
- **Service businesses on Flippa, BizBuySell, or Empire Flippers**
- **Brick-and-mortar businesses with retiring owners**

- **Digital assets (courses, blogs, affiliate sites)**

Tip: Look for businesses with **recurring revenue**, **low overhead**, and **clear growth potential.**

Using Credit to Start a Family Business

Once you've chosen the right business model, credit can help you move fast and with minimal risk.

Funding sources:

1. **0% APR Business Credit Cards**
    - Fund inventory, equipment, or marketing.
    - Many offer 12–18 months of interest-free financing.
    - Examples: Chase Ink Business, Amex Blue Business, Capital One Spark.
2. **Business Lines of Credit**
    - Revolving access to capital as needed.
    - Useful for hiring, expansion, or purchasing recurring supplies.
3. **Personal Credit Cards (carefully)**

- Best used for startup services: design, legal filing, web hosting.
- Avoid carrying long-term balances here; pay off quickly.

4. **Vendor Credit Accounts (Net 30)**
    - Build business credit by ordering and paying vendors on time.
    - Helps you qualify for larger credit lines later.

Example: Start a vending business using a $5,000 credit card to buy machines and products. Break even in 3–6 months. Profit for years.

Buying an Existing Business Using Credit

If you prefer to skip the startup phase, you can buy a business that's already running—using a mix of credit and negotiation.

How to do it:

1. **Find the Right Business**
    - Search Flippa, Empire Flippers, or local listings.

- Look for 2–3 years of profit history, low churn, and consistent customers.

2. **Use Business Credit for Purchase**

    - Some businesses under $25K can be purchased outright with credit cards or business credit lines.
    - Negotiate seller financing—many owners will accept 30–50% down, with the rest paid over time.
    - Use credit to fund the down payment or cover legal/accounting due diligence.

3. **Leverage the Business's Own Cash Flow**

    - Ideally, the business you buy should help you pay back the credit used to buy it.
    - Make sure the business covers its own debt within 12–18 months.

Involve Your Family in the Business

Once the business is launched or acquired, bring the family in.

Roles could include:

- **Spouse**: Accounting, marketing, customer service
- **Teenagers**: Tech, design, video, social media
- **Children**: Product assembly, labeling, cleaning, basic admin tasks
- **Parents/Relatives**: Delivery, bookkeeping, mentorship, vendor calls

This helps reduce hiring costs, build teamwork, and **teach real financial skills** in the home.

> Bonus: Children working in the business may qualify for **tax-free income up to $14,000/year**, depending on your entity structure.

Protect and Scale the Business with Credit

After the business is running:

- Use credit for **bulk inventory** or supplier negotiations
- Apply for a **business credit line** to cover seasonal dips
- Use **credit to invest in automation**, such as software, CRM tools, and email marketing

- Get an **LLC, insurance, and emergency credit fund** for legal and financial protection

Always keep **credit separate** from personal life to avoid overleveraging.

Pro tip: Create a separate "growth fund" credit card used only for things that generate ROI: ads, new equipment, or bulk inventory buys with discounts.

Chapter Summary:

- Family businesses build income, skills, and legacy—and credit makes starting or buying one faster and easier.
- Use credit strategically for startup or acquisition—not lifestyle expenses.
- Choose simple, scalable business models and involve your family in daily operations.
- Reinvest profits, build credit lines, and protect your business like an asset.
- Treat the business as a long-term tool for freedom—not just income.

"The Digital Rescue"

The Gutierrez family never planned on buying a business.

Luis worked as a warehouse supervisor. His wife, Daniela, ran a small Etsy shop selling handmade jewelry. Their teenage son, Nico, was a tech-savvy high schooler with dreams of starting a YouTube channel. They were a tight-knit family living in Central Texas—practical, humble, and cautious with money.

But in the spring of that year, everything changed.

The Fork in the Road

Luis's company announced layoffs.

He wasn't laid off—yet. But the writing was on the wall. Schedules were cut, overtime disappeared, and Luis was told to "start preparing for change."

That night at dinner, Daniela spoke first.

"What if this is our push?"

Luis looked up. "Push for what?"

"To finally own something. Something we control. Something that doesn't depend on someone else's schedule."

Luis shook his head. "We don't have the cash to open a store."

Daniela slid her laptop across the table. "We don't need one."

On the screen was a listing on Flippa.com: **"Profitable Children's Activity Blog with Passive Income — $9,800 OBO."**

A Family Business Online

The blog was run by a stay-at-home mom who was shifting careers. It had 200+ articles, 5 years of traffic history, email subscribers, and affiliate revenue from Amazon.

It was making **$400–$600/month**—consistently.

Daniela loved the niche. Luis was intrigued by the income. Nico? He immediately started brainstorming video content for a connected YouTube channel.

"We can buy this," Daniela said, "and make it ours."

They applied for a **business credit card** that came with 0% interest for 12 months. Luis had solid credit and was approved for a $15,000 limit.

They used **$9,800** to buy the blog. They spent another **$1,200** on legal review and transferring hosting. And they set aside **$500** for redesigning the site and buying content tools like Canva Pro, Jasper AI, and ConvertKit.

Total cost: **$11,500**, all on the card.

Monthly payment (at 0%): **$958**, which they planned to pay off using the blog's cash flow and Daniela's Etsy profits.

Making It a Family Operation

In the first 60 days, they:

- Rebranded the blog as *LittleExplorersClub.com*
- Added Daniela's printable craft guides from Etsy to boost affiliate earnings
- Started collecting emails and built an 800-subscriber list
- Connected Nico's new YouTube channel to the blog with simple how-to craft videos

Luis handled logistics and affiliate accounts. Daniela wrote blog content and newsletters. Nico handled SEO, thumbnails, and video edits—something he enjoyed more than homework.

They didn't have employees. They didn't even have office space. Just a corner desk, a free email platform, and a shared family calendar.

But they had something better: **ownership**.

The Tipping Point

By month five, traffic had grown 40% thanks to new blog posts and Pinterest promotion.

Their monthly revenue hit $980—just enough to cover the business card payment.

By month seven, they landed a small sponsorship from a toy brand.

By month nine, Nico's videos had passed 10,000 views, and the YouTube channel was monetized.

Luis was still at the warehouse—barely.

When the layoff finally came, he wasn't scared.

He was ready.

The Reinvention

Luis took a severance check and immediately paid off the remaining card balance—just over $2,000. Their credit score had gone up, not down, because of low utilization and on-time payments.

They reinvested into:

- A virtual assistant to manage Pinterest and email
- New video equipment for Nico
- An online course teaching how to start a craft blog (their own digital product)

The blog became a **business.** The business became an **asset.** The asset became a **family-owned income stream.**

By the one-year mark, they were earning over **$2,700/month** in a combination of:

- Affiliate income
- YouTube ads
- Sponsored content
- Their digital course
- Printable sales

They were no longer just reacting to layoffs and economic swings.

They were running their own economy.

Beyond the Business

At a family BBQ, Nico's uncle asked him, "What do you want to do after high school?"

Nico shrugged. "I'm already doing it."

Daniela smiled. "We built this together."

Luis added, "And credit made it possible—not because we spent wildly, but because we used it like a tool."

The Gutierrez family didn't buy a store. They didn't build a restaurant. They didn't open a franchise.

They bought a quiet little blog—and turned it into a business that made more than any job had ever offered them.

And now, they were ready to buy another.

Chapter 9: Automating and Delegating with Credit to Free Up Family Time

One of the greatest benefits of building family wealth through credit is the ability to **buy back your time**. As your income streams grow, you'll eventually hit a point where your most limited resource isn't money—it's time.

This chapter teaches you how to use personal and business credit to **automate, outsource, and delegate** the repetitive parts of your income streams or household management. The result? More freedom, less burnout, and a business that runs even when you're not working.

The Problem with Doing Everything Yourself

At the beginning of your journey, it's normal to wear multiple hats—entrepreneur, bookkeeper, marketer, tech support. But if you don't start automating or delegating, you'll quickly hit a wall:

- You'll become the bottleneck of your own business.
- Growth will stall because you can't scale yourself.
- Your family life will suffer as work consumes every free moment.

The solution isn't working harder. It's working **smarter**—with help from **systems, software, and strategic spending**.

What to Automate First Using Credit

Here are the **best tasks to automate first**, using affordable software or one-time purchases—funded with 0% APR cards or business credit:

Income Stream Automations:

- **Email marketing:** Use ConvertKit, Mailchimp, or Systeme.io to automate welcome emails, promotions, and abandoned cart recovery.
- **Online sales:** Shopify or Etsy integration to auto-fulfill digital products or notify for physical shipments.
- **Payments & invoicing:** Use Stripe, PayPal, or Square for recurring billing and client management.
- **Appointment booking:** Use Calendly or Acuity for service-based businesses.

Household & Admin Automations:

- **Bill pay:** Automate recurring bills and credit payments to avoid late fees.

- **Budget tracking:** Use Mint, YNAB, or Rocket Money to monitor finances.
- **Grocery delivery subscriptions:** Use Instacart, Amazon Fresh, or Walmart+ to save time.
- **Subscription management:** Use Truebill to track and cancel wasteful recurring charges.

Tip: Many of these platforms offer annual payment discounts—use a business credit card to lock in the savings upfront.

Strategic Delegation Using Credit

Once you've automated the basics, it's time to **outsource tasks** that don't require your direct involvement. This doesn't mean hiring full-time employees. You can start small:

Delegation Options:

1. **Freelancers on Fiverr or Upwork:**
    - Graphic design, video editing, email sequences, blog writing.
    - Use business credit to prepay for project packages.

2. **Virtual Assistants (VAs):**
    - Hire VAs from the Philippines, Latin America, or Eastern Europe for $4–$10/hour.
    - Use VAs for customer service, inbox management, content repurposing, and more.
3. **Local Help:**
    - Teens can pack orders or manage social media.
    - Family members can be paid tax-deductible wages through your business.

Consider paying monthly VA or freelancer contracts via credit cards to **earn points** while covering business expenses—just don't carry balances long-term.

Calculate the ROI of Buying Back Time

If you're hesitant to spend, use this formula:

What's your hourly value? Let's say you make $3,000/month from your online store. You work 60 hours. That's **$50/hour**.

If you spend 8 hours a week editing videos yourself (instead of working on strategy or sales), that's **$400/week** in lost opportunity.

Hiring a freelancer for $100/week returns $300 in time value to you.

Using credit to frontload that expense while the income continues flowing is not wasteful—it's **smart leverage**.

Automate and Delegate Without Losing Control

Automating and outsourcing doesn't mean disappearing. Stay involved by:

- Using project management tools like Trello, Notion, or ClickUp to manage freelancers.
- Holding a 30-minute weekly "business team" check-in with your spouse, VA, or kids.
- Reviewing income and expenses once a week to stay ahead of spending.

Use credit-backed services that allow **pause, control, and metrics**, like:

- Ad platforms with set spend caps
- Email tools with detailed open/click reports
- VA time-tracking software like Time Doctor

How Families Can Use Credit to Buy Time Together

The ultimate goal of building credit-funded income streams is **time freedom**. Use your improved credit to:

- Prepay for vacations using travel cards with cashback
- Invest in time-saving services like cleaning, laundry, or tutoring
- Buy devices and software that reduce repetitive work
- Use rewards to book flights, hotels, or meals as a family

Example: Use a travel rewards business card to fund your ecommerce growth. The points can cover family travel later—giving both income and memories.

Chapter Summary:

- Automate the repetitive tasks in your business and household to free up your time.
- Use credit to front-load time-saving software and outsource help without draining cash.
- Track ROI: spend $1 on automation or help that gives you $3–$5 in time or income back.

- Don't delegate everything—delegate strategically and stay involved.
- Use time freedom to invest in your family, health, and long-term goals.

"Time Bought Back"

The Patel family had a problem that didn't look like a problem to most people.

Business was booming.

Their digital planner shop on Etsy had crossed $7,000 in monthly revenue. Their YouTube channel—run by their 16-year-old daughter, Aanya—had just passed 25,000 subscribers. They had three online courses, a dozen printable products, and a growing customer base.

But they were exhausted.

The Breaking Point

It was a Saturday afternoon when Priya Patel finally snapped.

She sat at the dining table, buried in customer emails, watching cold tea sweat into a napkin. Her husband, Raj, had been troubleshooting the checkout page on their website for over an hour. Their kids were arguing about chores, and laundry sat untouched in a hallway basket.

This wasn't the freedom they envisioned when they started their business.

"We created this to get more time," Priya said, frustrated. "And now we have less of it than ever."

Raj sighed, rubbing his forehead. "We either shut half of this down… or we figure out how to run it **without** running ourselves into the ground."

The Automation Plan

That night, Raj reviewed their credit account. They had a **$12,000 business credit card** with 0% interest for 10 months.

They didn't want to use it to buy more stuff. They wanted to buy **time.**

So, they made a plan.

Phase 1: Automation

- Moved their courses from a clunky WordPress site to **Kajabi** (paid annually to save 20%)
- Switched email marketing to **ConvertKit**, automating all welcome emails, abandoned cart sequences, and weekly broadcasts

- Set up **Zapier** to connect customer actions across platforms (ex: new order triggers a review request + upsell email)
- Used **Canva Pro** to create and auto-schedule Pinterest and Instagram posts

All expenses? Charged to the business credit card—paid back monthly from business profits.

Total automation spend: **$2,400** Resulting time saved per week: **15 hours**

The Delegation Shift

With the basics automated, Priya tackled customer support—her biggest time drain.

They hired a **virtual assistant** from the Philippines for $6/hour, 20 hours/week. She handled:

- Etsy messages
- Refund requests
- Upload errors
- Positive review follow-ups

Next, they hired a **Fiverr freelancer** to redesign outdated thumbnails for their digital products and course pages.

Aanya, their daughter, took over weekly YouTube editing using **CapCut**, which they paid $75/year for via credit.

Delegation spend:

- VA: $480/month
- Fiverr: $300 one-time
- Software: $75/year

They tracked every ROI in a simple Google Sheet.

The Results

Within three months, they:

- Reduced weekly work hours from 50+ to 15–20
- Increased monthly sales by 18% (thanks to improved systems and follow-ups)
- Brought customer support response time from 48 hours to under 6

- Took their first **3-day weekend trip** in over a year—paid entirely with **credit card reward points**

Priya no longer felt chained to her inbox. Raj wasn't fixing broken links at midnight. Aanya was proud of being part of a real business—and finally had time for SAT prep.

And surprisingly, their **profit** didn't drop.

It grew.

Buying Back Their Life

With systems in place, they used the freed-up time to:

- Plan a second digital product line (student planners)
- Launch a podcast using their existing email list
- Start a weekend cooking class in their community—just for fun

But more than that, they got their **life** back.

They cooked together again. Took long walks. Played board games without someone checking Shopify notifications every ten minutes.

Their business didn't stop working when they stopped.

It ran **because they stopped micromanaging.**

A Family in Control

At their family meeting, Priya laid out their new weekly roles:

- Raj would monitor analytics and ads
- Aanya would handle creative tasks and YouTube
- The VA and freelancers would handle routine work
- Priya would oversee product development and partnerships

"This," Raj said, looking around the room, "is why we did all of this. To live, not just earn."

They had built a business that worked for them—not the other way around.

And they did it using credit **not to consume**, but to **free themselves**.

Time, they learned, is the most valuable currency.

And thanks to smart planning, they finally had enough of it.

Chapter 10: Scaling Wealth Through Credit-Funded Real Estate and Business Expansion

You've laid the foundation: credit is strong, income streams are flowing, and your family understands how to manage money and leverage wisely. Now it's time for the next step—**scaling**.

In this chapter, we'll cover how to use personal and business credit to **expand your wealth portfolio**, scale what's already working, and move from "extra income" to **true generational wealth** through **credit-powered growth**.

What Scaling Really Means

Scaling isn't just doing more—it's about:

- Multiplying income without multiplying effort
- Expanding successful models instead of starting over
- Using **credit, systems, and people** to increase profit and ownership

Whether you're growing your real estate portfolio or expanding your online business, the goal is the same: **use other people's money (credit)** to build more **assets**, not liabilities.

Scaling a Real Estate Portfolio with Credit

If you've acquired one rental, Airbnb, or BRRRR property using credit, scaling is simply a matter of **repeating the process—strategically.**

3 Ways to Scale Real Estate with Credit:

1. **Use HELOCs or Cash-Out Refinance**
    - Tap into equity from one property to fund down payments for others.
    - HELOCs can be interest-only and used flexibly.
    - Use the credit temporarily, then refinance after appreciation.
2. **Business Credit for Renovations**
    - Use high-limit business cards or lines of credit to cover:
        - Appliance purchases
        - Contractor payments
        - Airbnb furnishings
    - Pay them down with cash flow or refinance proceeds.
3. **Partner with Family Using Credit**

- Bring in relatives as co-borrowers or investors.
- Pool personal and business credit capacity.
- Set up an LLC with shared roles and profits.

Example: You buy one Airbnb using $15K from a HELOC. After a year of positive cash flow, use those profits and equity growth to purchase another—and repeat.

Scaling a Business With Credit-Funded Expansion

Your business doesn't have to be big to grow. Start with what's working, then pour fuel (credit) on it.

Methods to Scale a Business:

1. **Inventory Expansion**
    - Use 0% cards or vendor credit to buy inventory in bulk at discounts.
    - Improves profit margins and speeds up order fulfillment.
2. **Advertising & Marketing**

- Scale ad campaigns that already convert.
- Fund paid ads on YouTube, Facebook, or Google using business cards.
- Track ROI with tools like Hyros or Meta Ad Manager.

3. **New Product Lines or Services**
    - Use credit to test new offers without dipping into savings.
    - Launch a second digital course, product, or membership using previous profits and credit.
4. **System Upgrades**
    - Pay for CRM systems (like GoHighLevel, Kartra, or Kajabi) to automate sales pipelines.
    - Use credit to hire or upgrade fulfillment, bookkeeping, or virtual teams.

Tip: Apply for **multiple credit lines in a 2-week window** to minimize credit inquiries' impact and stack available capital.

Managing Credit and Risk as You Scale

Scaling increases opportunity—but also risk. Protect your growing business or real estate portfolio by:

- Keeping **utilization under 30%** to avoid score drops
- Setting up **LLCs for each property or brand** to isolate liability
- Building a **cash buffer** alongside credit expansion
- Using business insurance, umbrella policies, and contracts with clear terms
- Monitoring credit reports monthly (NAV for business, Credit Karma for personal)

Create a **credit dashboard** to track:

- Available limits
- Current balances
- Interest-free periods
- Payment dates

Use this dashboard to rotate credit usage, prevent overexposure, and preserve your ability to borrow again when needed.

Know When to Transition From Credit to Capital

Eventually, the goal is to shift from **credit-funded** to **cash-flow funded** growth.

Here's when to consider transitioning:

- Your business consistently generates $10K+/month
- You've built up 3–6 months of reserves
- Your assets can qualify for traditional lending (like SBA loans or commercial financing)
- You want to reduce exposure and improve debt-to-income ratios

At that point, you can use credit **strategically**, not out of necessity.

Scaling as a Family Mission

Scaling works best when it becomes a family mission—not just your solo hustle.

- Assign clear roles in real estate, ecommerce, or content creation
- Involve teens in outreach, marketing, or research
- Share the wins—track new income milestones together

- Celebrate with experiences, not just purchases
- Set new family goals each quarter: "Acquire one new asset," "Launch one new product," or "Pay off one funding source"

Scaling becomes legacy when it becomes **shared ownership**.

Chapter Summary:

- Scaling wealth is about multiplying what works—without increasing your stress.
- Use credit to expand real estate, inventory, ad spend, and automation.
- Protect your gains with legal entities, insurance, and proper risk management.
- Transition from credit to cash-flow-funded growth over time.
- Make wealth-building a family-centered, mission-driven process.

"The $250K Family Empire"

The Flores family didn't look like entrepreneurs.

Carla was a former dental assistant who started selling printable chore charts on Etsy to keep busy after being laid off. Her husband, Mateo, was a part-time landscaper who worked with his father's company. They lived in a modest home in Bakersfield, California, with their three kids—Luca (14), Mia (11), and baby Sofia.

Their first digital product sale brought in $6.74. Carla cried.

Not because it was a lot of money—but because it proved something they had started together could **work**.

They didn't know it yet, but that little Etsy sale would become the first spark of a **$250,000/year family business**—fueled by **credit**, teamwork, and a relentless commitment to growth.

From Kitchen Table to Online Shop

The first year was humble.

Carla made chore charts, homeschool printables, and teacher rewards for parents and educators. She learned how to bundle products, optimize keywords, and design in Canva. Mateo supported from the sidelines, picking up groceries, watching Sofia during nap time, and helping ship any physical versions they offered locally.

They used a **$3,500 personal credit card** to buy:

- Canva Pro and Creative Fabrica for assets
- An Epson EcoTank printer for test prints
- Their first Etsy ads campaign

Within 6 months, the shop was making $2,000/month.

They paid off the card in full—and **raised their credit limit**.

The First Scaling Decision

Late one night, after the kids had gone to sleep, Mateo asked a simple question: "What would happen if we really went for it?"

Carla paused. "You mean… like full time?"

They had $4,200 in savings. No safety net. But they had momentum.

They applied for a **business credit card** using Carla's growing income and were approved for **$9,000 at 0% APR for 12 months.**

They used it to:

- Hire a Fiverr designer to refresh their store branding
- Launch a Shopify site to sell directly

- Invest in bulk inventory for their new printable planners + bonus inserts
- Subscribe to **email marketing software** and start building a list

Mateo took a step back from landscaping. Mia and Luca helped organize orders and test new product ideas.

Family Business in Full Swing

By year two, their daily routine looked like this:

- **Carla**: Product creation, SEO, marketing
- **Mateo**: Shopify operations, supplier management, shipping
- **Luca**: YouTube tutorials on how to use printables (growing the channel to 15K subs)
- **Mia**: Product tester and TikTok clips with short tips and home hacks
- **Sofia**: Napping (most days)

They hired a **virtual assistant** for $350/month to:

- Handle customer service

- Send follow-up emails
- Monitor Etsy messages and reviews

They used credit to prepay the VA's contract for 6 months—saving $300 and earning cashback.

Real Estate Dreams & Scaling Up

With business profits reaching **$12,000/month**, they started looking at short-term rentals.

Mateo applied for a **home equity line of credit** (HELOC) on their primary residence—now worth $80,000 more than when they bought it.

They pulled **$50,000** from the HELOC and used it as a down payment on a **2-bedroom condo** in Big Bear, California, just a few hours from home. They furnished it with cashback points from their business card.

They automated the Airbnb listing, hired local cleaners, and set up remote check-in.

First month? Fully booked. Net profit: **$1,100** after expenses.

They now had two engines:

1. A growing digital products business

2. A credit-funded rental property

Managing Growth With a Plan

With systems in place, they built a credit strategy dashboard in Google Sheets. They tracked:

- Available limits
- Usage per card
- Due dates and grace periods
- Business ROI per expense

They rotated between 3 cards:

- One for **ads and marketing**
- One for **inventory and tools**
- One for **travel and rewards**

They never paid late. Never went over 30% utilization. And every dollar spent had a clear path to income.

Mateo handled the real estate side. Carla oversaw product launches and email sequences. The kids? They now had debit cards, budgeting apps, and biweekly "business review" meetings.

The Legacy in Motion

In year three, the Flores family business passed **$250,000 in annual revenue**.

They had:

- Over 400 products on Etsy and Shopify
- A monetized YouTube channel
- Two short-term rental properties
- Three high-limit business credit cards
- A growing list of over 12,000 email subscribers
- A written family financial blueprint

Carla no longer saw herself as a "mom who got lucky." She was a **CEO, creator, and investor.**

Mateo no longer saw his value as just physical labor. He had become a financial strategist and operations leader.

They hadn't just made money.

They made a **system**. A **structure**. A **legacy**.

And they did it by leveraging credit to create not debt—but **ownership**.

The best part?

They did it **together.**

FINAL WORDS FROM THE AUTHOR: "THE WEALTH IS ALREADY IN YOUR HANDS"

When I started this book, I didn't just want to write a guide—I wanted to create a mirror.

A mirror for the parent who lies awake at night wondering if they're doing enough. A mirror for the couple who works hard but never seems to get ahead. A mirror for the young adult afraid to start because they feel behind. And most of all, a mirror for the families—just like yours—who have more potential than they've ever been told.

Because the truth is this:

Wealth is not about being born into money. It's about being born into mindset.

And the mindset you choose—starting now—can change everything.

You Were Never Meant to Trade Time for Every Dollar

The system told you that to make money, you had to sacrifice time, energy, and presence.

You were taught to:

- Work harder, not smarter
- Save slowly instead of invest wisely
- Borrow only in desperation—not for growth
- Wait until you "have money" to start building wealth

But families who win—who build lasting wealth—**break those rules**.

They learn to:

- **Leverage credit to start income streams**
- **Automate and delegate to reclaim time**
- **Teach their children early** instead of shielding them from financial truths
- **Use structure to build legacy**, not just hustle to pay bills

And now that knowledge is in your hands.

What You've Built Throughout This Book

You haven't just read a book. You've built a toolkit.

Let's recap what you've done so far:

- Reframed credit as a tool, not a trap
- Rebuilt or optimized your personal credit file
- Learned to build business credit and use it to fund new ventures
- Started or acquired a family business or property
- Created multiple income streams that don't rely on a paycheck
- Protected your family's wealth with insurance, trusts, and LLCs
- Taught your children how credit works
- Automated your life so that you can **live**, not just earn
- Scaled with intention—not chaos
- Built a roadmap to make sure the wealth continues long after you're gone

You've gone from borrower to **builder**. From employee to **entrepreneur**. From worried parent to **family leader**.

That's no small journey.

If You're Feeling Overwhelmed, That's Okay

You don't have to do everything at once.

Some families start with fixing credit. Others launch a digital product. Some go straight into real estate or buying a business.

There is no "perfect order." There is only **consistent action.**

One smart move per week. One bill automated. One credit line secured. One conversation with your kids about money. One new idea tested.

Compound that over a year, and your entire life looks different.

You don't need a six-figure income. You don't need 100,000 followers. You don't even need a college degree.

You just need what you already have:

- Discipline
- Curiosity
- A plan
- And a reason

If your reason is your family—you're already wealthier than most.

What I Wish Someone Told Me Sooner

If I could go back 20 years and hand myself a letter, it would say this:

> "Credit isn't evil. It's a shortcut—if you treat it with respect.
>
> Start the business. Buy the duplex. Get the card with points.
>
> But only swipe if you know how the swipe pays you back.
>
> Teach your kids what you weren't taught. Show them a different life.
>
> Money isn't everything—but **freedom is**, and wealth is just freedom repeated across generations.
>
> Don't wait until you're desperate. Build while things are calm.
>
> Time is your greatest asset. Buy it back early. Use it well."

I now know that every dollar I borrowed—when used correctly—was actually a **down payment on freedom.**

And the faster you believe that, the faster you change your entire trajectory.

You Are the Blueprint Now

Here's what happens next:

Your family starts to ask questions. Neighbors start noticing you don't work weekends anymore. Your kids repeat phrases you've taught them: "Is this a liability or an asset?" Your spouse doesn't worry when bills come in—they ask, "How do we grow from here?"

That's the power of transformation.

And you're not just living it—you're leading it.

You are now the example someone else is waiting for. You are now the story your children will tell. You are now the **blueprint** for someone else's breakthrough.

Own it.

The Journey Doesn't End Here

This isn't the end. This is your beginning.

My challenge to you is simple:

- Choose the **first credit move** you'll make this week—big or small.

- Write out your **3-month family wealth goal**—and share it with someone.

- Schedule your **first (or next) family money talk**—even if it's just 15 minutes.
- And start tracking your progress like a real business—because your family is one.

If this book helped you, **pay it forward**.

Share it with a friend, a cousin, or a neighbor who's still stuck in survival mode. Show them the page that lit something up in you. Because there's enough for all of us to win.

The Quiet Revolution Happening in Homes Like Yours

There's a quiet revolution happening—not on Wall Street, not in Silicon Valley, and not in million-dollar boardrooms.

It's happening in **living rooms**, **kitchen tables**, and **home offices** all across the country.

Parents are learning what schools never taught them. Teenagers are launching businesses from laptops. Families are flipping the script—trading fear for financial literacy, debt for leverage, and survival for **ownership**.

And if you've made it this far in the book, you're part of it.

A New Type of Wealth Builder

Wealth used to look a certain way.

Suits. Stocks. Fancy terms. Old money.

But that's changing.

Today's wealth builder:

- Shops at Costco
- Uses reward points to buy groceries

- Builds LLCs on weekends
- Has a family bank account and a side hustle
- Reads their kid bedtime stories and teaches them about passive income
- Fixes credit, not to flash a lifestyle, but to **build freedom**

You are the new face of generational wealth. You are the new normal.

And you didn't wait for permission—you started.

What the Data Can't Measure

The statistics won't show the real transformation.

They won't show:

- The pride in a mother's eyes when she teaches her daughter how a credit score works
- The relief on a father's face when his side hustle covers the mortgage
- The giggles of a teenager opening their first debit card and logging a sale

- The notebook filled with credit card payment plans and business ideas
- The couple who argued about money last year now strategizing together every Sunday

These are the moments that redefine families—not just financially, but emotionally.

Wealth isn't just a number.

It's peace.

It's time.

It's options.

It's dignity.

And it's being passed down—one household at a time.

This Is Not About Perfection

You'll make mistakes.

You might overextend one month. Miss a payment. Launch a product that flops. Partner with the wrong person. Panic during a recession. Delay the trust paperwork. Forget to log expenses.

That's okay.

This is not about being perfect. It's about being **present**, **intentional**, and **resilient**.

There is no wealth builder on earth who didn't fall, adjust, learn, and come back smarter.

Your only job is to keep going—with wisdom and with purpose.

Look How Far You've Come

Let's take a moment to acknowledge what most won't.

You showed up. You made it to the final chapter. You absorbed uncomfortable truths and exciting possibilities. You opened your mind to tools that may have once scared or confused you. You made plans for your children—plans no one made for you.

That is extraordinary.

Wealth is not measured by how many dollars you make. It's measured by how many **limits you remove**—from yourself and from your family.

And you've removed a lot.

Take a moment. Breathe. Be proud. Because what you're building isn't temporary. It's not for show. It's not based on trends.

It's real.

The Next Generation Is Watching

You may not realize it now, but your kids are listening.

They hear you when you say, "That's not in the budget." They see you when you sit down with a calculator instead of buying impulsively. They feel the difference when money isn't a source of fear—but a tool of confidence.

They're learning how to treat credit. How to treat money. How to treat their own dreams.

Every smart decision you make today becomes a shortcut for their tomorrow.

They'll borrow wiser. Build faster. Fail safer. And dream bigger.

That's the gift you've given them.

Keep the Revolution Going

This is not the end. It's a baton pass.

Now you teach. You lead. You share.

Talk to your friends. Host a dinner where you walk through your new credit system. Email your sibling and offer to help them pull their credit report. Start a blog, podcast, or family YouTube channel. Print out your financial blueprint and put it in a binder on your desk. Record a short video message to your children explaining how you built what you built.

These are not small actions.

These are **seeds**.

And when planted, they grow into family trees that bear fruit for generations—fruit of ownership, discipline, creativity, and freedom.

You've taken the first step. You've stayed the course. You've built something real.

Now go share it.

Because this isn't just your wealth.

It's your **legacy**.

<u>CREDIT TO CAPITAL</u>

www.ingramcontent.com/pod-product-compliance
Lightning Source LLC
LaVergne TN
LVHW052011200926
848481LV00005B/1461